Fritz Reiner

PHILIP HART

Fritz Reiner

A Biography

Northwestern University Press
Evanston, Illinois 60208-4210

Copyright © 1994 by
Philip Hart. Published 1994 by
Northwestern University Press.
All rights reserved

Printed in the
United States of America

ISBN 0-8101-1125-X

Library of Congress
Cataloging-in-Publication
Data

Hart, Philip, 1914–
Fritz Reiner : a biography /
Philip Hart.

p.   cm.
Includes discography (p.   ),
bibliographical references
(p.   ), and index.

ISBN 0-8101-1125-X (alk. paper)

1. Reiner, Fritz, 1888–1963.
2. Conductors (Music)—
United States—Biography.
I. Title.
ML422.R38H37   1994
784.2'092—dc20
                    [B] 94-17316
                           CIP
                           MN

The paper used in this
publication meets the mini-
mum requirements of the
American National Standard
for Information Sciences—
Permanence of Paper for
Printed Library Materials,
ANSI Z39.48-1984.

For Margaret

CONTENTS

Fritz Reiner was one of the great conductors of opera and symphonic music in his time—the ultimate craftsman and consummate musician who set his performances before his public without podium histrionics or the ministrations of sycophantic publicists. No other conductor in America was more deeply committed to performing the music of his time and of his adopted country. Reiner was also involved in a historic evolution of concert and opera in America, in the development of characteristically American music, and in the education of musicians. He was a major participant in the electronic revolution—the new media of music dissemination—that profoundly changed American musical culture. As William Schuman observed in his eulogy in 1963, Reiner was a great teacher, not just in the classroom, nor on the podium, nor through the media, but in the broader sense of his dedication and the standards he set. Leonard Bernstein, his most famous pupil, declared, "Reiner is responsible for my own very high standards."

By naturalization, by marriage, by choice, and by commitment, Fritz Reiner's was a notably American career. Coming from Europe in 1922, he embraced the American musical environment, putting his artistry to the service not only of the "masterpiece" repertory of the past but also to the music of his own time and of his adopted country. In three cities—Cincinnati, Pittsburgh, and Chicago—he was a master orchestra builder. After distinguished opera conducting in Philadelphia and San Francisco, he spent five memorable seasons at the Metropolitan Opera.

However, Fritz Reiner's reputation for irascibility alienated a music world expecting at least a modicum of flexibility and rationality. Although he was sometimes the victim of circumstances beyond his control, much of the controversy surrounding him was deserved, the product of his own hermetic intransigence. If that inflexibility was essential to upholding the standards he set for himself and others, in carrying it to extremes he became self-destructive. His dour expression, acid tongue, and fiery temper alienated those whose support he needed and often obscured his intrinsic artistic achievement. Even in Chicago, where he shaped one of the greatest musical instruments of its time, he was a center of controversy and resentment that linger to this day. His most enduring legacy, the evidence that reminds us today of his greatness, remains in the recordings he made with the Chicago Symphony Orchestra. Focusing on his performances, they have dimmed the memory of the less endearing qualities of the artist who created them. Even among the players who made those recordings with him, the passage of time has mellowed the venom that once pervaded their feelings. They now recall him with a begrudging nostalgia of admiration: "That son-of-a-bitch could really conduct!"

As associate manager of the Chicago Symphony Orchestra, I observed closely Fritz Reiner's work with one of the greatest orchestras America has ever known. Though I was not spared the impact of his demands, we became friends then and remained friends during his last years after I moved to New York. I cherish the memory not only of his performances but also of the warm hospitality of Fritz and Carlotta Reiner at Rambleside, their home in Connecticut.

Carlotta Reiner survived her husband by nineteen years. She often spoke of a Reiner biography with me and other friends and writers. She had strong ideas of what should be written about him, for she remained to her dying day intensely, in fact obsessively, devoted to his memory. Carlotta insisted that a biography of her husband must "set the record straight," for she deeply resented what she regarded as aspersions on her husband's reputation. As time passed, she more and more idealized her husband's memory, to a point verging on fantasy. Obviously no biographer could work under her surveillance and still produce an honest and respectful account of the life and career of Fritz Reiner. She talked frequently of what she called "the Papers"—letters, programs, photographs, and other documents and memorabilia that would have been essential for any biography. But she never allowed me or any other writer to see this trove. My consolation was her repeated assurance that everything—the papers, the furnishings of her husband's studio, and his library of books and scores—would eventually go to Northwestern University as a Fritz Reiner memorial archive.

Although I had kept notes of my work in Chicago and of my conversations with both Reiners, I did not seriously undertake this biography until after Carlotta's death in 1983. By late 1986 Carlotta's executor had finally transferred Fritz Reiner's voluminous collection to Northwestern University. Since then, Don L. Roberts, the music librarian at Northwestern, has given me unrestricted access to this Fritz Reiner Library. I discovered this collection to be an extraordinary treasure documenting not only the career of Fritz Reiner but also the cultural context in which he worked.

Despite his celebrity, Reiner was intensely private. At the Chicago Symphony Orchestra, I learned how difficult it was to gain his cooperation in publicity and how unpredictable the result might be. Yet he collected and preserved, and had his wives and secretaries collect and preserve, an extraordinary documentation of his life and career, by conservative estimate some thirty thousand items. Along with letters from composers and professional correspondence, Reiner filed invoices for photographic equipment and custom-made shirts and shoes, as well as dog licenses. Reiner kept letters that by no means reflected favorably on him in some of his professional and personal relations. In addition to filing correspondence, Reiner preserved his annual red-bound diaries from 1931 onward. Though he occasionally jotted down his thoughts on matters of immediate concern, the diaries mainly recorded appointments and social engagements; for some years they included summaries of his income. By no means complete, they are invaluable in revealing the texture of Reiner's professional and social life and for establishing dates. Overwhelming as this archive is, one must ask in wonder why Fritz Reiner, such an intensely private man, amassed this collection. My own belief is that, for all his insistence on privacy, he wanted the unvarnished truth about his life and work to survive him.

These papers are now housed in a climate-controlled room in Deering Hall on the Northwestern University campus in Evanston, Illinois. They share the room with a few pieces of furniture from Reiner's Rambleside study. The room also contains Reiner's scores, those that he actually conducted and many that he did not. Reiner's personal library of books reflects his broad cultural interests. There are also bound volumes, season by season, of the printed programs of the three orchestras of which he was music director. Finally, there is what can be described as a general miscellany—press clippings loose and in scrapbooks, random concert programs, color slides taken by Reiner himself, and various publicity and personal photographs.

Yet there are significant gaps in the material at Northwestern. Many conducting scores of standard repertory never arrived there. Several file boxes from the Cincinnati years are missing, and there is little on Reiner's work at the Metropolitan Opera relative to what exists for other major posts he held. Columbia University has not permitted me to study the composer correspondence and other materials bequeathed by Carlotta Reiner to its Fritz Reiner Center for Contemporary Music. In the summer of 1983 some of Reiner's library found its way to a furniture auction in Portland, Maine. A used book dealer purchased one lot, containing two thousand books, letters, scores, and photographs. These items have been dispersed by resale. The Bagaduce Music Library in Blue Hill, Maine, received another lot of scores. I have not been able to trace the innumerable negatives and prints of black and white photographs that Reiner himself took over many years.

Although the rich archive at Northwestern University has been central to my work on this biography, I have supplemented it with research and interviews in the cities where Reiner worked, both at music organizations and in libraries to which they sent their archives. Much documentation is in press clippings. Having, as a public relations officer for such organizations, distributed information to the press, I have a well-developed skepticism about the accuracy of such self-serving material. Still, these sources, as well as the New York *Times* and other publications, have helped determine dates, names, and places. Thirty years after the death of Fritz Reiner, it has been my good fortune to encounter people who could cast significant light on my subject. To them and to the organizations and their staffs who guided and assisted me, I owe a great debt of gratitude.

I owe personal gratitude to Peg and Arrand Parsons and to Sally and Don Roberts for making my visits to the Chicago area an exceptional pleasure.

I dedicate this book to my wife, Margaret, both for her support of its creation and for the warm mutual respect and affection she enjoyed with Fritz and Carlotta Reiner.

CHAPTER I

Reiner Frigyes

Frederick Martin Reiner was born on 19 December 1888 in the Pest section of Budapest, the principal Magyar city of the Austro-Hungarian Empire. That was his legal designation when he became a United States citizen in 1928 and when his second wife divorced him in 1930; it was probably how the government of the Hapsburg Dual Monarchy named him in his birth certificate and in other official documents. As Friderik Reiner he conducted for one season in Laibach (now Ljubljana). But in Magyar he was Reiner Frigyes, so enrolled at the Franz Liszt Academy of Music in Budapest and later known professionally there. His close friends knew him as Frici.[1]

His parents, Ignácx and Vilma (Polak), were Jews, a heritage less important to Reiner than the Magyar. The family was apparently among those Jews who sought assimilation into the Hungarian middle class, by no means unusual in Central Europe then. Neither surviving documents nor family tradition indicates any significant Jewish identification or religious observance on Reiner's part. The Reiner family name probably originated in the late eighteenth century, when the Hapsburg emperor Joseph II decreed that all Jews take German names. Reiner's mother's family may have originally come from a Slavic region of the empire; a pencil notation in Reiner's handwriting on the back of a photograph of his maternal grandmother suggests that she came from Pressburg, now Bratislava in Slovakia but then a part of the Hapsburg domain. Some accounts refer to Ignácx as a tailor. In fact, according to his granddaughter Eva Reiner Bartenstein, he was a textile merchant of some means. Reiner's father was a stocky and formidable gentleman with a full dark beard. Reiner's mother was petite, vivacious, and loquacious.[2]

Accounts of the childhood of a celebrated public figure can be notoriously unreliable when based on the subject's own frequently self-serving recollection. Much "information" about Reiner's childhood stems from an interview he gave to Gertrude Guthrie-Treadway in Cincinnati in 1925. The account of his career in Hope Stoddard's *Symphony Conductors of the U.S.A.* contains further anecdotal information from a 1954 interview. Shortly before her husband took up his post in Chicago in 1953, Carlotta Reiner supplied Claudia Cassidy of the Chicago *Tribune* with further anecdotes. From these and other sources, most originating from Reiner himself, and through their permutations over the years, such "facts" and their elaboration grew into an official legend.[3]

Reiner had the good fortune to grow up in a family sympathetic to music and readily inclined to encourage his precocious talent. His mother, a talented amateur pianist, was the boy's first music teacher. The future conductor received his introduction to symphonies of Haydn, Mozart, and Beethoven from four-hand piano readings with his mother. Reiner traced his earliest encounter with music to a chiming clock in the hall of the family home. Its rendition of tunes from *Lucia di Lammermoor* so fascinated him that his parents took him to a performance of that opera. More impressed by the conductor than by the singers, the six-year-old boy returned home to imitate his gestures. With this introduction to the wonders of opera, young Frigyes visited the opera house regularly, and his family encouraged this interest by giving him vocal scores, which he learned to play at the piano by heart. Reiner later recalled:

I lived in a household which had a natural tradition of Rossini, Meyerbeer, the songs of Schubert, and the piano music of Chopin. This family diet of music might have remained unchanged but for the visit of a friend, an amateur musician. It was he who, playing the *Tannhäuser* Overture, introduced my family and me to the music of Richard Wagner—hardly a familiar name on the piano racks of the musical bourgeoisie of those days! The music made such an impression on me that I promptly borrowed a piano score of *Die Walküre* from a distant relative and, at the age of ten, could play the entire first act from memory.[4]

At nine, when he required more disciplined training than a mother could provide, his parents sent him to study with a professional piano teacher, whom he amazed by playing his own transcription of the overture to *Tannhäuser* from memory and by displaying an extraordinary ability to improvise. At the gymnasium he organized an orchestra, in which he played percussion and which he conducted in Beethoven's First Symphony at the age of twelve. He made his first public appearance playing the Mozart's Concerto in D Major (K. 537) at the age of thirteen.

One day during a summer vacation in the country village of Budakerz, he was playing the *Tannhäuser* overture on the piano. Through a window open to the street, a boy three years his senior heard the music and knocked on the door of the cottage to propose that they join in piano duets. He introduced himself as Leo Weiner. The two shared an enthusiasm for music and eventually became fellow students at the conservatory. Although their paths later diverged—Weiner's toward composition and teaching in Budapest and Reiner's toward performance on the international scene—theirs remained an especially close friendship.

Despite his son's musical talent, Reiner's father pressed the study of law on him as a more secure career. Three months before his fifteenth birthday, Frigyes enrolled simultaneously at the Royal University to study law and at the National Hungarian Royal Academy of Music. Founded in 1875, the academy was also known in Reiner's time as the Franz Liszt Academy of Music. It is hard to avoid contrasting Reiner's mother's musical inclination with his father's more practical pressure. After his father's death a year later, Reiner abandoned the law to devote his studies exclusively to music.

Reiner was baptized a Roman Catholic several years after his father's death. His mother converted to Roman Catholicism at the same time and remained an ardent communicant for the rest of her life. Such religious conversion was by no means unusual at a time when many Jews favored assimilation into Central European society. Although Reiner's daughter Eva Bartenstein was under the impression that her father had embraced Catholicism in 1911 to marry a Catholic, his baptismal certificate—in Latin and Magyar—is dated 10 November 1908.[5] Despite his conversion, Reiner's name appeared in the blacklist of Jewish musicians issued in the 1930s by the Nazi regime in Germany. Unlike many other converts, Reiner did not revert to his Jewish origins during World War II or upon the establishment of the state of Israel. He nevertheless resented anti-Semitic remarks, humorous or otherwise.

The Budapest of Fritz Reiner's youth was one of the most vital capitals in Europe. With a population in 1900 of 733,000, it was the sixth largest city in Europe, having nearly tripled its size in thirty-six years. Its economy relied on the manufacture of iron and steel, including armaments, and on the agriculture of the Danube basin. Until Minneapolis overtook it in 1900, Budapest was the largest grain milling center in the world. This rapid economic growth fostered public and private education and such urban amenities as an early underground railway and a proliferation of coffeehouses. Budapest supported a lively variety of performance activity ranging from restaurant-bars with entertainment, called "orpheums," to grand opera. In 1904 the city had sixteen thousand theater seats. Although German had been the official language of Budapest for some time, native Magyar was also in common use at the turn of the century; most residents were bilingual. Before World War I Budapest was relatively free of anti-Semitism, as compared to Warsaw or Vienna, for instance. That prejudice surfaced markedly after the self-styled regent, Admiral Miklós

Horthy, took control of the government in 1919, proclaiming a "Christian and nationalist" state.[6]

In the nineteenth and twentieth centuries Hungary produced a musical flowering quite out of proportion to its limited population and ethnic isolation. Although Franz Liszt received his training abroad and actually spoke little Magyar as an adult, his brilliant international career inspired young Hungarian musicians. After he retired from the concert platform, he took a great interest in the music of his native land. Although his "Hungarian" music owed more to a café style different from the authentic idiom later documented by Bartók and Kodály, his rich and generous personality made him a national hero. After Liszt, Hungary sent forth into the international music world such renowned artists as violinist Joseph Joachim and conductors Hans Richter and Arthur Nikisch. Some Hungarian musicians in Reiner's generation—Béla Bartók, Zoltán Kodály, and the great violin pedagogue Jenö Hubay—preferred to center their careers in their native land, while others, like Leopold Auer, Josef Szigeti, Reiner, and Eugene Ormandy, followed the trail of Liszt, Joachim, Richter, and Nikisch into the international music world.

The Royal Hungarian Opera, founded in 1873 and performing in one of Europe's most attractive opera houses since 1884, offered both staged performances and concerts by its Budapest Philharmonic Orchestra. Both Gustav Mahler and Arthur Nikisch had been musical directors there. During Reiner's youth, István Kerner held that post; a disciple of Richter and Nikisch, Kerner displayed elegance, musicianship, and economy of gesture that provided an early model for Reiner. Many years later, when Francis Robinson included a photo of the Royal Hungarian Opera auditorium in his book on Caruso, Reiner wrote him: "On page 44—that small figure high in the proscenium loge could have been me at 15 years—and twenty years later I was in the pit."[7]

At the Academy of Music admirers of Liszt and Wagner dominated the faculty, despite the emergence of an interest in authentic Magyar music among students and younger faculty. Ödon von Mihálovich, the director of the academy, was an ardent Wagnerian and an implacable foe of Magyar musical nationalism.

Reiner remained at the Liszt Academy until 1909, studying piano with István Thomán, piano pedagogy with Kálmán Chován, and composition with Hans Koessler.[8] During his last two years at the academy his piano teacher was the young Béla Bartók, who had returned to Budapest from the pursuit of an international career as a concert pianist and had recently joined Kodály in studying authentic Hungarian folk music in the field. The acceptance of these two young musicians by the conservative academy in 1906 marked a major change there.[9] Reiner's immediate elders—Bartók, Kodály, Ernö von Dohnányi, and Weiner—were all very much a part of the musical environment in which he studied and began his professional career. Throughout his later international activities he remained a loyal crusader for their music. When later pupils of Weiner, who revered him as an inspiring pedagogue, encountered Reiner as a conductor in the United States, they discovered an extraordinary correlation between the teaching of Weiner and the performance of Reiner.[10] Although Bartók had played his piano music outside Hungary, Reiner was among the first to conduct his early orchestral compositions abroad. The conservatory did not then offer instruction in conducting, but a young musician aspiring to become a conductor received a thorough grounding in composition, theory, and the mastery of his chosen instrument, usually the piano. Chamber music was an important part of this curriculum. Reiner played percussion in the student orchestra and may even have had a chance to conduct it. Its conductor, Jenö Hubay, was, according to Reiner, a very poor one. When the young percussionist asked for a cue at a difficult passage, Hubay responded, "Don't bother me. Can't you see I am busy conducting?"[11]

During his final years at the academy, Reiner accompanied several musicians on concert tours of Hungary, among them the singer Elena Gerhardt, the violinist Joan Manén, and the cellist David Popper. He also studied piano pedagogy and taught privately. A pupil from this time, Erzsébet ("Erzi") Szebestyén, recalled him as an excellent pianist but an impatient teacher. If Erzi played well, Reiner could be lavish in his praise, but he responded to poorly prepared playing with a violent display of temper that terrified the young girl. On one occasion, his teenage pupil so infuriated him that he threw the piano scores about the room. There they remained, since neither he nor his strong-willed pupil would stoop to recover them.[12]

It was Leo Weiner, already a *répetiteur* at the Népszinház Vigopera, one of the independent popular companies offering plays, operettas, and operas, who brought his young friend into that organization, where he served first as a rehearsal pianist and then as a conductor.[13] Reiner recalled joining this company in 1907–1908:

My friend, Leo Weiner, was a very excellent musician in every way but one. He could not conduct. To conduct is a special ability. It cannot be learned. One must be born with the tendency which would make you a conductor. Leo Weiner, although one of the best all-around musicians, was not a conductor. He was asked to become a coach for the comic opera at Budapest. He tried it, but after a while he came to me and said: "I want you to take my position. I am going to recommend you. I am going to resign. I am not a good conductor. I am not a success at the comic opera as a coach. You will succeed." . . . They put me on the chair and gave me a little stick. I could scarcely see anything but the pretty girls. I conducted and they were all wild about me, especially the girls. I got the position as coach for the comic opera.[14]

Fritz Reiner always maintained that the best place for a conductor to learn his craft was not in the classroom but in the opera theater. Only there could he encounter the full range of vocal and instrumental music. In coping with the diverse temperaments and limitations of singers, he could learn to meet the emergencies that every conductor would have to surmount in the opera pit or on the concert platform. Playing the piano well and being able to sight-read and transpose were indispensable qualifications for even the lowest rung on the ladder of the conducting profession—*répetiteur* or rehearsal pianist. That position trained a conductor in the score itself and gave him experience in working with that most treacherous of musical instruments, the human voice. Only after menial work as *répetiteur* did Reiner get his first chance to conduct a public performance in the spring of 1908, when a staff director suddenly became ill. He was nineteen, and the opera was *Carmen,* a work that he eventually conducted more than any other. It was, he said, "the hardest thing I ever did."[15]

While at the Vigopera, Reiner wrote to Imre Mészáros, director of the Royal Hungarian Opera, hoping to obtain a position there. Still at the Vigopera early in 1910, he accompanied some auditions for the director of the Municipal Theater in the Slovenian capital of Laibach, who was so impressed that he engaged Reiner as a staff conductor for the following season. Known there as Friderik Reiner, he was described on his engagement as a brilliant pianist from Budapest. Laibach was a provincial center of some musical importance, with a population of under fifty thousand. Mahler had conducted there in 1881 at the city's excellent Municipal Theater, where opera was sung in both German and Slovenian. The local orchestra, which served for concerts as well as opera and operetta performance, was small; Reiner recalled performing Beethoven's "Eroica" Symphony with fewer than thirty-five players. Václav Talich, four years Reiner's senior, was first conductor in Laibach. He and Reiner became close friends, and both were great admirers of Arthur Nikisch. The Municipal Theater offered a six-month season of plays, operettas, and operas, as well as occasional concerts by the staff orchestra.

For his Laibach debut on 2 October 1910, Reiner conducted Smetana's *Dalibor,* his sole performance of that opera. By the end of March 1911 Reiner had conducted fifty-four performances. His operatic repertory comprised *Dalibor, Tannhäuser, Der Freischütz, La bohème,* and *Faust*. He conducted thirty performances of operetta, a staple of the theater's repertory: Lehár's *Das Fürstenkind* and *Der Graf von Luxemburg*, Leo Fall's *Die Dollarprinzessen*, and Imre Kálmán's *Ein Herbstmanöver*. He also directed the incidental music for two plays by Slovenian writers.[16]

Among the patrons of the Laibach opera were the Jelacin family, who occupied a box visible from the podium. Seated in the front row of this box was their attractive daughter Elca. Reiner was welcomed in the Jelacin home, and in due course, he proposed marriage. They were married in October 1911 in Laibach after he had accepted a new post in Budapest.[17] Two years Reiner's junior, Elca was shy and, at least at the beginning of their marriage, an inexperienced housekeeper. She had studied piano at the Laibach conservatory and had also taken voice lessons. An album of snapshots, taken and labeled in German by Reiner, shows her and other young people on an alpine summer outing; these photos exude great joy and warmth.[18] As a young bride in Budapest Elca found herself in a strange city, confronted with a foreign tongue, and married to an ambitious young musician. Their first child, a daughter named Berta but called Bertushka or Tuśy (also spelled Tussy, but pronounced "Tushy"), was born in Budapest in September 1912.[19]

Reiner's new post in Budapest was at the recently reorganized Népopera, a private enterprise offering opera, operetta, ballet, and other performances to a popular audience. In Reiner's time the Népopera was separate from the Royal Hungarian Opera; it has since become a part of the state opera administration, still located in what is now the Erkel Theater. Performing in the Budapest Municipal Theater, which was considerably larger than the Royal Opera House, it could offer tickets at lower prices. The Népopera employed a full roster of resident performers and also presented touring companies from abroad. Although Reiner may have conducted operettas in his first year at the Népopera, his principal work was in grand opera.[20]

During 1913 and 1914 Reiner conducted more than fifty performances of twenty-three operas: Bizet's *Carmen*, Gounod's *Faust* and *Le médecin malgré lui*, Meyerbeer's *Les Huguenots*, Offenbach's *Les contes d'Hoffmann*, Planquette's *Les cloches de Corneville*, Donizetti's *La fille du régiment* and *Lucia di Lammermoor*, Puccini's *La bohème* and *Tosca*, Rossini's *Il barbiere di Siviglia*, Thomas's *Hamlet* and *Mignon*, Verdi's *Un ballo in maschera*, *Rigoletto*, *Il trovatore*, and *La traviata*, Wolf-Ferrari's *I gioielli della Madonna*, and four operas by Wagner—*Lohengrin*, *Die Meistersinger*, *Parsifal*, and *Tannhäuser*. The listing of the German repertory indicates that it was sung in the original. Other operas, notably those of French and Italian origin, were probably sung in Magyar or German, although foreign guest artists probably sang in their own tongues. Reiner conducted but one of the native Hungarian operas in the company's repertory—*Radda* by Károly Clement. Among the guest artists appearing with Reiner were Alessandro Bonci in *Rigoletto* and *Il barbiere di Siviglia,* Emmy Destinn in *Aida* and *Lohengrin,* Titta Ruffo in *Il barbiere di Siviglia,* Selma Kurz in *Mignon,* and Leo Slezak in *Faust* and *Les Huguenots.* The great German tenor Hermann Jadlowker sang with Reiner in *Parsifal, Tannhäuser, Lohengrin, Mignon, Faust, Carmen,* and *Die Meistersinger.*

The Népopera production of *Parsifal* made international news, for it was the first fully staged public performance of this opera in Europe after the expiration of its copyright in 1913. Earlier performances at the Metropolitan Opera in New York had been possible, over Cosima Wagner's protest, because the United States did not then adhere to international copyright code. In fact, there were several earlier performances of *Parsifal* outside Bayreuth sanctioned by the Wagner family, benefits or concert versions in Europe and South America, and eight private staged performances in Munich for King Ludwig. Reiner gave the downbeat for the Népopera *Parsifal* at 12:01 on the morning of New Year's Day in 1914—as soon as the copyright had expired. Fifty other European opera companies mounted the opera in the early months of 1914. Reiner conducted *Parsifal* eight times at the Népopera before leaving for Dresden in mid-May.[21]

Among the touring companies who performed in the Népzinház was the Diaghilev Ballets Russes. In a 1955 letter congratulating Pierre Monteux on his eightieth birthday, Reiner recalled: "We both conducted the same orchestra in Budapest (some forty years ago). I was spellbound by your absolute command, your virtuoso craftsmanship and eloquence of interpretation." Monteux's performance of Rimsky-Korsakov's *Scheherazade* made a strong impression on the young Hungarian. According to a Monteux letter to Stravinsky, he conducted the Népopera orchestra for Ballets Russes performances in 1913 "under bad conditions." Reiner may well have heard *The Firebird* on that occasion, probably his first encounter with Stravinsky's music.[22]

Occasionally the Népopera presented instrumental soloists either in recital or with orchestra. Reiner conducted the orchestral portion of several of these concerts that began with the orchestra and ended with solos. Jascha Heifetz, then aged twelve, made his Budapest debut on 1 March 1914 in such a concert, his first encounter with the conductor with whom he was to work in later years.[23] For Eugène d'Albert's appearance in the Liszt E-flat Concerto, Reiner also conducted music by Weber and von Mihálovich. A similar mixture of orchestral music and piano solos prevailed when Dohnányi played the Beethoven G Major Concerto and Reiner conducted the *Meistersinger* prelude and a new work by Leo Weiner.

During the autumn of 1913 Reiner had great success with the first Buda-pest production of Wolf-Ferrari's *I gioielli della Madonna*. The cast included as guest artists the soprano Eva von der Osten; her husband, the baritone Fried-rich Plaschke; and the tenor Fritz Vogelstrom, all from the Saxon Court Opera in Dresden. When the Dresden company later faced an emergency in the ill-ness and death of conductor Ernst von Schuch, Count Nikolaus von Seebach, the general director of music and court theaters, invited Reiner to Dresden to conduct three trial performances in late May and early June 1914. Although the recommendation of Reiner by the Dresden singers undoubtedly played a part in bringing him to Seebach's attention, the Népopera *Parsifal* and the young conductor's growing reputation in operatic circles as a Wagnerian must have also attracted attention to him.

Erzsébet Szebestyén shared the excitement of her young teacher. They discussed the Dresden invitation and speculated on which three operas he should conduct. When Erzi's father walked in on this conversation, he dismissed his daughter's views as those of a sixteen-year-old child, only to be contra-dicted by Reiner, who proclaimed his respect for her opinion. Both father and daughter predicted correctly that Reiner would not need all three trial perfor-mances to win an engagement and that he would be offered a contract after the first.

Leaving Budapest, the twenty-five-year-old Reiner had completed his musical apprenticeship. With the popular companies of Budapest and with the Mu-nicipal Theater in Laibach, Reiner had learned the routine of opera. The small Laibach orchestra and a few concerts at the Népopera had given him only lim-ited orchestral involvement except in opera, but his experience with some of Wagner's demanding scores, including *Die Meistersinger* and *Parsifal,* more than compensated for his lack of seasoning in concert.

Forty years later Reiner recalled that, when he approached the Royal Opera in Budapest for a job, he was told, "Young man, the best thing for you to do is to get out of Hungary and learn your profession elsewhere."[24] Ex-cept for a few guest appearances conducting opera and concerts some years later, Reiner played no further part in the musical life of Budapest, although he apparently twice sought a permanent post there. Henceforth he chose to be known, not in his native Magyar style, nor as Friderik of Laibach days, but as Fritz Reiner. If he now turned his back on his native land, he by no means forgot important elements of his heritage. His was not the fanatic nostalgia of many émigrés, but rather a deep affection for the friends and associations of his youth. Though Reiner was never an active hyphenated Hungarian-American, the anti-Communist uprising of 1956 moved him deeply, and he bitterly resented what he perceived as a lack of generosity by several of his colleagues toward the relief of Hungarians in their homeland. Subsequently in America he spoke and wrote English with idiomatic fluency but often exaggerated his Hungarian accent for emphatic effect. He manifested his ethnic roots most in loyalty to the best of Hungarian music—to that of Liszt from the past and to Bartók, Weiner, Kodály, and Dohnányi from his own time.

CHAPTER II

Florence on the Elbe

The Dresden that Fritz Reiner knew was partly medieval, but partly built in North German Baroque architectural style. One of the most beautiful cities in Europe, it was famed as "Florence on the Elbe" before its destruction in February 1945 by British and American fire bombing. Reputed to have sired more than one hundred and sixty children, the Saxon elector Frederick Augustus I "The Strong" was a passionate Italophile, as was his son Augustus II. They imported Italian artisans to design and build their court buildings in Dresden during the first half of the eighteenth century in a Saxon adaptation of the late Baroque. A masterpiece of German Baroque architecture, the ornate quadrangle of the Zwinger now houses great collections of painting, sculpture, and objets d'art. Between the Zwinger and the Elbe is another extraordinary building, the nineteenth-century Semper Theater. Its restoration was completed only in 1985, forty years after its destruction in the fire bombing of the city. A bronze tablet in its entrance reads "Semper fidelis" in honor of its durability.

Music always played an important role in the life of Dresden. Heinrich Schütz spent a major part of his career at the Saxon court. Although Augustus and his successors had favored Italian opera in their court theater, royal patronage introduced German opera early in the nineteenth century. Carl Maria von Weber was musical director of the German Department of the Saxon Court Opera from 1817 to 1826. He composed *Der Freischütz* in Dresden, where it has remained a staple of the repertory, although it actually received its first performance in Berlin. From 1843 to 1849 Richard Wagner held the same post as Weber, conscious of his role as Weber's successor in shaping a national operatic idiom. His *Rienzi* (1842), *Der fliegende Holländer* (1843), and *Tannhäuser* (1845) received their first performances in Dresden under his direction. Before his involvement in revolutionary activity forced him into exile,

Wagner composed *Lohengrin* and sketched the early scenarios for *Der Ring des Nibelungen, Die Meistersinger,* and *Parsifal* there.

Dresden stimulated Wagner's early thinking about the nature of opera, its staging, and the kind of theater most suited to its presentation. He worked in a theater designed by the Hamburg architect Gottfried Semper, finished in 1841 but destroyed by fire in 1869. Semper and Wagner collaborated on a never-realized project for Munich, but Semper's ideas influenced Wagner's design for his theater in Bayreuth. Fritz Reiner worked for more than seven years in the theater that Semper and his son built after the fire of 1869.

But a splendid opera theater alone could not create the operatic tradition that distinguished Dresden in the years bridging the turn of this century. This was the work of the Austrian-born conductor Ernst von Schuch, who joined the Saxon Court Opera as Kapellmeister in 1877, a worthy successor to the tradition of Weber and Wagner. Under Schuch, the Saxon Court Opera became one of the leading opera houses of Europe, rivaling those of Berlin, Munich, and Vienna. An excellent conductor, Schuch was also a man of cultivation and innovative musical ideas; as general music director, he introduced fifty contemporary operas to the Dresden repertory. Count Nikolaus von Seebach, general director of the Saxon court theaters, fully supported Schuch's efforts. Schuch is still remembered for introducing the early operas of Richard Strauss: *Feuersnot* (1901), *Salome* (1905), *Elektra* (1909), and *Der Rosenkavalier* (1911). Strauss oversaw these premieres and cited Schuch's direction as a model for all to follow. Although his career carried him farther afield after *Der Rosenkavalier*, Strauss never lost his affection for Dresden and continued to exercise a strong influence there.

Schuch died on 10 May 1914, his last major effort expended on the Dresden premiere of *Parsifal*. His illness and death left the conducting staff short-handed: a schedule of daily performances of opera or concerts required three principal conductors. Schuch's death left two competent but routine conductors—Hermann Kutzschbach and Kurt Striegler. Kutzschbach (1875–1938) had joined the Saxon Court Opera early in 1914 and remained with it until his death. Striegler (1886–1958), of lesser stature to judge by his title, joined the Dresden conducting staff in 1912 and remained there, through the regimes of Fritz Busch and Karl Böhm, until the destruction of the Semper Theater in 1945; he then taught at the conservatory at Coburg. Contrary to later accounts, Fritz Reiner did not succeed Schuch in Dresden, either as general music director or as first conductor.[1] Seebach first tried to replace Schuch with a general music director of major stature, reportedly receiving rejections from Karl Muck and Felix Weingartner. He settled in the end for adding another young conductor to the staff, retaining in his own hands the artistic direction that had been Schuch's domain.

Fritz Reiner, so named for the first time, made his Dresden debut *als Gast* on 24 May 1914, conducting *Rigoletto*. George Baklanoff, who had sung in the same opera with Reiner at the Népopera, made his Dresden debut in the title role. Although the critical notices relegated the new conductor to second place, they expressed admiration for his command of the performance.[2] On 1 June, Reiner conducted *Parsifal,* still a novelty that Schuch alone had conducted. His third "trial" opera was *I gioielli della Madonna,* with the same singers who had been guests at the Népopera; he never conducted it again. As the Szebestyéns had predicted, Seebach engaged Reiner after his first performance. Reiner signed a five-year contract on 27 May, for services from 1 August 1914 to 31 July 1919, with a provision for review and possible cancellation in 1916. His annual salary was nine thousand marks the first year, increasing to fifteen thousand the last. Both Reiner himself and his wives subsequently circulated reports of a "contract for life." It is possible that a later contract, after the republican government took control in 1918, may have carried such a provision as a prerogative of civil service.[3]

When he conducted *Die Walküre* on 4 June, he was a regular member of the company. In the three weeks before the theater closed for a summer recess, Reiner conducted eight more performances, all except *La bohème* by Wagner and including two—*Die Walkure* and *Götterdämmerung*—that he had never conducted before. Playbills in the present Dresden Opera library do not confirm Cesar Saerchinger's statement that Reiner conducted the entire *Ring* without rehearsal at this time.[4]

Reiner returned to Budapest during the summer recess to bring his pregnant wife and baby daughter to their new home in Dresden. The outbreak of war that summer delayed the usual late August opening of the opera season. During that interval, Reiner was one of several conductors who directed benefit concerts featuring singers from the Saxon Court Opera. Finally, on 27 September, the regular opera season opened with Reiner conducting *Lohengrin*. Less than a month later he conducted a new production of *Der Freischütz*.

Basking in his glory as the greatest composer of Italian opera, Giuseppe Verdi liked to describe his early years as "serving time in the galleys." Fritz Reiner might well have used the same terms to describe his seven and a half years in Dresden. Between his tryout with *Rigoletto* in May 1914 and his final performance conducting *Il barbiere di Siviglia* in November 1921, Reiner conducted more than eight hundred performances of forty-seven operas, plus some forty orchestral concerts. Except for a summer vacation of six weeks, the Saxon Court Opera performed seven days a week, either an opera or a concert by the Saxon Court Orchestra. Reiner often conducted three or four times a week, to say nothing of his daytime duties in coaching and rehearsal. He shared the conducting duties with Kutzschbach and Striegler, although occasionally chorus master Emil Pembaur conducted an opera otherwise assigned to the three staff directors. He also conducted most of the premieres of contemporary operas and many new productions of standard repertory through 1921. From 1915 until the overthrow of the Saxon king Carl Edward in 1918, the yearbook of the court theaters designated Reiner as Hofkapellmeister, or court conductor, a title also held by Kutzschbach but never by Striegler.

The Saxon Court Opera had a roster of principal artists and a full complement of *comprimarii,* chorus, and orchestra; during the war years at least, guest appearances by singers from other companies were rare, mainly to replace ailing resident artists. All performances, of course, were in German. The leading singers included Margarete Siems, Eva von der Osten, and Minnie Nast (the first Marschallin, Octavian, and Sophie, respectively), Friedrich Plaschke, Fritz Vogelstrom, Tino Pattiera, and the young Richard Tauber. After Reiner first heard the twenty-year-old Elisabeth Rethberg at the local conservatory, the cast listings at the Dresden Opera trace her rise from such small roles as Barbarina in *Le nozze di Figaro* to that of the Contessa. Reiner conducted many of her performances in Dresden, and she sang with him later in London and America.

The orchestra of the Saxon Court Opera also gave concerts as the Sächsische Hofkapelle or Saxon Court Orchestra. The three Kapellmeisters of the opera conducted most of these performances, although Richard Strauss, Arthur Nikisch, and eventually Fritz Busch appeared as guests. Among the soloists at Reiner's concerts were violinists Adolf Busch and Joseph Szigeti, pianists Elly Ney and Emil Sauer, and Polish soprano Claire Dux. The Saxon Court Opera and Orchestra received serious attention from the Dresden press. One senses a sort of family musical atmosphere: the annual Beethoven birthday concert on or near 16 December, his Ninth Symphony every Palm Sunday afternoon, and *Parsifal* at both Christmas and Easter. Much of the press comment on the familiar singers compared their performances from one occasion to another, or in their various roles. Except in commentary on important new productions, the conductors were mentioned only in passing, at the end of a review.

During his first two years in Dresden, Reiner conducted thirty-five operas. Although some were familiar to him from Budapest, he learned twenty-three that he had never conducted before, while carrying a heavy load of day-to-day work. In his last five years he learned another twelve operas. Under Seebach, the opera continued its tradition of offering works by contemporary German composers. Reiner conducted most of them. In his seven and a half seasons these included world or local premieres of eleven works by nine composers: Eugène d'Albert's *Die toten Augen* (premiere); *Rabab* by Clemens von Franckenstein; Karl Goldmark's *Die Königen von Saba;* Paul Graener's *Theophano* and *Schirin und Gertraude* (premiere); *Der Fremde* by Hugo Kann (premiere); Joseph Mraczek's *Ikdar* (premiere); Hans Pfitzner's *Das Christelflein* (premiere of a revised version); *Die ferne Klang* by Franz Schreker (premiere); and two operas by Siegfried Wagner, *Der Bärenhäuter,* and *Sonnenflammen.*

As might be expected, the operas of Richard Wagner played a major role in the repertory generally, and in Reiner's especially. *Der Ring des Nibelungen* was given as a cycle several times each year, and its more popular components, notably *Die Walküre,* more often. Reiner conducted a full *Ring* cycle at least once a year, sometimes conducting all four music dramas in one cycle, on other occasions sharing a cycle with Kutzschbach or Striegler. Thanks to the publicity surrounding the Budapest *Parsifal,* he naturally led many performances of it in Dresden as well. He directed the remaining Wagner operas frequently, from *Der fliegende Holländer* on, sharing this repertory with his two colleagues. For his first *Tristan und Isolde* he memorized the orchestration and wrote it out from the piano reduction. In 1919 he conducted a highly acclaimed revival of *Rienzi.*

From the non-Wagnerian standard German repertory, Reiner conducted two Mozart operas, *Le nozze di Figaro,* as *Figaros Hochzeit* with Hermann Levi's German recitatives, and *Die Zauberflöte;* Weber's *Der Freischütz;* *Hans Heiling* by Heinrich Marschner; *Die Fledermaus* of Johann Strauss; and Beethoven's *Fidelio.* From the Italian repertory, he played much Verdi—*Aida, Un ballo in maschera, Il trovatore, Rigoletto,* and *La traviata*—and Puccini's *La bohème* and *Tosca,* all in German, under such titles as *Der Troubadour* and *Amelia.* Reiner conducted Rossini's *Il barbiere di Siviglia* more frequently than any other Italian opera. His French repertory included forty-one performances of Bizet's *Carmen,* Offenbach's *Les contes d'Hoffmann,* and *Les Huguenots* and *L'Africaine* of Meyerbeer. In 1921 he presided over a very successful new production of *Faust* (as *Margarethe*) with Rethberg. Tchaikovsky's *Eugene Onegin* was another Reiner favorite; he conducted it twenty-five times in Dresden, but never afterward.

For all his later fame as a conductor of Richard Strauss's music, Reiner conducted only two Strauss operas there—a revival of *Salome* in 1916, which remained in the repertory for another five years; and the first production of *Die Frau ohne Schatten* after its Vienna premiere in 1919. Both *Der Rosenkavalier* and *Ariadne auf Naxos* were also in the Dresden repertory, but they remained in Kutzschbach's province. However, Reiner heard Strauss conduct *Der Rosenkavalier, Ariadne auf Naxos,* and *Elektra* as well as most of his symphonic poems during guest appearances in Dresden. He also traveled to Berlin, then the center of Strauss's activities.

Arthur Nikisch was even more important in the development of Fritz Reiner's conducting style. Since Dresden was but a short train journey from both Leipzig and Berlin, Reiner traveled to these cities to hear Nikisch rehearse and perform and to discuss musical matters with the older conductor. It is also possible that Reiner became acquainted in Leipzig with Hugo Riemann's study of Baroque music and the stylistic research of the Collegium Musicum.[5] On one of his Dresden programs Reiner included an "authentic" edition by Max Sieffert of a Handel concerto grosso with two keyboard instruments playing the continuo.

Although he received his musical training in Vienna, Nikisch was of Hungarian birth. Before his posts in Berlin and Leipzig, he had pursued a career at the Boston Symphony Orchestra, the Royal Hungarian Opera, and at other institutions in several German cities. He was by this time the greatest conductor in Germany, at the head of both the Berlin Philharmonic and the Leipzig Gewandhaus orchestras, posts he held until his death in 1922. Like Strauss, Arthur Nikisch conducted with great elegance and restraint. His example influenced Reiner throughout his career. "It was [Nikisch] who told me that I should never wave my arms in conducting, and that I should use my eyes to give cues."[6] Interpretively, both Nikisch and Strauss tended toward less personalized interpretations than those of such conductors as Gustav Mahler and Willem Mengelberg, although Sir Adrian Boult found Nikisch a "subjective conductor" given to "impetuous irregularities."[7]

The article on Reiner in the *New Grove Dictionary* errs in stating that, during his Dresden years, Reiner was also influenced by Mahler and Karl Muck.[8] Mahler had been dead for three years when Reiner went to Dresden, and Reiner later said that he had never heard him conduct. Mahler's temperament as a conductor was also completely at odds with Reiner's. Reiner probably knew Muck's work, possibly at Bayreuth in *Parsifal* or in Berlin, but in later years he never mentioned that conductor as an influence. On the other hand, he freely acknowledged his debt to Nikisch, whom he described to cellist János Starker, saying, "If Toscanini and Reiner [were] mixed together, Nikisch would come out of it."[9] Unlike those two conductors, Nikisch was good-natured and extremely courteous, even to players in his orchestras, whom he would address with "Excuse me, gentlemen, but . . ." The term most often applied to Nikisch was *hypnotic*. Tchaikovsky, whose music he conducted brilliantly, noted that he was "sparing of superfluous movements, and yet so extraordinarily commanding . . . small in stature [with] eyes that really must possess mesmeric powers."[10] His admirers made much of the fact that he conducted not in beats or bars but in phrases. Nikisch was held in awe as the paragon of conductors by such diverse musicians as Leopold Stokowski, Arturo Toscanini, and Sir Adrian Boult. The British conductor wrote of Nikisch's "stick of shining white that could be seen by everyone, actuated with the utmost restraint mostly by the thumb and two fingers, yet in a way that conveyed the pace and emotion of the music to perfection. . . . Behind the fingers was the wrist, and (rarely) the elbow to indicate the broader effects. . . . The left hand amplified the right at rare moments when the stick could not express all he wished."[11]

Harold Schonberg recognized the affinity between Reiner and Nikisch: "With his orchestra the conductor is, or should be, as one. If he has the knowledge and inner power, he can bend it entirely to his wishes. This cannot happen overnight, unless one is a Nikisch or a Reiner."[12] Nevertheless, Reiner learned the futility of trying to imitate Nikisch too closely:

I once watched Nikisch direct von Weber's *Oberon* Overture, and saw something which fascinated me. Just before the beginning of the *Allegro,* there is a *fortissimo* chord. The orchestra had been playing smoothly, quietly; then this sudden crash. Nikisch produced the effect in this way: he quickly drew two full circles in the air with his baton, and then came firmly down. Ordinarily, the crash would have come in with his downward gesture. But it did not. There was a brief instant of quiet—almost like a breath—and *then* came the chord. This fascinated me. I could hardly wait to get to the orchestra myself, to try this effect. I made the circles with my baton and came sharply down. And the crash came straight down with me, without any pause. . . . I have no idea *how* the orchestra knew the exact interval of time to wait before coming in with the chord.[13]

At Dresden Reiner had his first opportunity to conduct orchestral concerts regularly, adding some 150 works to his repertory. These included a solid representation of Bach (two Brandenburg Concertos, a suite, and orchestrations of organ works), of Beethoven (four concertos and seven symphonies), and of Brahms (three concertos, two symphonies, the Serenade in A Major, the *Tragic* overture, and the "Haydn" Variations). He programmed four symphonies of Bruckner, three by Haydn, a great deal of Mozart (including the last two symphonies), shorter pieces by Mendelssohn, two concertos by Schumann but only one symphony, two symphonies and one concerto by Tchaikovsky, and overtures by Berlioz, Weber, and Wagner. Of Mahler he conducted the Symphony no. 4, *Das Lied von der Erde,* and several songs with Claire Dux. As in opera, Reiner performed orchestral music by the composers in his immediate environment—Felix Draeseke, Eduard Erdmann, Paul Graener, Hugo Kaun, Jean-Louis Nicodé, Hans Pfitzner, Josef Rosenstock, Johannes Schanze, Georg Schumann, Julius Weismann, and Hermann Wetzler. But he also offered music from his native Hungary—by Liszt (including the *Faust Symphony* with Richard Tauber as soloist), his teacher Hans Koessler, Leo Weiner, Ernö von Dohnányi, and Béla Bartók.

Most of the press coverage of the opera concentrated on singers or interpretive discourses about the music. Despite the pride of the local press in

Kutzschbach and Striegler as native Saxons, Reiner received his share of serious comment. Especially during his early work, writers complained of Reiner's fast tempos, frequently praising subsequent performances as more relaxed and lyrical, more "spiritual." His conducting of *Tristan und Isolde* and Beethoven's Ninth Symphony, touchstone works that aroused typical German philosophizing, only gradually won over the critics as the years passed. On the other hand, Reiner was greatly admired in *Die Meistersinger* and in Italian opera generally. His conducting of a new production of *Un ballo in maschera,* in German as *Amelia,* drew unqualified praise, as did *Margarethe,* the German version of Gounod's *Faust.* Reiner's masterful direction of both *Rienzi* and *Die Frau ohne Schatten* received extensive coverage; these were major postwar productions. Poor staging and, except for Elisabeth Rethberg as the Empress, a weak cast detracted from the success of the Strauss opera.[14]

In August 1914 the Reiner family—Fritz, the pregnant Elca, and Tuśy—took up residence in an apartment at Hübnerstrasse 27, remaining there until mid-1916. Daughter Eva was born in January 1915. Both daughters heard in later years from their mother something of family life there. The friendship of Eva von der Osten, godmother of the younger daughter, was especially warm. Family tradition recalled evenings of Strauss playing intensely competitive games of skat with his host, and of his warm charm with Elca and the children. In such an informal setting, the two musicians discussed music and reviewed scores both of Strauss's own music and of such earlier composers as Mozart and Wagner, of whom Strauss was especially fond.[15]

But Reiner's responsibilities at the Semper Theater took their toll on his domestic life. In addition to daytime rehearsals and evening performances, the young conductor's duties included professional relations with attractive young women that easily became more than professional. The young wife, with two small children to care for, led a lonely life in Dresden. Her sheltered upbringing in Laibach scarcely prepared her for the artistic environment in which her ambitious husband moved. As their daughter Eva commented later: "Given the time in general with the social restrictions that were tighter than they are today; given the time in the couple's lives; my father gifted with all the great and difficult aspects of the artist's temperament, at the beginning of a brilliant career and intent to realize it—my mother as a young wife and mother, gifted with rich emotions—they were too young at the time to master what it would have taken to combine the developing career of the one with a marriage satisfying to both."[16]

Reiner was then, as he was later, by no means indifferent to feminine charms. His increasing inattention to his family aroused Elca's suspicions, and she resorted to spying on her husband during his unexplained absences.[17] Elca's suspicions may well have been confirmed by the birth on 11 February 1916 to Charlotte Benedict, a twenty-year-old singer in Dresden, of a baby daughter, Erika, whose father was Fritz Reiner. Erika was brought up by her mother's family as "Erika Rainer," her last name a variant of Reiner, but pronounced the same in German. There is no indication that Fritz Reiner ever acknowledged this child or continued any contact with the mother, who reportedly became a singer and later a prompter on the staff of the Dresden company. She never married but followed Reiner's career through press clippings sent her by friends in America; she died in Dresden in 1956.[18] Reiner's daughter Eva, when asked about this affair, replied: "I was told that before. I am doubting that [Charlotte] was the cause of my parents' separation."[19]

Both Elca's family and Reiner's third wife, Carlotta, believed that Berta Gerster-Gardini, a singer in the Dresden company, caused the dissolution of the Reiner marriage. According to their own later accounts to friends in Cincinnati, Reiner and Berta first met when they were entertaining troops of the German army of occupation in Lille, France. A pass issued by the Kommandatura in Lille to its Dresden counterpart authorized Fritz Reiner to travel to Lille between 18 April and 3 May. Although this pass does not indicate the year, 1916 was the only year when Reiner was not performing in Dresden during this interval.[20] Although Berta and Reiner later in Cincinnati gave the impression that she had been a member of the Dresden company, it is unlikely that she was. Although her obituary in the New York *Times* in 1951 identified her as a former singer at the Dresden Opera, this would have appeared only on the basis of the Reiners' accounts. Her name does not appear in the annual rosters of Dresden personnel for 1914–1921, nor in the directories of professional opera singers active in Germany then.[21] In 1911 *Musical America* described her as a singer and the wife of Walter Kirchhoff, a leading tenor with the Berlin Opera who later sang Wagnerian roles at the Metropolitan Opera.[22] She told her American friends that she had divorced Kirchhoff because of his liaison with a ballet dancer. Carlotta Reiner in later years attributed her husband's difficulties in Germany to his having "stolen" the wife of the Kaiser's favorite tenor at the Berlin opera.

Berta Gerster-Gardini was the daughter of the internationally renowned Hungarian soprano Etelka Gerster, who had retired to live and teach in a handsome villa at Pontecchio near Bologna with her Italian impresario-conductor husband, Carlo Gardini. Etelka Gerster (1855–1920) enjoyed a brilliant career in opera in both Europe and America, frequently the rival of Adelina Patti. She made her American debut in 1878 as Amina in *La sonnambula* at the Academy of Music in New York, where she returned several times. She sang in Theodore

Thomas's 1882 festivals in New York, Cincinnati, and Chicago. Her daughter Berta accompanied her when Oscar Hammerstein brought Gerster to New York in 1907, when she also taught at the Institute of Musical Art. In Berlin she reportedly arranged for her daughter to sing at the imperial court. Gerster had been a pupil of Mathilde (Graumann) Marchesi de Castrone, who had studied in turn with Manuel Garcia. In her teaching Gerster followed the bel canto method of Garcia and Marchesi. Berta, as a teacher in Berlin, Dresden, Cincinnati, and finally in New York, proclaimed herself an exponent of the Garcia-Marchesi tradition handed down through her mother.[23]

Also a soprano, Berta made her debut in a secondary theater in Berlin as Gilda in *Rigoletto* but never established a career in opera. She was an occasional recitalist, possibly to attract singing students.[24] When she and Reiner met, she was probably teaching in Berlin. A photograph, dated summer 1916, shows an impish Reiner with two women, one of them holding a small child, who was probably Eva. When she saw this photograph for the first time in 1988, Eva Bartenstein identified the woman holding the child as Berta; she could not identify the other woman, probably the child's nanny.[25] This could indicate that Berta figured in some way in the Reiner household in the summer of 1916.

In July 1916 Fritz and Elca Reiner terminated their marriage. He rented an apartment in Berlin for his wife and the two girls, visiting them once a month.[26] During a visit in mid-1917 Elca told him that she was returning to her family in Laibach with the girls. After moving from Hübnerstrasse to Lilienstrasse, Reiner took rooms at the Hotel Bellevue in 1919.[27] A year later he moved to an apartment in Hospitalstrasse, where Berta leased an apartment.[28]

For the next five years, protracted and acrimonious negotiations ensued between Reiner and his wife, over a divorce, alimony, and custody of the children. Correspondence between Reiner and his lawyers charged that Elca was living with a married man in Laibach/Ljubljana.[29] Claiming that she was an unsuitable parent for the two girls, Reiner sought sole custody of them. Since both Reiners had been citizens of Austro-Hungary, they required lawyers in Dresden, Budapest, and Laibach/Ljubljana, arrangements complicated by the breakup of the Hapsburg empire. According to settlements of January 1920 in Budapest and May 1921 in Dresden, Elca retained custody of the children and received a monetary settlement, apparently for child support. She also agreed that the girls would learn music and English.[30]

In the summer of 1922, as Reiner prepared to go to Cincinnati, Elca brought the children to Dresden to see their father for the first time since their parting in Berlin in 1917. Reiner again brought up the issue of custody, urging his lawyer to seek a modification of the divorce agreement to permit more frequent visits with the children. He again insisted that Elca was morally unfit as a mother. So antagonistic were the relations between the parents that their lawyers made elaborate arrangements for the children to pass from one parent to the other in a lawyer's office, without their meeting face to face. According to Eva Bartenstein, this was the only time she met Berta, though Tuśy later lived with the Reiners in Cincinnati. On this occasion Reiner had studio portraits taken of the girls with their stepmother.[31]

Although the circumstances surrounding the divorce were the first documented instance of Reiner's vindictive intransigence, they undoubtedly reflect a deep-seated psychological insecurity in his character. The surviving correspondence, despite its legal objectivity, scarcely shows Reiner sympathetically. His righteous indignation at his wife's living with a married man hardly squared with his own conduct, unless, of course, he was applying a different standard to his wife. Equally noteworthy was his obsessive effort to gain custody of the two girls. In this Reiner was exhibiting a self-righteous isolation and lack of empathy that would persist later in his life. Reiner's retention of such documents as would put his position in the best light was also typical of him. The surviving correspondence with the lawyers is incomplete: there are no letters from Elca's lawyers, telling her side of the dispute. One must assume that Reiner himself or one of his later wives purged these materials.

Despite Carlotta Reiner's assertion that Berta and Reiner married only to establish "respectability" before they went to Cincinnati, papers filed for Berta's 1930 divorce in Cincinnati report that they were married twice—in Berlin in November 1921, some months after the divorce from Elca, and in Rome in May 1922.

The end of World War I in November 1918 brought drastic changes in Dresden. Because of riots in the streets and general political instability, the Dresden opera closed for more than two weeks, reopening, not as the Saxon Court Opera but as the Saxon State Opera (later Dresden Opera), under the newly established Saxon republic. With the deposition of the Saxon monarchy, Seebach was removed. A succession of bureaucratic officials, generally identified as "Professor" or "Doktor," followed him as superintendent of the state theaters under a variety of titles. Nor did the republican government immediately strengthen the artistic administration of the Saxon State Opera by appointing a general music director, a position that had remained vacant since the death of Schuch in 1914. By early 1921 the local press was calling for that post to be filled. Reiner and Kutszchbach, in a joint letter in February 1921, pressed the state administration to appoint a general music director, citing artistic needs.[32]

Unquestionably Reiner aspired to that post, but he failed to attain it. Promotion from within the ranks was unlikely: he was an all too familiar figure, both to the public and to the musical staff he would have to command. More-over, the turmoil in Germany following the Armistice significantly increased anti-Semitism, from which Reiner's conversion to Catholicism would scarcely protect him. He was also a foreigner working in an increasingly nationalistic country; there were plenty of native Germans who were qualified for such a post. Finally, he was not popular personally, especially toward the end of his tenure in Dresden. The sole Reiner anecdote surviving there sixty years later, in several versions, told of a performance of *La bohème,* in which the orchestra played the entire first act at a monotonous *mezzoforte.* When the enraged con-ductor confronted the players during the intermission, their spokesman replied, "Well, that is how you conducted it." Even so, during these years Reiner con-ducted prestigious new productions of *Rienzi, Un ballo in maschera, Faust,* and *Die Frau ohne Schatten,* and, to celebrate the 150th anniversary of Beethoven's birth, a new *Fidelio* in December 1920.

Reiner became increasingly dissatisfied with his Dresden post, possibly because of working conditions there but also because Berta was prodding him to seek wider activity. As early as May 1918, he returned to the Városi The-ater in Budapest for six performances of opera—two each of *La bohème, Tann-häuser,* and *Rigoletto*—with singers from Berlin, Dresden, and Vienna. At the end of 1920 he wrote to a Berlin manager that his position in Dresden had be-come "untenable." Although there were openings for general music director in other German cities—Cologne, Darmstadt, Mannheim, and Frankfurt, among others—Reiner received no invitations, even to perform *als Gast.* He wrote to managers in Berlin, Hamburg, Prague, and Vienna proposing orchestral con-certs, some of them featuring such Dresden singers as Elisabeth Rethberg, Richard Tauber, and Tino Pattiera. A concert without singers materialized with the Hamburg Philharmonic early in 1921, when he conducted a Locatelli con-certo grosso and music by Beethoven and Richard Strauss. There was also a concert in Lübeck in 1922. Reiner applied, unsuccessfully, to head the Royal Hungarian State Opera.[33]

During the summer of 1920 Reiner received an invitation, at the sugges-tion of Ottorino Respighi, from the Accademia Santa Cecilia in Rome, which closed with best wishes to the "Signora." This indicates Berta's active role in Reiner's career as early as 1920, when she was already identified as his wife before their actual marriage. He appears to have made at least two proposals to Berlin managements, probably through the firm of Louise Wolff, the most influen-tial agent in Germany. In the fall of 1921 he conducted one or more concerts in Berlin, for which he programmed some Baroque music and, more signifi-cantly, compositions by Respighi and Weiner. When Reiner proposed for one Berlin program the Bartók Suite no. 1 and Richard Strauss's *Eine Alpensinfonie,* the manager urged a more conservative repertory—Beethoven, Schumann, or Brahms. In his memoirs, Joseph Szigeti recalled a performance in Berlin of the Dohnányi Violin Concerto with Reiner conducting the Berlin Philharmonic Orchestra.[34] This concert was probably in early 1922.

In the spring of 1921 Fritz Busch appeared as guest conductor of the Saxon State Orchestra. The following fall the orchestra announced two series of six concerts each, one to be conducted by Busch, the other by Reiner, who protested to the official administration against the engagement of an outside conductor.[35] In the detailed prospectus of the repertory for each series, Reiner's included the annual all-Beethoven concert in December, with Walter Gieseking as soloist. It became apparent that Fritz Busch would become general music director of the Saxon State Opera as soon as he could leave Stuttgart.

Reiner's deteriorating relations with the Dresden opera came to the breaking point in the fall of 1921, when he asked for a leave of absence to conduct eight performances of *Die Meistersinger* at the Teatro Costanzi in Rome, beginning in December. When the Dresden administration refused to grant him this leave, Reiner resigned his position, conducting *Il barbiere di Siviglia* as his last performance there on 22 November 1921.

While he was rebuffed in Germany, Reiner began to receive inquiries from America. During the summer of 1921, while Reiner and Berta vacationed at Pontecchio, the conductor heard from two American agents. Both Jules Daiber and Milton Diamond expressed interest in arranging appearances in the United States. Daiber offered twenty weeks at five hundred dollars a week but did not specify the kind of conducting. In his letters, Diamond mentioned meeting Reiner in Germany and sent his respects to "Frau Reiner." Of greater significance was Reiner's contact with Cesar Saerchinger, then European correspondent for the *Musical Courier*. Though born in Germany, Saerchinger grew up in America. He returned to Europe in 1919, when he attended the new Dresden production of *Rienzi*.[36] Saerchinger was also an adviser to Anna Sinton Taft, president of the Cincinnati Symphony Orchestra. In several letters, Saerchinger urged Reiner not to accept Daiber's offer. He also warned that the Wolff agency might not necessarily serve his best interests because of its representation of Wilhelm Furtwängler and Felix Weingartner.[37]

After conducting *Die Meistersinger* in Rome in late December and early January, Reiner was reengaged to return the next year for *Tannhäuser*. He then went, without Berta, to Barcelona for an engagement in early May at the Gran Teatre del Liceu to conduct *Lohengrin, Die Meistersinger, Die Walküre,* and *Tristan und Isolde.* [38] While Reiner was vacationing in Majorca before the Barcelona performances, an offer from the Cincinnati Symphony Orchestra reached Berta in Dresden or Italy. When Reiner received garbled telegrams, he gave Berta carte blanche to respond affirmatively to Cincinnati on his behalf. On 24 May the executive committee of the Cincinnati Symphony Orchestra agreed to Reiner's engagement. Saerchinger was traveling about Europe, but kept in touch with both Reiners in Rome and Dresden to settle the details of the conductor's engagement in Cincinnati.

During the summer, possibly at Marienbad, where he and Berta vacationed, Reiner met with Emil Heermann, the Cincinnati concertmaster, to plan programming and to arrange for several European players to join the orchestra the next fall. According to press reports, based on self-serving publicity material, Reiner may have conducted the Berlin Philharmonic and the London Symphony Orchestra before boarding the *Caronia* for New York. Neither engagement can be verified, but there is some evidence of a concert in Zurich.

Joining the Cincinnati Symphony Orchestra at the age of thirty-four, Reiner was a thoroughly seasoned conductor, with intensive experience in that most effective of musical training grounds—the pit of a major opera theater. His Dresden post also gave him significant experience with an orchestra in concert. His close contacts with Nikisch and Strauss provided models for his own conducting style and musicianship. On a personal level, Berta had clearly established the role she would play for the next few years in his career, but his family relationships foreshadowed the tempestuous tensions that would prevail later. Although he could not then recognize explicitly the decisiveness of his departure from Europe, his career for the rest of his life would be primarily an American one.

CHAPTER III

Orchestra Builder

Fritz Reiner had the good fortune to launch his American career under exceptionally favorable circumstances. The conjunction of three personal forces—Reiner himself, Charles and Anna Sinton Taft, and Arthur Judson—produced with the Cincinnati Symphony Orchestra during the 1920s one of the finest moments in the history of symphonic music in the United States. All of Reiner's previous training and experience found their realization in creating a major American orchestra and putting it to the service of music old and new. Important as that artistic achievement was, it could not have happened without the Tafts' enlightened and dedicated financial support. In all this, Judson was a catalytic adviser—to the Tafts in supporting their orchestra and to Reiner in shaping his career, not only in Cincinnati but also by introducing him to Philadelphia and New York.

In Cincinnati Reiner joined an orchestra that was part of a strong local musical tradition. In the 1850s the traveling orchestras of Louis Antoine Jullien and the Germania Society visited Cincinnati, which later became an important stop on the tours of Theodore Thomas and his orchestra. Many of the settlers in Cincinnati were German immigrants, who brought with them a devotion to amateur choral music. Their Sängerfeste stimulated an interest among the wealthier element of the city, who supported Thomas's organization of the first May Festival in 1873.[1] To house this festival, the community built the Music Hall in 1878, the home of the Cincinnati Symphony Orchestra for much of its history, though not in Reiner's time. The success of the May Festival may well have delayed the establishment of a strong resident orchestra, and it unquestionably fostered an unhealthy rivalry between the festival and the Cincinnati Symphony Orchestra that was still rife during Reiner's tenure there.

It remained for a group of women from the uppermost strata of Cincinnati society to lay the foundation for a major professional orchestra. In 1894 the Ladies Musical Club followed its successful presentation of the touring Boston Symphony Orchestra with the incorporation of the Cincinnati Orchestra Association Company, with a female board of directors. Texas-born Frank van der Stucken was the orchestra's first conductor. Sensing the need for business guidance, they also established an advisory board of businessmen. An executive committee drawn from both groups made major decisions, but three of the ladies made major contributions of money and leadership. Helen (Mrs. William Howard) Taft headed the association until President McKinley called her husband to be high commissioner of the Philippines. Her successor, Bettie Fleischmann (Mrs. Christian) Holmes, survived confrontations with the local musicians' union and with the orchestra's second conductor, the young Leopold Stokowski, before he resigned in 1912 to direct the Philadelphia Orchestra.[2] Following the departures of Holmes and Stokowski, Anna Sinton Taft began a long and distinguished presidency of the orchestra. During Anna Taft's presidency, the association found the old Music Hall too large and socially inappropriate and moved into a new Emery Auditorium, built with contributions raised to match an initial gift from the Emery family. This remained the home of the Cincinnati Symphony Orchestra, except for special events and popular concerts in the Music Hall, until 1937.

Charles and Anna Taft were the principal benefactors of the orchestra for eighteen years, during which they gave well over five million dollars in gifts to the orchestra, its conductors, and players and ultimately by donation or bequests to the Cincinnati Institute of Fine Arts.[3] Charles Phelps Taft was the eldest son of Alphonso Taft (1810–1891), who had come from New England in 1838 to practice law in Cincinnati and to establish a family "dynasty" that has been prominent in the community and in national politics ever since. Anna Sinton was the daughter of a wealthy Cincinnati family with extensive holdings in real estate, transportation, and banking. Charles Taft was most visible as owner and publisher of the *Times-Star,* a position of great influence in the community. The Tafts also owned one of the largest ranches in Texas and a summer home at Murray Bay in Quebec. They traveled extensively in Europe, hearing music and collecting art for their Cincinnati home. Although Charles Taft shared his wife's interest in music, theater, and the arts generally, she was the prime mover in supporting the Cincinnati Symphony Orchestra.

Anna Taft relied for advice on Arthur Judson, who became well acquainted with the Cincinnati Symphony Orchestra as early as the Stokowski era there.[4] Moving on to New York and thence to management of the Philadelphia Orchestra, he kept in touch with Cincinnati. Given his remarkable affinity for people of wealth and power, Judson could scarcely have missed the opportunity to cultivate the Tafts and Cincinnati as a sphere of activity ancillary to his expanding managerial empire. Judson had extensive contacts in European music circles, either personally or through a network of local intermediaries. He had ample opportunity to hear of Reiner through managerial colleagues or from such musicians as Nikisch and Strauss. However, there is no indication that he actually handled the Cincinnati negotiations with Reiner, since Cesar Saerchinger was another on whom Anna Taft relied.

After Stokowski's successor, the Austrian Ernst Kunwald, fell victim to World War I hysteria, his successor, the Belgian Eugene Ysaye, proved to be less persuasive as a conductor than as a violin virtuoso. By early May 1922 the Cincinnati executive committee had narrowed its list of seventeen mainly European applicants and nominees down to four names—Wilhelm Furtwängler, Felix Weingartner, Serge Koussevitzky, and Fritz Reiner. Neither of the German conductors would give up a major European career to be resident conductor of a midwestern American orchestra, and the Cincinnati board balked at Koussevitzky's demand for a seasonal salary of thirty thousand dollars. Although Reiner countered with a proposal for only half a season, he readily accepted the offer of twenty thousand dollars for a seven-month period that included the 1923 May Festival. Robert A. Taft, nephew of Charles Phelps Taft and later a United States senator, drew up the contract. The Cincinnati press, undoubtedly inspired by the orchestra's management, reported that Reiner willingly canceled an engagement for the following season in Rome because "from my childhood days I always wanted to go to America."[5]

Fritz and Berta Reiner arrived in New York on the *Caronia* on 27 September 1922, after a rough crossing from England. A. F. Thiele, manager of the Cincinnati Symphony Orchestra, went down New York harbor on the customs launch and climbed up a rope ladder to welcome the Reiners on deck. He later reported that Reiner was puffing on a pipe and that, as the ship passed the Statue of Liberty, the immigrant conductor raised his hat. After Thiele had settled them in a suite at the Hotel Martinique, the Reiners gave their first interview in the United States. Although Berta, with her better knowledge of English, assisted with translation, Reiner impressed the reporters with his command of the language, which he had studied intensively during the summer. Having expressed curiosity about American jazz, Reiner was taken on a tour of New York night spots. From this exposure he declared that jazz was not a fad but had "come to stay for at least fifty years." In New York and later at a similar gathering at the Sinton Hotel in Cincinnati, Reiner held forth with his views of modern composers. Igor Stravinsky, Arnold Schoenberg, and Paul Hindemith were, in his opinion, replacing Richard Strauss in the European avant-garde. He also spoke warmly of his friends in Italy—Ottorino Respighi, Alfredo Casella, and Goffredo Petrassi. His promise to "give modern composers of all schools, American as well as others, liberal representation" on his programs must have struck fear in the hearts of conservative Cincinnati concertgoers.[6]

After meeting the players of the Cincinnati Symphony Orchestra at an informal gathering arranged by the Tafts, Fritz Reiner got down to business with them at their first rehearsal on 8 October. Reading from penciled notes in English on the back of a piano score of "The Star-Spangled Banner," he greeted the musicians, promising to create a great orchestra in Cincinnati.[7] From the beginning he was exacting, requiring more than an hour to get through only a portion of the Beethoven *Leonore* overture no. 3. He and the players had more than two weeks to take one another's measure before the opening concert on 27 October: the Beethoven overture, Brahms's Symphony no. 4, and two standard Wagner excerpts, the *Meistersinger* prelude and the prelude and "Isolde's Transfiguration" from *Tristan und Isolde*. The concert was enthusiastically received by a capacity audience and by most of the critics. An exception was J. Herman Thuman of the *Enquirer,* who found that Reiner's *rubato* "displayed a high disregard for phrasing."[8] Outspoken and opinionated, Thuman had been first a supporter and then a foe of Stokowski. He relished exercising his power and regarded the May Festival as his personal domain. He would continue to harbor outspoken reservations about Reiner for the next nine seasons.

In November Berta and Fritz Reiner applied for United States citizenship, an early indication of Reiner's commitment to an American career; they received their final papers in 1928. Berta joined the faculty of the Cincinnati Conservatory of Music as a vocal instructor and coach in operatic repertory. The press showed intense interest in the Reiners' personal lives. Considerable, though vague, references to the two daughters in Europe implied that they were Berta's, without explicitly saying so. Several papers published the photograph, taken the previous summer in Dresden, of Berta with Tuśy and Eva. Any public mention of both Reiners' previous marriages would have offended the conservative sensibilities of Cincinnatians of that time.

After an intensive schedule of five pairs of subscription concerts, three popular concerts, and twelve concerts on tour, the Reiners spent the Christmas holidays in New York. Arthur Judson introduced them to important music figures in Manhattan. They attended a concert of the New York Symphony conducted by Walter Damrosch, who greeted them backstage after the performance. At the Philharmonic they sat in the Carnegie Hall box of Bettie Fleischmann Holmes, by then an active patron of music in New York. A month after the Reiners returned to Cincinnati, there was a gala "Louis XVI" benefit for the musicians' pension fund in the Grand Ballroom of the Hotel Sinton. Looking uncomfortable in a white wig, a brocade suit, and shoes with silver buckles, Reiner conducted a similarly attired orchestra in Haydn's "Farewell" Symphony by candlelight.

In February the composer-critic Deems Taylor visited orchestras in Detroit, Cleveland, Chicago, St. Louis, Minneapolis, and Cincinnati, reporting on them for the New York *World*. He heard a Cincinnati program that included none of the standard repertory in which he could compare this orchestra with others: the local premieres of Pizzetti's *La pisanella* suite and Respighi's *Ballata delle gnomidi;* Wolf's *Italienische Serenade;* and Elena Gerhardt in songs by Gluck, Marcello, and Richard Strauss. Reiner, he wrote, was a "real find." In a few years he would no longer be "Little Nikisch" but rather "Big Reiner." Like Stokowski, he "convey[s] a sense of restless, almost ferocious, nervous vitality." Such an imprimatur from a New York authority carried great weight in Cincinnati, where the Taft-owned *Times-Star* reprinted the entire article.[9]

More important than these outward manifestations of success was Reiner's immediate grip on his position as music director. In November he asked the executive committee for information on the orchestra's financial affairs. Its chairman, Louis T. More, pointedly advised Reiner that it was not customary for a conductor to involve himself in such matters. More, a professor of physics and dean at the University of Cincinnati, would remain hostile to Reiner, but his attitude was more than tempered by Anna Taft's strong support. After reviewing the financial report, Reiner saw no reason why the Cincinnati Symphony Orchestra should not become one of the "four best" orchestras in the country. He promised to take it to New York the next season to prove his point. He also urged the executive committee to explore the possibility of presenting operas in the Music Hall. Rather than arousing resentment, his interest in the minutiae of the orchestra's affairs was welcomed as a contrast with his predecessor's indifference toward such matters. In a series of meetings of the executive committee and of the full board, over which Anna Taft presided, Reiner suggested achieving his goal by reducing touring to smaller cities, enlarging the orchestra, and importing better players.[10]

In late February the executive committee and board offered Reiner a four-year contract, through April 1927, at twenty-five thousand dollars annually for the first two years and thirty thousand dollars for the last two. There would be a "bonus" of five thousand dollars if he reduced the annual operating deficit by twenty thousand dollars. The Tafts agreed to raise their annual contribution to one hundred thousand dollars as their commitment to a major orchestra.

Reiner received broad power over allocating financial resources, hiring orchestra personnel, and determining players' salaries. The board replaced Thiele as manager with Anna Taft's former personal secretary, Jessie Darby, who would handle Cincinnati operations while Arthur Judson would book touring through his New York management office. The orchestra also engaged him as "advisory manager" for the same four-year term as the conductor's. A month later Judson submitted to the board the first of several reports supporting Reiner's authority, emphasizing the importance of improving orchestra personnel, and urging a long-range effort to secure an endowment.[11]

As an exception to its contentious relations with the orchestra, the May Festival invited Reiner to participate in its May 1923 Golden Anniversary, his sole appearance at this biennial event. Frank van der Stucken, still commanding a loyal following since succeeding Theodore Thomas, conducted four choral events. Reiner was on the Music Hall podium for two orchestral matinees. One of these concerts featured a newly installed organ in the Saint-Saëns Third Symphony and included Wagner excerpts sung by Florence Easton and Clarence Whitehill. The other was a "heroic" program of Beethoven's Third Symphony and *Ein Heldenleben* by Richard Strauss. According to the critic of the New York *Times,* in Cincinnati for the occasion, "This performance verifies the splendid reports we have heard of Mr. Reiner. He is indeed one of the great conductors."[12]

Before returning to Europe for the summer, Reiner came to what may have been his first confrontation with the Cincinnati board, which shared his desire to take the orchestra to New York the following season. For some years the Cincinnati Symphony Orchestra had had a contract with the Columbia Record Company to make recordings whenever it visited New York. Unlike Ysaye, who had made several discs for no fee, Reiner insisted on extra compensation. Since the orchestra could not play in New York without recording, the 1924 visit was canceled. The newspapers learned of the cancellation only after Reiner's departure. When the subject came up in an October interview, Reiner disingenuously explained that no hall in New York was available at a suitable time.[13]

During Reiner's summer absence the Cincinnati press speculated about changes he planned to make in the personnel of the orchestra. There were rumors that he was hiring players in Europe and much conjecture about local musicians to be released. Despite Jessie Darby's denials, the conductor was in fact auditioning players in Europe. When the 1923–1924 season opened in October, twenty-nine new players were in the orchestra, which had been increased by three overall. Most of these newcomers came from New York, recruited with the help of Judson's staff. Moreover, when the musicians' union raised objections to Reiner's hiring foreigners, Charles Taft used his political influence in Washington to expedite immigration procedures.[14]

The Reiners returned to Europe in May, stopping at Pontecchio and visiting with Respighi and Casella in Italy. In Dresden they encountered bureaucratic obstacles to removing their belongings from Germany. Faced with demands for taxes on their earnings abroad, the Reiners fortunately had valuable foreign funds with which to bargain with German officials.[15] They arrived in New York in late September on the *Conte Russo* with four large dogs. In Cincinnati they told the press of invitations for Reiner to fill future engagements in Vienna, Palermo, London, and Rome.

With the security of a four-year contract, Reiner settled in to build a major orchestra in Cincinnati, where he first earned his reputation for high turnover in personnel. There is no question that the goals of the Cincinnati Symphony Orchestra required changes in personnel significantly exceeding normal attrition. To this end, Reiner pursued a draconian policy of weeding out overage players, professionally marginal musicians, and "troublemakers." By his fourth season, in 1925–1926, he could confidently say that the Cincinnati Symphony Orchestra was truly *his* orchestra. Of ninety-two players, only twenty-six had been in the orchestra when he arrived. In that season, the minimum weekly pay was fifty dollars for twenty-eight weeks. Many of the players had contracts above that minimum, and both the association officially and Anna Taft unofficially supplemented players' income. Out-of-town players often received twice the pay of local members. A good number found part-time work in theaters, nightclubs, ballrooms, and restaurants, and the more prominent principal players taught at the conservatory or privately. It was not unusual for some Cincinnati Symphony players to earn, from all sources, as much as seven to ten thousand dollars a season. Under Reiner's pressure, the size of the orchestra reached a high of over one hundred players under contract in 1927; that figure declined after the change in organizational structure in 1929.[16]

Arthur Judson fully supported Reiner's efforts to improve the personnel of the orchestra. While the local press printed rumors of extensive replacements planned by Reiner, Judson explained through the orchestra's office that such changes were imperative if the Cincinnati Symphony Orchestra was to attain a status worthy of the community. He went to some pains to point out how few players were involved and how many Americans, not Europeans, would be brought in. Judson was building his own network of control, not only of conductors and soloists but of orchestral players as well. Through much of his management of the New York Philharmonic Orchestra, its personnel manager, Maurice Van Praag, also contracted free-lance work in New York, including early radio studios. Reiner relied, at Judson's urging, on Van Praag to engage out-of-town musicians for the Cincinnati Symphony Orchestra. Judson assured Reiner and the Cincinnati committee that he had instructed Van Praag not to recruit for New York openings players whom Reiner wanted to keep in Cincinnati. At the same time, Van Praag relieved Reiner of players that he did not want by offering them jobs elsewhere. When the local union objected to the "importation" of players from outside, Judson assured Reiner that he would intercede with Joseph Weber, then president of the American Federation of Musicians.[17]

Long after Reiner was in Cincinnati, a writer recalled, "Any day on which he failed to lose his temper was a day on which he was actually too sick to conduct."[18] Although Reiner may have been on his good behavior with the musicians during his first season in Cincinnati, he became more authoritarian once he had his four-year contract. In rehearsal, he singled out individual players for withering abuse in German, Italian, and English. He submitted many of them, especially string players, to the indignity of playing difficult passages alone. Listening grim-faced from the podium, his highest praise was "NOT impossible." He would ask a player where he had studied and, on being told, would reply, "You were cheated! You should get your money back!"

Cincinnati players recalled at least two occasions when Reiner's treatment of their colleagues backfired. While demanding that the first trumpeter repeat the famous passage in *Also sprach Zarathustra*, Reiner insisted that he play *pianissimo*, whistling the passage as an illustration. The player finally approached Reiner and handed him his instrument, saying, "You play it. I can whistle too!" On another occasion, Reiner demanded that the tambourine player bring his instrument to the podium. Attempting to demonstrate how he wanted the instrument played, he pushed his knuckle through the membrane. Without a word of comment, he handed the broken tambourine back to the player. Many musicians were convinced that Reiner abused them out of sheer sadism. Some players became physically ill in Reiner's orchestra; others dropped out rather than suffer his abuse. In protecting its members from such treatment, the Cincinnati union, like others of the time, was largely ineffective. Yet many players agreed that Reiner was the best conductor they had ever encountered.[19] Once Reiner had the musicians he wanted, the personnel of the Cincinnati Symphony Orchestra stabilized appreciably, especially from 1927 onward.

In Cincinnati Reiner had to learn an orchestral repertory for at least twenty different programs a season. Its foundation was the traditional Central European repertory from Bach through Brahms, including a generous representation of Wagner. To this Reiner added his personal expansion and elaboration of non-

German music and, most characteristically, a strong commitment to the music of his own time and national environment. Especially in his first years in Cincinnati, this required that Reiner learn a great deal of new repertory. From his Dresden programs he drew approximately a quarter of the four hundred compositions he conducted in his nine Cincinnati seasons. His programs included an extraordinary number of composers—at least ninety-five.[20] Wagner was by far the most frequently played composer, with twenty-one works in Reiner's programs, some of them requiring such singers as Alexander Kipnis, Florence Austral, and Lauritz Melchior. In Cincinnati Reiner did not hesitate to extract the kind of excerpts from Wagner's operas that Sir Donald Francis Tovey dubbed "bleeding chunks." The program of one concert listed "Siegfried Ascending Brünnhilde's Rock."

When Reiner played harpsichord continuo in the Bach B Minor Suite on the opening program of his second season, it was an isolated case of "authenticity" in his performance of Baroque music, possibly influenced by the Collegium Musicum in Leipzig. He was more likely to offer Bach in modern orchestrations of his organ music. He programmed all nine Beethoven symphonies, all four of Schumann and all four of Brahms, seven of Haydn, five of Mozart, and two of Schubert. At a time when the music of Bruckner and Mahler was seldom heard from American orchestras, Reiner offered Cincinnati performances of four Bruckner symphonies (the Fourth, Seventh, Eighth, and Ninth); of Mahler he programmed songs with orchestra and the Second, Fourth, and Seventh symphonies. He played the major symphonic poems of Richard Strauss, the popular ones more than once, but no operatic excerpts; both Elena Gerhardt and Claire Dux sang Strauss *Lieder* with the orchestra. Reiner's Russian repertory included not only popular works by Rimsky-Korsakov and Tchaikovsky but also music by Glazunov and Liadov. In addition to the Cello Concerto in B Minor with Pablo Casals, he programmed Dvořák's Violin Concerto and the E Minor Symphony. Of the music of Debussy, still something of a novelty on American symphony orchestra programs, he played *Prélude à l'après-midi d'un faune,* "Ibéria," "Rondes de printemps," *La mer,* and the two orchestral *Nocturnes.* More significantly, he offered his own first performances of Maurice Ravel's music, which he found especially congenial, including *La valse, Rapsodie espagnole, Ma mère l'oye, Le tombeau de Couperin,* the second suite from *Daphnis et Chloé, Boléro,* and the orchestration of Mussorgsky's *Pictures at an Exhibition.* Despite the disdain of the critics, *Boléro* was a tremendous success with the public, repeated in a popular concert and on the request program that concluded the season.

Equally important was Reiner's commitment to new music, explicit from his arrival in Cincinnati, despite resistance from both the press and his audiences. One-fifth of his Cincinnati repertory was by composers still living. Among four compositions by his friend Respighi was the world premiere of *Gli uccelli*. With the Orpheus Club Chorus and a local soloist, he gave the first American performance of Busoni's monumental Piano Concerto. Other American "firsts" included the Violin Concerto of Kurt Weill, Milhaud's Viola Concerto, the Glazunov Third Symphony, and *Italia* by Casella. Reiner also engaged Stravinsky, Respighi, and Dohnányi as guest conductors of their own music.

From his first months in Cincinnati, Reiner developed an involvement with American composition, less by way of explicit crusading zeal or publicity-seeking than as a matter of ingrained professionalism. In addition to the music of such earlier composers as Edward MacDowell, Henry Hadley, and Arthur Foote, he played music by Deems Taylor and John Alden Carpenter. He conducted orchestral music of Edgar Stillman Kelley, both in Cincinnati and at the Hollywood Bowl. On one of his first concerts in Cincinnati, he offered *The Twenty-second Psalm* of Ernest Bloch, then a fellow Ohioan teaching in Cleveland. He also played Bloch's "epic rhapsody" *America,* when the Cincinnati Symphony Orchestra was one of five orchestras to give its "simultaneous premiere" in 1928. Toward the end of his Cincinnati tenure, Reiner began to play music by such younger Americans as Roger Sessions, Louis Gruenberg, George Gershwin, Daniel Gregory Mason, and Aaron Copland. His premieres of American works in Cincinnati included Gruenberg's Jazz Suite, Mason's Third Symphony, and Sessions's suite from *The Black Maskers*. He offered Copland's *Scherzo* in Cincinnati after giving its premiere in Philadelphia. He corresponded with both Copland and Sessions regarding the premieres of their music, his exchange with Sessions including discussion of scoring for alto flute in *The Black Maskers*.[21]

In March 1928 George Gershwin appeared as soloist with Reiner and the Cincinnati Symphony Orchestra, playing his *Rhapsody in Blue* and Concerto in F. Ever since introducing the *Rhapsody in Blue* at his historic concert with Paul Whiteman in 1924, Gershwin had attracted attention for his fusion of popular and concert music. Although the Cincinnati critics were inclined to patronize Gershwin, he was a favorite with the audiences. He and Reiner established a good working relationship and a warm personal friendship. Reiner programmed *An American in Paris* a few months after Walter Damrosch had introduced it with the New York Philharmonic-Symphony.

Of Stravinsky he not only played suites from *The Firebird* and *Petrushka,* but also *The Song of the Nightingale,* a suite from *Pulcinella,* and several shorter works. Reiner first encountered the composer in person when Arthur Judson brought him to the United States in January 1925 for his first concert tour as conductor and piano soloist performing his own music. Stravinsky made his first Philadelphia appearances not under the auspices of the Philadelphia Orchestra but sponsored by the Philadelphia Philharmonic Society. After conducting players from the Philadelphia Orchestra for the society, he returned as soloist in his Concerto for Piano and Winds. Of that occasion Stravinsky wrote in his *Autobiography:*

Most conductors devote several rehearsals to the preparation of my Concerto, but on this occasion we had barely half an hour. And there was a miracle. There was not a single hitch. It was as though Reiner had played it time and again with that orchestra. Such an extraordinary phenomenon could never have occurred, notwithstanding the prodigious technique of the conductor and the high quality of the orchestra, if Reiner had not acquired a perfect knowledge of my score, which he had procured some time before. One could apply to him the familiar saying: he has the score in his head and not his head in the score.[22]

In addition to the Stravinsky concerto, this formidable program included the Berlioz overture to *Benvenuto Cellini,* the Suite no. 1, opus 3, of Béla Bartók, and *Till Eulenspiegel* of Richard Strauss. This concert was Reiner's first in Philadelphia and marked the beginning of an important association with that city.

Stravinsky conducted the Cincinnati Symphony Orchestra three weeks later in a program of his own music. Charles Ludwig, a Cincinnati critic who attended his rehearsals, wrote: "Stravinsky was suffering from the cold. He came to Emery Auditorium heavily bundled in sweater and overcoat, and even carried a huge shawl to protect himself against drafts. He was so indisposed Wednesday that he had to remain in his room at the Hotel Gibson while Fritz Reiner took his place on the conductor's stand at the rehearsal. Stravinsky said before he took the baton Thursday that he still felt ill—and he asked Reiner to hold his bottle of medicine for him."[23]

Although Reiner objected strongly to touring with his orchestra to the "provinces" of the Ohio Valley and beyond, he placed extraordinary emphasis on taking the Cincinnati Symphony Orchestra to such major East Coast centers as New York and Philadelphia. After he forced the cancellation of a New York appearance by the Cincinnati Symphony Orchestra in the 1923–1924 season, it was two more years before Reiner and his orchestra appeared together in New York. He had meanwhile conducted the New York Philharmonic in Lewisohn Stadium in the summers of 1924 and 1925. Reiner's program on 6 January 1926 consisted of the *Benvenuto Cellini* overture, the Brahms Fourth Symphony, *Till Eulenspiegel,* and the Dance Suite of Bartók, of which the orchestra had recently given the first American performance in Cincinnati. Critical reception for Reiner and his orchestra ranged from Leonard Liebling's enthusiasm in the *American* and high praise from Olga Samaroff in the *Post* to Lawrence

Gilman's qualified approval in the *Herald-Tribune*. At the other extreme were Olin Downes's harsh words in the *Times:*

Mr. Reiner has brought his orchestra to a considerable pitch of efficiency . . . [but] the tone quality is often forced till it becomes shrill and hard. . . . There is a constant tendency to dramatic extremes. . . . [He played] the Brahms symphony with little ritards and diminuendos . . . sufficiently significant to spoil the symmetry of movement. . . . This was a concert in which the orchestra showed a considerable degree of virtuoso technique; but the performance did not enhance musical values or leave the impression of an original or creative interpreter.[24]

Following this concert, Bettie Holmes gave a supper party at her Park Avenue apartment in honor of the Reiners; the guests included Adolph Lewisohn, the Walter Damrosches, the Frederick Steinways, the Artur Bodanzkys, the Herbert Witherspoons, and the Arthur Judsons. Bettie Holmes was a generous supporter of the International Composers Guild, which had presented a concert of contemporary music in Aeolian Hall the Sunday preceding the Cincinnati Symphony Orchestra concert. Reiner participated in a program that included a variety of solo and ensemble music, "of dubious value" according to Downes. The program opened with Reiner conducting the Hindemith *Kammermusik* no. 3, with Cornelius Van Vliet, principal cellist of the Cincinnati orchestra, as soloist, and closed with Casella's *Pupazzetti.*

Returning to Cincinnati after this tour, Reiner told the *Times-Star* that he had never heard finer playing in his entire career than the Cincinnati players had given in New York. If anything, "their playing in Philadelphia reached even greater heights." (In the latter city one critic ranked the Cincinnati Symphony Orchestra as one of the four best in the country.) In the same interview, Reiner, noting that every orchestra reflected the style of its conductor, described the special character of his Cincinnati ensemble. "Some orchestras, for example, may specialize in smoothness. I have specialized in range of dynamic values— and contrast. So that on the one hand we have developed a rare and unique pianissimo, really the softest and most delicate whisperings, and on the other hand a dazzling forte, not of mere loudness, but of power and brilliancy."[25]

A year later in Carnegie Hall, Reiner again challenged conservatives like Downes with a program including Bartók's Suite no. 1, Casella's *Italia,* and *The Song of the Nightingale* by Stravinsky. Downes, again dismissing Reiner as a "modernist," liked the Bartók Suite no. 1 better in 1927 than he had the Dance Suite in 1926; he was under the impression that the latter was an earlier composition. He also reported that Casella sat in a box seat at this concert and that Wilhelm Furtwängler's towering figure was seen among the standees.[26] This tour also included appearances in Cleveland, Philadelphia, Pittsburgh, and Washington. In the nation's capital, President Coolidge received the entire orchestra at the White House, shaking hands with every player and inquiring politely of Reiner as to who financed the orchestra. He was pleased to learn of its impeccably Republican sponsorship. The Coolidges did not attend the concert in Constitution Hall, but Chief Justice William Howard Taft was his elder brother's guest of honor. On their return to Cincinnati, the orchestra and its conductor received much praise in the press. Responding on the stage of Emery Auditorium to a glowing tribute from the mayor of the city, Reiner compared the Cincinnati Symphony Orchestra favorably with the New York Philharmonic.[27]

For his third and last appearance in New York with the Cincinnati Symphony Orchestra in February 1928, Reiner offered a program of contemporary Hungarian music. This was during Béla Bartók's first visit to the United States, after his debut as piano soloist with the New York Philharmonic under Willem Mengelberg's direction. He was originally scheduled to play his Piano Concerto no. 1, but Mengelberg could not or would not prepare the music in time. Instead Bartók played his earlier Piano Rhapsody, opus 1, on 22 and 23 December 1927. A few weeks later, with Reiner and his Cincinnati Symphony Orchestra in Carnegie Hall, Bartók played the concerto that Mengelberg and the Philharmonic had canceled. The entire program on 13 February, under the auspices of the Hungary Society, consisted of music by living Hungarian composers: Bartók's Concerto and *Deux images, Carnival* by Leo Weiner, the suite from Kodály's *Háry János,* and *Ruralia hungarica* by Dohnányi. Thanks to its sponsorship, this concert drew a near-capacity audience in Carnegie Hall, and Toscanini personally congratulated Reiner on the program.[28]

Ten days later, after the orchestra had completed its tour to Buffalo, Erie, and Toronto, it returned to Cincinnati, where Bartók again played his concerto. Thuman described it in the *Enquirer* as "either a colossal joke [or] unbridled ravings of a rash experimenter. . . . If it were not so tragic, it would be humorous." The following October Bartók wrote to Reiner from Budapest: "I have played my piano concerto a few times since I came home; the performances have been as diverse as the receptions! . . . The Berlin performance—under Kleiber—had lots of life, but the orchestra had a few misadventures. Of course, not one of the European performances came up to the standard of precision shown in Cincinnati." [29]

Bartók had written to thank Reiner for his cabled congratulations on winning one of four prizes in a competition for a chamber music composition offered by the Musical Fund Society in Philadelphia. Both Reiner and Mengelberg were among the judges. They became embroiled in a widely publicized dispute over an award to Bartók.

It has been impossible to learn anything specific about the "Budapest proposition" to which Bartók also referred in this letter. Apparently Reiner had discussed a position in Budapest that had not materialized. "I am sorry that the Budapest proposition came to nothing, although who knows whether you would have been able to bear it here. As regards membership in the Upper House [of the Hungarian parliament], this is one thing that—in my opinion— you shouldn't have asked for. This question wasn't brought up in the winter when we talked the matter over, so I don't know if you really made it one of your conditions." [30]

It is worth noting at this point the extent of Fritz Reiner's commitment to the music of Béla Bartók, a commitment unmatched by any other contemporary composer, for Reiner had an understanding and devotion to Bartók's music that no other conductor of his time equaled. He persisted in programming this music in Cincinnati and New York in the face of critical contempt and audience hostility. With his Cincinnati orchestra he programmed the American premieres of five major orchestral works in nine seasons: the Suite no. 1, opus 3, in 1923; the Dance Suite in 1925; *Deux images* in 1926; the suite from *The Miraculous Mandarin* in 1927 (a world premiere of the concert suite following the first performance in 1926 of the complete ballet in Cologne); and the Piano Concerto no. 1 in 1928. Each time he conducted his Cincinnati Symphony Orchestra in New York he included an important Bartók work on the program. Although he introduced Bartók's Hungarian Sketches in Philadelphia, he played nothing else by this composer during his guest-conducting years in the 1930s. Once established with his own orchestra in Pittsburgh, he gave the first American performances of the revised version of the Suite no. 2, opus 4. As guest conductor of the New York Philharmonic-Symphony in 1943, he conducted the first American performance of the Concerto for Two Pianos with the composer and his wife as soloists. His Bartók repertory also included the Concerto for Orchestra, the Second and Third piano concertos, the Divertimento, the Music for Strings, Percussion, and Celesta, the Violin Concerto no. 2, the Viola Concerto, and Leo Weiner's orchestration of Two Rumanian Dances. No other conductor in America did as much for Bartók's music.

Despite his early interest in the total operations of the Cincinnati Symphony Orchestra, Reiner soon left such details as finance, publicity, and concert presentation to the board, the Tafts, and Judson. However, when the orchestra's operation affected his own work or his personal convenience, he exerted pressure in at least three areas—choruses, touring, and popular and children's concerts.

The May Festival dominated choral activity in Cincinnati, drawing the best choristers from the churches and singing societies. It rehearsed regularly for two years under Frank van der Stucken's direction to prepare for the biennial event. When Reiner made his sole appearance at the festival of 1923, he conducted completely orchestral programs. In 1924 the Tafts made a special effort to bring the two organizations together with Reiner as musical director, but Thuman recalled that Reiner had been "indiscreet" during the 1923 festival. Although the May Festival needed the Cincinnati Symphony Orchestra, it did not need or want its conductor. Only once did the May Festival chorus appear in the winter series of the Cincinnati Symphony Orchestra, in the finale of the Mahler Second Symphony. For other choral repertory in the winter season, Reiner had to work with inferior local groups. He engaged the Orpheus Club for the Brahms *Alto Rhapsody* in 1926 and for the Busoni Piano Concerto in 1930. A combined chorus from the high schools sang in Bloch's *America*. Such occasional improvisation did not meet Reiner's artistic goals, nor did it satisfy his competitive instincts vis-à-vis the May Festival.

In 1926 the Cincinnati Symphony Orchestra solved this problem by arranging for joint appearances with the Toronto Mendelssohn Choir in both cities, the featured work being the Beethoven Ninth Symphony. The Tafts paid fifteen thousand dollars to underwrite these joint appearances, which continued through 1931 as a part of the association's regular budget. Herbert A. Fricker, the Toronto director, conducted the purely choral concerts. Reiner always conducted at least one full program on the Cincinnati subscription series featuring the chorus with the orchestra and well-known soloists. The annual Toronto trip during these Prohibition years in the United States challenged the ingenuity of both players and conductor to smuggle alcohol across the border. Reiner once preempted the orchestra's timpani as a hiding place for his contraband and on another occasion chose the innards of the phonograph used to play the nightingale recording in Respighi's *I pini di Roma*.

After his first season in Cincinnati, Reiner sought to reduce the number of concerts he conducted himself and to concentrate his energies on the subscription concerts. His immediate targets were touring to smaller cities and such nonsubscription concerts in Cincinnati as the Sunday afternoon popular concerts in the Music Hall and the programs for children. Judson agreed that musicians' services on tour could be better used for rehearsals. He also suggested that it was scarcely appropriate for a twenty-five-thousand-dollar-a-year music director to conduct concerts for which the top admission price was twenty-five cents. The obvious solution was to employ an assistant conductor. In 1925 Reiner corresponded with Eugene Ormandy, then a violinist-conductor at the Capitol Theater in New York. Negotiations collapsed over the fee requested by the younger Hungarian for his services as assistant conductor and principal second violin and for his wife's as harpist in the orchestra.[31]

Two years later Reiner achieved a successful solution in the person of the

Russian violist-conductor Vladimir Bakaleinikoff, who had extensive experience in chamber music and conducting at the Moscow Art Theater. "Bak" proved to be an ideal assistant to Reiner, personally congenial but, more important professionally, completely reliable. He played principal viola in the orchestra and took on work that Reiner shunned. The engagement of Bakaleinikoff not only relieved pressures on Reiner in Cincinnati but also gave him an opportunity to expand his activities in Philadelphia.

CHAPTER IV

An Expanding Career

With the assurance of her husband's four-year contract in the spring of 1923, Berta began house-hunting. She settled on a house at 3818 Winding Way in Avondale, a suitably fashionable residential area on the escarpment rising northeast of downtown Cincinnati. During the summer the Reiners had the home remodeled to suit their requirements, at a cost of twelve thousand dollars, which Anna Taft paid as a personal gift.[1] The three-story house provided ample space for the entertaining that Berta enjoyed arranging, personal accommodations and a large study for Reiner, and, on the third floor, quarters for servants and Berta's "live-in" students. A garden surrounded the house, and the backyard contained a swimming pool, which Reiner enjoyed when weather permitted.[2]

Most of Berta's students at the Cincinnati Conservatory of Music were young women, to whom she became strongly attached in a quasi-maternal way. Childless herself, she insisted that her "girls" call her Mumsie. One or two of Berta's students lived in the Avondale home, often arousing Reiner's suspicion that they were spying on him. Respected and popular in the highest social circles, Berta was a distinct social asset to Reiner in his role as the leading musician of Cincinnati. Fritz was a charming, if somewhat reserved, host and expected Berta to entertain in a style befitting their place in the community. When such visiting artists as Ottorino Respighi and his wife or George Gershwin came to appear with the orchestra, the Reiners entertained them at their home.

Berta was three years older than Reiner and, to judge from photographs of them together, taller than him. (Carlotta Reiner characteristically referred to her predecessor as Big Bertha.) Just as she manipulated her students, Berta wanted to play a strong role in shaping her husband's career. She was opinionated on musical matters and criticized her husband's performances and views in the presence of her students and guests. She took credit for discovering Reiner in Dresden and for persuading him to reject the narrow provincial life of the Saxon capital. Sometimes claiming to have taught Reiner "everything that he ever knew about music," she took credit for having introduced him to such important Italian musicians as Respighi and Toscanini. Berta was probably, though with Reiner's tacit approval, the source of reports released to the press of the various opportunities—real and fictitious—that her husband had rejected. In the spring of 1926 the Cincinnati *Post* quoted her saying that Reiner had turned down an offer with the Roxy Theater orchestra in New York at an annual salary of fifty thousand dollars.[3] Apparently Berta, herself of limited talent, needed to associate herself with more gifted artists such as her mother and husband. Fiercely loyal to Reiner, she refused even to see her former husband, Walter Kirchhoff, in New York when he made his debut at the Metropolitan Opera as Loge in *Das Rheingold* in January 1927.

During his Cincinnati years, Reiner sent one hundred dollars a month to his mother in Budapest and, intermittently, ten dollars a month to Elca, probably for child support.[4] Reiner enjoyed what was for that time a substantial income. In 1926 he earned close to forty thousand dollars from the Cincinnati Symphony Orchestra and from guest appearances in Buenos Aires, Budapest, and elsewhere. Berta had her own financial resources, from her teaching and from her parents' estates. Reiner enjoyed his creature comforts—custom-tailored clothing, good food, and fine wine. His secretary attended to orders for handmade shirts and shoes and for special blends of cigarettes and pipe tobacco. Soon after settling on Winding Way, Reiner bought a Cadillac Imperial sedan; the press reported with some awe that it had cost eight thousand dollars! The Reiners traveled first class as celebrities on transatlantic liners to Europe and booked suites in the best hotels. Preparing for a trip to Europe in 1927, Reiner made elaborate arrangements for the voyage, including shipment of a Pierce-Arrow touring car, for which he required an insurance "triptych" covering travel in Hungary and Yugoslavia. On his return, he reported that he had driven more than six thousand miles all over Europe. It was probably beside this automobile that someone took a snapshot of Reiner and Arturo Toscanini in motoring garb.

Reiner's absorbing hobby was photography, which had fascinated him from childhood. The Avondale home contained a well-equipped darkroom in the basement. For many years he was an active member of the Circle of Confusion, an exclusive group of celebrity amateur photographers in New York. Reiner kept abreast of the latest developments in cameras, lenses, and film. (Some years later he rejected his broker's advice to buy Polaroid stock because he doubted whether a system could succeed that did not permit flexible processing by the amateur photographer.) He owned an early Bell and Howell movie camera, which he used at home and on his travels. In the summer of 1928 the press reported that he had been taking pictures of "bathing beauties" at Virginia Beach and that Pathé News had bought his film of the Kentucky Derby. He sent photos of life in Cincinnati to his children in Yugoslavia and, on his visits there, took pictures of his daughters to show to friends in Cincinnati.

Sailing for Europe immediately after his second Cincinnati season in the spring of 1924, Reiner went to Budapest to conduct the Philharmonic there during a Beethoven festival.[5] A few days later he was in Prague for the second annual festival of the International Society for Contemporary Music. He conducted a program that included Prokofiev's First Violin Concerto with Joseph Szigeti as soloist. In his memoirs Prokofiev credits this performance with having established this concerto in the concert repertory after an unsuccessful premiere in Paris under Koussevitzky. Szigeti also reported this success, remarking that "Reiner was a glutton for new music." In Prague, Reiner heard the first performance of *Erwartung* by Schoenberg. He also heard *Pacific 231* by Arthur Honegger, which he later introduced in Cincinnati.[6]

During the summer of 1926 Reiner was again active abroad, conducting opera for the first time in this decade. In May he made first appearances at the Royal Hungarian State Opera in Budapest, conducting *Die Walküre* and *Die Meistersinger*.[7] He then sailed from Europe to Buenos Aires, where he spent more than a month conducting German opera with distinguished international casts. His repertory included *Die Walküre*, sung in German for the first time at the Teatro Colón, *Der Freischutz*, *Tannhäuser*, *Die Meistersinger*, and *Tristan und Isolde*. His casts included Friedrich Schorr, Meta Seinemeyer, Alexander Kipnis, and Gustav Schützendorf. This was Reiner's first working encounter with these major postwar German singers, some of whom worked with him subsequently in America and in London. Some years later Reiner responded to an interviewer's question about making cuts in performances of Wagner's operas, recalling that, when he conducted *Die Meistersinger* in Buenos Aires, the performance lasted only three and a half hours, including intermissions. This, he suggested, was going too far. The press agent for this Colón season was Bruno Zirato, who was to play an important part in Reiner's later career.[8] This was Reiner's only engagement in South America.

The annual arrival interviews in the Cincinnati press often referred to Reiner's having conducted extensively in Europe, even suggesting in 1924 that he had turned down a major engagement at the Berlin opera. It has been impossible to verify other reports of concerts in London, in Vienna, and in Russia.[9] Such stories frequently originated with Berta, directly or through the orchestra. Berta also took credit for Arturo Toscanini's inviting Reiner to conduct the orchestra of the Teatro alla Scala in Milan. It is equally possible that Arthur Judson encouraged these invitations, for the Italian conductor was now firmly established at the New York Philharmonic.[10] When Reiner returned to Cincinnati after his first La Scala engagement in the fall of 1927, there were reports that his commitments in the United States had made it necessary for him to turn down opera engagements in Italy and Egypt.

Looking back many years later, Judson recalled Fritz Reiner as "one of the most difficult" of the many conductors he had managed, but also one of the most exceptionally talented.[11] Although he may have intended his frequent statements hailing the young Reiner as one of the most important conductors in America for local Cincinnati consumption, his own promotion of Reiner's career elsewhere spoke eloquently of his high regard. Already a dominant manager of concert artists and conductors, Judson was even more powerful as manager of both the Philadelphia Orchestra and the New York Philharmonic.

On one of Reiner's first visits to New York, probably during the 1922 Christmas holidays, Judson took him to an evening musicale at the Fifth Avenue home of the philanthropist Adolph Lewisohn, an amateur singer and an ardent patron of music. Judson later recalled how the young conductor completely captivated Lewisohn by his ability to sight-read and transpose the piano accompaniments of German *Lieder* set before him by his host, who had taken his first singing lessons in his seventieth year. This favorable impression resulted in Reiner's being engaged as guest conductor at Lewisohn Stadium for two weeks each in the summers of 1924 and 1925.

At the instigation of a family friend, Mrs. Charles S. ("Minnie") Guggenheimer, Lewisohn had in 1918 underwritten a series of summer symphonic concerts at an outdoor stadium he had built on a steep eastward-facing hillside on the campus of the College of the City of New York. By 1923 Judson and Lewisohn engaged the New York Philharmonic for the summer season at the Stadium, an arrangement that continued through 1951. In its time, the Stadium Concerts, unlike some other popular concerts, performed complete symphonies and concertos, rather than lighter short pieces. But the most truly popular aspect of these concerts was the low admission price, as little as twenty-five cents for general admission to the steeply raked concrete amphitheater. Generations of New Yorkers owed their introduction to "classical" music to these concerts in Lewisohn Stadium.[12]

For these concerts Reiner programmed standard symphonic works from his Cincinnati repertory, interspersed with such lighter music as overtures and ballet and dance music from his popular concert programs. Departing from standard Stadium fare, he conducted the American premiere of Leo Weiner's Serenade for Small Orchestra and the first performance in New York since 1916 of Richard Strauss's *Eine Alpensinfonie,* for which it was necessary to add 28 players to the orchestra's usual 106 personnel.[13]

In 1925 Reiner also appeared at the Hollywood Bowl, where Artie Carter Mason had established a counterpart to the New York summer concerts with the Los Angeles Philharmonic Orchestra. Originally Mrs. Mason had engaged Reiner to conduct sixteen concerts for an overall fee of twenty-four hundred dollars, with additional concerts at two hundred dollars each. Probably because of his crowded schedule, he conducted only twelve programs in three weeks, opening the fourth season of these concerts before an audience numbering twenty-five thousand. Reiner's repertory there was similar to that of the Stadium Concerts, except that, during the three-week period, two American composers appeared on Reiner's programs conducting their own music: Edgar Stillman Kelley with his symphonic poem *The Pit and the Pendulum* and Howard Hanson with his *Lux aeterna.*[14] The Reiners traveled to Los Angeles by motorcar. With friends in a second car, the party made a leisurely sightseeing trip together. However, Reiner's final concert in Los Angeles was to occur shortly before his first rehearsal in New York for a two-week stint in Lewisohn Stadium. To meet that schedule, Reiner had to fly from Los Angeles to New York. Before regular commercial transcontinental service, one flew as a passenger on a mail plane during the day and took a Pullman sleeper overnight, because planes could not fly at night. Reiner must have found this trip unpleasant, because he avoided further airplane travel until the last years of his life.

On Judson's recommendation that Cincinnati should release its conductor to enhance his own and his orchestra's reputation, Reiner had made his Philadelphia debut in 1925 accompanying Igor Stravinsky. When Arturo Toscanini fell ill two months later, Judson arranged for Reiner to conduct one week of New York Philharmonic concerts, including a Saturday morning program for children. For this winter season New York Philharmonic debut, Reiner's fee was five hundred dollars. In Carnegie Hall and the Metropolitan Opera House, Reiner offered music by Beethoven, Richard Strauss, Wagner, Debussy, and Dukas, as well as a suite from Stravinsky's *The Firebird.*[15]

Judson then arranged for Reiner to take three weeks away from Cincinnati in January and February 1927 to conduct the Philadelphia Orchestra in that city, Baltimore, New York, and Washington, while Leopold Stokowski took a midseason vacation. During Reiner's engagement in Philadelphia, Toscanini delayed his arrival from Italy. The Philadelphia Orchestra "loaned" Reiner to the New York Philharmonic for concerts in Carnegie Hall, the Metropolitan Opera House, and the Brooklyn Academy of Music. Although his programs for the subscription concerts with the Philadelphia Orchestra were conventional as compared with his Cincinnati repertory, they included two of his specialties that Philadelphia had not heard for many years—Debussy's *La mer* and Strauss's *Also sprach Zarathustra,* which received an "ovation." Despite his success with the Philadelphia Orchestra, when Reiner brought his own Cincinnati Symphony Orchestra to Philadelphia for its second visit a few weeks later, one critic complained of "the same faults as last season . . . lack of cohesion, blurred strings, uneven playing. Reiner sought to overcome these deficiencies by the spritely and effervescent quality of his direction . . . but such makeshifts were not necessary when he conducted the Philadelphia Orchestra." [16]

Reiner became better acquainted with the Philadelphia Orchestra in the fall of 1927, when he conducted the first thirteen weeks of the season while Leopold Stokowski took a sabbatical. Other guests that season included Sir Thomas Beecham, Ossip Gabrilowitsch, Frederick Stock, Willem Mengelberg, and Pierre Monteux. Reiner's engagement—nearly half the season—was the longest of any guest conductor, an indication of Judson's high regard for him. When Reiner submitted his repertory for Philadelphia, he proposed for his first program Strauss's *Eine Alpensinfonie.* Judson objected strongly to this music as unsuitable to get Reiner "off on the right foot" in Philadelphia. Accordingly, the Strauss selection on his opening program was the familiar *Till Eulenspiegel.* Arriving in Philadelphia in September 1927, Reiner expressed views that must have struck a responsive chord with Arthur Judson and conservative Philadelphians but were also an implied criticism of Stokowski: "I believe Philadelphia audiences prefer classical music to extremely modern selections and, as this coincides with my own musical tastes, I am not planning to play much else. Of course, I shall play some modern music on my programs, but there are so few good moderns." [17]

This cautious approach was what Judson wanted and may well have been a welcome relief to Philadelphia patrons upset by Stokowski's crusading zeal for new music. Reiner's Philadelphia programs were not entirely devoid of innovation, however. On 4 November he conducted the world premiere of Aaron Copland's *Scherzo* for orchestra, beginning a long association with that composer. His programs also included the Prokofiev Violin Concerto in D Major with Szigeti, and Casella's *Italia* rhapsody. In his last concert at year's end, Reiner was reunited with Béla Bartók, as soloist in the same Rhapsody for Piano and Orchestra, opus 1, that he had played a week earlier for his American debut with the New York Philharmonic. In less than three weeks early in 1928, Reiner had conducted three orchestras in fifteen concerts—the Philadelphia Orchestra, the New York Philharmonic as a substitute a second time in less than a year for Toscanini, and his own Cincinnati orchestra on its third East Coast tour.

After conducting the last half of the Cincinnati season, Reiner returned to close that of Philadelphia. The preceding guest, Pierre Monteux, had expressed himself undiplomatically on the subject of the Philadelphia audience, following the departure of some patrons during his performance of Stravinsky's *The Rite of Spring*. Ninety-five percent of the orchestra's audiences, he said, "know nothing about this art of music. . . . Philadelphians want a tall, slim conductor who pays a great deal of attention to his tailor . . . [not a conductor] so short and stout." Philadelphians were not mollified by Monteux's subsequent protestations of his admiration for Stokowski: "We are dear and close friends." Reiner delighted them by coming to their defense: "Monteux is a fool—talking bunk—and what I think of him is unprintable. . . . Philadelphia is the music centre of America. . . . [Walking out] is the inalienable right of the person who pays to hear the music. . . . People in Philadelphia know more about music than in any other city." The interviewer described Reiner as "of medium stature, about five feet, six, and inclined to plumpness . . . wearing a finely-tailored wine-colored suit, a yellow shirt, and a tie with alternating lavender and black diagonal stripes."[18] No wonder, then, that many who claimed to be knowledgeable on orchestral affairs in Philadelphia began to talk of Reiner as a possible successor to Stokowski.

As early as his first season in Cincinnati, Reiner began his long involvement with radio. In January 1923 he conducted his orchestra in a broadcast over WLW, the station of the Crossley Radio Company, a pioneer in radio manufacturing and broadcasting and the most powerful station in the nation. From time to time there were other broadcasts, sometimes with the full orchestra, sometimes with selected personnel.

But it was Arthur Judson who introduced Reiner to network radio. In the mid-1920s Judson had recognized the potential of promoting artists under his management over the radio, but David Sarnoff rejected his proposal to supply "talent" to the National Broadcasting Company. Judson then leased telephone lines and studio facilities for nationwide broadcasting that he called the Columbia Broadcasting System in 1927. Suffering from underfinancing and lack of marketing expertise, this project had a precarious existence until William Paley rescued it in 1928. Although Paley took over CBS, Judson remained a substantial stockholder, and the artist management conglomerate that he organized in 1932 was first known as Columbia Concerts Corporation. It remained an affiliate of the network until 1940, when the Justice Department took antitrust action against it and a similar artist management affiliated with the National Broadcasting Company.[19]

In the fall of 1927 Judson began presenting a series of weekly concerts "radiated over the CBS chain."[20] These broadcasts featured concert artists under his management with a studio orchestra contracted by Van Praag. Reiner inaugurated this series on 9 October with soprano Sophie Braslau and tenor Charles Hackett as soloists. In these early days of network radio, Judson booked many of the soloists heard on such programs as the Dutch Masters Hour, the Atwater Kent Hour, and the Cadillac Hour. On one of these programs—the Firestone Hour—Richard Tauber appeared with his old Dresden colleague in 1931. Their staff conductors included Eugene Ormandy, Howard Barlow, and André Kostelanetz, all of whom Judson managed. These broadcasts were long a showcase for his concert artists, culminating in the weekly CBS broadcasts of the Sunday afternoon concerts of the New York Philharmonic-Symphony Orchestra.

Reiner's insistence on a special fee to make disc recordings with the Cincinnati Symphony unfortunately prevented any documentation of his work with that orchestra. However, he did make "recordings" of a sort in 1925 and 1926, "conducting" two pianists for Welte-Mignon Licensee player-piano rolls in popular symphonies for De Luxe Record Company at the Autopneumatic Studios in New York. A 1928 royalty statement includes the Dvořák "New World" Symphony, Mozart's "Jupiter," the Tchaikovsky Fifth, the Haydn "Surprise," and the Beethoven First, Fifth, and Sixth symphonies. Probably because of an annual guarantee, Reiner earned three thousand dollars in royalties from these piano rolls in 1926.[21] Reiner was listed as one of the pianists in Beethoven and Mozart symphonies. A cover letter with this statement apologizes for declining sales attributed to competition from phonograph recordings.

As Anna Taft grew older and became less directly involved in the affairs of the Cincinnati Symphony Orchestra, its governance rested increasingly with the executive committee. To its chairman, Louis T. More, fell the task of negotiating with Reiner for the renewal of the four-year agreement that the orchestra had signed with him in the spring of 1923. Anticipating its expiration at the end of the 1926–1927 season, Professor More discussed renewing the contract with Reiner in December 1926. We know the substance of these talks only one-sidedly, from the conductor's letters to More following their meetings. Reiner delayed for several months his agreement to More's offer of a one-year contract. Finally, in April, he signed it at a salary of thirty-five thousand dollars for sixty concerts. The association agreed to engage an assistant conductor and to relieve Reiner of the popular and children's concerts.[22]

In a letter to Judson a year later, Reiner gave a more candid account of his next discussion with More regarding a contract for 1928–1929. While expressing his appreciation for the Cincinnati Symphony Orchestra's releasing him for the Philadelphia engagement, he had asked that the association reduce his commitment from sixty to fifty-four concerts for the next season. Advising Reiner not to expect more than a one-year contract, More had denounced the conductor's "high living" requirement of three-room hotel suites on tour and his insistence on an unnecessarily large orchestra. Conductors, he told Reiner, contribute nothing to the community "commensurate with the high salaries they receive." For his part, Reiner wrote Judson, he "just listened calmly."[23]

More's failure to offer Reiner contracts for more than one year at a time reflected growing concern for the financial stability of the Cincinnati Symphony Orchestra. For Fritz Reiner's artistic achievement in Cincinnati had carried its price: after four seasons, the orchestra's operating deficit was over $240,000 out of expenditures of $383,000. The Tafts met over two-thirds of it, $166,000. Although Charles and Anna Taft never wavered in their devotion to Reiner and the Cincinnati Symphony Orchestra, they and others concerned with its future could not ignore the possibility of their no longer being around to help. In 1922, when Reiner arrived, Charles Taft was seventy-eight years old, and his wife was seventy.

From his earliest consultations as adviser to the Cincinnati Symphony Orchestra, Arthur Judson had urged the establishment of an endowment fund of at least four million dollars to provide perpetual support for the orchestra. After much consultation, the Cincinnati Institute of Fine Arts was incorporated in March 1927. Its objective was to assure permanent support for musical and other artistic culture in Cincinnati by endowing art education, music and drama, museums, and the symphony orchestra. The four incorporators were Lucien Wulsin of the Baldwin Piano Company, Louis T. More, Robert A. Taft, and banker John J. Rowe. Two months later Charles and Anna Taft announced a gift to the Institute of $1 million in market securities and real estate for the benefit of the orchestra. They also gave to the institute their extensive art collection to be housed in their Pike Street home as a museum. These gifts were conditional on the institute's raising another $2.5 million for its endowment. Although the total of $3.5 million was significantly less than the $4 million Judson had recommended as a minimum for the orchestra alone, he expressed enthusiasm for this effort, hailing Reiner as "one of the three great conductors in the world."[24]

For more than a year the leaders of the new institute planned an aggressive fund-raising campaign. This culminated in November 1928, when, in nine days, three hundred teams of solicitors raised $2,682,633 for the institute. On the first day of 1929 the Cincinnati Institute of Fine Arts assumed control of the Cincinnati Symphony Orchestra Association Company. Its board of directors consisted of men who had played a prominent role in its establishment, drawn, except for More, from the business community. Robert A. Taft, nephew of Charles and Anna, represented the Tafts. One of the stipulations embedded in the institute's original fund-raising was that the orchestra would not independently undertake its traditional annual fund-raising, leaving it largely dependent on the institute for financial support. Although the institute's board was not responsible for the operation of the orchestra, it wielded decisive influence through its allocation of the income from its endowment funds. The orchestra was now governed by a board of trustees of seven men and two women, one of them Anna Taft. There was also an advisory board of eighteen women, reversing the genders of the original governing structure.[25]

Of immediate importance to Reiner was the shift from the benevolent generosity of Anna Taft to a board of businessmen, lawyers, and bankers as the controlling power behind the Cincinnati Symphony Orchestra. In fact, the orchestra's trustees shortly authorized a survey of leading European conductors in anticipation of the possibility of the expiration of Reiner's contract.[26] Reiner may well have sensed some insecurity in his Cincinnati position when he discussed the "Budapest proposition" with Bartók early in 1928. Having just completed thirteen highly successful weeks in Philadelphia, he may have seen a future unfolding before him with which a long-term commitment to Cincinnati might interfere. If so, it would not be the last time in his career that his expectations were overly optimistic.

To open his eighth Cincinnati season, Reiner conducted the Brahms Second Symphony and Strauss's *Ein Heldenleben,* a program honoring Charles and Anna Taft for their devotion to the orchestra. Two and a half months later, on 29 December 1929, Charles Phelps Taft died at the age of eighty-six. After a year in mourning, Anna Taft returned to her box at Emery Auditorium on 30 January 1931; she died the following day at her home at the age of seventy-nine. In her will, she bequeathed another one million dollars to the Cincinnati Institute of Fine Arts.[27]

Meanwhile, major changes affected Reiner's family affairs. When they first arrived in Cincinnati, Fritz and Berta gave the impression that the two daughters in Europe would shortly join them in Cincinnati. Berta shared her husband's desire to achieve a concrete family unit. (Berta's reported epilepsy may have prevented her having children of her own.) Reiner continued to press Elca to allow one or both of the girls to join him in Cincinnati. In July 1926, while Reiner was in Buenos Aires and Berta was at Pontecchio, Tuśy wrote to her stepmother in English, addressing her as Mutzi. Instead of returning from Buenos Aires directly to the United States, Reiner joined his wife and daughter in Europe for the transatlantic voyage.[28]

Tuśy remained in the United States until December 1929, living at Winding Way during the school year of 1926–1927. Meeting George Gershwin at the

Avondale home in 1927 remained one of the highlights of her American visit with which she regaled her family and friends in Ljubljana. She was at camp in Maine in the summer of 1927, while her father and Berta took an extensive motor tour of Europe. She later attended the Mater Misercordiae Academy in Merion, a suburb of Philadelphia.[29] In the summers of 1928 and 1929 Tuśy was again at camp, while her father was traveling with Carlotta Irwin, with whom he had by this time established an amorous liaison.

Something of Tuśy's relationship with her father is evident in letters she wrote him from Mater Misercordiae as a sixteen year old, a few weeks after he had finished his extended engagement with the Philadelphia Orchestra.[30]

March 14, 1928

Dear Father:
It has been about four days since I received your kind letter and the ten dollar bill, which certainly was a big surprise. I am glad you feel sure that the whole amount is not going to be spent for candy. I would only like to know, if the money is intended for the pair of shoes, which you promised me in New York, but since we did not have enough time could never get them, or for my pocket money. . . . Since this coming Saturday is my only chance to go to town, I would certainly appreciate an immediate answer, with the necessary sum of money. Don't you think I deserve it after playing Bach for one month, and all the other acts that I have been doing since Lent began? I am glad to hear that Eva is improving her letter writing. She also wrote to me, that her only wish is to see me this coming summer. Well, it is also Tuśy's chief wish! I hope Papa will appreciate the wishes of his two little daughters.

March 28, 1928

Dear Father:
I thank you very much for the ten dollars, which I received today. . . . How about your summer plans? Have you decided yet what you are going to do? I am very anxious to hear about it. I also hope some inspiration will make you decide in favor of Eva and myself.

These letters reveal an early manifestation of a nexus that was to dominate Tuśy's relations with her father for the rest of his life. There was on her part a recurring concern for money and clothing cast in wheedling alternating with abject gratitude. Reiner, for his part, doled out funds in small amounts as if he did not trust her to spend money properly. Nor was she insensitive to the deterioration of her father's marriage that had become an open scandal. Tuśy's distress became excruciatingly explicit in a letter of 11 November 1929 from Mater Misercordiae: "Please take me away from this place. . . . I refuse to put up with any more of this ridiculous arguing with the narrow-minded nuns. . . . Papa, I am imploring you. . . . And, Papa, this divorce proposition is also getting to be a big trouble."

By this time Berta was no longer in the picture to mediate between father and daughter. Reiner had become deeply involved with Carlotta Irwin, who apparently tried to comfort Tuśy by suggesting that the girl stay in America and live with Carlotta's mother, Amelia.[31] Ultimately Reiner relented and arranged for his daughter to return to Ljubljana. In a letter written from the *Mauretania* on her voyage home in December 1929, Tuśy returned to a lighter mood. After telling about the voyage and her cabinmate from "Sack's on fifth avenue," she lists some records she would like to have to play for her friends in Ljubljana: "I'm a Dreamer, Aren't We All?" "If I Had a Talking Picture of You," and "Pagan Love Song," among others. She then closes: "Oh Daddy, I can hardly wait to be at home amongst my old friends. Yes, its [*sic*] going to be wonderful! But I'm also looking forward to the time when you come over in May, and you and Eva and I will all go some place, or rather go places and do things." Reiner had tried to persuade his younger daughter, Eva, to join her sister in America. As she recalled later, what she heard from her sister did not make her want to join her father and stepmother there.[32]

The uncertainties in Reiner's professional position in Cincinnati coincided with the disintegration of his domestic situation on Winding Way. Possibly as early as the fall of 1926, Fritz Reiner attended a dinner party in Cincinnati at which another guest was the young American actress Carlotta Irwin. She was the leading lady in Brock Pemberton's production of *Loose Ankles,* trying out in Cincinnati before opening on Broadway. In 1929 she joined the Cincinnati company of the Stuart Walker Players, a theatrical stock company resident at the Cox Theater. Carlotta Irwin's father was a Pittsburgh fabricator of steel-frame skylights; since her mother came from a German family, Carlotta had learned that language as a child. After completing finishing school in Pittsburgh, she went to New York to study at Sargent's Academy of Dramatic Art, eventually acting on Broadway, usually in *soubrette* roles.[33]

Carlotta enjoyed recalling how Fritz Reiner was totally captivated by her charm and vivacity and how her "playing hard to get" merely fueled his ardor. Players from the Cincinnati Symphony Orchestra recalled his rushing four blocks from Emery Auditorium after concerts to wait for her backstage at the Cox Theater. On evenings when he was not conducting, he sat in a box there, much to the distress of pit musicians who also played in his orchestra.

Carlotta was everything that Berta was not. She was twelve years younger than Reiner and petite, whereas Berta towered over her husband, who was three years her junior. She was a sophisticated American, without Berta's obsessive attachment to the Garcia-Marchesi-Gerster bel canto tradition. Whereas Berta had tried to influence Reiner musically, Carlotta worshiped his artistry without qualification. It was impossible for Reiner's passion for Carlotta to avoid providing fodder for gossip, although Cincinnati propriety kept their affair out of public mention. Players in the orchestra, aware of their conductor's new amour, found him less tense. "She made a man of him," recalled one musician.

The Reiner marriage was already strained. Berta did not accompany Reiner to Buenos Aires in the summer of 1926; instead she took a small group of her pupils from the conservatory to Pontecchio for a summer of instruction and exposure to Italian culture. In February 1927, when the Cincinnati Symphony Orchestra played in New York, she presented her pupils in a well-publicized recital as a benefit for an Etelka Gerster Scholarship Fund. She later told friends of efforts to secure a position at the Metropolitan Opera for Reiner. When she reported success, he turned on her savagely and demanded a divorce.[34] There were reports of domestic turmoil on Winding Way, even of physical violence. On one occasion Reiner appeared at rehearsal with a bandaged head, a black eye, and his right arm in a sling. It was rumored that Berta had thrown him down the stairs.

In the fall of 1927, while Reiner was in Philadelphia, his secretary wrote to a realtor that he wanted to sell the Avondale home.[35] During the summer of 1928 Reiner did not go to Europe, declining another invitation from Toscanini to conduct the La Scala Orchestra. Carlotta probably accompanied him on his vacation at the Kentucky Derby and Virginia Beach. The following summer, when her husband was in Europe, Berta wrote from Cincinnati to a friend in New York that he was traveling with Carlotta, introducing her as Mrs. Reiner.[36] From Europe Reiner cabled his secretary to rent an apartment to be ready on his arrival in Cincinnati. Returning in the fall in high spirits, he announced that he had "discovered" yachting while vacationing at an island off the Dalmatian coast.

On 20 January 1930 a Cincinnati court heard Berta's divorce complaint, charging her husband with mental and physical cruelty, citing his objection that she was "too old for him," and claiming that he had attempted to take Pontecchio away from her. Reiner did not contest the divorce or make an appearance in court. The proceedings listed his annual income at fifty thousand dollars and Berta's at ten thousand dollars and reported no financial settlement, but Reiner later maintained that Berta had been well provided for. The court entered a final decree of divorce on 5 February 1930.[37]

Berta moved to New York, where she attempted with little success to give vocal instruction. Obviously shattered by the breakup of her marriage, she became a pathetic figure. At one time she taught at a WPA-supported music school in Harlem. As a teacher, she had theories about the physical element of vocal production that led her to work for a while as a physical therapist. Reiner ignored her completely, indifferent to pleas for financial help that came directly from her or indirectly through her friends.

Despite the scandal, the trustees of the Cincinnati Symphony Orchestra offered Reiner another one-year contract for the 1930–1931 season, which he accepted. However, their patience came to an end with what was regarded as Fritz Reiner's all too hasty and furtive marriage to Carlotta Irwin in Bridgeport, Connecticut, on 26 April 1930, immediately after the conclusion of the orchestra's season. Friends in Cincinnati first learned of the wedding from printed announcements in the mail. The Reiners sailed for Europe. In Berlin, Reiner introduced his *jetzige Frau* to Richard Strauss. When the composer asked her to name her favorite character in his operas, she replied, much to his and her husband's delight, that it was Klytemnästra in *Elektra,* adding that she sang the part in the bath.[38] Returning to Cincinnati in the fall, Reiner reported that they had visited Maurice Ravel at his home at Ciboure in southern France during a three-week stay in the Basque country. The composer showed Reiner the two piano concertos he was working on and stressed the importance of maintaining an unchanging moderate tempo in *Boléro.* [39]

Carlotta's devotion to Fritz Reiner was total and fanatical. She proudly proclaimed that she had given up her career in the theater to marry her Fritz, and there is no question that she devoted her life single-mindedly to him. If there is one word to describe Carlotta Reiner, it would be *spirited.* She exhibited spirit not just in the sparkle of her bright blue eyes or in the vivacity of her speech and bearing, but also through the inner strength that enabled her to bear her husband's mercurial alternations of affection, dependence, and abuse. In the process, she built a wall around him, shielding him from outside distraction and cutting him off from a fuller life in his career. Carlotta was her husband's match when it came to rudeness and selfishness. She could, when she wished, be a person of dignity and charm, playing the grande dame of impeccable breeding. Or she could be a veritable harridan, mouthing the foulest obscenities of the gutter. In either case, she was playing a role as if on the stage.

Carlotta had little direct impact on his music-making: she knew better than to interfere with his artistry. Although he relied on managers and accountants for career and business advice, Carlotta's concern for his reputation and for his comfort and convenience influenced his career decisions. Her sharp tongue and rude behavior, often reflecting feelings that Reiner might suppress, seriously offended people on whom he had to depend for his advancement. She bitterly resented the success of other conductors, especially when she perceived a consequent neglect of her husband. As the mirror of Reiner's own psychological idiosyncrasies, she was also a reinforcing distortion of them. When he faced serious crises in his career, she could support and encourage his worst impulses.

Yet Carlotta had a profound effect on his working arrangements and everyday life. A good cook herself, she knew how to direct household help around her husband's needs. When they traveled, she went to extremes to demand the utmost in special attention for her celebrated husband. In building a wall about him, she became indispensable to his career. Although he hired part-time secretaries, Carlotta supervised their work and handled personal and confidential matters. Although he had been collecting and filing his correspondence and other papers before he married Carlotta, she continued this process more thoroughly, under his supervision. Toward his former wives she had nothing but hatred, and she deeply resented the demands they and his daughters made on him. Though on polite terms with Eva, she resented Reiner's children and grandchildren as an intrusion into her marriage and as a burden on him. She begrudged Reiner's attentions to other women that seemed to her to be more than casual—especially when the women were young and attractive.

As the Reiners sailed on their honeymoon, a storm of indignation engulfed the Cincinnati Symphony Orchestra. The news of the marriage reached Cincinnati just as the orchestra began its subscription campaign for the following season. At their meeting on 5 May 1930, the trustees heard that subscription cancellations had amounted to $1,353. The Indianapolis committee warned that it would not sponsor the appearances of the Cincinnati Symphony Orchestra as long as Reiner was its conductor.[40] These reactions reflected a lack of underlying personal support for him in a very conservative community. It was the "unanimous decision" of the board (in the absence of Anna Taft) not to reengage Reiner after the 1930–1931 season. The board then tried to persuade him to withdraw even from the coming season. When he received their request in Europe, Reiner was at first inclined to defer to it, but Carlotta dissuaded him by reminding him of his obligation to "his men." "The show," she proclaimed, "must go on!"[41]

The board was already negotiating with the British conductor of the Rochester Philharmonic, Eugene Goossens, to succeed Reiner. A client of Judson's, Goossens had appeared in 1927 as guest conductor in Cincinnati during one of Reiner's absences. By mid-August the symphony trustees had signed a contract with Goossens for two years beginning in 1931–1932. They agreed with Judson to delay announcement until the following Christmas season, after he had terminated Goossens's Rochester contract. However, what had become general gossip in Cincinnati became a newspaper scoop in the Cincinnati *Post* on 19 December. The trustees had no choice but to announce officially the next day that "Fritz Reiner, director of the Cincinnati Symphony Orchestra for nine years, has resigned, effective at the close of the present orchestral season, and

Eugene Goossens, now director of the Rochester Philharmonic Orchestra, has been engaged to succeed him." Accompanying this announcement was a letter that Reiner had written to the trustees "some time ago":

I am very reluctant to inform you that with the end of this season, I shall resign my position as conductor of the Cincinnati Symphony Orchestra. It seems to me that all I could do for the musical growth of the orchestra has been accomplished in the past nine seasons, and, since I have been negotiating with another organization, it is my duty to let you know of the change which I contemplate to make, so that you may proceed to procure some one else to take my place for the coming season.

Please rest assured that it is with the greatest regret that I made up my mind to this decision, and that Cincinnati's fine orchestra and understanding public will always be remembered by me with interest, affection, and sympathy. My best wishes for your success always.[42]

On 10 February 1931 Fritz Reiner announced that he would go the next season to Philadelphia as the head of the orchestra department at the Curtis Institute of Music, as principal conductor of the Philadelphia Grand Opera Company, and as guest conductor of the Philadelphia Orchestra. Reiner's announcement of his plans came less than two weeks after the death of Anna Taft. It was indeed the end of an era in Cincinnati.

For his final season in Cincinnati, Reiner outdid himself in his programming: Howard Hanson's "Romantic" Symphony, the Milhaud Viola Concerto, and the Mahler Seventh Symphony. To honor the memory of Anna Taft, he conducted a stirring performance of the Beethoven Fifth Symphony. Having established the custom of responding to requests in his final program of each season, Reiner bade his farewell to Cincinnati with Leo Weiner's orchestration of the Bach Toccata, Adagio, and Fugue in C Major, the Brahms First Symphony, the Polka and Fugue from Weinberger's *Schwanda, Don Juan* of Richard Strauss, and the prelude to *Die Meistersinger*. There were floral offerings on the stage and gifts of a silver service and diamond-set shirt studs and cuff links. The press followed the next day with extravagant tributes to Reiner's achievement in building a great orchestra in Cincinnati. He never appeared in that city again.

CHAPTER V

Teacher

Carlotta Reiner later maintained that Fritz Reiner's career began only after he left Cincinnati in 1931: "Everything before that was merely preparation." Although Carlotta's personal perspective ignores his earlier achievements, Reiner's departure from the Cincinnati Symphony Orchestra unquestionably marked a major watershed in his career. It took him decades to recover from the setback. His operatic activity with the Philadelphia Grand Opera Company proved to be brief, his commitment at the Curtis Institute of Music was both flexible and light, and his hopes of succeeding Leopold Stokowski at the helm of the Philadelphia Orchestra were unavailing.

Leaving Cincinnati in April 1931, the Reiners went briefly to Philadelphia, where they boarded their dog at a kennel in suburban Radnor; a publicity release reported that they took turns sitting up with their pet in the baggage car. Before embarking on the *Augustus,* Reiner gave the Curtis office a rough itinerary, which included 24 April at the Teatro San Carlo in Naples, 4 May at La Scala in Milan, 22 May in Ljubljana, 29 May in Vevey, and 11 June at Marienbad.[1] This clearly established his presence at Milan in May 1931, when events occurred that did not, at least in hindsight, put Reiner in the most favorable light. On 14 May Arturo Toscanini was beaten by Fascist thugs in Bologna for refusing to open a concert with *Giovinezza,* the party anthem. This marked a decisive confrontation with Benito Mussolini by this son of a fervent socialist and follower of Garibaldi. In Budapest, Béla Bartók took the lead in drafting a protest from the New Hungarian Music Society. Serge Koussevitzky canceled his guest appearance with the La Scala Orchestra, and Ossip and Clara Gabrilowitsch interrupted a holiday in Switzerland to hurry to Milan to visit Toscanini.

Reiner visited his Italian colleague in the Via Durini before his 27 May engagement with the La Scala Orchestra.[2] It is inconceivable that the Bologna incident was not mentioned, for Toscanini talked of it freely with other visitors.[3] Nevertheless, when a member of the La Scala audience called out for *Giovinezza* at the beginning of Reiner's concert, he conducted it.[4] This incident takes on added significance: a penciled copy of an undated cable in Carlotta's handwriting states that Fritz Reiner had a half-hour audience with Benito Mussolini.[5] The following February, King Victor Emmanuel made Reiner an officer of the Order of the King of Italy in recognition of his "great musicianship and standing as a conductor."[6]

Apart from its reflection of Fritz Reiner's susceptibility to flattery and the bestowal of honors, this affair must be viewed as an interplay of several forces. Following his divorce from Berta, Reiner may well have been anxious to shore up his professional opportunities in Italy, where her family contacts had been so important to his career. Against that must be set his friendship with Toscanini, whose earlier invitations had led to his conducting concerts of the La Scala Orchestra. In 1931 many foreigners admired Mussolini's regime, and not just for his running the trains on time. Igor Stravinsky was not the only outspoken admirer of Mussolini among musicians in the early 1930s.[7] In Cincinnati and elsewhere in the United States, Reiner's social and business contacts were with the conservative establishment. Arthur Judson constantly urged his artists to avoid anything remotely associated with political sentiments that might offend the business power structure. To be sure, Reiner early in 1933 joined Toscanini and other leading conductors in America in a well-publicized cable to Adolf Hitler protesting the treatment of Bruno Walter and other Jewish musicians. However, his conducting *Giovinezza* in Milan could scarcely have improved his relations with Toscanini, who wielded great influence on the American musical scene. Although it is impossible to assess its impact on his career in America, this incident could scarcely have helped it. In any event, Reiner's accommodation certainly facilitated his conducting regularly in Italy until 1938.

Returning to America in July 1931, the Reiners established their principal home in New York City—at first at the Dorset Hotel and eventually in an apartment at 815 Park Avenue leased at an annual cost of twenty-eight hundred dollars.[8] Although his Philadelphia duties initially prompted them to take an apartment briefly in suburban Merion and later in downtown Philadelphia, the Park Avenue apartment became the Reiners' home. Reiner first filled a two-week engagement with the New York Philharmonic-Symphony Orchestra in Lewisohn Stadium, where one of his programs comprised American music. He then went to Philadelphia for a week in the second season of concerts at Robin Hood Dell in Fairmont Park. In the fall he took up his duties at the Curtis Institute of Music, which remained a professional haven for him until 1941.

Mary Louise Curtis Bok Zimbalist was one of those extraordinary women who have made lasting contributions to the development of American musical culture, supplementing an enlightened commitment to music with generous financial assistance.[9] Her father, Cyrus Herman Kotschmar Curtis, had built a successful publishing empire, based on such magazines as the *Saturday Evening Post, Ladies Home Journal,* and *Country Gentleman.* An ardent amateur musician, he had a full-size pipe organ installed in his home and played it every day. His only child, Mary Louise, was born in Boston on 6 August 1876. Brought up to share her parents' devotion to music, her education included courses in music theory as well as piano lessons. The family ardently supported their close friend Leopold Stokowski. At the age of twenty, after a three-year engagement, Mary Louise married Edward Bok, the notably progressive editor of her father's *Ladies Home Journal.*

In 1924 the family founded the Curtis Institute of Music, of which Josef Hofmann became director in 1927. Hofmann had long been a giant among the pianists of his time, a supreme virtuoso of Romantic persuasion. His leadership bestowed on the Curtis Institute an instant cachet in the music world, attracting a prestigious faculty and the most talented students. The Curtis faculty included violinists Leopold Auer and Leah Luboschutz, violoncellist Felix Salmond, pianist Isabelle Vengerova, harpist Carlos Salzedo, soprano Marcella Sembrich, and baritone Emilio de Gogorza. In 1939 Rudolf Serkin joined the Curtis faculty as head of the piano department; he later served as director of the institute from 1968 to 1976. The school also drew on the Philadelphia Orchestra, employing flutist William Kincaid, oboist Marcel Tabuteau, and horn player William Horner, among others, establishing a symbiotic relation between the orchestra and Curtis. From its inception, the Curtis Institute admitted only the most talented students, to whom it gave full scholarships. Although students had to meet their living expenses, Mrs. Bok—as she is known in the history of American music—frequently subsidized these from her own resources. Until her death in 1970 Mrs. Bok took a keen, extremely personal interest in the institute, its faculty, and its students. She wielded absolute control over faculty and staff and closely followed the progress of the students. The Philadelphia Grand Opera Company, the Philadelphia Orchestra, and the Settlement Music School also received her generous support.

Fritz Reiner established cordial relations with the Boks during his first guest engagement with the Philadelphia Orchestra early in 1927. In 1929, with his divorce from Berta imminent, Reiner actively sought a position at Curtis. The death of Edward Bok on 9 January 1930 prevented Mrs. Bok from concluding arrangements with Reiner when he was under pressure to settle with the

Cincinnati board for another year. A year later and after the announcement that Reiner was leaving the Cincinnati Symphony Orchestra, Hofmann and Reiner signed a one-year contract, which took effect in the fall of 1931, at a salary of nine thousand dollars for the school year from September through May. Reiner paid a 15-percent commission on this engagement to Arthur Judson. During the next ten years Reiner renewed this contract annually at salaries ranging from four thousand to nine thousand dollars.[10]

At the Curtis Institute, Reiner was in charge of the student orchestra, which he trained, conducted, and administered; and he taught a small class of advanced students, whom he personally selected, in the technique of conducting. Reiner had additional responsibilities in the opera department, which existed from time to time. When other engagements did not interfere, he spent a minimum of one day a week in Philadelphia. He also auditioned orchestra players, conducting students, and student singers for opera classes, sometimes at his Park Avenue apartment. Curtis permitted Reiner a very flexible schedule; the variations in annual salary probably reflected professional engagements he anticipated when signing his contract each spring. At a time of uncertainty in his career and throughout the Depression years, Reiner could count on the Curtis Institute of Music professionally and financially.

Despite some disagreements, Reiner enjoyed cordial relations with Mrs. Bok, who regarded him as an illustrious member of her faculty. Mrs. Bok had purchased two collections of Richard Wagner's letters, known as the Pusinelli and Burrell collections. After going through these materials in 1935, Reiner wrote her that their importance was of greater musicological value than of practical performing interest. He expressed his pleasure at having spent "a day with Richard the First." A year later Reiner sent Mrs. Bok a copy of the American edition of Igor Stravinsky's *Autobiography,* calling attention to the composer's laudatory comments about his conducting in 1925. Mrs. Bok replied, congratulating the conductor. With the menacing political situation in Europe, Reiner interceded successfully with Mrs. Bok to add Elisabeth Schumann to the Curtis faculty but failed to persuade her to engage Béla Bartók.[11]

Boris Goldovsky, one of Reiner's first conducting students, has written of encountering him at Curtis: "From the moment Reiner mounted the podium and faced the student orchestra, there was a silence in that hall such as I had never heard before. The man's look was terrifying. He had a gimlet eye that could pierce you like a dagger, even when he was looking at you from the side, and he had a tongue to match."[12] Reiner made no concessions to his players' youth: he expected the same professionalism he did from the players in the Philadelphia Orchestra. Many students who played in Reiner's orchestra at Curtis later pursued careers as major orchestra players, including Leonard Rose, oboist John de Lancie in Pittsburgh and Philadelphia, flutist Julius Baker in Chicago and New York, and tubist Arnold Jacobs in Pittsburgh and Chicago. Later, when Reiner filled vacancies in his own orchestras, he frequently turned for advice to Curtis faculty or to graduates who had played under him.

The student orchestra at Curtis generally met once a week, dividing its time between reading orchestral repertory and preparing public concerts and broadcasts. The orchestra appeared occasionally in the Academy of Music, usually under the auspices of the Philadelphia Forum. On such occasions, free-lance players or members of the Philadelphia Orchestra, preferably Curtis graduates, augmented the student orchestra. In January 1932 it gave a concert in Carnegie Hall, with Jorge Bolet as soloist in the first movement of the Tchaikovsky Piano Concerto in B-flat Minor. Bolet later studied conducting in Reiner's class. In November 1937 Mrs. Bok sponsored a concert at the Metropolitan Opera House in New York honoring the fiftieth anniversary of Josef Hofmann's American debut at the age of eleven. The orchestra included not only current Curtis students but also alumni from orchestras as far away as Kansas City. Reiner began with the Brahms *Academic Festival* overture and conducted the orchestra for Hofmann's performances of the D Minor Piano Concerto of his teacher Anton Rubinstein and his own *Chromaticon*. [13] In March 1939, on his retirement as director of the Curtis Institute, Hofmann played the Beethoven "Emperor" Concerto with the augmented Curtis orchestra in a concert at the Academy of Music.

Although the student orchestra gave few public concerts, it appeared in several of the weekly broadcasts from Curtis over the CBS network. Reiner conducted the student orchestra in three or four broadcasts each school year. His programs were very conservative, the most adventurous repertory being some Weiner folk-song arrangements and a movement from the Second Symphony of Randall Thompson, who succeeded Hofmann as director in 1939. Some broadcasts consisted of substantial operatic excerpts—the second act of *Le nozze di Figaro*, the beginning of act III of *Die Meistersinger*, or an excerpt from *Fidelio*. [14] Occasionally some of Reiner's conducting students led the orchestra for a broadcast, usually sharing a program. In April 1941, however, Leonard Bernstein conducted an entire program in the series.

Reiner's most important work at Curtis was as teacher of conducting. The rigorously selective standards at Curtis and Reiner's reputation as a superlative technician attracted a group of exceptionally talented students to his class. They guaranteed him an illustrious place in the history of music education in America.

Morton Gould had vivid memories of his audition for Reiner's conducting class in the early 1930s. When he appeared at the New York apartment, Reiner curtly asked him to play "anything" on the piano. While Gould responded with his best pieces, the conductor wandered about the room, opening his mail and picking his teeth, seemingly oblivious of the young man. Then he challenged Gould, "So you want to be a conductor! What do you know about conducting?"

"Well, I can beat 5/4."

"Any pig can beat 5/4. Play this." Placing a large opera score on the piano rack, he pointed his finger at a passage. Every time the young musician began to feel in command of the score, a complex one that he had never seen before, Reiner would turn a few pages and jab his finger at a new place. At one point he asked Gould to sing a passage. (The score was *Elektra*.) After doing the same with another opera score, Reiner exclaimed, "Now you know that conducting is more than beating 5/4!" and showed the young man to the door. A few weeks later, Gould received a letter from Curtis offering him a full scholarship in Reiner's conducting class. Because of family problems, Gould had to turn down the scholarship. Later he and Reiner became friends and colleagues, the conductor being one of the first to program his compositions with a major orchestra.[15] Similar accounts by Boris Goldovsky, Lukas Foss, Leonard Bernstein, and others confirm that the conductor-teacher was looking for a combination of solid musicality and skill in sight-reading at the piano. Students whom Reiner accepted generally spent two years in his class, which met once a week on the morning of the day when he also rehearsed the student orchestra.

Reiner's teaching was primarily technical, based on the student's previous musical training and innate ability. He expected awareness of historical and national musical styles as well as a general knowledge of history and literature. For his early pedagogical work at Curtis he prepared an "Outline for Course in Conducting," written out in his own longhand to be typed in carbon copies on onionskin paper. Reiner's outline began: "The technic of conducting must be learned and practiced BEFORE actually conducting an orchestra. Pupils must be capable of conducting an important work clearly and musically WITHOUT previous rehearsing with an orchestra." He recommended study of the orchestration treatises of Hector Berlioz and Richard Strauss as well as a comprehensive acquaintance with contemporary repertory. He expected thorough grounding in harmony, counterpoint and formal analysis, the ability to sing (or whistle) at sight in *solfège* complicated rhythms and difficult intervals. The conductor's gestures, he wrote, should be direct and natural, both clear and expressive; the conductor should "sing" the music mentally. Conducting involved both the control of the orchestra and the re-creation of the music. He sought, rather clumsily in this document, to define phrasing in terms of pitch, dynamics, duration, tone, and balance, all synchronized by the conductor. At one point he declared that the conductor was "the conscience of the orchestra."[16]

Although Reiner may not have followed this outline exactly in the classroom, it provided important insight into his concept of conducting. The accounts of one of his first pupils, Boris Goldovsky, and one of his last, Lukas Foss, nearly a decade later, agree remarkably on how Reiner managed his class. He began with recitatives from Mozart operas, which the student had to "conduct" while singing each part from memory. According to Goldovsky, Reiner declared at the first class: "Conducting is basically a simple business as long as the tempo doesn't change. Anyone can beat time evenly and it's nothing to be proud of, because any fool can do it. And I'm not going to waste your time and mine teaching you easy things. What I am going to do first is teach you how to conduct operatic recitatives. Because until you've conducted opera, you don't know what conducting really is."[17] Elsewhere Reiner observed:

Each conductor has his own gestures and special signals. He develops these for himself, out of his own physical and suggestive power. It is this power which reveals the true conductor; not the things he does. The gestures which bring out the musical effects are as gestures *per se,* quite unimportant. The technique of conducting has value only after it has become unconscious second nature. The best conducting technique is that which achieves the maximum of musical result with minimum of effort. . . . The conducting of *recitatives* involves short cuts. I do not conduct the whole measure, only certain beats. . . . At the start of the "Magic Flute" Overture there are pauses. You don't conduct pauses—you simply wait, counting time for yourself. . . . The only general rule is to infuse all gestures with precision, clarity, and vitality. Without these, the music will not come to life. . . . The precise nature of the down-beat must be made clear in advance. . . . It must be clear through the up-beat that goes before.[18]

As the course progressed, Reiner would assign movements from the standard repertory for students to memorize and then "conduct" or play at the piano. From time to time Reiner would interrupt, demanding to know what a particular instrument was playing at a particular bar. Sometimes he would trick a student by asking for an instrument that was not playing the passage. Sometimes he would play a passage himself at the piano for the students to comment on musically. He required not merely memorization by rote but, more important, total comprehension of the music for which memorization was but the first step. Reiner conveyed his instruction with economy and, most frequently, with devastating criticism and withering sarcasm. It was not so much what he said that made Reiner so fierce as how he said it. The simple German phrase *total unbegabt,* completely untalented, could be devastating when Reiner uttered it with sardonic cruelty in an exaggerated Hungarian accent. With these students, as with the players in his orchestras, the generation of fear was a fundamental pedagogical method.

Supplementing their weekly classes with Reiner, the conducting students also played in the student orchestra. Since there was at best but one piano part, they also played percussion instruments. As Reiner had learned as a student in Budapest, this was a vantage from which one could see the master conductor demonstrate the precepts he was teaching in the classroom. The student conductors also coached singers in operatic repertory. Reiner seldom gave his students opportunity to conduct the student orchestra and assigned only the most advanced and most talented students to conduct on the radio broadcasts.

Many of his students became important in the musical life of America in coming years: Goldovsky in a variety of operatic activities, Saul Caston in Denver, Ezra Rachlin in Pittsburgh and Kansas City, Hugo Weisgall and Vincent Persichetti as important composers, Jorge Bolet as a pianist and teacher, Max Goberman as a conductor of ballet and chamber orchestra, Lukas Foss as a composer and conductor, Walter Hendl in Dallas and Chicago, and, of course, Leonard Bernstein. Bernstein's relations with Reiner have been the subject of considerable speculation. They became strained during the summer of 1940, following Bernstein's first year at Curtis. With Reiner's strong recommendation he had joined Serge Koussevitzky's conducting class at Tanglewood. On 27 August 1940 he wrote to Reiner from Sharon, Massachusetts:

I have just spent the most wonderful six weeks of my life at the Berkshire Music Center. From the first day to the last it was crammed full of exciting work—real work. And I feel a great debt to you for the success I enjoyed there. As soon as I arrived I was informed that I was to conduct the Randall Thompson Symphony in a few days. That seemed like an incredible order for my very first attempt at conducting, and I am sure I could never have done it without just the kind of preparation you gave me last year. It was a preparation that set a standard that I had to live up to. As it was, the Thompson went off very well, and to me it was the greatest moment in my life. It seemed significant, too, that the first work I should conduct in life was a modern American work. Appropriately, the last work I conducted there was the Outdoor Overture of Copland.
    In between I did the Histoire du Soldat of Stravinsky (with original words about Tanglewood), the Brahms-Haydn Variations, the Bach Double Concerto, the Haydn Symphonie Concertante, Scheherazade (2nd & 4th movements). All this actual conducting, and intensive rehearsing, besides the personal success with the orchestra (which I was sure would resent me as a student conductor, but instead coöperated magnificently) and the excitement which Koussevitzky always arouses—all these gave a great lift to my Weltanschauung. At present I am waiting for word from Koussevitzky about the coming year. He has some plan for assembling a young orchestra in Boston, & getting a few pupils to work with it (and him). (I think his only pupils are Foss and myself.) I am sure you will agree that the main thing for me now is actual conducting—as much of it as possible. Therefore, if this plan succeeds, I shall no doubt be in Boston next year, but I won't know the verdict for some weeks. So please don't forget me, or think me ungrateful, if I don't return this year.
    I owe a tremendous lot of thanks for the discipline you gave me, and for the glorious standard of knowledge, will, and skill that you have always represented to me. Only you could have done the impossible task of teaching me to conduct without an orchestra.
    And you did.

In an undated letter from New York, obviously after the preceding one and apparently following a face-to-face confrontation, Bernstein undertook to explain himself more precisely:

In view of what happened last Friday, I realize that I owe you an explanation and an apology. I feel that there must be some misunderstanding involved, and I want above all to be as clear and honest with you as I know how. Let me assure you that whatever you may have read or heard to make you doubt my loyalty, I have consistently regarded you as my teacher; and that my work this summer was as your pupil, and in line with your theory that I must avail myself of every possible opportunity for practical conducting.

When the vague possibility arose of my continuing this summer's work into the winter, I was tempted to consider it for two reasons, both of which I hope you will understand. Primarily, it afforded me of a chance of living at home in Boston, thereby reducing my financial obligations to a minimum. The financial problem is more acute this year than last and there was considerable doubt whether sources on which I drew last year would again be forthcoming. This has since been solved by a loan.

Secondarily, as your student, I had come to realize the importance of actual conducting and I was probably swayed unduly by this vague possibility; but I should never have allowed myself to be so swayed if I had thought for a moment that you would see in it any disloyalty to you or to your teaching.

I offer you my sincere apology for any offense I may have given you. There is nothing in the world that could make me knowingly offend you; my devotion to you is far too great for that. I fervently hope that this year will enable me to prove that devotion.[19]

Two points are worth noting here—Reiner's apparent anger at what he perceived as his student's disloyalty, and the importance Bernstein placed on "actual conducting" not offered in Reiner's class. Bernstein's contrition and the intercession of Mrs. Bok and Randall Thompson persuaded Reiner to keep him in his conducting class for another year, which turned out to be Reiner's last at Curtis. In the fall of 1940 Mrs. Bok arranged for the conducting class, including Bernstein, Foss, and Hendl, to travel to Chicago to observe their teacher preparing a production of *Der Rosenkavalier*. Thompson drove them out from Philadelphia, writing Reiner that he would introduce them as "Dr. Koussevitzky's most promising students."[20]

If Reiner later gave pungent expression to his annoyance with Bernstein, he also had great respect for his pupil. He not only engaged him as a guest in Pittsburgh but also recommended him as a possible guest in Chicago. But Bernstein contributed to Reiner's bitterness with his extravagant public declarations of devotion to Koussevitzky. Reiner could never have matched Koussevitzky's active promotion of the young American as his successor in Tanglewood and Boston. Especially after Reiner's death, Bernstein became more specific in acknowledging his debt to Reiner, more evenhanded in defining the significant differences between his two teachers in their influence on him: "Reiner's way of teaching was tyrannical in the extreme. . . . Whereas Koussevitzky's way of teaching was inspirational . . . more in terms of emotion and 'it must be warm like the sun coming up in the morning, . . .' whereas Reiner would say: 'What is the second clarinet playing?' . . . Reiner is responsible for my own very high standards."[21]

In the summer of 1984 Bernstein paid even more explicit tribute when he met Reiner's grandson Vladimir Assejew in Ljubljana while touring with the Bavarian State Radio Orchestra. Embracing the young man with characteristic exuberance, he effusively proclaimed his debt to the young man's grandfather.[22] On the other hand, after a telecast of one of Bernstein's more athletic conducting exhibitions, Reiner commented wryly, "He didn't learn *that* from me."

With a faculty including de Gogorza, Sembrich, Schumann, and Reiner, it would have been impossible to ignore opera at Curtis. Until its demise in 1932, the Philadelphia Grand Opera enjoyed a close relation with Curtis. Reiner's pupils coached the advanced students who sang supporting roles with the company. After the collapse of the Philadelphia Grand Opera in the spring of 1932, Curtis continued opera training on a less professional scale, with workshops and concert performances of opera scenes. Much of this involved Reiner, sometimes as conductor but also administratively in auditioning students and advising on repertory to be studied. It was at his urging that Mrs. Bok engaged Ernst Lert, with whom Reiner had worked in Buenos Aires, to head opera training at Curtis for several years.

During Reiner's years at Curtis, the school undertook two full-scale productions of opera. In early 1935 Reiner conducted a performance of *Il barbiere di Siviglia,* sung in Nathalie McFarren's English translation by a cast of Curtis students and graduates. The director was Herbert Graf, whom Reiner had brought from Europe to stage productions in the Philadelphia Orchestra's opera season. According to a press release, Graf "originated a new form of presentation" for this performance, adding three new scenes. The Philadelphia Forum presented the production in the Academy of Music on 18 January, where most of the orchestra were Curtis students, supplemented by players from the Philadelphia Orchestra. A performance at the Juilliard School in New York required special arrangements with the local musicians' union to bring students and professional players into its jurisdiction. Consequently, the performance at Juilliard was labeled "private." Among the distinguished guests, according to the press, were Mrs. Bok, Hofmann, Walter Damrosch, Artur Bodanzky, Leopold Auer, Edward Johnson, Felix Warburg, and Eugene Ormandy. Broadway was represented by Blanche Yurka, an old friend of Carlotta's.[23]

In 1937 the Curtis Institute of Music produced the world premiere of *Amelia Goes to the Ball* by the twenty-six-year-old Gian Carlo Menotti. Reiner conducted it in an English translation of the composer's original *Amelia al ballo*. This marked the first performance of a work by a composer destined to be a major figure in twentieth-century opera. He was a special favorite of Mrs. Bok, who continued to assist him and his endeavors financially for many years. Menotti's opera, which one critic described as "a whimsical satire on women," shared a double bill with the American premiere of Darius Milhaud's *Le pauvre matelot*. Reiner apparently agreed to do the Menotti opera only under pressure from Mrs. Bok herself. He would have preferred to couple the Milhaud opera with Bartók's *Bluebeard's Castle*.[24] After this production, he never again programmed any of Menotti's music.

In October 1938 Josef Hofmann stepped down as director of the Curtis Institute of Music. In the fall of 1939 Randall Thompson faced the unenviable task of succeeding Hofmann. A composer, especially for the voice, Thompson came to Curtis with a strong academic orientation, quite different from the virtuoso commitment that had prevailed there since its founding. His career at Curtis was brief: in February 1941 his long-rumored departure from the school became a reality; he left, but not without airing his advocacy of a broader academic education for musicians.

The day before the publication of Thompson's forced retirement from Curtis, there was a brief announcement that Fritz Reiner would leave its faculty. He was in fact complying with Mrs. Bok's request for his resignation. Citing necessary changes for financial reasons that would require dropping the orchestra program and conducting class, she suggested that he write her, giving as his reason for resigning the pressure of his commitments to the Pittsburgh Symphony Orchestra and other institutions. Reiner's response followed her request precisely and proposed that they meet soon for lunch.[25] Press coverage of Reiner's resignation explicitly pointed out that it was not related to Thompson's and called Reiner "one of the greatest conductors of opera in the world." To succeed Thompson, Mrs. Bok appointed the violinist Efrem Zimbalist, whom she married in 1943.

CHAPTER VI

Opera and the Philadelphia Orchestra

As he arrived at the Curtis Institute of Music, Reiner simultaneously prepared for his North American opera debut, on 22 October 1931, conducting the Philadelphia Grand Opera in *Tannhäuser*. [1] Active between 1926 and 1932, the Philadelphia Grand Opera Company offered an ambitious repertory of operas, as many as twelve to fifteen productions a season, sometimes in the Metropolitan Opera House, sometimes in the Academy of Music. Many of the singers in Philadelphia were fixtures in "provincial" opera in America and with such touring companies as Fortune Gallo's San Carlo Opera Company. Before Reiner, the company's conductors included Eugene Goossens and Leopold Stokowski's assistants Sylvan Levin and Artur Rodzinski. The resident stage director was William von Wymetal, son of a famous Viennese director, whose inadequacies have been amusingly chronicled by Boris Goldovsky. Although the company's list of sponsors prominently included Leopold Stokowski, he participated only in two of the company's presentations—the first American performance of Alban Berg's *Wozzeck* on 19 March 1931, and the United States premiere in 1932 of Carlos Chavez's ballet *HP*. The former was, of course, a historic occasion for music in America. It was repeated in Philadelphia the following November and in New York's Metropolitan Opera House on 24 November 1931 under the auspices of the League of Composers. An augmented Philadelphia Orchestra, 116 strong, was in the pit, and 25 students from Curtis constituted the stage band. Reiner, to be sure, was not involved in this production, first staged before he came to Philadelphia, but he was in the city during its revival.

A week after the *Tannhäuser* and three weeks before the revival of *Wozzeck* under Stokowski, Reiner conducted *Elektra*. This was his first performance of an opera with which he would become closely associated. Philadelphia had not heard this opera since Hammerstein's Manhattan Opera Company had performed it in French twenty-two years earlier. Reiner presented it now for the first time in the United States in German. This Philadelphia production preceded by more than a year its first Metropolitan Opera performance. Anne Roselle, who was to sing the title role, visited Richard Strauss at Garmisch and sang for his approval, which the composer conveyed to Reiner in a letter:

I am glad to learn that you have now found your way back to opera and that you will conduct "Elektra" with the Philadelphia Orchestra, whose extraordinary achievements still linger in my memory.

Miss Roselle sang her part today for me. It is a marvelous part for her, and I am certain that she will have a tremendous success with it.

In reference to the orchestra, please proceed according to your best judgment and the same with the dynamics marking, so that the voice shall not be drowned. Only in the final duet, C major, 6-4 time, I have cut myself some of the "pianos" and let the orchestra break loose. This is better for the total effect.

Well, good luck in Philadelphia. I hope that I will hear some good news from you soon. With best greetings.[2]

After Reiner's public assurance that Strauss's music would not shock Philadelphia and with the first three rows of seats removed to accommodate the augmented orchestra, *Elektra* was staged in the Academy of Music on 29 October 1931. Besides Roselle, the cast included Margaret Matzenauer (Klytemnästra), Ingrid Bjoerner (Chrysothemis), Nelson Eddy (Orest), and Bruno Korell (Aegisth). Although the great Hungarian mezzo-soprano was near the end of her operatic career, Matzenauer's interpretation of Klytemnästra created a sensation. The young American baritone, who was also rehearsing in the revival of *Wozzeck,* was on the threshold of a brief operatic career that would soon give way to his becoming one of the first singing idols of radio and cinema. The orchestra, drawn mainly from the Philadelphia Orchestra, numbered ninety-six players. Goldovsky remembered Wymetal's staging as singularly ludicrous. The director conceived the idea of electronically amplifying the death shrieks of Klytemnästra and Aegisth with loudspeakers placed in a box close to the stage. Given the state of audio at that time, the effect was hardly realistic. Reiner's direction was long remembered as one of the most electrifying performances heard in that era. Olin Downes, who had heard *Elektra* in Europe, declared that he had "never heard such a reading of the score, one distinguished by such complete mastery and dramatic fire as displayed tonight by Fritz Reiner, who is palpably an opera conductor first and a symphonic conductor afterward, and whose reading is one of the memorable experiences of twenty-five years of reviewing musical performances."[3]

Reiner conducted four more operas in what was to be the last season of the Philadelphia Grand Opera. Ivan Steschenko sang the title role in *Boris Godunov* on 10 December, with Nina Koshetz as Marina and Dimitri Onofrei as the Pretender; this was Reiner's only performance of that opera. Roselle was back in February for *Lohengrin* with Cyrena Van Gordon (Ortrud), Paolo Marion (Lohengrin), and Eddy (Telramund). A month later the company repeated *Elektra* with the October cast. On 7 April 1932 Coe Glade sang as Carmen, with Aroldo Lindi and Chief Caupolican (whom Goldovsky described as a full-blooded American Indian). With Reiner conducting *Aida* a week later, the Philadelphia Grand Opera gave its last performance. During this season, Reiner had conducted seven performances of six operas. *Elektra* and *Boris Godunov* were new to his repertory.

Three years later the Philadelphia Orchestra included ten full-scale opera productions in its Academy of Music subscription series. By 1934 the orchestra felt the impact of the Depression acutely. Ticket sales declined precipitously, and dwindling donations to the annual operating fund endangered a zealously husbanded endowment. Despite cuts in musicians' pay, as well as Stokowski's, the orchestra faced serious financial problems that it shared with others throughout the country. Facing similar problems, the Metropolitan Opera canceled its visits to the Philadelphia Academy of Music on nights when the orchestra was in New York or other cities. Confronted with a genuine crisis, the directors and Arthur Judson sought fiscal relief in a major innovation.[4]

The collapse of the Philadelphia Grand Opera Company in 1932 and the Metropolitan's cancellation left an operatic void that Judson saw an opportunity to fill with the Philadelphia Orchestra's 1934–1935 subscription season. Opera under the orchestra's auspices, he suggested, would alleviate declining subscriptions to its concerts by combining both in one package. In New York, Judson had made a similar proposal to merge the Philharmonic-Symphony and Metropolitan Opera and to offer a combined concert and opera season in the Metropolitan Opera House. This scheme failed because of the adamant opposition of Arturo Toscanini.[5] On the Philadelphia board, Mrs. Bok and her son Curtis welcomed filling the educational gap left by the demise of the Philadelphia Grand Opera. Leopold Stokowski's position was detached at best: he neither supported nor opposed Judson's proposal, assuming the lofty attitude that he was interested only in opera produced "in new ways."[6] Besides, his one venture into opera, the American premiere of *Wozzeck* with the Philadelphia Grand Opera in 1931, was hardly the kind of success that the manager counted on to ease the financial problems of the Philadelphia Orchestra.

Unquestionably another attraction of this operatic scheme was the availability of Fritz Reiner, who had already shown Philadelphia that he was an extraordinary opera conductor. Therefore, besides several orchestral subscription and popular concerts, Judson had him conduct five of the ten operas scheduled at three-week intervals through the orchestra's 1934–1935 season; Alexander

Smallens conducted the other five. Their assistants were Boris Goldovsky and Sylvan Levin. Reiner was not only the principal conductor but also the "general musical director," in fact if not in name. During the spring and summer of 1934 Reiner was busy planning the season, not merely musical details but all phases of production. He called on the technical staff at the Academy of Music for details on stage facilities, the strength of the overhead fly loft, and the availability of electrical power. At one point he considered offering the American premiere of Richard Strauss's *Die schweigsame Frau*. He settled finally on *Der Rosenkavalier* despite Judson's objection to what he viewed as the composer's exorbitant fee. Reiner brought Herbert Graf from Europe to stage all the operas he conducted and consulted with him on musico-dramatic coordination. It was Graf who required a specially built revolving stage, also used in *Carmen,* to place the final trio and duet of *Der Rosenkavalier,* not in a dingy inn, but in a handsome formal garden.

Reiner visited Berlin and Vienna to audition and engage singers, for he planned to introduce several who had not yet appeared in America. His first choice for Isolde was a Norwegian soprano, whom he did not audition but of whom he had heard good reports, but Kirsten Flagstad had commitments in Norway for the fall.[7] She made her Metropolitan debut the following February. For *Der Rosenkavalier* he engaged Lotte Lehmann, Elisabeth Schumann, and Emanuel List. For *Die Meistersinger* he "borrowed" Friedrich Schorr from the Metropolitan. He also engaged American singers, many of them former or current Curtis students. The young Julius Huehn sang several important roles, including Faninal, Kurvenal, Kothner, Count Almaviva, and Falstaff. Both *Falstaff* and *Le nozze di Figaro* were sung in English. Just as his Philadelphia Grand Opera *Elektra* and *Boris Godunov* were new to his repertory, Reiner was conducting two of the five operas in this season for the first time in his career—*Der Rosenkavalier* and *Falstaff*.

During the summer of 1934 Reiner had shown interest in Shostakovich's *Lady Macbeth of the Mzensk District*. He asked Goldovsky to study the piano score and Russian text to advise him whether it might be suitable to present in an English translation.[8] Goldovsky told Reiner that *Lady Macbeth* was a lurid subject portrayed in explicit dramatic and musical terms that would offend the Philadelphia audience. But Alexander Smallens saw in it an opportunity to create a scandal matching Reiner's successes. (There apparently was no love lost between the two conductors: when he heard that Smallens had boasted that he would need only one rehearsal for the entire *Ring,* Reiner commented, "He wouldn't know what to say at the second rehearsal."[9]) With interest heightened by the publicity attending the January 1935 American premiere in Cleveland, Smallens conducted the Shostakovich opera in a considerably toned-down translation.

For the opening *Tristan und Isolde,* Reiner first selected the sculptor Alexander Archipenko as designer to implement his ideas of staging:

Ist Act. . . . Steeply inclined VIKING boat—Tristan at the rudder sharply etched against the horizon. At the end of the act landing coast with castle to be seen. There must be an exit provided from the Rudder deck into the hold of the boat so that the crew can disappear. Also staircase from upper deck to lower deck (on right side of boat).
IInd Act. . . . Two symbolic trees entwining forming perhaps a NATU-RAL SEAT. Terrace of castle on high plateau. Torch must be center of action first scene—low enough for ISOLDE to take hold of. Castle and terrace (reality) to be submerged in darkness. As soon as love duet begins a sense of unreality must come over the entire stage through use of lighting and gauze. No shadow-graphs for duel.
IIIrd act. . . . 1. Towering ruins of castle—sea to be seen beneath.
2. Symbolic inclined pathway from Tristan's bed to doorway of castle, where Isolde appears at end of act.
3. At the end everything dissolves—only Tristan and Isolde to be seen mid stage.
In general I would like to use Gauze throughout the whole opera WITHOUT CURTAIN AT THE BEGINNING—darkened stage curtained by Gauze.
What do you think of *not* using curtain at the end of the opera to create same atmosphere as during the prelude? [10]

Reiner's comments may indicate acquaintance with Adolphe Appia's seminal observations on the staging of this opera. They may have reflected what he had heard from Appia's assistant Ernst Lert of Toscanini's production in 1923 at La Scala, which Appia had designed.

When Archipenko's project proved to be too expensive to produce, Reiner turned to the Broadway designer Donald Oenslager for a more conventionally "pictorial" design. According to Goldovsky, a huge sail that was raised and lowered as the action shifted from Isolde's cabin to Tristan's post at the rudder dominated the design of act I. This kind of production creativity was then uncommon in American opera and, in many respects, anticipated innovations that did not reach the Metropolitan Opera for another two decades. Reiner wanted to perform *Tristan und Isolde* without cuts—unprecedented at that time in America—and did so at the Thursday afternoon performance on 19 October 1934 that began at 1:30 and ended at 6:35. After the performance, according to Goldovsky, oboist Marcel Tabuteau exclaimed, "Is Roosevelt still president?" For two more performances in five days, Reiner shortened the performance by twenty-five minutes.

Both Judson and the orchestra's directors had serious misgivings about their opera venture as early as the spring of 1934. They urged Reiner to save money, but he won out on many issues, probably with Mrs. Bok's support. Although the Philadelphia Orchestra's venture into opera was an artistic success, recalled for years as a great event in the city's music history, it was a financial disaster. Herbert Graf's revolving stage, Oenslager's massive set for *Tristan,* hundreds of new costumes, specially constructed properties, and staggering rehearsal overtime for the orchestra and stagehands produced a loss on the ten opera productions of a reported $250,000, almost depleting the orchestra's reserves. The Great Opera Fiasco, as it came to be known, contributed significantly to an upheaval in the orchestra's governance and in the destinies of three conductors, not least Fritz Reiner.

Between 1927 and 1936 Fritz Reiner appeared as a guest with the Philadelphia Orchestra more frequently than any other conductor. In five years after leaving Cincinnati, Reiner conducted the Philadelphia Orchestra in three subscription seasons, popular concerts in a fourth season, and two summers at Robin Hood Dell. When Reiner was omitted from the 1932–1933 season, Samuel L. Laciar of the *Public Ledger* wrote a long article recalling memorable performances of *Also sprach Zarathustra* and *Petrushka:* "It is a matter of keen regret that Fritz Reiner will not be among the conductors of the orchestra this season, for he is . . . one of the best living orchestra leaders (and of opera as Philadelphians had occasion to find out last season) . . . two magnificent performances of Elektra the memory of which will not soon fade."[11] It is not surprising that he came to be talked of as a possible successor to Leopold Stokowski.[12]

Founded in 1900, the Philadelphia Orchestra had by 1931 attained extraordinary eminence under Stokowski's leadership, which began in 1912. To Philadelphians, Stokowski embodied the ultimate in conducting glamour, matching his personal charisma with a consummate genius for building and conducting the symphony orchestra and with a crusading zeal for new music. By 1931 he was growing restless; his sabbatical in 1927, when Reiner filled in for him, was an indication of a certain ennui on his part. In spite of Reiner's commitment to contemporary music in Cincinnati, he became, as a guest in Philadelphia, a conservative counterweight to Stokowski, who was then challenging his audiences with Arnold Schoenberg's *Gurrelieder* and Anton von Webern's Symphony. Although Reiner's Philadelphia debut in 1925 had been with Stravinsky in a program also including music by Bartók, he offered only suites from *The Firebird* and *Petrushka* on his later programs there.

In a musical comment rare in his correspondence, he wrote to Rochester Philharmonic manager Arthur See, apparently responding to an inquiry about Stravinsky's recent "neo-classical" music: "I have played the *Pulcinella* Suite many times, but find the incongruence of the style with the idiom of the 18th century makes this music stand only on one half of a leg. It is sophisticated but not genuinely good entertainment. Yes, I find it dull and boresome in stretches. I am sorry! I prefer Stravinsky the Muscovite."[13] Searching for novelty in Reiner's repertory at this time, one finds such undemanding contemporary music as Malipiero's *Concerti* and Toch's overture, *The Fan.* Surprisingly, his 1936 Philadelphia performance of the second suite from *Daphnis et Chloé* introduced that Ravel work into the orchestra's repertory. Harpist Edna Phillips, who joined the orchestra that season, recalled Reiner's receiving a standing ovation from the orchestra at the first rehearsal for his brilliant mastery of the score. Although he programmed Kodály's suite from *Háry János,* Dohnányi's *Ruralia hungarica,* and Weiner's Divertimento in Philadelphia and elsewhere, he offered little Bartók, playing only the Hungarian Sketches. At the very end of his guest affiliation with the Philadelphia Orchestra in 1936, he conducted a special choral concert consisting of Kodály's *Psalmus hungaricus* and Honegger's *Le roi David.*[14]

During his last sequence of subscription concerts with the Philadelphia Orchestra, Reiner also raised more than a few eyebrows by reversing the order of the two middle movements of Beethoven's "Eroica" Symphony. In a long interview with Laciar, the conductor justified this unusual procedure: "In the first place, there is the great length both of the first movement and of the funeral march to be considered. . . . In the Ninth Symphony and the B-flat Sonata Op. 106, when confronted by exactly the same situation, Beethoven placed the scherzo second and the slow movement third, precisely what I have done in the 'Eroica.'"[15]

The Philadelphia Orchestra sought to supplement its winter subscription season with summer concerts at Robin Hood Dell. These concerts in Fairmont Park began during the summer of 1930, and the series included a significantly successful debut by Eugene Ormandy. Reiner made his first appearance with seven concerts in August 1931, returning in 1934 and again in 1951. These Robin Hood Dell concerts began precariously in the depths of the Depression: in 1934, when the Judson office attempted to collect its commission on his fee, Reiner had to point out that he had not received any payment. During the 1934–1935 winter season he conducted several popular concerts, for which he received one hundred dollars each, plus hotel and train fare from New York. In 1936 he received two thousand dollars for a package including two subscription pairs and another of these popular concerts.

On the flyleaf of his 1935 diary, Fritz Reiner copied a bitter aphorism of Papini's, asserting that all human activity is a promissory note requiring payment in cash. With the thwarting of his hope to succeed Leopold Stokowski as music director of the Philadelphia Orchestra, Reiner suffered a devastating disappointment. Until 1931 every major change in his career had been upward—from Budapest to Dresden and from Dresden to Cincinnati. He had every reason to expect that the next step would lead to one of the greatest orchestras in the world. That failure must have had a profound impact on both Reiner and his new wife. It was she who was reduced to writing begging letters describing his situation as "desperate."

By the early 1930s the power structure of the Philadelphia Orchestra began to break up. There was increasing tension between the orchestra's board of directors and their glamorous conductor. Not only was Stokowski's repertory too adventurous for the conservative board and audience, but worst of all, it was expensive. In their eyes it was bad enough for him to press for expensive innovation; it was even worse when he threatened to resign and denounced them from the stage of the Academy of Music and in the press. In their efforts to control Stokowski, the board had an effective deputy in their long-time manager, Arthur Judson. Although he shared their businesslike approach to the orchestra, his skillful management of the conductor prevented a serious rupture. In all this, a key figure was Alexander Van Rensselaer, the orchestra's board president since its founding in 1900. "Mr. Van" enjoyed the respect and friendship of the diverse elements in the organization. Stokowski, devastatingly critical of the Philadelphia board in his later years, always made an exception of Van Rensselaer, whom he called a "remarkable" man. Despite his extensive business commitments elsewhere, Judson remained with the Philadelphia Orchestra out of loyalty to this leader. When Van Rensselaer died in 1933, the directors, responding both to his expressed wish and to pressure from Mrs. Bok, chose her son Curtis as their president. Like his parents, the younger Bok was an ardent admirer of Stokowski, to the point of idolatry: the conductor especially enjoyed his young devotee's addressing him as "Prince."

In October 1934 Judson announced that he would resign as manager of the Philadelphia Orchestra at the end of the season. His announcement coincided with the beginning of the combined concert and opera season that he and the board by this time anticipated as a financial disaster, whatever artistic distinction it might bring. Two months later Leopold Stokowski announced that he too would leave the Philadelphia Orchestra, disclosing publicly his disagreements with the directors of the association. A dismayed public expressed support for the conductor and outrage toward the board. Curtis Bok called on all his fellow directors to resign in favor of new leadership more supportive of the conductor. However, the board was merely reorganized with some "new blood" in the blue-hued Philadelphia tradition. Reginald Allen, whom Stokowski had known as a publicist at the RCA-Victor record company, became manager, and the conductor was persuaded to remain. This accommodation in early 1935 lasted only one year, for Stokowski submitted his final resignation in 1936. This time there was no public demonstration in his favor, and he agreed for the next year to appear on a limited schedule as co-conductor with Eugene Ormandy.[16]

By the early 1930s Eugene Ormandy had become the favored protégé of Arthur Judson, who carefully guided the young Hungarian's career from the orchestra pit of the Capitol Theater, to conducting radio programs, to successful guest appearances with the Philadelphia Orchestra and Minneapolis Symphony, and ultimately to the musical direction of the Philadelphia Orchestra. Even so, Ormandy was not unanimously popular in Philadelphia: when Linton Martin of the Philadelphia *Inquirer* lamented the absence of Reiner from the 1932–1933 season, he spoke disparagingly of Ormandy, the "brisk young Hungarian conductor" who, despite "agreeable gasps and gurgles [that] may greet performances," was not building a major reputation.[17]

Reiner lost out as successor to Stokowski for several reasons. He was too closely associated with the opera fiasco, whereas Ormandy showed no interest in conducting opera. Although Reiner softened his repertory considerably for his guest engagements with the Philadelphia Orchestra, he was well known for an espousal of new music; nor was his intransigence on behalf of Bartók on the Musical Fund jury in 1928 easily forgotten. If less flamboyant than Stokowski, he was certainly more committed to new music than many in the Philadelphia power structure then wanted. If Ormandy could evoke "gasps and gurgles" from an audience enthralled for many years by Stokowski, he offered no threat to its conservative sensibilities. Harpist Edna Phillips recalled that, though Reiner was highly respected by the players, he was not similarly appreciated by the audiences. Socially, the Reiners made little effort to ingratiate themselves in Philadelphia, especially while Reiner "commuted" to the city from Park Avenue in New York, scarcely evidence of commitment to the Quaker City. Nor did the circumstances of his departure from Cincinnati endear him to "proper" Philadelphia society. Moreover, Arthur Judson, still influential in Philadelphia, was now committed to his protégé Ormandy. Judson was not one to stand by a probable loser, and though he continued to represent Reiner as personal manager, he no longer promoted his career as energetically as he had a decade earlier. After conducting the Philadelphia Orchestra early in 1936, Fritz Reiner did not appear again during its winter subscription series in the Academy of Music for another twenty-two years.

CHAPTER VII

Lean Years

It would be all of seven years before Fritz Reiner would find a "permanent" post with another American orchestra. Only such a close affiliation between an orchestra and its music director could enable a conductor to build a cohesive performing ensemble and to develop his own, and his orchestra's, distinctive repertory and style. This lack of his own orchestra was a frequently disappointing, desperate, and even humiliating experience for the ambitious conductor who had received such strong support in Cincinnati. As early as October 1932 Claire Dux, now married to Harold Swift in Chicago, replied to a letter from Carlotta, expressing sympathy that "our Fritz has had to go through such a disappointing experience with Stokowski. I am sure he had too great a success with the Philadelphia audience to please Mr St, and especially as he added so much to his reputation by giving those brilliant *Elektra* performances. What has Mr. Judson to say? Isn't it entirely up to him?" [1]

With the opening in 1932 of the Radio City Music Hall, Reiner actively sought to be conductor of its large concert orchestra; the post went to Erno Rapee. When Issay Dobrowen canceled his Philadelphia guest engagement in 1933, the Reiners sought Mrs. Bok's intercession with Stokowski. She assured them of Stokowski's "good will." Carlotta sent invitations to a long list of New York musical notables urging them to attend Reiner's opera performances in Philadelphia; few, if any, made the journey. Early in 1935 Carlotta wrote Mrs. Bok asking her intercession with Herbert Witherspoon, who had succeeded Giulio Gatti-Casazza as general manager at the Metropolitan Opera. She described Judson as "apathetic, indifferent (choice). . . . I am so disturbed and unhappy. . . . I see nothing encouraging happening to [Reiner's] future." Reiner wrote directly to Witherspoon proposing the American premiere of Alban Berg's *Lulu*. Such was their desperation in these years that there is a pencil draft in Carlotta's handwriting of a petition to be signed by players in the New York Philharmonic-Symphony Orchestra asking its directors to appoint Fritz Reiner to succeed Arturo Toscanini when he retired.[2] Constance Hope, whom Reiner retained as a publicist, was in touch with Edward Johnson, Witherspoon's successor at the Metropolitan, to sound out possibilities for Reiner there. The only position would have been as assistant to Artur Bodanzky, a post shortly filled by the young Erich Leinsdorf.

In these efforts the Reiners were often working through the wrong people. After 1935 Mrs. Bok's influence with the Philadelphia Orchestra had waned. One cannot read these appeals without gaining an impression of an extraordinary naïveté on the part of both Carlotta and Fritz Reiner, a simplistic belief that his very renown would automatically open doors for him. These years were difficult financially as well. Reiner had to suffer the embarrassment of advising the executors of Charles Taft's estate that he could not repay a loan. After falling in arrears with his dues, he resigned from the Lotos Club in New York and from the Cincinnati musicians' union. Nonetheless, the Reiners still traveled first class to Europe and kept their Park Avenue apartment in New York.

Family matters remained a constant concern. Reiner's two daughters were in Vienna pursuing professional studies—Tuśy in acting and Eva in dance —and they saw their father during his visits there. In the summer of 1934 Reiner arranged for Eva to sing for Elisabeth Schumann, who heard enough talent to recommend a good Viennese teacher whom Reiner paid for his daughter's lessons. He continued to send money to his daughters, usually ten dollars each month, but discontinued his remittances to their mother. Reiner also continued monthly remittances, usually fifty dollars, to his mother in Budapest until her death in 1939, and he occasionally sent money to his uncle Sándor. A major crisis developed in 1938 when Eva informed her father that she intended to marry Werner Bartenstein, a young Swiss. Reiner reacted characteristically with preaching and admonition, expressing doubts about Eva's competence to judge her feelings and Werner's sincerity. At one point Eva turned for help to her grandmother in Budapest. Ultimately Eva gave up all thought of a career and married Werner, with whom she enjoyed a happy marriage and had three children.[3] Tuśy continued her acting and enjoyed some success in the theater before the outbreak of World War II.

Lacking a central focus for his work, Reiner had to rebuild his career with a variety of activities. One area increasingly open to him was in the electronic revolution that was having a profound effect on the music profession. Radio broadcasting became an important part of Reiner's work in the 1930s, financially if not artistically. During this period he also made his first recordings, either experimentally or anonymously, but not for commercial distribution. His work with the Philadelphia Grand Opera Company and the brilliant opera season with the Philadelphia Orchestra eventually led to seasons at Covent Garden and the San Francisco Opera. Although Reiner no longer had Pontecchio as a European base after his divorce from Berta, he visited Europe with Carlotta at least once a year until 1938.

In New York Reiner became involved in various professional activities. In 1933 he was in touch with Aaron Copland and Roger Sessions about some unspecified project in which he would conduct programs of new music for no fee.[4] After Arnold Schoenberg came to the United States in 1934, he visited Reiner several times before moving to Los Angeles. Although Reiner never conducted any of Schoenberg's twelve-tone music, they enjoyed a cordial professional friendship. Still, without an orchestra of his own during these years, Reiner performed little exacting contemporary music, especially compared with his programming in Cincinnati. A notable exception was a Stravinsky-Hindemith ensemble program for the League of Composers at Town Hall in New York on 30 January 1934. It included Stravinsky's *A Soldier's Tale,* the Kammermusik no. 1 for twelve solo instruments, opus 24, no. 1, and the Kammermusik no. 2 (Klavierkonzert), opus 36, no. 1, of Hindemith, the latter with Frank Sheridan as soloist. Claire Reis at the League of Composers tried several times to interest Reiner in programs of contemporary music with Curtis students, but Mrs. Bok shared the antipathy of many music patrons to modernism.

Unless his personal prestige was at stake, as it was in Italy in 1931, Reiner seldom involved himself publicly in the political and social causes that dominated the 1930s. His most overt action was to join Toscanini, Koussevitzky, and others in a 1933 letter to Adolf Hitler protesting the treatment of such Jewish musicians as Bruno Walter. When the American Music League asked Reiner to join in publicly endorsing Béla Bartók's refusal in 1937 to allow his music to be broadcast in Nazi Germany, Judson approved of Reiner's refusal, expressing his opposition to mixing music and politics.[5] In 1938 Reiner asked that his name be removed from a list of sympathizers with republican Spain that included Virgil Thomson, Aaron Copland, Pablo Casals, Samuel Chotzinoff, Sol Hurok, and Walter Piston.

Reiner received honorary doctorates from the University of Pennsylvania in Philadelphia in 1940 and the following year from the University of Pittsburgh. When he learned of the University of Pennsylvania honor, Reiner wrote to Mrs. Bok expressing appreciation for what he recognized as her efforts on his behalf. Both Reiners set great store by these degrees, as well as those Fritz later received from Northwestern University and Loyola University. He and Carlotta insisted on his being addressed as *Doctor* Fritz Reiner. With his musicians and other professionals, he was no longer Maestro or Meister, but Doctor Reiner. In Reiner, who took such pride in being an American, this insistence on the honorific betrayed a vanity rooted in insecurity.

Reiner of necessity welcomed opportunities to appear as guest conductor, either of an established orchestra or of an ad hoc group, as a stepping-stone to a resident post. In this the support of Arthur Judson was indispensable, for he was then the sole American manager of conductors. With a network of orchestra managers and influential board members friendly or obligated to him, his recommendations carried decisive authority. In the 1930s the American market for soloists and conductors of international stature assumed increased importance. This was especially the case with Jews fleeing Germany and frequently discriminated against in other European countries. Many non-Jewish musicians also restricted their European activity on principle. Reiner of course was hardly a 1930s émigré, having lived in the United States since 1922.

While managing the Philadelphia Orchestra, Judson had shifted his headquarters to New York. He had become manager of the New York Philharmonic and the Lewisohn Stadium Concerts in 1922 through a series of manipulations and consolidations of orchestras. These would culminate in 1928 with the merger of the Philharmonic with Walter Damrosch's New York Symphony. Henceforth the New York Philharmonic-Symphony Orchestra would dominate that city's symphonic activity.[6] As a self-styled "salesman of fine music," Judson assembled a roster of concert artists and conductors by personal persuasion or by merging with other managements. He used the weekly broadcasts of the New York Philharmonic-Symphony to promote his concert artists and conductors over the CBS network, of which he was a major stockholder.

This strategy of consolidation culminated in 1932, when Judson joined five of his competitors in organizing the Columbia Concerts Corporation, affiliated with CBS. Columbia Concerts, in turn, had its "organized audience" affiliate, Community Concerts, which arranged the booking of concert artists throughout America. A similar organization affiliated with the National Broadcasting Company, the National Concert and Broadcasting Bureau, had its "organized audience" outlet in Civic Concert Service. Although these two corporations were theoretically competitors, they had informal agreements to divide the territory they served. However, Judson still controlled the management of conductors.[7]

At the height of their power, Judson, the Philharmonic administration, and his partners at Columbia Concerts occupied the top floors of the Steinway Building across from Carnegie Hall on West 57th Street. From Philadelphia, Judson had brought Ruth O'Neill, whom he placed in charge of scheduling singers and instrumentalists under his management. In addition to booking concert engagements, she wielded great influence over appearances by conductors and soloists on the "Hours" of semiclassical music on all four radio networks. She scheduled many of Judson's conductors' guest engagements with orchestras until 1937, when Judson assigned this responsibility to Bruno Zirato, who had been and remained the assistant manager of the Philharmonic.

Zirato was a large and voluble Italian, at one time associated with Caruso and other Italian singers. Reiner worked with him during the summer season at the Teatro Colón in 1926, when Zirato was in charge of publicity. Although both were impressive physically, Zirato and Judson differed in temperament and style. Whereas Judson was always the corporate "man of distinction," Zirato was the Italian extrovert, outspoken, openly ruthless, and, on occasion, devastatingly earthy. Igor Stravinsky, whose conducting engagements Zirato handled for many years, called him Sparafucile, after the hired assassin in Verdi's *Rigoletto*. Zirato returned the compliment by suggesting that the composer's business monogram consisted of his first initial superimposed on the last, forming a dollar sign. Reiner and Zirato got on well with one another, peppering their correspondence with Italian phrases and addressing one another as "caro amico." When Zirato wanted to pass on confidential information to Reiner, he wrote in Italian.

Aside from work with the Philadelphia Orchestra until 1936, Judson and his staff obtained for Reiner guest engagements with seven orchestras and one opera company in America between 1931 and 1938. They arranged many radio appearances and worked on some of his European engagements. Still, there was constant friction between the two strong-willed men. Judson was frustrated by what he perceived as the conductor's intransigence, and Reiner was more resentful of the manager's failure to advance his career than of his meddling in artistic matters. Nor were relations between the two men eased by Carlotta's outspoken resentment at Judson's failure to promote her husband's career more successfully. Although her tactless rudeness to Judson may have reflected her husband's feelings, it did his career no good.

While still in Cincinnati, Reiner had apparently bypassed Judson in rejecting an inquiry from the St. Louis Symphony. When Carlotta attempted to revive St. Louis's interest in Reiner in 1933, she learned that the community was happy with Vladimir Golschmann. Reiner finally appeared there, as guest rather than candidate, in 1936. Between 1931 and 1936 Reiner was a guest conductor of the Rochester Philharmonic in four seasons out of five, while that orchestra sought a replacement for Eugene Goossens. That courtship ended when the orchestra selected José Iturbi, a Spanish pianist with conducting ambitions who was then a great favorite of Judson. For two seasons beginning in 1935, the Detroit Symphony Orchestra engaged Reiner as a guest and apparently seriously considered him as its music director, but eventually settled on Franco Ghione. Less promising were two summer engagements in San Francisco in 1933 and 1934. The symphony orchestra there was in the throes of financial problems and reorganization that eventually led to the engagement of Pierre Monteux in 1936.

In such "audition" engagements with unfamiliar orchestras, Reiner inclined toward safe programming. In Rochester he shared the podium with Howard Hanson as a diplomatic gesture toward the influential director of the Eastman School of Music. He also favored that audience with the world premiere of Leo Weiner's suite of Old Hungarian Folk Dances and with the first American performance of excerpts from Casella's *La donna serpente*. During his London visit in 1936 he had encountered the suite from William Walton's *Façade*, which he offered on a number of his programs.

Reiner conducted the Stadium Concerts in both 1931 and 1937. As before, he could trust the players of the New York Philharmonic-Symphony Orchestra with such repertory as Strauss's *Sinfonia domestica* and the Ravel orchestration of Mussorgsky's *Pictures at an Exhibition*. His 1931 programs included an evening of American music. In 1937 he devoted four evenings to extended excerpts from Wagner's *Der Ring des Nibelungen* tetralogy, with Florence Easton, Göta Ljungberg, and Paul Althouse among the featured singers. In that same year he first encountered the Chicago Symphony Orchestra at its summer home at Ravinia Park, where he offered substantial programs that included *Also sprach Zarathustra*, the *Façade* suite, and the Weiner Divertimento. To Ruth O'Neill he reported sold-out houses but an orchestra inferior to the New York Philharmonic-Symphony. From Ravinia he proceeded westward by motorcar for his first appearances in the Hollywood Bowl since 1924. There Howard Hanson conducted his own music on part of one program. The soloist on another evening, in songs by Max Reger, was the young Helen Gahagan, still appearing as a singer before turning to acting and finally, after her marriage to Melvyn Douglas, to the United States Senate. Reiner followed his Bowl engagement with a leisurely trip to San Francisco via Yosemite Park.

Aside from summers in Lewisohn Stadium, Reiner conducted rarely in New York. His most important appearance was a concert on 2 November 1932 at the Metropolitan Opera House. He conducted the Musicians' Symphony in excerpts from *Salome* with Maria Jeritza and Nelson Eddy. *Salome* had scandalized the backers of the Metropolitan Opera in 1907, and its music still enjoyed a certain notorious novelty in New York; the Metropolitan would not revive it for another two years. According to Olin Downes, the selections offered were "especially made [for Jeritza] and endorsed by the composer" to give a "fairly unified" notion of the opera.[8] Reiner began the program with the Brahms *Aca-*

demic Festival overture and preceded the *Salome* excerpts with the andante from Mahler's Second Symphony, the Bach-Respighi Passacaglia in C Minor, and Johann Strauss's *Emperor* waltz. As encores, Jeritza sang Brünnhilde's "Ho-jo-to-ho" from *Die Walküre* and the orchestra played the *Blue Danube* waltz. Reiner made one or two other appearances in New York during the 1930s. Leopold Stokowski was announced in advance as one of the conductors of a "mammoth" symphony concert, featuring an orchestra variously stated to be of two hundred or four hundred players, to be broadcast internationally on New Year's Day 1933, as part of the celebration of the opening of the Radio City Music Hall at Rockefeller Center. According to the newsletter of the Curtis Institute of Music in November 1933, Reiner substituted at the last minute for Stokowski.[9] In 1938 Reiner joined John Barbirolli and Philip James as one of several conductors in a memorial to Henry Hadley; Reiner conducted the concert overture *In Bohemia*.

Such concerts as these New York appearances were less important in introducing Reiner to a larger audience than was his increasing exposure on the radio and, to a lesser extent, on phonograph recordings. By the 1930s the public media—radio, cinema, and recording—were assuming an importance that would increasingly pervade music in the next decades. Eventually Reiner would become involved in all these media, including the adaptation of cinema to television, but during the 1930s his principal activity was in radio.

He was only abortively involved in sound film, the "talkies," which in the late 1920s aroused great hope that the cinema might become a vehicle for concert music and opera in Hollywood. In July 1934 the New York *Times* carried an announcement that Reiner would be musical director of a color film version of Gounod's *Faust*. In an editorial three days later it hailed this project for its artistic potential.[10] The moving force behind this project was George Bailhe, who appears also to have enlisted the composer George Antheil, theater designer Lee Simonson, and the German director G. W. Pabst. As general musical director, Reiner was to have a three-year contract, including other operas, and to be a shareholder in the corporation, Music Guild Productions. The more the project evolved, the more it moved away from the Gounod opera toward something like Marlowe's *Doctor Faustus* or Goethe's *Faust,* with incidental music. Nor could Bailhe raise the necessary capital. Writing later to Carlotta, Antheil's wife, Boske, called Bailhe the "Phantom of the Opera." Of more eventual consequence was an approach in 1936 to Reiner by a Hollywood agency concerning a *Carmen* film to be produced by Boris Morros. Although that project never materialized, Morros was a producer some years later of *Carnegie Hall,* in which Reiner took part.

Other than the Welte piano rolls, there is no documentation of Reiner's conducting before 1931–1932, when fragments of three of his performances at the Academy of Music were recorded experimentally. These owed their existence to Leopold Stokowski's fascination not only with the mass-culture possibilities of the phonograph but with the technical process as well.[11] During the Philadelphia Orchestra's 1931–1932 season, J. P. Maxfield of the Electrical Research Products division of Western Electric brought technicians to the Academy of Music for a series of experimental recordings. Maxfield had worked earlier on the development of electrical recording and was also interested in the cultural implications of his work. These recordings demonstrated a degree of audio fidelity then unknown in commercial techniques; some were actually in stereophonic sound. They included fragments from two Reiner concerts with the Philadelphia Orchestra: a program of orchestral Wagner and a Russian program including the Tchaikovsky Piano Concerto no. 1 with Vladimir Horowitz as soloist. A substantial portion of the February 1932 *Lohengrin* with the Philadelphia Grand Opera was also recorded. Because there was only one recording lathe, the continuity of the music was broken.[12] With some Stokowski performances on successive identical programs, it was possible to assemble an entire work.

Reiner's correspondence with Maxfield about these "test recordings" showed a more than passing interest on his part. At one point they discussed a proposal to make sound films of *Parsifal* and Rimsky-Korsakov's *Scheherazade*. The conductor even obtained from Maurice Van Praag information on union fees for the orchestra players. His contact with Electrical Research Products may also have resulted in experimental recordings (not with orchestra) with Elisabeth Rethberg, Jascha Heifetz, and Gregor Piatigorsky.[13] Maxfield and his colleagues also made experimental recordings of some radio programs, which may be the source of a brief excerpt from a 1931 Firestone Hour in which Richard Tauber sang a Grieg song and reminisced briefly with Reiner about their days in Dresden.

Not until 22 November 1938 did Fritz Reiner make recordings for commercial distribution, and then only anonymously, for a series of discs sold by the New York *Post* as a promotional scheme. With sixty players from the New York Philharmonic-Symphony Orchestra in Carnegie Hall, RCA-Victor recorded Reiner in two three-record sets of music by Debussy and Wagner, without disclosing the identity of the orchestra and conductor. Other newspapers across the country sold these recordings for promotion, and eventually discount music stores remaindered some discs. Reiner, Ormandy, and Rodzinski considered legal action to halt retail sale, but since none of them had any contractual understanding with the promoters, they could not proceed. Reiner contended that he had made the recordings only as a personal favor to *Post* publisher David Stern, and not as a commercial venture.[14] Though these recordings brought

Reiner in touch with Charles O'Connell, director of classical recording at RCA-Victor, the company's commitments to the orchestras of New York, Boston, and Philadelphia and to their respective conductors precluded making recordings with Reiner. When RCA-Victor scheduled Lauritz Melchior to record with the Philadelphia Orchestra in 1938, the tenor wanted Reiner to conduct these sessions, but it was contrary to the orchestra's policy to record with anyone except its own music director.[15]

It was in radio, then unquestionably the major electronic medium for disseminating concert music and opera, that Reiner was most active. By the 1930s Arthur Judson's early use of the medium for promoting his artists had led to a proliferation of one-hour broadcasts of lighter concert music in such programs as the Firestone Hour, the Dutch Masters Hour, the Cadillac Hour, and the Carnation Hour, featuring concert artists. The artists and repertory of these broadcasts complemented the nationwide chains of the Community Concerts and Civic Music Association "organized audiences" that reached into thousands of American communities. These radio programs used union musicians under contract to the network studios, usually with such staff conductors as Frank Black, Don Vorhees, Howard Barlow, Alfred Wallenstein, or André Kostelanetz. Sometimes the producers brought in "name" conductors like Reiner who conducted such programs for fees of five to seven hundred dollars. Qualitatively the performance and repertory of these "Hours" fell far short of the standards of established performing organizations.[16]

But it was the Ford Sunday Evening Hour that most widely broadcast the performances of Fritz Reiner. Begun in 1934 with Ossip Gabrilowitsch conducting the Detroit Symphony Orchestra in local broadcasts, this weekly series moved in the fall of 1936 to the CBS network at nine o'clock on Sunday evenings. Between September 1936 and early 1942 Reiner conducted forty-two of these broadcasts. He conducted another four after Ford briefly revived the series in 1946.[17] Major concert artists of the caliber of Jascha Heifetz, John Charles Thomas, Lawrence Tibbett, Grace Moore, Helen Traubel, and Kirsten Flagstad appeared on the program. The orchestra was the Detroit Symphony, and the conductors were Judson clients. Though some soloists came from rival managements, most came from Judson and his partners in Columbia Concerts. The program paid good fees, one thousand dollars to conductors like Reiner and Ormandy, and more for the top soloists of that era.

The Ford Sunday Evening Hour was so rigidly structured as to approach a ritual. The program opened with a "signature" theme, the "Prayer" from Humperdinck's *Hänsel und Gretel*. Before the first appearance of the soloist, a lively overture was obligatory. A short orchestral or choral selection sometimes preceded the station break at midprogram. There then was a brief talk by

W. J. Cameron, spokesman for Henry Ford's sometimes eccentric but always ultraconservative political and social views. The soloist's appearance during the second half of the program was lighter, sometimes with piano accompaniment. A lively orchestra selection was followed by a mandatory "Closing Hymn," in which the audience, five thousand in the auditorium and millions over the air, was invited to join a local chorus, the orchestra, and soloist. The printed program and the radio announcer added a personal touch by acknowledging the contribution of Henry and Edsel Ford.

In organizing these programs, the Ford Motor Company's advertising agency worked with Ruth O'Neill at the Judson office and with other managers to schedule the "talent" and to make protracted arrangements for the repertory. Edsel Ford took a keen personal interest in the program, exercising a taste in music as conservative as his father's politics. The producers repeatedly admonished Reiner not to suggest music by Bartók, Stravinsky, or Mahler and to avoid "expensive music" by Richard Strauss. At one point there was an edict that scores and recordings of "unfamiliar" music had to be submitted four weeks in advance of the broadcast for approval. Edsel Ford also objected to playing the same music too frequently, thus challenging the ingenuity of the conductors to maintain familiarity without too much frequency. On another occasion, Ford forbade opening the program with any selection lasting more than seven minutes; Reiner met this restriction by abbreviating longer selections. At the outset, Reiner warmly embraced the Ford Sunday Evening Hour. Early on Reiner met Edsel Ford and Cameron in Detroit for a tour of the River Rouge assembly plant, where he took pictures that he later sent to the Fords. Although he had purchased a Packard touring car early in 1936, he loyally arranged to replace it with a Lincoln Zephyr a year later. He had it driven to New York for the installation of a custom sliding roof.

After a while, tension developed along the lines of communication from the Fords through the advertising agency and the Judson office to Reiner and then back to Edsel Ford. When Cameron and another Ford executive heard phonograph recordings of the suggestions for one program, they disliked all of Kodály's *Háry János* music except the "Musical Clock" section. They frequently recommended changes in the order of the music, because of "rhythmic contrast," and especially favored Johann Strauss waltzes. The *Emperor* waltz replaced the objectionable Leo Weiner orchestration of two Bartók Rumanian Dances on one program. In 1939 Judson reported to Reiner that the agency was having trouble with Edsel Ford, who had "blown up completely," threatening to cancel the entire project.

Reiner also had to deal with William J. Reddick, who directed the Detroit chorus but also worked as a musical coordinator and liaison with Edsel Ford.

He infuriated Reiner at rehearsals by standing behind him and signaling instructions to the orchestra; Reiner tried with varying success to have him banished to the control room. In the spring of 1941 the advertising agency asked Judson to submit a list of proposed conductors for the following season, but explicitly told him to omit Ormandy and Reiner. Still, Judson had booked some Reiner dates for the first half of 1942 before the cancellation of the program shortly after Pearl Harbor. With the conversion of the Ford plants to war work, there was no need to advertise the Ford product to consumers. The company may well have been happy to soften its isolationist image in the interests of wartime patriotism. After the war Ford briefly revived the Sunday Evening Hour, and Reiner conducted several programs in the spring of 1946.

Why did Reiner continue to conduct these programs that offended his artistic sensibilities and sorely tried his patience? Enthusiasm for a new project may have motivated him at first, but as the pressures of the series ground on, only the money could have held him there. The schedule was easy: he took an overnight train to Detroit, conducted the Sunday rehearsal and broadcast, and returned on the late night train to New York, Philadelphia, or Pittsburgh. For this he received a fee of one thousand dollars, the same as for a full week of rehearsing and conducting two or three concerts as a guest with an orchestra. The Ford Sunday Evening Hour fees often amounted annually to more than he earned at Curtis.

Reiner spent most summers in Europe, combining concerts and holidays, sometimes returning early enough to fill summer engagements. Carlotta invariably traveled with him, taking charge of arrangements with hotels, chauffeurs, and steamship lines and looking after his comfort. On some trips he visited his daughters in Ljubljana and Vienna or his family in Budapest. He and Carlotta had a particular fondness for luxurious spas—Bad Gastein, Marienbad, or Semmering near Vienna. The Lido also had a great attraction for them, and they stayed there either for holidays or during working engagements at the Teatro La Fenice in Venice.

It was there that he participated in a 1932 festival of contemporary music, at which he conducted the La Scala Orchestra in a program of American music.[18] Although the entire program cannot be reconstructed, Irving Kolodin later told George Gershwin that it included his Concerto in F, played by Harry Kaufman, then a member of the Curtis faculty. Kolodin reported that the La Scala Orchestra had found the concerto very difficult but that Reiner's command assured its success.[19] This program also included the first performance anywhere of *Golem* by Joseph Achron, in which the last movement was a repetition of the first movement, repeated backward, describing the creation and destruction of the monster of Jewish mythology.[20] For several summers, Reiner also conducted concerts regularly in Palermo, Naples, Rome, Florence, Milan, and, for the Italian government radio, in Turin. His Italian programs included a substantial representation of such Italian composers as Respighi, Casella, Malipiero, Lualdi, and Pizzetti. He also conducted occasionally in Vienna and Budapest.[21] In January and February 1937 his Paris agent arranged a series of concerts in Stockholm.

Despite its financial disaster, Reiner's operatic work in Philadelphia led to artistic success that firmly established him as a major conductor of opera, although not in Italy or Germany. The Italians would not accept a foreigner in Italian opera, and after the Fascist-Nazi rapprochement, conductors of German opera had to be approved by Josef Goebbels in Berlin. Only Mario Labroca in Florence showed any interest in Reiner for opera.[22] One of Reiner's more curious operatic efforts in Europe was his effort to secure a post in Berlin, possibly with the help of Richard Strauss. A 1931 telegram from Hans Tessmer at the Charlottenburg Opera indicates Reiner's interest in becoming general music director there.[23] A 1932 New York *Times* dispatch from Berlin reported that he had declined the post of general music director of the Municipal Opera.[24] The latter story, probably inspired by his publicist Constance Hope, was untrue. In fact, during May and June of that year Reiner was seeking a meeting with Karl Ebert, the director of that theater, and it is obvious from the correspondence that Ebert was avoiding such a meeting.[25] This is all the more curious because Reiner never conducted in Germany after 1922, although not for want of effort to secure engagements through various agents. It may well be that the circumstances of his departure from Dresden were held against him. When Miklós Radnai died in Budapest in 1935, leaving open the post of director of the Royal Hungarian Opera, Reiner made inquiries about obtaining that position. Apparently the authorities would not consider him unless he agreed in advance to accept the invitation.[26] For whatever reason, nothing came of this possibility, and Reiner limited his Budapest appearances to single orchestra concerts in 1935 and 1936.

Early in 1936 Sir Thomas Beecham encountered difficulty in securing Hans Knappertsbusch for his spring opera season at Covent Garden; Knappertsbusch was out of favor with the Nazi government, which refused to assure his return to his Munich post. Sir Thomas then approached Artur Bodanzky of the Metropolitan Opera, whose fee was too high, £250 for each performance. Probably at Judson's suggestion, Beecham lunched with Reiner when he was in New York for concerts with the Philharmonic-Symphony. While Reiner was guest conducting in St. Louis, Carlotta wired him that Sir Thomas had told her that he would be in touch if Knappertsbusch was not available. Beecham shortly offered Reiner *Tristan und Isolde, Parsifal,* and *Der Rosenkavalier* between mid-April and the end of June, for a fee of £600, then somewhat more than three thousand dollars.[27]

Parsifal, with Frida Leider, Torsten Ralf, Ludwig Weber, and Herbert Janssen, was Reiner's London debut opera on 29 April 1936. It was repeated five weeks later. According to Harold Rosenthal, it was given uncut and aroused the admiration of the eminent Wagnerian Ernest Newman: "The best thing that Covent Garden has ever given us but as good, on the whole, as anything we could hear in Europe today. The orchestra under Fritz Reiner's sure and sensitive guidance played superbly."[28] The cast for *Der Rosenkavalier* included Elisabeth Rethberg, Tiana Lemnitz, Stella Andreva, and Emanuel List; there were three performances, one of them broadcast over the BBC. The sensation of the season was Kirsten Flagstad's London debut in *Tristan und Isolde,* with Lauritz Melchior, List, and Janssen; it received four performances, on 18 and 22 May and 2 and 11 June. As Isolde, Flagstad was in her prime, and Melchior offered an extraordinary interpretation of Tristan. Despite Flagstad's suffering from a bad cold at the first performance, there were eight curtain calls after act I, nine after act II, and fifteen at the conclusion of the performance.

During Reiner's two seasons at Covent Garden, the Gramophone Company (His Master's Voice) made experimental performance recordings of an entire *Tristan und Isolde* with Kirsten Flagstad and Lauritz Melchior in 1936 and portions of *Der fliegende Holländer* and *Parsifal* in 1937. This was a major undertaking, requiring two gravity-driven recording lathes with carefully synchronized wax masters. These became the source of a number of underground tapes and long-playing records. During the 1936 *Tristan,* HMV executive Fred Gaisberg planned to capitalize on Flagstad's London debut by recording act II with Fritz Reiner conducting the Vienna Philharmonic Orchestra the following September. When this proved impossible, Gaisberg proposed a commercial release of act II from the Covent Garden performances, which none of the artists, including Reiner, would approve.[29]

Since England was in mourning for the death of George V, social activity during the 1936 opera season was sharply curtailed. However, Fred Gaisberg arranged for a limousine to drive the Reiners to visit Glyndebourne, where John Christie entertained them cordially before and during a performance of *Così fan tutte.* The conductor took pictures there, as well as in London, and later sent prints to his English colleagues. Mrs. Bok came to London for some of Reiner's performances and also visited Glyndebourne, later thanking the conductor for his help in arranging her visit.[30]

As impresario at Covent Garden, Beecham was notoriously casual in his commitments to artists: he would promise the same operas to several conductors and then extricate himself most charmingly. For the gala season honoring the coronation of George VI in the spring of 1937, he first offered Reiner a repeat of *Tristan und Isolde* and then sought the services of Wilhelm Furtwängler for all German operas. Having booked the German conductor for the *Der Ring des Nibelungen*, he offered Reiner *Tristan und Isolde*, *Prince Igor*, *Parsifal*, and a new production of *Der fliegende Holländer*. Reiner turned down *Prince Igor*, countering with *Falstaff* instead, which Beecham took over himself along with *Tristan und Isolde*. Reiner finally wound up with *Parsifal*, *Der fliegende Holländer* with Flagstad and Janssen, and Gluck's *Orphée et Euridice* more or less in the 1774 Paris version, which Beecham had originally planned to conduct himself; Harold Rosenthal describes Reiner as having been "pitchforked" into conducting it.[31] Maggie Teyte was a last-minute substitute for Ninon Vallin as Euridice, and the De Basil Ballet Russe de Monte Carlo appeared in the Gluck opera and filled out the evening with Massine's *Le beau Danube*. *Parsifal* was given with the 1936 cast except that Kerstin Thorborg replaced Leider. Reiner's conducting of the *Der fliegende Holländer* with Flagstad and Janssen won high praise from Richard Capell: "The credit for the exceptional effect made at this performance belongs first to the conductor, a musician of powerful grip and practiced judgment."[32]

During the coronation season the Reiners enjoyed the lively social whirl of London and country house weekends, including another visit to Glyndebourne. Through friends they had a good location from which to view the coronation procession. A BBC broadcast of Wagner excerpts with Florence Easton and Walter Widdop in February 1937 was a direct consequence of Reiner's Covent Garden success the previous season. Several agents and London orchestras were already seeking to schedule him there in 1938 and 1939. Had the war not intervened, Reiner could have built a substantial career in London.

The Covent Garden engagement was the beginning of a friendship between Sir Thomas and Fritz Reiner, who is credited with having evoked one of Beecham's more outrageous witticisms by thanking him for "a wonderful night with Mozart and Beecham." To this Sir Thomas replied, "Why drag in Mozart?"[33] After he became music director of the Chicago Symphony Orchestra, Reiner engaged his British colleague as guest in two seasons.

Other operatic opportunities for Reiner in the United States were slow to develop, largely because of a lack of stable companies at that time. René Devries, the Chicago correspondent for the *Musical Courier*, wrote frequently to the Reiners about his efforts to persuade Paul Longone to engage Reiner in his attempts to revive opera in Chicago after the collapse of the Civic Opera in 1932. Other inquiries, directly to Reiner or through the Judson office, were typical of prevailing conditions. On an undated leaflet announcing Reiner's appearance in opera in Boston, a friend scribbled the advice, "Get your money first!"[34] In fact, the Metropolitan in New York and the San Francisco Opera were then the only stable companies in the United States. At the same time that Beecham was negotiating for Reiner's services for the spring of 1936, Gaetano Merola was arranging through Judson for him to conduct in San Francisco during the following autumn season.

Born in Naples and a disciple of Puccini, Merola had founded the San Francisco Opera in 1924.[35] He had the support of the local Italian-American community and others in a city that had long shown a passion for opera. By scheduling a concentrated fall season before the Metropolitan began for the winter, Merola relied heavily on artists appearing in New York. For a decade the company performed under makeshift arrangements in the Civic Auditorium, before the War Memorial Opera House opened in 1934. True to his Neapolitan heritage, Merola concentrated on a repertory of Italian opera for the first years of his company's existence. Alfred Hertz, then director of the San Francisco Symphony Orchestra, conducted an occasional German opera, including a 1933 *Tristan und Isolde* in which Ezio Pinza sang the role of King Mark.

In 1935 the San Francisco Opera undertook a full presentation of Wagner's *Der Ring des Nibelungen*. Creating its own scenery, it imported singers and the conductor Artur Bodanzky from the Metropolitan. The singers included Kirsten Flagstad, Elisabeth Rethberg, Lauritz Melchior, Friedrich Schorr, and Emanuel List. Bodanzky brought with him four players from the Metropolitan Opera orchestra for the special tubas required by Wagner's scoring. The success of the 1935 *Ring*, given but once, inspired immediate plans to offer more Wagner opera in 1936, including *Tristan und Isolde* with Flagstad and Melchior. Bodanzky had not endeared himself with his patronizing view of the community and his contemptuous treatment of the orchestra and the company. When he tried to raise his fee, Merola looked elsewhere. Merola and Judson then settled on Reiner's engagement to conduct *Tristan und Isolde, Die Walküre,* and *Götterdämmerung* the following fall. Nearly all the 1935 singers were reengaged, but Lotte Lehmann replaced Rethberg as Sieglinde in *Die Walküre*. This was the only occasion when both she and Flagstad sang in the same production of any opera. Melchior, Schorr, and the American Kathryn Meisle rounded out this extraordinary 1936 cast. Kurt Reidel assisted Reiner and conducted *Das Rheingold*.

The four special tubas for the *Ring* operas became a nagging problem, for the local union would not allow the importation of musicians from New York. The problem concerned not only the players themselves but also the instruments for them to play. Merola claimed that at preliminary discussions in New York Reiner had agreed to adapt the parts in question to be played on regular horns. He pointed out that Otto Klemperer had apparently done this in a recent Los Angeles performance of the Bruckner Seventh Symphony. Reiner insisted on the proper instruments, as Bodanzky had the year before, and threatened to cancel his appearance. He knew, in fact, that Curtis owned a set of these tubas and prevailed on Mrs. Bok to lend them to the San Francisco Opera. Merola assigned to Reidel the task of coaching four local brass players on the unusual instruments. In September, Reiner and Reidel corresponded concerning progress with the tuba players and the cuts that the conductor planned in the three Wagner operas. For *Die Walküre* he specified "the usual Metropolitan mutilation" and substantial deletions in the second and third acts of *Tristan und Isolde* and in the prologue to *Götterdämmerung*.[36]

Reiner made his debut at the San Francisco Opera on 2 November 1936, conducting *Tristan und Isolde*. *Götterdämmerung* followed on the fourth and *Die Walküre* on the thirteenth. *Die Walküre* and *Tristan und Isolde* each received a second nonsubscription presentation. Although Flagstad and Melchior had appeared in the 1935 *Ring*, their appearance in *Tristan und Isolde* created a sensation. Both public and press acclaimed Reiner's conducting as the finest ever heard at the San Francisco Opera. During the stage rehearsals for *Die Walküre*, Reiner objected vehemently to the noisy steam machine in the "Magic Fire Music." He threatened to withdraw and eventually persuaded Merola's cousin, stage director Armando Agnini, to omit the steam.[37] For the first time the NBC network broadcast portions of several San Francisco Opera performances; Marcia Davenport was an effusive commentator. Despite cuts, the second act of *Die Walküre* ran past the allotted broadcast time; some underground recordings from the 13 November performance have Davenport describing the curtain falling before the end of the act.[38]

In 1937 the American Julius Huehn replaced Schorr in a repetition of *Tristan und Isolde*. None of the *Ring* was repeated that year, but Reiner conducted *Lohengrin* with Flagstad, Melchior, Meisle, and Huehn, and *Fidelio* with Flagstad and René Maison. This season also saw the inauguration of annual visits by the San Francisco company to the vast Shrine Auditorium in Los Angeles. *Tristan und Isolde* was the obvious choice to open this engagement, and *Lohengrin* was included to capitalize on the popularity of the fabled Wagnerians.[39] By this time Reiner was something of a fixture during the brief fall season of the San Francisco Opera, an important force in establishing the German repertory in a city where the Italian had long reigned. However, he was also notoriously difficult, demanding more rehearsals and larger orchestras than Merola was inclined to finance. Several of Reiner's productions required expansion of the orchestra pit by eliminating the first rows of seating, thus reducing ticket sales. His demands and threats to leave created increasing pressure on Merola. For protection in 1938, Merola engaged the young Austrian Erich Leinsdorf to conduct Debussy's *Pelléas et Mélisande* and to assist Reiner. When asked to explain his making the unusual assignment of the Debussy opera to a specialist in German opera, Merola explained that he wanted to have another conductor of Reiner's repertory in the house just in case he threatened to quit.

Flagstad and Melchior did not return in 1938, and Wagner was represented by *Die Meistersinger,* marking Schorr's return, with Irene Jessner and Charles Kullman. Rose Pauly, Kerstin Thorborg, Huehn, and Karl Laufkötter sang in *Elektra* (with the borrowed Curtis tubas). *Elektra* and *Die Meistersinger* contributed to what was, for the San Francisco Opera, a staggering deficit of eighty-eight thousand dollars. The company's first *Don Giovanni* had Rethberg, Jessner, Mafalva Favero, Pinza, and Salvatore Baccaloni on stage and Reiner in the pit. This was the conductor's first performance of the opera. In Los Angeles Reiner conducted *Elektra* and *Die Meistersinger,* with Rethberg as Eva. With his engagement in Pittsburgh, Reiner no longer needed the San Francisco Opera, and Merola was happy to replace him in the German repertory with the more accommodating Leinsdorf.

Reiner's fortunes and prospects had reached their nadir in the months after the end of the Philadelphia Orchestra opera season in the spring of 1935. Nevertheless, his two operatic projects in Philadelphia had established him as a major conductor of opera leading to engagements at Covent Garden and the San Francisco Opera, where they marked the turning point in his fortunes in the 1930s. They provided welcome relief from guest engagements with second-rate American orchestras and from constant wrangling over radio programs of questionable artistic merit. Covent Garden and San Francisco, plus a busy summer with outdoor concerts in 1937, found Reiner more active than he had been earlier. Finally, a guest appearance with the newly reorganized Pittsburgh Symphony Orchestra in January 1938 resulted two months later in his engagement as its music director. Fritz Reiner again had the kind of resident post so necessary for the full realization of his talent.

Bartcky Victor   BUDAPEST.

Reiner Frigyes with his mother, Irma.

The young huntsman.

Friderick Reiner with Angela (Elca) Jelacin, his first wife, Laibach/Ljubljana 1910.

Reiner with his grandson Vladimir Assejew in front of the Ljubljana Municipal Theater, summer 1954.

*Conductor at the Saxon State Opera,
Dresden, c. 1920.*

Richard Strauss, c. 1916.

Burkard caricature of Arthur Nikisch.

Reiner and Berta Gerster-Gardini, his second wife, c. 1923.

Anna Sinton Taft, president of the Cincinnati Symphony Orchestra.

Reiner's daughters Eva and Berta (Tuśy).

Igor Stravinsky, Paris 1929.

Studio portrait by Kossuth, Wheeling, West Virginia, c. 1925.

Arturo Toscanini and Reiner on vacation in Italy, c. 1927.

Carlotta Irwin, Reiner's third wife, c. 1926.

Reiner, George Gershwin, Deems Taylor, and Robert Russell Bennett at All-American concert, Lewisohn Stadium, New York, 10 August 1931.

Herbert Graf, Arthur Judson, and Reiner during Philadelphia Orchestra opera season 1934–35.

Pittsburgh Challenge

Apparently Fritz and Carlotta Reiner never considered establishing a residence in Pittsburgh. On the contrary, with the security of a "permanent" post in Pittsburgh, the Reiners could realize their dream of a home in the country. They purchased twenty-six acres on Davis Hill Road in Weston, Connecticut, in the rolling hills north of Westport. They owned jointly the initial twenty-six acres purchased in 1938, as they did another eighteen acres bought in 1946. Shortly after that purchase, they sold several homesites from the southwest portion of their land along Davis Hill Road. In 1956 Fritz Reiner deeded his interest in the remaining thirty-five acres to Carlotta, who owned the property until her death in 1983.[1] The site was one of idyllic beauty: gently rolling countryside with rock outcroppings, open meadows, and scattered clumps of trees bordering the Aspetuck River. In the summer of 1939 the Reiners moved into their newly constructed home, which they named Rambleside.

Except for landscaping around the house and building a large swimming pool, the Reiners left the Rambleside property unspoiled. Its meadows and woods were ideal for walking, needing few formal trails. The house was in French country style, faced with white-painted brick and wood trim, and roofed with slate. A spacious but informal living room, with a high peaked ceiling, ran the width of the house with windows on each side. A sylvan scene painted by the Reiners' friend Willy Pogány over the large fireplace dominated one wall. The Reiners' Irish setter, Rambler, was observed from a lower corner by an elf modeled on Oscar Levant. Shelving and drawers for a library in four languages and storage of music filled the two end walls. At one end of the living room were the kitchen and dining room; above them, on the second floor, were the Reiners' private quarters. From the other end of the living room, a glass-enclosed passage led to a separate wing for a guest room, bathroom, and Reiner's studio, another large high-ceilinged room. At its entrance, a shallow upper level acted as a platform, with a bookshelf and Reiner's desk, overlooking the large room. In the shelf behind the old desk from Dresden were snapshots of his parents. To his left, on the wall, hung an oil portrait of Richard Strauss. Near the door stood a "low-fidelity" RCA phonograph. Down a few steps was the main portion of the well-lighted studio with comfortable furniture facing a fireplace and a grand piano on loan from Steinway. There were more shelves for records, scores, and books. In the basement under the study wing was a fully equipped darkroom.

The Reiners' choice of property in the Westport/Weston area reflected the presence there of writers, musicians, and theatrical figures from New York. Esther Adams, the wife of the New York *Herald-Tribune* columnist Franklin P. Adams, was the realtor who arranged their second purchase of land and may have handled the first. Richard and Dorothy Rodgers lived a few miles away. Theresa Helburn and Lawrence Langner of the Theater Guild were nearby; they tried unsuccessfully to persuade Carlotta to return to the stage in the role of Aunt Eller in *Oklahoma!*

The isolation of Rambleside appealed to the Reiners. The house itself was well back from Davis Hill Road, invisible and secluded. At Rambleside, Carlotta was the presiding chatelaine, an enchanting hostess and an excellent cook, but also the possessive guardian of her husband's privacy and career. He, in turn, showed an old-world charm and courtliness seldom displayed in his professional life. Never a voluble conversationalist, he could command his hearers' attention with leisurely reminiscences and caustic wit. In the summer, Carlotta organized weekend parties around the swimming pool, sometimes for musical and theatrical friends, and occasionally for such professional celebrations as a cast party after recording *Carmen* in 1951. The Reiners controlled such social occasions to preserve their privacy and his freedom from distraction. The conductor found varied relaxation from his work: a daily swim in the pool, a walk through the meadows and woods, an hour or two reading in the house or in a shady spot in the garden. His most frequent recreation was work in his darkroom. For Reiner continued and intensified his interest in photography; he was a true amateur with fully professional skills.[2]

Rambleside allowed Reiner to withdraw from the urban pressures and the distractions of the social activity that accompanied a conductor's career. It also became essential to Carlotta's protecting her husband, shielding him not only from interference with his work but also from personal contacts that might compromise the invisible wall she built around him. Although Reiner employed part-time secretaries who came to the house to help with his correspondence, Carlotta supervised their work and herself handled personal business and family correspondence, for both Reiners were intensely secretive about such matters.

If Fritz loved Rambleside for the seclusion and privacy it gave him to work and for its freedom from everyday annoyances, Carlotta came to love it as the symbol of their marriage.

It was from Rambleside that Fritz Reiner emerged to conduct the Pittsburgh Symphony Orchestra and to Rambleside that he returned with what many viewed as unseemly haste. The Pittsburgh years were in many respects the most fruitful and constructive of his career. In other respects, they were the most frustrating. In his sixth decade, Reiner was physically active and artistically mature, ready to face the musical and practical challenges of converting a part-time provincial orchestra into one of major stature. Seven years in an "orchestral wilderness" had built up in Reiner a pressure that could be released only by the challenge of a resident position.

Although the Pittsburgh Symphony Orchestra later became one of the wealthiest American orchestras, supported by a multimillion-dollar endowment and playing concerts in its own downtown home, this was far from the case when Reiner was its conductor between 1938 and 1948. Then he encountered what the music profession regarded as a "mediocre provincial orchestra," performing in a cavernous lodge hall on the fringes of downtown Pittsburgh. The country was just beginning to recover from a devastating depression when Reiner went to Pittsburgh and was soon to become embroiled in a world war. Nor did he find in Pittsburgh any single major philanthropist as unswervingly devoted to the orchestra's growth and survival, and to him personally and artistically, as Anna Taft had been in Cincinnati.

An earlier Pittsburgh Symphony Orchestra had existed between 1896 and 1910, at first under Victor Herbert and then under Emil Paur. For many years afterward symphonic activity relied on touring orchestras and on ad hoc local ensembles drawn from a lively music profession working in theaters, hotels, dance halls, and nightclubs. In May 1926 these local musicians played a free concert in Syria Mosque to introduce the orchestra of a new Pittsburgh Symphony Society. Richard Hageman, Elias Breeskin, and Antonio Modarelli were at various times conductors of this orchestra. It gave from three to eight concerts a year, sometimes with such guests as Eugene Goossens, Walter Damrosch, Hans Kindler, and Bernardino Molinari.[3] Of the founders of the 1926 Pittsburgh Symphony Society, Edward Specter was by far the most important in his commitment to the establishment and perpetuation of the Pittsburgh Symphony Orchestra. A native of Pittsburgh, Specter worked his way through the University of Pittsburgh and its law school by playing trumpet evenings in cabarets and dance halls, all the while hoping for a symphony orchestra in the city. After serving briefly as president of the society, he became its first manager, dividing his time between it and his law practice, which withered away as the orchestra consumed more and more of his life.

The only time the Pittsburgh musicians could assemble to play concerts was on Sundays. This brought them into conflict with blue laws in Pennsylvania dating from the 1790s that prohibited commercial activity on Sundays. After various subterfuges designed by the lawyer-manager, the orchestra openly defied the law, resulting in the arrest of Specter, Breeskin, and nine board members. The ensuing publicity persuaded the legislature to repeal the offending statutes. The first ticket legally sold to a Sunday symphony concert in Pennsylvania was autographed by George Gershwin, the soloist on that occasion in 1927.

In his determination to establish a fully professional orchestra, Edward Specter consulted Arthur Judson and other members of a loosely organized conference of major orchestra managers that predated the American Symphony Orchestra League. Judson, of course, was a source through whom Specter engaged guest conductors and many soloists. For such customers Judson could be very generous with advice. By 1937 Specter and his board had concluded that it was impossible to build an orchestra solely from local personnel. Despite traditional union opposition to the importation of nonresident players, Specter persuaded his fellow members in the local to allow the new orchestra to hire twenty players from outside Pittsburgh. In exchange Specter agreed to hire seventy local musicians on a guaranteed weekly pay scale.

A reorganized board with wider representation of business leadership set out to underwrite the deficits anticipated in the first seasons. A local foundation made a major contribution of $240,000 to underwrite concerts for schoolchildren. Early in 1937 Specter and the society announced the first season of a new Pittsburgh Symphony Orchestra—thirteen pairs of concerts to be conducted mainly by visiting conductors, some of them candidates for the new resident post. To audition and organize this orchestra, the society engaged Otto Klemperer, conductor of the Los Angeles Philharmonic since 1933. Traveling by train from Los Angeles in the heat of August 1937, Klemperer spent a week in Pittsburgh auditioning local players before going on to New York to hear and engage the permitted imported players.[4]

Klemperer conducted the first three concerts of the new season; the initial program was broadcast nationally. To follow him, the society engaged Eugene Goossens, Carlos Chavez, Fritz Reiner, and Georges Enesco for two pairs of concerts each, and Walter Damrosch and concertmaster Michael Gusikoff for one each. The orchestra played its concerts in pairs in Syria Mosque, on Friday afternoons and Saturday evenings. After Reiner had conducted his two programs in January 1938, Damrosch canceled his appearance and Enesco conducted but one of his scheduled weeks, giving Reiner an opportunity to conduct two additional pairs. His programs were conservative, typical of his guest engagements with orchestras he did not know. They included symphonies by Beethoven and Brahms and accompaniments of Nino Martini in tenor arias and of Nathan Milstein in the Tchaikovsky Violin Concerto. He offered the Leonardi transcription of the Bach Toccata and Fugue in D Minor, symphonic poems by Tchaikovsky and Richard Strauss, and plenty of Wagner. His last concert was on 3 February, a week before the end of the short initial season of the reorganized orchestra. It had been a highly successful engagement for Reiner, and he had established cordial relations with Specter from the outset.

The society first invited Otto Klemperer to be its resident conductor at a substantial increase over his Los Angeles salary. The German émigré decided to remain in Los Angeles. Specter was also in touch with Reiner by letter and in person at Rambleside, and with Judson in New York. Although the Pittsburgh board first considered another season of guests, with Reiner included, by late March it announced his engagement as the orchestra's new music director. Reiner, according to a pencil notation on a letter, apparently sought a three-year contract with an annual salary increasing from twenty-five thousand dollars to thirty thousand dollars and a fee of seventy-five hundred dollars if the society canceled a season. He readily settled for one year at the lower figure.[5] Because of Reiner's prior commitment to the San Francisco Opera for the fall of 1938, the Pittsburgh season did not begin until mid-November. Meanwhile, Carlotta had been in touch with realtors in Pittsburgh to lease a house or apartment for the coming season. This search led her first to a rented apartment and later to the Schenley Hotel, where the Reiners lived seasonally for most of their years in Pittsburgh.

Throughout his Pittsburgh tenure, Reiner worked under difficult physical and financial limitations. The orchestra played in Syria Mosque, which was too large for orchestra concerts (3,750 seats) and too wide and shallow for good acoustics. The largest audience for any Pittsburgh Symphony concert in the 1940s numbered 3,100, for a special concert in 1946 with Oscar Levant playing Gershwin, which Reiner did not conduct. Yet the orchestra played pairs of subscription concerts in this hall to audiences that frequently filled fewer than half the seats! In his first months in Pittsburgh, Reiner asked Specter to look into the possibility of remodeling the smaller Carnegie Music Hall as a home for the orchestra. But the orchestra's precarious finances prevented any serious consideration of an estimated cost of $950,000. As Reiner opened his first season in the fall of 1938, Specter had to announce publicly that the previous season's deficit had been $82,000. This pattern prevailed throughout Reiner's years in Pittsburgh, as Specter and the board continuously played a catch-up game of symphony finance. In April 1940 Reiner apologized to Judson for being late in transmitting his commission, because the orchestra was a month late in paying him. A year later Reiner insisted to Judson that his salary be $30,000, but offered to contribute $2,500 of it to the orchestra's fund "if necessary."[6]

During his first season with the Pittsburgh Symphony Orchestra, Reiner arranged for his old associate from Cincinnati, Vladimir Bakaleinikoff, to join him in Pittsburgh as assistant conductor and as principal of the viola section. This remained one of the most harmonious relations that Reiner enjoyed with any colleague. "Bak" was helpful with auditions and in taking over concerts that Reiner did not want to conduct, especially several weeks of school concerts each season that were indispensable to the orchestra's community relations and foundation support. Reiner could be difficult with these programs, at one point refusing to conduct in a school auditorium that was too warm for his comfort. Bakaleinikoff was a skillful diplomat both with his colleague and with school officials. After the war, when the orchestra expanded its season, Bakaleinikoff took over a Tuesday night series of popular concerts. Reiner always included him as conductor and often as soloist in the subscription series.

Bakaleinikoff was also the first conducting teacher of Pittsburgh's child prodigy on the violin and podium, Lorin Maazel. After conducting in New York and Hollywood, Maazel made his hometown debut at the age of twelve, conducting a children's concert in 1943. A year later he conducted a special concert with another Pittsburgh prodigy, Byron Jannes (originally Yanks and later Janis), as soloist. Although Maazel's parents wanted Reiner to teach their son conducting, he recommended study with Bakaleinikoff instead. In 1988, by this time an international celebrity, Maazel became music director of the Pittsburgh Symphony Orchestra.

In Pittsburgh Reiner faced the challenge of building an orchestra that he, Specter, and the community envisioned as a second major orchestra in Pennsylvania on the foundation of admittedly inferior local material. Specter's addiction to long letters gives a vivid picture of this problem, recapitulating what he and Reiner had discussed in meetings in New York or at Rambleside.[7] But Reiner's pursuit of high quality pushed the limits of what the society could afford and what the union would permit. Early in his correspondence with Specter, he was already impatient with the local union's twenty-player limit on importations.

Reiner's friend Goddard Lieberson certainly had him in mind when he said, "Show me an orchestra that likes its conductor and I will show you a lousy orchestra." It was in Pittsburgh that Fritz Reiner definitively enhanced his previous reputation for ruthless and even brutal treatment of musicians. Long after his departure, Pittsburgh Symphony players, with typical musicians' black humor, credited Reiner with having fired three pallbearers at his funeral. He still ordered players to play difficult passages by themselves and reacted caustically to their performance. By his Pittsburgh years, he had developed to a fine point his systematic testing of every player and was merciless in weeding out players who did not meet his standards.

Not all of Reiner's difficulties with the Pittsburgh personnel were of his own making. He could not offer imported players compensation comparable to that available at the four major American orchestras. For some young instrumentalists, fresh out of Curtis or other conservatories, a weekly salary of seventy-five dollars for twenty-five weeks exerted a certain attraction. A few principal players might earn from twenty-five hundred to three thousand dollars a year, but unlike Cincinnati in the 1920s, Pittsburgh could offer little outside work, as the electronic revolution had by this time decimated live music performance. Still, playing under Reiner, for all his sinister reputation, could be something of a postgraduate course professionally. Dimitri Mitropoulos is said to have observed that the education of an American orchestral musician was incomplete without exposure to the ministrations of Fritz Reiner. A young player who survived working under Reiner had a good chance of moving on to a better job elsewhere. What with Reiner's firing players and natural attrition, turnover in the Pittsburgh Symphony Orchestra was very high—frequently well over 50 percent from one season to the next. In his first season Reiner retained fewer than half of the players from the previous year, bringing in forty-six new musicians, but by 1940–1941, there were only twenty-six changes in personnel. Such recordings as Strauss's *Don Juan* and *Don Quixote* give an idea of the quality of the orchestra in Reiner's third season in Pittsburgh.

However, beyond Reiner's or the society's control was the military draft, which affected all orchestras as early as 1941–1942 and became a serious problem in the following years. In Pittsburgh, as elsewhere, there was an increase in the number of women in the orchestra, which Reiner hailed publicly but privately resisted. The draft made it necessary to retain older men and foreigners not subject to military call. The Pittsburgh Symphony Orchestra, with its low pay, was vulnerable to losing such safe players to wealthier orchestras. Although Specter had to use his powers of persuasion to gain local union approval for imported players in Reiner's first years, importation became a moot question after the draft took its toll. During the war years, personnel turnover rose to 55 percent or more each year: in 1944–1945, of a roster of eighty-nine (twenty-four of them women), forty-eight players were new. But by 1947–1948, Reiner's last season in Pittsburgh, turnover was down to 31 percent.[8] With postwar demobilization, federal law required that returning veterans be restored to their former positions, even if that required bumping wartime replacements. In at least one case, Specter had to pay a musician a full season's wage for not playing. Some players returned to Pittsburgh to hold a job there while looking for something better elsewhere. Others returned with wives who also wanted to play in the orchestra.

John S. Edwards, Specter's assistant in Reiner's last two seasons, recalled that the conductor's attitude toward his players at times approached paranoia. Reiner once became so convinced that a particular player planned to murder him that the musician in question had to be given a leave of absence. Edwards also recalled an older player in the orchestra, who should have received his pension if the orchestra could have afforded it, whom Reiner drove to a nervous breakdown. "His look was like a stigmata. It could turn a fellow to stone!"[9] Engendering fear, even if accompanied by hatred, was a basic technique in Reiner's handling of his orchestra. Rare indeed was the double-bass player who had the effrontery to use a telescope to decipher Reiner's legendary minuscule beat; he did not return the following season. A player who survived Reiner's baptism of fire could well be a more professional musician. Those who played under Reiner never forgot the experience, both for the indignities to which they were subjected and for the training they received.

Between his arrival in Pittsburgh in the fall of 1938 and his departure in the spring of 1948, Reiner programmed, in Pittsburgh and elsewhere, some five hundred compositions. He conducted more than half of these for the first time in his career. Contemporary works figured on more than half of his Pittsburgh programs, and half of these were by Americans.[10] By the time he reached Pittsburgh, Reiner had developed a reasonably complete command of the standard symphonic repertory. Among the Haydn symphonies, Reiner never developed any special favorites: in Pittsburgh, he conducted eight, five of them for the first time. With a local chorus but with visiting soloists, he programmed *Ein deutsches Requiem* of Brahms and Verdi's *Messa da Requiem*. Mendelssohn and Schumann had never figured prominently in Reiner's repertory, so it is not surprising that Pittsburgh heard his first readings of the Mendelssohn Third and Fourth symphonies and, in his own "revision," the Second Symphony of Schumann.[11] In 1942 he received the Bruckner Society medal, less for his own first performance of that composer's Fourth Symphony than for repeating several works of Mahler he had first performed in Dresden and Cincinnati. He began to explore the major repertory of Sibelius with the First and Second symphonies and the Violin Concerto, with Jascha Heifetz. In addition to the symphonic poems of Richard Strauss, he programmed extensive concert excerpts from *Der*

Rosenkavalier, Salome, and *Ariadne auf Naxos.* He also supplemented his usual Wagner orchestral excerpts with extended passages from *Die Walküre, Tristan und Isolde,* and *Siegfried.*

Reiner expected his players, many of them holding their first symphony jobs, to play a great deal of new music, not just the standard repertory they learned in school. In 1947 the National Music Council surveyed the performance of contemporary music by the major American symphony orchestras. It reported that the Pittsburgh Symphony Orchestra under Reiner ranked first in the nation in the performance both of contemporary music generally and of American music.[12] Reiner deeply resented his being ignored for his commitment to contemporary music, especially when other conductors built highly publicized reputations for such support. When a Chicago critic later complained of the scarcity of new music on Reiner's programs there, he replied, "I did my share in my time." Some of Reiner's resentment at not being sufficiently recognized for his commitment to contemporary music arose from a certain reticence on the part of Specter and the Pittsburgh board, who apparently felt that publicizing new repertory could be counterproductive in the box office and in contributions. Specter once wrote Reiner that the head of the women's committee had complained of the difficulty of selling subscriptions to a season that opened with Hindemith's *Mathis der Maler* symphony. Reiner testily questioned her knowledge of music but postponed the Hindemith work to later that season.[13]

Much of Reiner's extensive correspondence with composers was blandly routine—sending and retrieving scores, rehearsal and performance schedules, and program details.[14] An interesting exception was a blistering letter from Arnold Schoenberg in 1944 regarding Koussevitzky's performance of his Theme and Variations, opus 43b, in which he complains of that conductor's disregard of metronome indications, his concentration on the upper voice of the score, and "his general ignorance as a musician and as a man."[15] These variations, *Pelleas und Melisande,* and *Verklärte Nacht* were the only Schoenberg works that Reiner ever programmed. Despite his earlier proposal of Alban Berg's *Lulu* to the Metropolitan Opera, Reiner actually performed little music from the Second Viennese School: apart from the Schoenberg pieces, the concert excerpts from *Wozzeck* with Rose Bampton in 1945 were his sole venture into that repertory before 1957.

As Russian wartime allies, both Prokofiev and Shostakovich figured prominently in Reiner's Pittsburgh programs, although he had to yield American premieres to such conductors as Koussevitzky and Toscanini. Of Prokofiev he played the then-new Fifth Symphony, the *Lieutenant Kijé* and *Semyon Kotko* suites, and the Second Violin Concerto (with Heifetz). When he scheduled

Peter and the Wolf, Serge Koussevitzky was distressed that Reiner had obtained a copy of the score when he was under the impression that the composer had entrusted it to him exclusively.[16] Reiner performed Shostakovich's First, Fifth, Sixth, and Ninth symphonies in Pittsburgh, as well as the Piano Concerto no. 1. Among his rare performances of British music were the Sea Interludes and Passacaglia from Benjamin Britten's recent *Peter Grimes,* and Ralph Vaughan Williams's Fantasy on a Theme of Thomas Tallis. He introduced Casella's *Paganiniana* to the United States and gave the world premiere of Darius Milhaud's Concerto for Two Pianos, featuring Vitya Vronsky and Victor Babin.

In Pittsburgh Reiner again played music by Bartók. When the composer came to the United States in 1940 as a refugee from Nazi-oriented Hungary, Reiner was one of his official sponsors in the immigration procedures. The Pittsburgh Symphony Orchestra was one of the few that engaged Bartók as soloist; he played his Second Piano Concerto there in 1941. When Reiner was guest conductor of the New York Philharmonic-Symphony Orchestra in January 1943, Bartók and his wife played the American premiere of the Concerto for Two Pianos, an adaptation of his Sonata for Two Pianos and Percussion. In Pittsburgh, Reiner offered more music of Bartók than of any other contemporary composer. Among nine compositions played in Pittsburgh were the first performance anywhere of the revised version of the Second Suite, opus 4; the suite from *The Miraculous Mandarin;* the Violin Concerto (no. 2) with Yehudi Menuhin; and the Divertimento for Strings. It was Reiner who, with Joseph Szigeti, persuaded Koussevitzky to offer Bartók the thousand-dollar commission that resulted in the Concerto for Orchestra. The Pittsburgh Symphony Orchestra performances on 18 and 20 January 1946 were the first after the Boston premiere, and Reiner conducted the concerto's first recording. Reiner also tried to find employment for Bartók, most notably, but unsuccessfully, at the Curtis Institute and at the Juilliard School of Music.[17] The composer, his wife, and son Peter visited the Reiners at Rambleside, where Reiner took photographs of them.

In November 1946 Reiner invited Zoltán Kodály, then visiting America, to conduct his Galánta Dances in Pittsburgh, having himself directed a performance there two years earlier. Reiner apparently still preferred the "Muscovite" Stravinsky during his Pittsburgh years. The suites from *The Firebird* and *Petrushka* continued to figure in his programming. He repeated from his Cincinnati repertory *The Song of the Nightingale* and the suite from *Pulcinella,* ignoring Stravinsky's music from the intervening fifteen years. He added but one work of Stravinsky to his repertory, the first American performance of the Concerto for Strings in D Major, then known as the Basle Concerto, having been commissioned by Paul Sacher for his Basle Chamber Orchestra.

With an instrument of his own forging in Pittsburgh, Reiner became a major force in the presentation of American music. Some of the composers with whom he worked were well known, but others are now largely forgotten in the process of cultural survival in which testing in actual performance is so important. One need only review the roster of Americans whose music Reiner programmed between 1938 and 1948: Samuel Barber, Robert Russell Bennett, Ernest Bloch, Henry Brant, Charles W. Cadman, John Alden Carpenter, George W. Chadwick, Aaron Copland, Paul Creston, Norman Dello Joio, Alvin Etler, Lukas Foss, George Gershwin, Morton Gould, Charles T. Griffes, Edward Burlingame Hill, Robert McBride, Edward MacDowell, Daniel Gregory Mason, Burrill Phillips, Walter Piston, Gardner Read, Wallingford Riegger, Richard Rodgers, William Schuman, David Stanley Smith, William Grant Still, Randall Thompson, and Virgil Thomson.

Composers knew they could count on Reiner for a thoroughly prepared performance of their music. Players in the Pittsburgh Symphony Orchestra marveled at Reiner's complete command of a new score from his first downbeat in rehearsal. He never used a rehearsal to try out new compositions, having made his decisions in the privacy of his study. Reiner formed friendships with such American composers as Norman Dello Joio, William Schuman, Virgil Thomson, and Morton Gould, who were visitors at Rambleside. Among his most frequently performed American works was *El salón México* by Aaron Copland, whose *Appalachian Spring, Outdoor Overture,* and suite from *Billy the Kid* he also introduced to Pittsburgh. He conducted the world premieres of two compositions by Norman Dello Joio, Concert Music for Orchestra in 1946 and Three Symphonic Dances in 1948. Although Morton Gould could not study conducting with Reiner at Curtis, the two men became good friends in later years, partly because of Gould's connections at NBC and with publishers. Pittsburgh heard four Gould compositions under Reiner, including the world premiere of the Symphony no. 1 in 1943. On one occasion, when Reiner played a short work by Gould, the composer did not trouble to make the overnight train trip to Pittsburgh for the concert. When he offered the excuse that it was "just a little piece," Reiner replied, "But it was a *Reiner* performance!"[18] The conductor retained his interest in Gershwin, programming both the Concerto in F and the *Rhapsody in Blue* with Pittsburgh-born Oscar Levant as soloist. He also commissioned and gave the first performances and made the first recording of Robert Russell Bennett's "Symphonic Picture" based on *Porgy and Bess.* Another of Reiner's lighter favorites was the waltz from *Carousel,* by his neighbor Richard Rodgers.

In 1945 Reiner offered the suite from *The Plow That Broke the Plains* by Virgil Thomson, then music critic of the New York *Herald-Tribune.* In December 1946 Thomson conducted the Pittsburgh orchestra in his *Six Portraits,* and three weeks later he lavishly praised Reiner: "No other conductor now working before the American public, save only Pierre Monteux, is at once so sound a musician and so completely a master of his art." [19] The Reiners remained friends with Thomson, attending the 1947 premiere of *The Mother of Us All,* which delighted the conductor. The Reiners enjoyed Thomson's company and they visited one another at Rambleside or at the composer-critic's apartment in the Chelsea Hotel.

William Schuman enjoyed a special relation with Reiner beginning with a 1941 performance of the *American Festival* overture. Reiner conducted the world premieres of *Prayer in Time of War, 1943* and *Side Show for Orchestra.* He repeated the former with the New York Philharmonic-Symphony Orchestra in 1943 and the latter during a guest engagement in Cleveland in 1945. Upon becoming president of the Juilliard School of Music in 1945, Schuman tried to involve Reiner in summertime orchestra and conductor training. After extended discussions, Reiner conducted a pair of concerts in August 1948 with a student orchestra prepared by Walter Hendl. Reiner had scheduled a Schuman work for the Chicago season that was curtailed by his illness. William Schuman delivered the eulogy at Reiner's funeral in 1963.

Reiner maintained a friendly professional contact with some of his Curtis pupils. Both Ezra Rachlin and Max Goberman benefited from his recommendations for positions with orchestras or opera and ballet companies. After Leonard Bernstein's sensational debut with the New York Philharmonic-Symphony Orchestra in November 1943, Reiner engaged him the following January to conduct the world premiere of his own *Jeremiah* symphony with Jennie Tourel. Bernstein returned a year later to conduct a concert that included the suite from his *Fancy Free* and the Ravel G Major Concerto, conducted from the keyboard. In February 1945 the conductor-teacher offered the premiere of the Symphony in G Major of Lukas Foss. Foss appeared a year later as soloist in the Fifth Brandenburg Concerto and conducted his own *Ode for Orchestra.* A similar pianist-conductor role brought Walter Hendl to Pittsburgh in the Mozart D Minor Piano Concerto, Tchaikovsky's *Romeo and Juliet,* and the Third Symphony of Peter Mennin.

The recordings Reiner made with the Pittsburgh Symphony Orchestra, the first with his name and approval, were for the newly revived Columbia Masterworks label. That label had had a motley history in the United States under several foreign and domestic owners. It ran a distant second to the Victor Talking Machine Company and its successor after 1928, RCA-Victor. During the 1930s it had been primarily an American outlet for the Columbia division of the British Electrical and Musical Industries. In 1938 Isaac Levy and Edward Wallerstein, an RCA-Victor executive, persuaded William Paley of CBS to purchase the label, catalog, and releasing rights.[20] In August 1939 Wallerstein stunned the recording industry by drastically reducing the retail price of classical phonograph records and dramatically established Columbia as a major force in the American recording industry. To head the Columbia Masterworks division, Wallerstein employed, in succession, Boston critic Moses Smith, another RCA-Victor alumnus Charles O'Connell, and finally Goddard Lieberson. The latter proved to be one of the most successful and innovative recording executives of his time. A graduate of the Eastman School of Music in composition, Lieberson combined business and promotional shrewdness with a sense of artistic mission in his direction of Columbia Masterworks. He balanced a commitment to unprofitable recordings of contemporary American music with such commercially successful projects as original cast recordings of *South Pacific* and *My Fair Lady*. Reiner enjoyed Lieberson's brilliant mind, keen musicianship, and outrageous humor. Lieberson and his first wife were frequent houseguests at Rambleside.

Wallerstein's first step in rebuilding the Masterworks label was to record several major American orchestras. Thanks to Arthur Judson's affiliation with CBS, the New York Philharmonic-Symphony Orchestra was one of the first under a Masterworks contract. Since RCA-Victor had long-term contracts with the orchestras of Philadelphia and Boston, as well as with the new NBC Symphony Orchestra under Arturo Toscanini, Columbia had to look to the orchestras of such cities as Chicago, Rochester, and Cleveland. Thus the Pittsburgh Symphony Orchestra under Fritz Reiner became one of the prime orchestras on the new Columbia label.

From the beginning Reiner himself was the main attraction to Columbia, for Moses Smith expressed doubts about the quality of the Pittsburgh orchestra, especially in Wagner, suggesting that other opera material might be more suitable.[21] He also raised the possibility of Reiner's recording with the New York Philharmonic-Symphony Orchestra. Nevertheless, a session devoted to Wagner orchestral excerpts was held on 14 March 1940 in Pittsburgh's Carnegie Music Hall, to avoid the poor acoustics of Syria Mosque. Because of fluctuations in electric power that showed up only when Smith listened to the test pressings, ten of fourteen 78-rpm sides had to be discarded. Three others were damaged, and only one, the "Ride of the Valkyries," was suitable for release. The next Pittsburgh recording session ten months later was more productive. In January 1941 Columbia re-recorded some of the Wagner music, along with Richard Strauss's *Don Juan* and the Johann Strauss, Jr., *Wiener Blut,* the first of several best-selling Strauss waltz recordings by Reiner. In November of the same year there was more Wagner, Debussy's "Ibéria," and, with Gregor Piatigorsky, *Don Quixote* of Richard Strauss. By this time Columbia was ready to sign an extended agreement with both conductor and orchestra rather than contract from session to session.

Power supply at Carnegie Music Hall was not the only technical problem with the Columbia Masterworks recordings of the 1940s. A major irritant was the variable quality of Columbia's processing. Through the 1940s Columbia cut its original recordings on lacquer or acetate sixteen-inch discs at 33⅓ rpm, standard for radio transcriptions. From these Columbia copied 78-rpm masters, which they processed onto shellac discs. Lacquer/acetate discs were easier to handle and transport than the fragile wax blanks previously used. It was also possible to play back a performance immediately. Meanwhile Columbia was developing a long-playing microgroove record for which masters could be copied from the sixteen-inch transcriptions. Such dubbing to 78-rpm masters resulted in some degradation of the sound, and Columbia's laminated records frequently suffered from hairline cracks, especially with poor-quality shellac during wartime. Reiner frequently complained about the quality of the finished product and refused to approve several test pressings.[22]

Viewing the electronic distribution of music to be in direct competition with their live efforts, recording musicians sought to gain some share of the profits accruing to radio stations and recording companies. The American Federation of Musicians had successfully bargained for higher compensation for musicians playing on national radio networks and had established a substantial hourly fee for recording sessions. In an effort spearheaded by AFM president James C. Petrillo, it also sought to levy a royalty of its own on the sale of records.[23] When the recording industry, then concentrated in three companies, resisted Petrillo's efforts, he banned all recording by union musicians in the United States effective 1 August 1942. At first the ban had minimal effect: there were plenty of unreleased recordings "in the icebox." For a time wartime allocations sharply limited the manufacture of records. When the War Production Board lifted restrictions on the use of shellac, pressure increased on the companies to come to terms with Petrillo, and in 1944 the industry agreed to meet his demands. However, the recording ban had so tarnished the image of Petrillo and his union that they became a target of the Taft-Hartley Act in 1947, which specifically forbade the kind of royalty the union had obtained. A brief stoppage in 1948 was quickly resolved by a new royalty paid into an independent Performance Trust Fund to encourage the performance of live music—by union musicians, of course.[24]

During the ban a major development at Columbia Masterworks had a significant impact on Reiner's recording fortunes. Early on, both Columbia and Reiner continued to plan recordings to be made when the ban would be lifted. These included possible sessions with the New York Philharmonic-Symphony

Orchestra. There is no doubt that, at this point, Columbia considered Reiner one of its prime conductors. However, after decades as an exclusive RCA-Victor recording orchestra under Leopold Stokowski and Eugene Ormandy, the Philadelphia Orchestra switched to the Columbia label in 1943.[25] Once the recording ban ended, that orchestra began to record intensively as the primary orchestra on the Columbia roster. Moreover, the New York Philharmonic-Symphony Orchestra, after Artur Rodzinski replaced John Barbirolli in 1943, provided further competition for Reiner at Columbia, which also had Bruno Walter under contract. So Reiner found himself limited in the music he could record in Pittsburgh.

The initial Pittsburgh recordings after the ban reflected these limitations: in March 1945 short Russian "pops" selections, the *Porgy and Bess* arrangement, Beethoven's Second Symphony, and compositions by Weiner and Kodály that were never released. In the next year there were the Shostakovich Sixth Symphony, the Brahms D Minor Concerto with Rudolf Serkin, the Bach Suite in B Minor, the suite from Richard Strauss's *Le bourgeois gentilhomme,* and the Bartók Concerto for Orchestra. Further recordings in several crowded sessions included Carol Brice in Mahler's *Lieder eines fahrendes Gesellen* and Falla's *El amor brujo,* both recorded for the first time, Bartók's Hungarian Sketches (never released), Ravel's *La valse,* and the Mozart G Minor Symphony, K. 550. In November 1947 *Ein Heldenleben* was Reiner's last recording with the Pittsburgh Symphony Orchestra. A scheduled *Verklärte Nacht* of Schoenberg was canceled. None of this repertory produced the sales—and royalties—that Reiner felt other conductors were earning. His own net income from recording royalties ranged, after the ban, from thirty-five hundred to seven thousand dollars a year. When he sought to improve his position by recording with other orchestras, in the United States or abroad, the Pittsburgh board adamantly refused. Lieberson and others at Columbia took pains to explain to him that, as long as there was a backlog of unreleased Pittsburgh material, he could not expect to make more until sales justified additional sessions. After Reiner left Pittsburgh, Columbia made no more recordings there.

CHAPTER IX

New Directions

The once cordial relations between Fritz Reiner and Edward Specter
deteriorated seriously, especially after the end of the war, when the Pittsburgh Symphony Orchestra failed to attain financial stability. Recordings were by no means the only source of friction between Reiner,
Specter, and the Pittsburgh board. Reiner and Carlotta detested touring. Yet Specter was responsible to his board to generate as much earned
income as possible: touring was a means of getting the most out of the
salaries the orchestra had to pay its players to attract them to Pittsburgh.
In Reiner's early years there, the orchestra toured little, at first because
it was not yet well known and later because of wartime restrictions on
travel by rail or bus. With the relaxation of restrictions in 1943, the Pittsburgh Symphony Orchestra made a modest tour to upstate New York.
In the immediate postwar period, some orchestras played as many as
eight concerts a week in communities served by the "organized audience" affiliates of the two major concert management companies, for fees
that produced a significant "profit" after travel expenses and net payroll.
Traveling by bus and rail, the Pittsburgh orchestra expanded its travel,
making an extended tour to the South in 1946.[1] Reiner expressed his
views on touring in a telegram, drafted in pencil but not sent, to Zirato,
complaining that touring was "contrary to my ideas of orchestra's success. Find out if [Edward] Johnson still interested in having me as a
permanent fixture [at the Metropolitan Opera]. Could get Pittsburgh
release on grounds of health."[2]

Reiner created constant problems with touring, either by having
Specter schedule tour concerts with Bakaleinikoff or by calling on his assistant at the last minute. It was then up to Specter and his assistant, John
Edwards, to mollify local sponsors when the orchestra's music director
did not appear. Edwards recalled one city where Reiner had canceled his
appearances the two previous years and where the local sponsor insisted
on a doctor's certificate if the conductor canceled again. Punctually at

six o'clock, Edwards received the expected telephone call. He pleaded with Reiner to make an effort to fill the engagement unless he could convince a doctor of his inability to conduct. "I have just dropped the phone on my foot," declared Reiner, as the line went dead with a loud thud. In this case the local doctor determined that Reiner was suffering heart palpitations, but nothing could convince Edwards that he had not been doing push-ups or other exercises to accelerate his pulse.[3]

Reiner's refusal to give local sponsors any choice in programs was another irritant, as was his and Carlotta's objection to the obligatory postconcert parties. In later years Carlotta Reiner recalled what an imposition such touring had been on her husband: the incessant travel by train or bus, the acoustically inferior halls, the terrible hotels and meals, and the players' physical exhaustion that made proper performances impossible. Specter and Edwards did their best to mollify the Reiners with special train accommodations, suites in hotels, and chauffeur-driven cars. Reiner's demands on tour sorely taxed the managers' ingenuity. In one town, Reiner announced that he had to spend the night after a concert in the *next* town on the itinerary, probably to avoid postconcert social obligations. Ignoring the lack of train, bus, or taxi service, he merely replied to the managers, "It's up to you to get me there." The Reiners made the midnight trip in a hired hearse. On another occasion, the management had to purchase drawing room accommodations for the Reiners from Detroit to Miami on a train trip of less than two hundred miles through Ohio. What rankled Reiner most was that, with all its touring, the Pittsburgh Symphony Orchestra never performed under his direction in such major centers as New York, Chicago, Boston, or Philadelphia.

In April 1946 Mayor David Lawrence announced that the Pittsburgh Symphony Orchestra would visit Mexico early the following year, the first orchestra from the United States to make such a tour. This announcement followed resolution of a ban on performances by musicians from the United States by the Mexican musicians' union in retaliation against a similar exclusion imposed on Mexicans by Petrillo's American Federation of Musicians. The Pittsburgh Symphony Orchestra played five concerts in Mexico City and one in Monterey. It preceded and followed the Mexican visit with an extensive tour through the South, including Alabama, Arkansas, Texas, Tennessee, Louisiana, and Georgia. The tour began on 20 January 1947 in Columbus, Ohio, and ended in Pittsburgh nearly six weeks later. The schedule, booked by Columbia Artists Management, sometimes called for concerts on ten consecutive days. With only occasional overnight stops in hotels, the musicians lived on the train. The Reiners, of course, occupied two drawing rooms. John Edwards later recalled making special arrangements for the Reiners' comfort. He was in charge of crates of bottled water carried with the baggage for Reiner's exclusive use. When the supply was exhausted, Edwards—unbeknownst to Reiner—simply refilled the bottles with local water.[4]

Because Columbia Records assisted the Mexican tour financially, Lieberson urged that Reiner's programs include a generous representation of the orchestra's recorded repertory, especially the Wagner excerpts, *Don Juan,* Debussy's "Ibéria", and many lighter short selections. Reiner also played the *Galánta Dances* of Kodály and the Bartók Hungarian Sketches. Barber's overture to *The School for Scandal* was the sole American work played on this tour.[5]

This Mexican tour was a major undertaking for an orchestra that was, throughout Reiner's tenure in Pittsburgh, running at a constant deficit. A leitmotiv of Specter's letters to Reiner was the difficulty of raising money. The 1943 fund drive for $150,000 fell $60,000 short of its goal. According to a press release, the Pittsburgh Symphony Society could not muster volunteer workers in competition with wartime causes. By 1945, with the season expanded to twenty-eight weeks, the goal was $225,000, again not met. When the orchestra visited Dallas, John Rosenfeld wrote enviously in the Dallas *News* that the Pittsburgh Symphony Orchestra's annual budget of $600,000 ranked fifth among American orchestras—just behind those of Boston, Chicago, New York, and Philadelphia.[6] That same year, the society set an objective of $285,000, including a carryover of $60,000 from the past. Despite the great corporate wealth of Pittsburgh, business leaders there still preferred to give in their own names or through family foundations rather than through the corporations they directed. There remained a strong reluctance, there as elsewhere, to indulge in corporate philanthropy at stockholders' expense, even when such contributions were tax-deductible.

The Pittsburgh Symphony Orchestra may well have depended too much on Edward Specter himself. His personal commitment to the orchestra as far back as 1926 was so pervasive that others were inclined to relax and "let Eddie do it." This perception of his indispensability also made him invulnerable to Reiner's attacks. Reiner, for his part, never enjoyed widespread personal loyalty in Pittsburgh, although residents had an unquestioned respect for his ability as a conductor. When he left Curtis in 1941, giving as the ostensible reason his responsibilities in Pittsburgh, there were many in that city who hoped that he would now make his home there, at least for the duration of each season. Instead the Reiners remained commuting visitors, arriving in time to prepare for the orchestra's first concert. They took a midseason holiday at Rambleside and returned home after the last concert. In Pittsburgh they never established a domestic headquarters for work and social life such as Reiner had maintained with Berta on Winding Way in Cincinnati. To judge from his diary, most of their social activity consisted of parties after concerts as guests of board members. From Carlotta's accounts in later years, they had few close friends in Pittsburgh, certainly nothing comparable to the social and professional activity they enjoyed at Rambleside.

Such was the attraction of Rambleside that the Reiners traveled no further afield than Chicago between 1938 and 1949. He conducted summer concerts in New York, Philadelphia, and Chicago and fitted winter-season appearances with three important orchestras into his Pittsburgh vacation. On the radio he continued to conduct the Ford Sunday Evening Hour regularly through 1941 and again with its resumption in 1946. Of greater importance were his engagements to conduct the NBC Symphony Orchestra and the New York Philharmonic-Symphony Orchestra during several summer seasons of broadcasts. Since traveling in Europe was out of the question during the war, Reiner made his first trip abroad in an elaborately planned itinerary to see his daughters in the summer of 1949. But he was not inclined to accept the economic limitations of postwar Europe necessary to reestablish himself professionally there. Even a 1946 invitation from Glyndebourne failed to arouse his interest. Nor could Mario Labroca lure him to the Florence Maggio Musicale in 1949.

Except for fulfilling his commitment to the San Francisco Opera in the fall of 1938, Reiner conducted but three opera productions, all in the United States, during the decade he was in Pittsburgh. Early in 1939 a group trying to establish an American Lyric Theater in New York, by offering music theater productions on Broadway, enlisted Reiner as its music director. Its board of directors included Claire Reis of the League of Composers, Walter Damrosch, Nelson Rockefeller, and Robert Edmond Jones. The first and only production by this organization was a double bill at the Martin Beck Theater in May 1939 consisting of the Ballet Caravan in William Dollar's *Filling Station,* with a score by Virgil Thomson, and the world premiere of Douglas Moore's *The Devil and Daniel Webster,* a one-act opera with a libretto by Stephen Vincent Benét. Reiner prepared and conducted the first three performances of the new opera for a fee of twenty-five hundred dollars. He later recalled how John Houseman's staging placed the singers where they could not see the conductor, a typical complaint on his part about theatrical directors deficient in musical background.

Over the years Reiner had been in touch with various impresarios in Chicago striving to revive opera there after the collapse of the Chicago Civic Opera in 1932. A succession of companies enjoyed a precarious existence offering a few performances each season, mostly with singers from the Metropolitan. Both René Devries, the Chicago correspondent for the *Musical Courier,* and May Valentine, the long-time opera librarian, wrote the Reiners periodically to relay the latest gossip about the operatic situation.[7] On 12 November 1940, when Henry Weber was in charge of the Chicago Opera Company, Reiner finally made his operatic debut there with the first of two performances of *Der Rosen-kavalier* to which Mrs. Bok sent the Curtis conducting class. Given a weak cast except for the young Risë Stevens, this was not an especially auspicious occasion for Reiner, though many in Chicago regarded it as the "pinnacle of the season."[8]

With his primary commitment to the Pittsburgh Symphony Orchestra, Reiner was not under pressure to appear as guest conductor with other orchestras, unless such engagements would advance his career. Such advancement could only come with a major American symphony orchestra. Although Philadelphia was out of the question, changes in leadership among other orchestras might have created an opening for Reiner. In the turmoil in Chicago following Frederick Stock's death in 1942, it would be some time before Reiner would be offered a hearing in Orchestra Hall. With the orchestras of Boston and New York, the prospect was more promising, as it was in another attractively stable orchestra of increasing stature in Cleveland.

Following the departure of Arturo Toscanini in 1936, the New York Philharmonic-Symphony Orchestra went through a period that might be described as a combination of retrenchment and stagnation.[9] Its music director was the overburdened John Barbirolli, who yielded increasingly to guest conductors until his departure in the spring of 1943. Reiner was not one of the ten distinguished conductors engaged by Judson for the orchestra's hundredth anniversary season in 1941–1942. However, he was included during the 1942–1943 season that offered a parade of possible successors to Barbirolli. Four subscription weeks early in 1943 were Reiner's longest wintertime engagement ever with that orchestra. Leading an orchestra he knew well from summers at Lewisohn Stadium, Reiner could confidently program a distinctively varied repertory. Once again in New York, a highlight was music by Béla Bartók, who appeared with his wife, Ditta, in the American premiere of his Concerto for Two Pianos and Orchestra. This was the composer's last public appearance as a pianist. The concerto was heard only on the Thursday and Friday concerts of 21 and 22 January; in its place on the following Sunday, concertmaster John Corigliano played the Dvořák Violin Concerto, to avoid offending the radio audience with Bartók's music. Reiner also offered a program of Russian music: Stravinsky's *The Song of the Nightingale,* the Ravel orchestration of Mussorgsky's *Pictures at an Exhibition,* the Prokofiev "Classical" Symphony, and lighter pieces by Tchaikovsky and Shostakovich. Reiner wrote to Stravinsky that Bartók had heard his piece and admired it highly.[10] Yielding to pressure from Columbia Records, Reiner programmed on all four concerts of his final week the Robert Russell Bennett arrangement of the *Porgy and Bess* "Symphonic Picture." Reiner's concerts received a predictably mixed reception in the press. Olin Downes in the *Times* took special exception to the Bartók concerto, but Virgil Thomson in the *Herald-Tribune* was more tolerant of the new music and otherwise lavish in his praise of Reiner.

Although Reiner would not conduct the Philharmonic-Symphony's subscription concerts for another seventeen years, he conducted the orchestra frequently in nonsubscription concerts. For three summers, 1943 through 1945, the Philharmonic played radio programs from Carnegie Hall over CBS, to extend its Sunday afternoon broadcasts following the end of its regular season in May. Sponsored by the United States Rubber Company, the programs lasted ninety minutes and concentrated on familiar repertory that could be prepared with minimal rehearsal and sixty-five players. Reiner conducted three broadcasts in 1943, five in 1944, and two in 1945. Despite Zirato's admonitions to avoid unfamiliar music, Reiner managed to give the first New York performances of Copland's *El salón México* and excerpts from Shostakovich's version of *Boris Godunov* with Alexander Kipnis in the title role.

Similar programs prevailed in Reiner's four summer engagements in Lewisohn Stadium. Each year when Judson pressed Reiner to accept a Stadium engagement, the conductor would first plead the need for a rest after an exhausting season. He would then request a fee that would send Minnie Guggenheimer "into orbit," declaring that she would never again invite Reiner. Ultimately— in 1939, 1941, 1942, and 1948—he agreed to two-week engagements. In 1939 he offered a six-concert Beethoven series of all nine symphonies, four concertos, and various overtures. That season opened with a Wagner program, with Florence Easton and Jan Peerce singing excerpts from *Tristan und Isolde, Die Walküre,* and *Götterdämmerung*. In 1942 he offered Wallingford Riegger's *New Dance* and Silvestre Revueltas's *Janitzio,* both of which he had programmed in Pittsburgh and on his NBC broadcasts. Otherwise Reiner's Stadium programs contained few departures from the standard repertory.

For Reiner in 1944 the Cleveland Orchestra must have compared attractively with Pittsburgh: the orchestra had its own Severence Hall and a substantial endowment. In three weeks at the end of 1944 and the beginning of 1945, Reiner offered safe repertory: Bach, Brahms, Mozart, Mendelssohn, and Wagner. Only in his second and third programs did he venture into newer repertory with William Schuman's *Side Show* and the Shostakovich Sixth Symphony. Under pressure from the Pittsburgh board, Reiner turned down Columbia's suggestion that he record with the Cleveland Orchestra. After his visit, he asked the company to send some of his Pittsburgh recordings to members of the Cleveland board. Not long afterward, Zirato wrote to Reiner that he had been seriously considered for the post to which George Szell was appointed. Reiner never conducted the Cleveland Orchestra again.

A year later Reiner was guest conductor of the Boston Symphony, his only engagement there. The one-week engagement in December 1945 included a concert in Providence and a pair in Symphony Hall. Reiner showed his respect for the Boston Symphony Orchestra with an exacting program—the Mozart "Haffner" Symphony, Debussy's "Ibéria," and two works by Richard Strauss, the *Sinfonia domestica* and Salome's Dance. He arrived in Boston early enough to hear Koussevitzky's preceding concert and to join him at his home for supper afterward. A few months after his visit to Boston, Reiner asked Zirato about the possibility of a reengagement there, reporting that Koussevitzky had indicated he wanted him back. He was apparently unaware of the Russian conductor's habit of promising guests a reengagement even if he did not intend one.

Reiner's correspondence indicates a number of engagements that either did not materialize or that he turned down because of insufficient fees. He dismissed both South America and a return to London after the war with notations of "offer inadequate." He declined a staged version of *Elektra* in the Hollywood Bowl in 1939. He rejected persistent invitations to conduct outdoor concerts at Grant Park in Chicago, although at one point he was even offered a position as musical director of the summer season.

Throughout the 1940s radio broadcasting assumed increasing importance in the dissemination of concert music. Although the earlier "Hours" continued, several symphony orchestras broadcast all or part of their regular concerts, including the Cleveland, New York, and Boston orchestras, which Reiner conducted as a guest.[11] Each of the four major radio networks developed its own in-house orchestra, responding less to artistic altruism than to musicians' union pressure. They hired excellent musicians at salaries often exceeding what symphony orchestras could pay. In addition to fulfilling union requirements, programming "serious" music on the networks was a decided advantage when affiliated stations applied for license renewals to the Federal Communications Commission at a time when public service was still an important consideration. In addition to its weekly broadcasts of the New York Philharmonic-Symphony Orchestra, the Columbia Broadcasting System maintained a regular staff orchestra that broadcast regularly with Howard Barlow, Alfredo Antonini, Bernard Herrmann, André Kostelanetz, and occasional guests. During the Philharmonic's summer off season, it offered full symphonic programs on Sunday afternoons. Reiner conducted two broadcasts of the CBS Symphony in late August and early September 1945. Broadcast from Liederkranz Hall, they included the Shostakovich Sixth Symphony and Falla's *El amor brujo* with Carol Brice, repertory obviously reflecting Columbia Records releases. In May 1947 he again conducted the CBS orchestra in a Russian program that included the Shostakovich Ninth Symphony.

The most important of these network staff orchestras was that of the National Broadcasting Company, which in 1937 lured Arturo Toscanini back to the United States to conduct its NBC Symphony Orchestra. Contrary to his and the general public's impression, this orchestra was not necessarily "created" for him. Its personnel, hired to meet union requirements, also played under Frank Black and in other configurations as a part of the union contract. Toscanini was extremely annoyed to discover that the NBC Symphony Orchestra was not exclusively his, and for the season of 1941–1942, he refused to conduct its regular weekly concerts.[12] In view of Reiner's having conducted *Giovinezza* in Milan in 1931, it may be significant that he did not conduct the NBC Symphony Orchestra until the season when Toscanini was on the sidelines. The artistic administrator of the NBC Symphony Orchestra was Samuel Chotzinoff, formerly Heifetz's piano accompanist and later a music critic in New York. "Chotzi" had been David Sarnoff's emissary to Toscanini in arranging to bring him to NBC. With the sometimes explicit and sometimes tacit approval of Toscanini, he generally selected the guest conductors, who seldom had the generous rehearsal time Toscanini received. Nor did they perform, as Toscanini eventually did, in Carnegie Hall, but rather in the acoustically dry Studio 8-H in the RCA Building. In his correspondence with Reiner, Chotzinoff took pains to admonish him to play familiar music. For his first two programs in March 1942, Reiner bent those rules somewhat, programming Riegger's *New Dance* and the Revueltas *Janitzio* on his first broadcast and Strauss's *Don Quixote,* with Frank Miller as soloist, on the second. He did not return to Studio 8-H until December 1946, when he conducted four broadcasts, which included the suite from Bartók's *The Miraculous Mandarin,* Hindemith's *Mathis der Maler* symphony, and Kodály's Galánta Dances, one on each of his first three programs. The following April, Chotzinoff wired Reiner: "SORRY NOT NEXT YEAR." Only after he changed his personal management did Reiner return to the NBC Symphony Orchestra; he went back in December 1949 and again for more engagements through 1952.

In 1946 the independent Hollywood producer Boris Morros, who had earlier tried to involve Reiner in a film of *Carmen,* assembled a motley collection of concert and popular music celebrities for a film about Carnegie Hall.[13] The plot concerned a cleaning woman who had brought up her violinist son to be a great concert artist, only to have him become a jazz musician. On this slim story the producers hung appearances by such performers as Walter Damrosch, Bruno Walter, Leopold Stokowski, Artur Rodzinski, Lily Pons, Gregor Piatigorsky, Risë Stevens, Artur Rubinstein, Jascha Heifetz, Harry James, and

Vaughan Monroe. Reiner's contribution was conducting players from the New York Philharmonic-Symphony Orchestra and others in a twelve-minute version of the Tchaikovsky Violin Concerto with Heifetz as soloist. Reiner and Heifetz, assisted by stand-ins, went before the cameras in Carnegie Hall on 5 and 6 September 1946, "playing" in synchronization with a previously recorded sound track. Reiner also appeared in a brief scene in Heifetz's dressing room, during which he spoke two lines describing stage fright, "that funny sensation at the pit of the stomach." A *Variety* reviewer called *Carnegie Hall* "a musical treat in every sense of the word. . . . Film carries heavy exploitation values, for modern music is blended with the classics." James Agee was less impressed by the twelve-track recording, an "aural compromise between the Johnstown flood and the Black Hole of Calcutta."[14]

For a few days' work in *Carnegie Hall* in 1946 Reiner received a fee of twenty-five hundred dollars, the same as he received from the American Lyric Theater in 1939 for learning a new score and spending several weeks of preparation, or for a week of concerts in Lewisohn Stadium. Such figures, often appearing at the end of an annual diary, give some idea of Reiner's finances. In the 1939 diary, he entered fifteen hundred dollars for the swimming pool at Rambleside and a total cost for the house of thirty-three thousand to forty thousand dollars. On one occasion, he told Judson that he would need many engagements to pay for his swimming pool and house. Both the New York Philharmonic-Symphony Orchestra summer broadcasts and the NBC Symphony Orchestra paid one thousand dollars a concert, or, if the latter was not sponsored, half that amount. In 1947 Reiner's royalties from Columbia Records brought him a net of approximately fifty-five hundred dollars for the year. During his Pittsburgh years, such miscellaneous income plus his Pittsburgh salary earned him between forty and fifty thousand dollars a year.

Such financial resources enabled the Reiners to live comfortably at Rambleside and to carry on a social life that mixed his colleagues from the music world and Carlotta's friends from the theater. Although Reiner traveled to and from New York, the center of his and Carlotta's life was Rambleside. He meticulously entered in his diary trips to the veterinarian or boarding kennel with their Irish setter, Rambler, and the time required to fill or empty the swimming pool with its sophisticated filtering and chlorinating system. Gadgetry and the mechanical aspects of housekeeping fascinated Reiner. In the kitchen the Reiners had an early automatic dishwasher and a large stainless steel stove. A gasoline-powered electric generator provided standby power for the house and for the well. Outfitting the darkroom in the basement required constant perusal of the latest equipment catalogs. In 1947 Reiner bought a Chrysler Town and Country four-door, wooden-sided, convertible sedan, which he enjoyed driving.

He set aside a substantial part of each summer to read new scores and to prepare his programs for the coming season. When he was working, there were few visitors or trips to New York City. Judson, Zirato, and other business acquaintances visited for a Saturday or Sunday lunch or for an entire weekend of swimming, walking in the woods, and good food and drink. Occasionally the Reiners entertained such out-of-town visitors as the Robert Watt Millers from San Francisco; Mr. Miller was president of the opera there. Other weekend guests were young musicians like Lukas Foss and William Kapell. In 1947 Reiner frequently saw John Selby, an editor at Rinehart, to discuss a book on conducting. He prepared an outline for this book but never wrote it.

The fate of his family and friends in Europe was a constant concern to Reiner. He sent monthly payments to his brother János and his uncle Sándor until hostilities in Europe made it impossible to send funds directly to Budapest. For a time Reiner relied on Eva in Zurich and on the Red Cross to get money and food through to Hungary. Early in 1941 Reiner wanted to bring János to the United States, but red tape in Hitler-dominated Hungary prevented this. In March 1945 Reiner clipped and filed a story and picture from the New York *Times* on the destruction of Dresden a month earlier. At his suggestion, after peace came to Europe the players in the Pittsburgh Symphony Orchestra collected strings and reeds to send to orchestra musicians in Budapest. By the summer of 1946 he was sending food parcels regularly through CARE and other agencies to Tuśy in Ljubljana and to his relatives in Budapest; he also sent occasional food packages to Leo Weiner. For Reiner, the discharge of these obligations was his contribution to postwar relief. When a Pittsburgh friend chided him for the modesty of his contribution to the United Jewish Fund for refugee relief in 1946, Reiner cited his obligations to his family and friends in Europe and enclosed a check for two hundred dollars.

Reiner's relations with Tuśy, strained since her stay in America, remained aggravated by concern and annoyance on his part and by a feeling of neglect on hers. Even after she had married a Russian, Vladimir Assejew, and had a son, Reiner continued to treat her as a child, alternately scolding and indulging her. In addition to clothing and food for her and baby Vovček, Reiner sent her a bicycle that was lost in transit. For a time Reiner established a "stocking fund" with Eva in Zurich, to whom he periodically sent twenty dollars with which to purchase lingerie for her sister in Ljubljana. To Tuśy's letters of complaint over his neglect, he replied that she was ungrateful. He was especially annoyed when she left her husband to return to her family home. He threatened to stop sending funds, which she did not acknowledge. Such was his impatience with his elder daughter that he often left it to Carlotta to type his letters to her. When Tuśy sent her father a list of clothing she needed, Carlotta replied that the cost of one hundred dollars was "out of the question" and mailed her a package of her own old clothing for Tuśy to alter for herself. The Reiners' impatience with Tuśy was probably further aggravated by their realization that she was becoming an alcoholic. With Eva, Reiner's relations were more cordial, and most of their correspondence was handwritten; he had now come to treat her as adult. He was delighted in 1945 to learn of the birth of her first child, Hans.[15] Two years later, she and her son spent two months at Rambleside.

Reiner also received appeals from Berta, directly and through the Reverend Ralph S. Thorn, father of one of her former pupils. Thorn described Berta as impoverished and suffering from delusions and a sense of humiliation, either escaping psychologically into daydreams or seized with suicidal impulses. To one especially pressing letter from Thorn, Reiner had his lawyer respond that he had paid in full a very generous settlement to his former wife and could not be responsible for Madame Gardini's inability to manage her resources.[16]

By the end of 1946 Fritz Reiner had been music director of the Pittsburgh Symphony Orchestra for eight seasons, half of that time under wartime conditions. Whatever hopes he may have had of building a great orchestra in western Pennsylvania had become frustrated by the orchestra's recurring annual deficit. Despite more stable personnel and a longer season, a decline in 1945–1946 subscriptions prompted Specter to suggest to Reiner that his programming was to blame. In the back of his 1946 diary Reiner listed topics to be discussed with Thruston Wright, president of the Pittsburgh Symphony Society. These notes focused on his dissatisfaction with Specter. He suggested that differences between himself and Specter should be resolved by the board itself. He anticipated the risks of the Mexican tour, objecting especially to giving a concert in a bull ring. He also wanted to enlarge the orchestra with five more string players.[17]

During his Pittsburgh years, Reiner's personal relations with Arthur Judson deteriorated steadily after a high point when the Reiners visited him at his camp in the Canadian Laurentians in 1938. Carlotta apparently fueled her husband's antagonism. Nora Shea, Judson's secretary who was friendly with the Reiners, once wrote Carlotta that she had offended him on a recent occasion.[18] Reiner's contract with Judson, which he had renewed automatically since 1922, expired in the spring of 1946. On 20 April he wrote to Bruno Zirato that he was "thinking about" renewal. The following day he wrote Zirato, "Renewal not feasible."[19] By this time Reiner sensed that he could get on without Judson, who no longer enjoyed his unchallenged control of conductors' American careers.

For a short time Reiner was without management, although he frequently communicated with Andrew Schulhof. A fellow Hungarian, Schulhof had worked with the music publishers Boosey and Hawkes in the management of Béla Bartók's concert activity in the United States. Although he had represented Reiner in the negotiations for *Carnegie Hall,* they signed a management agreement only in September 1946. For the next few months Schulhof explored various possibilities with the London Philharmonic Orchestra and Decca Records. He eventually took over Reiner's negotiations with the Pittsburgh Symphony Orchestra and Columbia Records. In many respects Schulhof was the worst possible manager for Reiner. Unlike Judson, whose curbing of Reiner's more unreasonable impulses could be advantageous, Schulhof shared Carlotta's tendency to support his less temperate and more suspicious reactions. When Schulhof failed to deliver major engagements, Reiner terminated the services of the manager in July 1947.[20] Reiner had already made contact with another independent manager, James A. Davidson, who had had considerable experience in larger management agencies. Davidson already represented several important singers at the Metropolitan Opera and had booked transcontinental tours of the Philadelphia Orchestra. He also represented Margaret Truman in her brief concert career.

One festering issue between Reiner and the Pittsburgh board concerned recording. When his Pittsburgh recordings did not satisfy him artistically or financially, Reiner sought to record with other orchestras, but both the Pittsburgh board and Columbia refused at various times. In October 1946 Specter wrote testily to Reiner that Schulhof was "misrepresenting" the problem between Columbia Records, the conductor, and the board. He maintained that only Koussevitzky had a more favorable contract with respect to division of royalties and sharing of recording costs and that Reiner's Pittsburgh salary was higher than those of conductors anywhere except in New York, Philadelphia, and Boston.[21] In a generally conciliatory reply the conductor accepted Specter's proposal to allow him to record in Europe, where Reiner still had no solid base. In ensuing months relations between Reiner and Specter deteriorated further. Reiner frequently avoided speaking directly to Specter, using Edwards as an intermediary, and eventually tried to replace Specter with Edwards as manager.[22] In this Reiner made a serious misjudgment, for the Pittsburgh community and the board had a high regard for Specter. If a showdown were to come between manager and conductor in Pittsburgh, the odds had to be in favor of the manager.

That consideration seems to have made little impression on the Reiners. Through the fall and winter of 1947 Davidson was trying with Specter to make the best of a worsening situation. After Reiner returned from his midwinter vacation at Rambleside early in 1948, there were meetings in Pittsburgh with the society's executive committee, Specter, Reiner, and Davidson. Specter and a divided board determined to take draconian steps to solve their chronic financial problems. Guest conductors would be selected, not by Reiner, but by Specter and the board. They would reduce the season from twenty-eight to twenty-five weeks, and the orchestra from ninety to eighty-five players. Both Specter and Reiner would receive a 10-percent cut in salary. Recording issues remained unresolved, but the board rejected Reiner's demand to limit touring to six days at a time. Finally on 20 February Davidson wrote to Specter advising him of Reiner's resignation, citing his efforts to hold the orchestra together in wartime and the success of the Mexican tour.[23]

The board announced Reiner's resignation publicly on the twenty-third, expressing regret and assurances of goodwill. Initially, the official position was that Reiner's resignation was not related to the orchestra's accumulated deficit, variously given as forty or sixty thousand dollars. However, it was soon apparent that Reiner had been unwilling to accept reductions in the length of the season and in the number of players, which would have jeopardized the quality of the orchestra. The press expressed the fear that these reductions would impair the orchestra's ability to retain its best players.[24]

For some time, Davidson had been in touch with Edward Johnson at the Metropolitan Opera concerning Reiner's joining that company. These discussions had probably progressed to the point where Reiner felt more confident in taking a strong position with Pittsburgh. In its report of Reiner's Pittsburgh resignation, the New York *Times* mentioned rumors about his possible engagement at the Metropolitan.[25] At first Reiner evaded questions from the press: "I am going back to Connecticut to raise vegetables." However, in an interview two days after the announcement, he declared: "Unless a concerted effort is made to provide an endowment and a good hall for the orchestra, the picture is cloudy. . . . The orchestra must have a hall of its own. We are constantly being shifted about under the present arrangement. And an endowment would give the Symphony a security it lacks now."[26] These were prophetic words indeed regarding the future of the Pittsburgh Symphony Orchestra.

Reiner's weekend subscription program following the announcement of his resignation was an ambitious evening of selections from Wagner's *Ring*— the entire first act of *Die Walküre* and excerpts from *Götterdämmerung*, with Astrid Varnay and Set Svanholm and an expanded orchestra of one hundred players. The end of the season in April brought special tributes. Following the final pair of subscription concerts—an all-Beethoven program—the players gave Reiner a farewell party. A week later, the society's board of directors honored Fritz Reiner at a reception following a special nonsubscription "farewell concert," at which Thruston Wright expressed the community's gratitude and presented the conductor with an engraved sterling silver tray. The next evening, ironically on tour to Beaver Falls, Reiner conducted the Pittsburgh Symphony Orchestra for the last time. He did not appear again in Pittsburgh.

Even before Reiner's final concert, the orchestra announced its plans for a season of guest conductors: Leonard Bernstein for three weeks in Pittsburgh and four weeks on tour, Artur Rodzinski, Charles Munch, Victor de Sabata, Erich Leinsdorf, and Paul Paray, all, except Rodzinski, clients of Judson. The fund goal, announced in April, was again $285,000, including a $60,000 carry-over from the past. When the orchestra opened its next season the following October, the drive was still $100,000 short of its goal.

The Pittsburgh experience was chastening to Reiner. Approaching his sixtieth birthday, he had failed to realize the full potential of a "resident" position at the head of a major American orchestra. Only after an interval of five years in the pit of the Metropolitan Opera would Fritz Reiner finally achieve the goal he had sought since 1931.

CHAPTER X

The Metropolitan Opera

Fritz Reiner's five seasons at the Metropolitan Opera brought him back to musico-dramatic activity to which he had been committed since his youth, not merely as a guest in London, San Francisco, or Philadelphia, but as a full-fledged member of one of the world's great opera companies. They also marked his achievement of an important post in New York City, which he regarded as the preeminent American musical center. If the Philharmonic was to be denied him, the Metropolitan gave him a regular exposure to the New York audience that was impossible as a guest conductor.

The most important development in Reiner's career during his transition from Pittsburgh to the Metropolitan was the completion of his change in personal management. Beginning in 1946 with his dismissal of Arthur Judson, it ended two years later with his arranging for representation by Sol Hurok. A flamboyant impresario, Hurok marketed himself as skillfully as he promoted his clients. With such artists as Marian Anderson, Artur Rubinstein, Jan Peerce, and Isaac Stern, he showed a distinctive flair for personal management. His most spectacular achievement was his promotion of Russian-style ballet as art and entertainment throughout the United States. Reiner's initial representation contract, signed in April 1948, was for one year. Reiner relied on Hurok directly and on his staff, dealing with the impresario's principal associates, Mae Frohman and Walter Prude, and with Martin Feinstein on publicity. Though the two men disagreed occasionally, Reiner's association with Hurok was fruitful, for there was a strong mutual respect between them professionally. Hurok seems never to have irritated Reiner as Judson did with strong musical opinions, but he impressed Reiner with his keen sense of business and promotion. In representing Reiner, Hurok had the distinct advantage of not having been involved in the difficult days of Pittsburgh and earlier. Yet he could build on the conductor's recognized achievement in having brought two American symphony orchestras to special musical eminence.

Possibly out of concern for his personal finances following his departure from Pittsburgh, Reiner took on a busier summer schedule than usual. He opened the 1948 season at Lewisohn Stadium with eight concerts in two weeks, including the obligatory all-Beethoven and all-Wagner programs. Among his soloists was William Kapell, playing the Rachmaninoff C Minor Concerto on an all-Russian program. Kapell had been a soloist with Reiner in Pittsburgh and had become one of his favorite young American musicians. Carol Brice, who had recorded Falla's *El amor brujo* with Reiner in Pittsburgh, repeated it for the New York summer audience. Kodály's Galánta Dances and Weiner's arrangement of Two Rumanian Dances by Bartók offered some Hungarian novelty. Richard Rodgers's waltz from *Carousel* and Virgil Thomson's *The Seine at Night* represented American music on these programs.[1] Reiner went from Lewisohn Stadium almost directly to Ravinia Park in the northern suburbs of Chicago, where he conducted the Chicago Symphony Orchestra in a week of four concerts. On this occasion he offered neither contemporary nor American music. He enjoyed a warm reception from both audience and press.

Even before Reiner had resigned from the Pittsburgh Symphony Orchestra, James A. Davidson had arranged for him to conduct the opening four weeks of the Minneapolis Symphony Orchestra season in 1948, while Dimitri Mitropoulos was a guest with the New York Philharmonic-Symphony. The Rodgers *Carousel* waltz was the only American work on his programs, and the second suite from Ravel's *Daphnis et Chloé* the most exacting repertory in demands on the orchestra's ability or the audience's tolerance. Afterward Reiner returned to New York, stopping in Chicago to meet Claudia Cassidy, the formidable critic of the *Tribune,* as Hurok had arranged.[2]

Although Reiner's engagement at the Metropolitan was widely accepted as a fact in New York, the company itself delayed official verification until announcing its 1948–1949 season in October.[3] Reiner realized after twenty years an ambition to conduct America's premier opera company. It had been a long and circuitous path, involving Berta's efforts with Giulio Gatti-Casazza in the 1920s, Reiner's own proposal to Herbert Witherspoon of Berg's *Lulu,* and intermittent contact with Edward Johnson by Constance Hope and Bruno Zirato. Early in 1946, before Reiner dropped Judson as his manager, Zirato wrote a note to Reiner in Italian suggesting that he develop *ajuti sociali*—social support—for his engagement at the Metropolitan.[4]

After Reiner had instructed Hurok associate Marks Levine to accept the Metropolitan's terms in late May, the manager reported that there would be no decision until mid-August. An added complication was that, for the first time in its history, the Metropolitan Opera faced serious labor union negotiations. Only on 30 September did Reiner, Levine, and Hurok meet with Edward Johnson to confirm contractual details. In a telegram to Reiner, Richard Strauss reportedly hailed his appointment to the Metropolitan as a "great day for opera!"[5] The contract, dated 1 October, called for Reiner to conduct ten performances between January and mid-April 1949 for a fee of ten thousand dollars, with a thousand dollars for each additional performance. The one-page typewritten contract was in the then-standard mimeographed form. As was customary, there was no compensation for rehearsals, which, in Reiner's case, began in late November.[6] These arrangements were typical of the operation of the Metropolitan Opera under Edward Johnson's direction.

Reiner arrived at the Metropolitan in the thirteenth year of Johnson's tenure, when the former tenor was already talking of retirement. The war and its aftermath had two important artistic consequences for the Metropolitan under Johnson: the integration of new American singers into a predominantly foreign roster and the employment, usually for a full season, of such conductors as Bruno Walter, George Szell, Sir Thomas Beecham, Pierre Monteux, Fritz Busch, and Fritz Reiner. (Reiner was not, as suggested in some sources, one of the émigré conductors engaged by Johnson; he had been in America for a quarter of a century and a United States citizen since 1928.) Such American singers as Risë Stevens, Jan Peerce, Richard Tucker, Jerome Hines, Frank Guarrera, Charles Kullman, Leonard Warren, Rose Bampton, Nadine Conner, Margaret Harshaw, Dorothy Kirsten, Patrice Munsel, Regina Resnik, Eleanor Steber, Blanche Thebom, and Astrid Varnay were already on the roster when Reiner arrived in the fall of 1948. He already knew many of them as students at Curtis or as soloists in Pittsburgh.

Reiner's initial assignments were *Salome, Falstaff,* and the traditional spring performances of *Parsifal.* He began *Salome* rehearsals and completed *Falstaff* casting with Johnson's assistant Max Rudolf in late November 1948. By mid-December, more than six weeks before his first performance, he was rehearsing those two operas almost daily. Meanwhile, he started to work with Charles Kullman and other principals on *Parsifal.* Regina Resnik recalled that, as soon as Reiner had the entire *Falstaff* cast together, he began each rehearsal with the final fugue.[7] Reiner's diary shows appointments for interviews with national news magazines and local critics in anticipation of his debut on 4 February 1949.

Salome on that night is still remembered as "one of the most spectacular [occasions] the Met has ever known."[8] It marked the double debuts of Reiner and Ljuba Welitsch, who brought to the title role the voice, histrionics, and animal temperament that created a sensation. Yet even the Bulgarian Bombshell, as Reiner referred to her, could not detract from the conductor's comparable triumph in the pit. Together they shared a fifteen-minute ovation. Irving Kolodin wrote that Reiner's contribution was "as tense and comprehending a performance of the orchestral score as the Metropolitan has ever known."[9] Although Olin Downes complained of "certain excessive fortissimos of Mr. Reiner's orchestra," he acknowledged that "his reading of the score was exciting and symphonic, flexible and remarkably salient of detail, charged with inspiration too. He had the orchestra in the palm of his hand."[10] The highest praise came from Virgil Thomson, who hailed the occasion as "one of the great musico-dramatic performances of our century."[11] Welitsch sang all five performances in New York, plus one in Philadelphia. The final performance, a Saturday matinee on 12 March 1949, was broadcast.

Meanwhile, at an earlier Saturday matinee on 26 February, Reiner conducted *Falstaff* in Italian, with Leonard Warren in the title role. This was Reiner's first broadcast from the Metropolitan. Thomson hailed this *Falstaff* as "the kind of performance generally believed to be beyond the capability of the Metropolitan."[12] Olin Downes was equally enthusiastic, calling it "a performance of *Falstaff* that we have not seen equalled on this side of the Atlantic."[13] Never a "box-office" opera, *Falstaff* played only three times that season. Despite the pleas of Warren and Reiner, the company did not mount this opera again during their years there.

The Metropolitan traditionally presented *Parsifal* each spring, as close to Holy Week as its schedule would permit. Tradition was served by three performances in March and April 1949, the first with Charles Kullman in the title role, the last two with Set Svanholm. Rose Bampton appeared as Kundry throughout, and Joel Berglund was Gurnemanz. After his successes in *Salome* and *Falstaff,* Reiner did not come up to critical expectations in his first local performance of an opera by Wagner. This foreshadowed a coolness toward Reiner's Wagner through much of his time at the Metropolitan. Thanks to his late arrival after his Minneapolis engagement, Reiner conducted but eleven performances at the Metropolitan Opera House in early 1949, plus *Salome* in Philadelphia and Boston. In addition, he conducted *Le nozze di Figaro* in Baltimore and Boston, preparing it in two days, with a performance of *Parsifal* on the evening between.

Reiner was consulted in the management of the orchestra, especially in auditioning new players and in casting the operas he conducted, but his word was by no means final. Although he had to accept the staging of revived operas, he was consulted on new productions. Such limits on his authority did not temper the demands he made on singers and orchestra musicians. On at least one occasion he was so abusive of the musicians in rehearsal that their representatives were on the point of filing formal charges against him with the local union. Only the diplomatic skill of Max Rudolf averted a major crisis.

After his first trip to Europe since the war, Reiner spent the rest of the summer of 1949 at Rambleside studying scores for the coming season, all of them repertory he had conducted previously: *Der Rosenkavalier, Die Meistersinger, Le nozze di Figaro, Don Giovanni,* and *Salome.* There were several meetings at Rambleside with Eleanor Steber, who was to sing her first Marschallin in *Der Rosenkavalier,* having previously sung Sophie. Early in August, Reiner signed a standard contract for a minimum of twenty performances of five operas between 21 November 1949 and 16 April 1950, with three weeks off in March for a guest engagement with the Chicago Symphony Orchestra. His fee was one thousand dollars per performance, the same for additional ones. There was an option for a three-week tour, with rail fare for one person to be paid by the Metropolitan. He actually conducted twenty-three performances, including two on the postseason tour. A month before Reiner began rehearsals for *Der Rosenkavalier,* Richard Strauss died in Bavaria. Earlier that summer Reiner had encountered the composer's son Franz at an Italian hotel and learned that the old man was declining rapidly.

Der Rosenkavalier on 21 November 1949 was the only occasion on which Reiner conducted an opening night at the Metropolitan, but the event was more in honor of Steber than of Reiner. The cast included Erna Berger, in her American debut, as Sophie, Risë Stevens as Octavian, and Emanuel List as Ochs. In his *Sun* review, Kolodin described Reiner's *Der Rosenkavalier* as an orchestra piece with singers, quite different from his recollection of the Philadelphia performances in 1934. Although Olin Downes found it "by no means the conductor's best effort with the score," he reported in the *Times* that "the orchestra sounded as we don't ever remember to have heard it sound before at the Metropolitan in this opera." [14] For a second year, opening night was telecast over a network limited to six cities as far west as Detroit and Chicago; this was Reiner's first appearance on television.

In November and December Reiner rehearsed *Le nozze di Figaro* and *Die Meistersinger.* The Mozart opera opened on 4 January 1950 with a cast including Steber as the Contessa, Bidú Sayão as Susanna, Jarmila Novotna as Cherubino, Italo Tajo as Figaro, and John Brownlee as the Conte. Although the production by Herbert Graf dated back several years, it was one of the more distinguished stagings of the Johnson era. The third and final performance on 4 March brought an unusual change in cast: Brownlee sang Figaro, and Giuseppe Valdengo the Conte.

Die Meistersinger also reached the stage in January, after extensive ensemble and orchestra rehearsals. Gunther Schuller played first horn in this production. When Reiner stopped to correct him in rehearsal, he replied, "But Maestro, I have not played this piece before." While the rest of the orchestra held its breath awaiting a Reiner explosion, the conductor responded with feeling, "What I would give to hear *Die Meistersinger* for the first time!" Schuller and his partner, Alan Fuchs, must have played very well, for Reiner stopped them during the "Fliedermonolog" in act II. He exclaimed that theirs was the most beautiful rendition he had ever heard of that haunting horn passage and requested that they play it again, alone, for the benefit of the entire orchestra. As Schuller pointed out, Reiner was seldom in a such a mellow mood.[15] As with *Parsifal* the previous season, the critics again expressed some disappointment in Reiner's Wagner. Kolodin was typical in his view that Reiner had not conveyed "the big line."

At the end of January *Salome* was repeated. Because of Welitsch's delay in arriving from Vienna, Astrid Varnay sang the title role in the first of three performances. Paul Schoeffler, who later sang Sachs in *Die Meistersinger* and the title role in *Don Giovanni,* made his American debut on 26 January 1950 as Jokanaan. Again the Strauss opera enjoyed a great success. Schoeffler's Don followed his Jokanaan by one week, on 3 February. Mozart's *dramma giocoso* was given three times (including in Philadelphia) with Welitsch as Donna Anna. On the 1950 postseason tour, Reiner conducted *Die Meistersinger* twice, in St. Louis (20 April) and in Chicago (11 May). The latter performance, following a successful three-week engagement with the Chicago Symphony Orchestra, enhanced his exposure in that city. This was his only appearance in Chicago with the Metropolitan Opera and, in fact, his last fully staged opera in that city. Between the St. Louis and Chicago performances, Reiner returned to Rambleside, but he went to New York City on 25 April to have lunch with Rudolf Bing, who had been "observing" the 1949–1950 season before taking over as general manager of the Metropolitan Opera in the fall.

The Metropolitan Opera did not monopolize Reiner's professional life. During three summers he accepted outdoor concerts in New York, Philadelphia, and Chicago. He conducted the NBC Symphony Orchestra more frequently than previously, in the winter and in the summer. His only winter-season orchestra engagement, an obviously important one, was for three weeks in Chicago in March 1950. In the fall of 1951 he went to Mexico for a series of concerts, and in 1949, 1952, and 1953, he and Carlotta traveled to Europe, combining family visits with a few professional engagements.

Early in October 1951 Reiner returned to Mexico, the scene of his success with the Pittsburgh Symphony Orchestra four years earlier. His sponsor was José Yves Limantour, a wealthy young conductor who had organized his own Orquesta Sinfónica de Xalapa.[16] In protracted preliminary negotiations, Reiner insisted on train accommodations—a drawing room and an adjoining bedroom from New York to Mexico City for himself and Carlotta. They would not leave New York until his fee had been deposited in a New York bank. The Reiners left New York on 10 September, arriving three days later in Mexico City. Before rehearsals began, they motored to Taxco and Acapulco for four days, returning to Mexico City, where they changed hotels. Although Limantour's orchestra was a rival to Carlos Chavez's, Reiner had a cordial visit with the composer-conductor. Rehearsals began on 28 September for a 3 October concert.

These were interrupted when Reiner was in an auto accident on the twenty-ninth, with "Pepe" Limantour driving. Reiner was bruised badly enough to require a wheelchair, but not enough to prevent his attending a reception at the Prado Hotel given in his honor by RCA-Victor. After two more rehearsals, the postponed concert took place on 7 October—the prelude to *Die Meistersinger,* the Schumann Piano Concerto with Esperanza Pulido as soloist, and the Brahms Fourth. On the tenth Reiner conducted Mozart's G Minor Symphony, *Don Juan,* Weiner's arrangement of Bartók's Two Rumanian Dances, Casella's *Paganiniana,* the prelude to *Irmelin* by Delius, and the march from Berlioz's *Les Troyens.* The day following this concert, the Reiners entrained for New York, but they were delayed for twelve hours by a derailment at Chirimoya. From the train window they bought for one hundred pesos a small harp, now at Northwestern University. They finally arrived home on 16 October.

During the opera season the Reiners moved to Manhattan, where they leased a succession of apartments. These apartments were large enough to accommodate a piano, so that singers could come from the Metropolitan for rehearsals. Otherwise, while Reiner was working, he insisted on privacy, which Carlotta zealously protected. They entrusted Rambleside to various caretakers: some lived in, and others checked the premises regularly. Whenever possible, mostly on weekends, the Reiners returned to the country. During the off season their guests at Rambleside included many friends and professional colleagues from the music world and the theater.[17] There were several visits from Reiner's piano pupil in Budapest, Erzi Szebestyén Klinger, then a surgeon in New York. Reiner's appointment book also listed frequent visits to therapists for massage and treatment of muscular pain.

In that diary there was also an entry on 7 August 1951, "Berta died in Roosevelt Hospital," and, on the following day, the location of the funeral home and cemetery. According to Berta's friends, she had season tickets at the Metropolitan Opera and could have heard her former husband conduct from the upper reaches of the theater on Thirty-ninth Street. The obituary in the *Times* mentioned her parents and her marriages to Walter Kirchhoff and Reiner, stating erroneously that she had been a member of the Dresden opera.[18] Although his diary does not indicate that Reiner attended Berta's funeral, Carlotta in later years maintained that he called privately at the funeral home to pay his last respects.

Although Reiner did not travel to Europe until 1949, he was eager to see his daughter Eva Bartenstein, who came to Rambleside in 1947 for a six-week stay, bringing her elder son, Hans. This was Reiner's first encounter with a grandchild. Eva visited Rambleside again in 1954, bringing her younger son, Fritz.

In late July 1949 the Reiners sailed on the *Vulcania,* arriving in Genoa on 2 August. After two weeks at the Hotel Excelsior on the Lido, they traveled by hired car and driver to Eva's home in Zurich. Early in his planning, Reiner had considered also visiting Tuśy and her son Vladimir ("Vovček") in Ljubljana, but he eventually decided that he could not face another confrontation with his older daughter. Had he made such a visit to Ljubljana, he planned to "park" Carlotta at the Lido.[19] Instead the Reiners vacationed in Tarasp and Bad Gastein before motoring to Milan for a concert on 21 September with the orchestra of La Scala. He offered a conventional program, including Weiner's orchestration of the Bach C Major Toccata, the Brahms Second Symphony, "Ibéria" of Debussy, and Strauss's *Till Eulenspiegel.* From Milan the Reiners proceeded to Genoa, where they boarded the *Saturnia,* arriving in New York on 4 October.

Reiner originally planned his next trip to Europe in 1952 to include a production of Milhaud's *Christophe Colomb* in an outdoor arena on the outskirts of Naples. However, because it was impossible to complete an Italian translation of the text in time, Reiner's appearance in Naples was postponed for a year. Nevertheless, the Reiners embarked on the *United States* for Le Havre and traveled thence by car to Paris and by the Aarlberg Express to Zurich for a visit with the Bartenstein family. After a few days there, they motored to Kitzbühel and Bad Gastein, where they stayed some three weeks before going to Salzburg to hear the premiere of Strauss's *Die Liebe der Danae.* In addition to the Strauss opera, which Clemens Krauss conducted, they heard *Don Pasquale* and *Le nozze di Figaro.*

This time the Reiners visited Tuśy in Ljubljana, where they found the hotel uncomfortable and noisy. They moved into the Jelacin family home, where Tuśy was living with her son and mother. In Ljubljana Reiner visited the Municipal Theater where he had conducted forty-two years earlier and had a snapshot taken of himself and young Vovček standing in front of the building. After two nights in Ljubljana, the Reiners resumed their motor trip, traveling to the Lido via Trieste. They remained there for more than two weeks, during which they visited with Gian Francesco Malipiero and George Szell. After returning home, Reiner sent them color photos of these visits. From Venice they went by train to Genoa, where they embarked on the SS *Constitution* for New York.[20]

In 1949, for the second summer in succession, Reiner accepted Minnie Guggenheimer's invitation to conduct in Lewisohn Stadium. He appears to have been on cordial terms with that formidable lady, lunching with her several times the previous spring and accompanying her out to the Stadium for the first rehearsal of the season. William Kapell, always a Reiner favorite, was soloist on opening night, in the Rachmaninoff Second Concerto. Reiner's programs were not very enterprising, although he repeated Virgil Thomson's *The Seine at Night*. On an all-Beethoven program, there were two concertos, the Fourth for piano with Eugene Istomin and the Violin Concerto with Joseph Fuchs.[21]

Reiner also conducted the Chicago Symphony Orchestra at Ravinia Park in the summers of 1948 and 1949. William Kapell was again one of his soloists, this time in Mozart's K. 453 in G Major and Falla's *Noches en los jardines en España*. Otherwise Reiner's programs were typical of what he could offer his summer audiences with the limited rehearsal at his disposal. The only novelty was Robert McBride's *Swing Stuff* with Mitchell Lurie as clarinet soloist. Once again, he visited with May Valentine and René Devries in Chicago, and with Florence Lackner and Margaret McClure in Highland Park. Although Ravinia gave Reiner exposure to the audience from Chicago and its vicinity, particularly from the wealthy suburbs of the North Shore, it was scarcely comparable to appearing in Orchestra Hall during the subscription season of the Chicago Symphony Orchestra. Only with four or five rehearsals for every weekly pair of concerts could a conductor place his own interpretive stamp and discipline on the performance.

That milestone was reached when Hurok arranged for Reiner to conduct the Chicago Symphony Orchestra for three subscription weeks in the spring of 1950. He arrived in Chicago with Carlotta on the Twentieth Century Limited on 6 March 1950. He was apparently in some discomfort, because his appointment book shows visits to an osteopath throughout his Chicago stay.[22] Knowing that he was under consideration for the post of music director of the orchestra, Reiner gave much thought to his Chicago programs, jotting down possibilities in the front of his 1950 diary, apparently weeding out any repertory that might prove controversial. He offered little contemporary music: Casella's *Paganiniana* and suites from Stravinsky's *Petrushka* and Falla's *El sombrero de tres picos* were his most modern repertory. Mahler's *Kindertotenlieder* with Kathleen Ferrier was especially memorable. In his programs in Orchestra Hall, Milwaukee, and Ann Arbor, he offered three Brandenburg Concertos—the First, Third, and Fourth—reflecting his recent recordings of all six for Columbia.[23] Otherwise, he offered a standard fare of Mozart, Beethoven, Schumann, Saint-Saëns, and Wagner. All of Reiner's concerts were well received by the local audience and press. Claudia Cassidy of the *Tribune* was exceptionally enthusiastic.

In the summer of 1951 Reiner returned to the Philadelphia Orchestra, not at its Broad Street home in the Academy of Music, but in Fairmont Park at Robin Hood Dell. This was now securely established as the summer home of the orchestra under the guidance and support of Frederic Mann. RCA-Victor, for whom Reiner had been recording for a year, arranged this reunion. Although the Philadelphia Orchestra did not permit conductors other than Eugene Ormandy to record with it, its personnel could benefit financially by recording for RCA as the Robin Hood Dell Symphony Orchestra. This arrangement dictated the choice of soloists and repertory for Reiner's programs in late June. Kapell played the Rachmaninoff Rhapsody on a Theme of Paganini on one program, and Nathan Milstein and Gregor Piatigorsky the Brahms Double Concerto on another. The concert on 26 June included selections from Mendelssohn's incidental music for *A Midsummer Night's Dream*. RCA-Victor recorded all three pieces at the Academy of Music. The most adventurous repertory of the three concerts was the three dances from Falla's *El sombrero de tres picos*. The press responded respectfully, with Max de Shauensee praising Reiner's "control and authority."[24]

Now that he was managed by Hurok, Reiner appeared more frequently on the weekly one-hour radio broadcasts of the NBC Symphony Orchestra. Between late 1948 and the end of 1950, Reiner conducted at least twelve broadcast concerts.[25] Since Arturo Toscanini's influence on this series depended on his declining health and relations between him and NBC, Samuel Chotzinoff was more than ever in charge of the program, wielding considerable influence over the choice of conductors and soloists. Guest conductors generally received a two-hour rehearsal during the week before a performance. On the day of the broadcast, there was a one-hour run-through of the program for final timing and the announcer's rehearsal. Reiner received a fee of fifteen hundred dollars for a sustaining program, which increased to two thousand if the program was commercially sponsored.

Despite the limited rehearsal available, Reiner offered some unusual repertory, a recognition of the high quality of the orchestra personnel, many of whom Reiner had known as far back as his Curtis days. Under these conditions he programmed the suite from Bartók's *The Miraculous Mandarin* on 15 December 1948, the Kodály Galánta Dances the following week, and then, on 29 December, Hindemith's *Mathis der Maler* symphony. The broadcast of

19 June 1949 featured Lauritz Melchior, by this time a Hollywood celebrity, in Prokofiev's *Peter and the Wolf.* Later that summer Reiner programmed the *Bachianas brasilieras* no. 5 of Heitor Villa-Lobos with Bidú Sayão. In October 1950 one of his programs included Bartók's Hungarian Sketches, and on 6 November Benny Goodman played the world premiere of Aaron Copland's Clarinet Concerto. During 1951, though Reiner conducted no NBC broadcasts, there was discussion of a broadcast featuring Mahler's *Das Lied von der Erde,* probably instigated by RCA-Victor. In January 1952 his NBC Symphony Orchestra program included Ravel's *Le tombeau de Couperin,* Debussy's Petite Suite, the Weiner arrangement of Bartók's Two Rumanian Dances, and Strauss's *Till Eulenspiegel;* RCA-Victor recorded the Debussy and Ravel selections for commercial release.

These NBC Symphony Orchestra programs and the Saturday matinee broadcasts from the Metropolitan Opera gave Reiner a nationwide exposure of a quality that he had not enjoyed so consistently previously. The weekly Saturday matinee radio broadcasts over ABC included all of Reiner's Metropolitan repertory except for *Parsifal.* [26]

Reiner's last years in Pittsburgh coincided with Columbia's development and introduction of the 33⅓-rpm long-playing record. This important innovation required considerable investment of capital and extensive commitment of technical personnel to make new masters of previously recorded material and to retool processing and pressing equipment at the Columbia plant in Bridgeport. Moreover, Reiner's closest contact at Columbia, Goddard Lieberson, moved up the corporate ladder, having inaugurated a series of highly successful original cast recordings of Broadway musical hits. The phenomenal success of his LP recording of *South Pacific* with Mary Martin and Ezio Pinza played a major part in the initial acceptance of the new format. Richard Gilbert, a former executive at RCA-Victor, became Reiner's working contact at Columbia Records.

Columbia introduced its new long-playing recordings in 1948 with heavily orchestrated publicity involving endorsements by its leading artists. Reiner was the subject of several photo sessions, alone and with such other Columbia artists as Dinah Shore and George Szell. Although most of the recording industry, including many small companies, soon accepted Columbia's innovative LP, RCA-Victor countered with a new system of its own, a small 45-rpm vinyl record with its own player for both popular and classical repertory. The "battle of the speeds" dominated the record market for two years, ending only when RCA-Victor capitulated by releasing its first LP records early in 1950. This remained the standard format for classical music for the next thirty-five years, while the 45s continued as the medium for popular single discs. For a time at least, these technical and marketing preoccupations had a dampening effect on recording new material. With their resolution in 1950, the recordings of classical music enjoyed an extraordinary growth in aggregate sales and also in an unprecedented diversification of repertory.[27]

Less than a month after his Metropolitan debut, Reiner recorded the final scene of *Salome* with Ljuba Welitsch and the Metropolitan orchestra on 14 March 1949 at Columbia's studios in Liederkranz Hall on East Fiftieth Street. Reiner signed a separate contract for this recording, as he did for others after leaving Pittsburgh. Initially issued both in the older 78-rpm format and on a ten-inch LP, this recording continued to appear in various reissues for many years. In 1952, two years after Reiner left the company, his royalty income from Columbia Records was over seventeen thousand dollars, most of it attributable to this *Salome* excerpt.[28] One of the ironies of Fritz Reiner's association with Columbia Records was the company's failure to recognize the potential of recording complete operas on long-playing records with him. As Dario Soria demonstrated with his imported Cetra opera recordings from Italy, the long-playing record created an entirely new market for complete recordings of opera. Columbia had a contract with the Metropolitan Opera to record "complete" operas under an exclusive arrangement that guaranteed the Metropolitan twenty-five thousand dollars a year against royalties.[29] At this time, when Columbia had both the Metropolitan and one of the premier conductors of opera under contract, it could have recorded a complete *Salome* with Reiner and Welitsch.

In July 1949 Reiner and Oscar Levant, then one of Columbia's most popular artists, recorded the Honegger Concertino for piano and orchestra with free-lance musicians, most from the staff of CBS. In six sessions between late October and early December 1949 Reiner recorded the six Brandenburg Concertos of Bach for Columbia. In an effort, pioneering at the time, to achieve Baroque proportions—and incidentally to save musicians' pay at high recording rates—he used a small ensemble of hand-picked free-lancers and Metropolitan players. The soloists included his former Pittsburgh concertmaster Hugo Kolberg, flutist Julius Baker, cellist Leonard Rose, oboist Robert Bloom, trumpeter William Vacchiano, and harpsichordists Sylvia Marlowe and Fernando Valenti. The instruments were, of course, modern, and Reiner's style can best be described as a modified "authentic" approach to Bach. In February 1950, again with the Metropolitan orchestra and Welitsch, Reiner recorded Donna Anna's arias from *Don Giovanni*. Following these sessions Reiner remained in touch with Gilbert. On 25 April 1950 Reiner noted in his diary that Columbia could not afford to record him that summer.[30]

Six weeks later Reiner lunched at the Plaza with Hurok, Samuel Chotzinoff of NBC, and Alan Kayes of RCA-Victor. Having lost the "battle of the speeds," RCA-Victor needed to strengthen its orchestral roster. In Boston, Charles Munch had just replaced Serge Koussevitzky and, at this point, could not be counted on for major sales. Eugene Ormandy and the Philadelphia Orchestra had defected to Columbia Masterworks. RCA-Victor's star conductor, Arturo Toscanini at the NBC Symphony Orchestra, was eighty-three years old and talking of retiring. Even if Reiner had no orchestra of his own, his experience and broad repertory offered much to RCA-Victor, which could assemble free-lance orchestras for him to conduct for recordings. Nor could RCA-Victor ignore the possibility that Reiner might eventually take over the Chicago Symphony Orchestra. Reiner's RCA-Victor contract, dated 20 July 1950, called for recordings of Tchaikovsky waltzes, *Das Lied von der Erde,* the Haydn Symphony no. 100, and Tchaikovsky's *Tempest* and *Hamlet.* Abandoned projects would prove to be the rule in RCA-Victor's planning with Reiner. However, early correspondence regarding possible complete recordings of *Carmen* and *Der Rosenkavalier* indicate that the company recognized Reiner as a potential director of opera recordings. The conductor received a 10-percent royalty on noncopyright repertory, 6 percent on copyright material, and 5 percent or 3 percent if there was a soloist. He would also share in the cost of the musicians, under the usual complicated formula.

RCA-Victor knew that Rudolf Bing planned to present Johann Strauss's *Die Fledermaus,* with Reiner conducting, as one of the new productions of his first season at the Metropolitan Opera and that Columbia planned a complete recording of the production. By having Reiner record enough excerpts for one LP with a cast of important Metropolitan singers, even before the company opened its season, RCA-Victor laid the groundwork for a major competitive coup. Reiner began rehearsals on 6 September and completed the recording on the twenty-sixth. Richard Mohr and Lewis Layton, who worked on most of Reiner's recordings for the next thirteen years, were producer and engineer respectively.[31]

During the *Die Fledermaus* sessions, Reiner also recorded Tchaikovsky waltzes, and shortly afterward, he recorded Richard Strauss's *Till Eulenspiegel* and *Tod und Verklärung.* By late October, Reiner had also recorded the Brahms *Alto Rhapsody* with Marian Anderson and the Robert Shaw Chorale, and short selections by Wagner and Humperdinck. In December, he and Gregor Piatigorsky recorded the Saint-Saëns A Minor Violoncello Concerto. Reiner resumed recording in March 1951, beginning with the Liszt *Totentanz* with Alexander Brailowsky. He continued with excerpts from Gluck's *Orfeo ed Euridice* and Mozart's *Le nozze di Figaro* with Risë Stevens and from *Der Rosenkavalier* with Stevens and Erna Berger. In May and June at Carnegie Hall, Reiner conducted a recording of the Rachmaninoff Third Concerto with Vladimir Horowitz.

Between 16 May and 22 June Reiner rehearsed and recorded Bizet's *Carmen* in Manhattan Center, returning in July to re-record a few passages. Made in advance of the new production planned for the Metropolitan's next season, the recording used the version of that opera current there, including the Guiraud recitatives and ballet music from *La jolie fille de Perth* and *L'Arlésienne* in act IV. This was Reiner's only complete opera recording, made and published with his approval. For all these recordings, Reiner conducted the RCA-Victor Symphony Orchestra, drawn from New York free-lance players, the Metropolitan Opera, and the New York Philharmonic-Symphony. With the Philadelphia Orchestra, under its "alias" as the Robin Hood Dell Symphony Orchestra, he recorded concertos with William Kapell, Nathan Milstein, and Gregor Piatigorsky, as well as the excerpts from *A Midsummer Night's Dream,* all in the Academy of Music. Returning to Rambleside after this heavy schedule of recording, the Reiners gave a party there for the cast of *Carmen,* RCA-Victor executives, Kapell, Ania Dorfmann, and New York *Post* critic Emily Coleman.[32]

During the next few months, while listening to his recording tests, Reiner discussed with RCA-Victor executives possible future recordings, including *Das Lied von der Erde* and the third act of *Die Walküre*. However, a less ambitious repertory materialized: Ravel's *Le tombeau de Couperin* and Busser's orchestration of Debussy's Petite Suite, both recorded with the NBC Symphony Orchestra following the broadcast in January 1952. In April Reiner again recorded with Horowitz, this time the Beethoven "Emperor" Concerto, and there were discussions of recording the Liszt E-flat Concerto later. In October 1952 Reiner and a small ensemble recorded three of the four Bach orchestral suites, leaving the B Minor until early January 1953. By this time, Reiner's engagement by the Chicago Symphony Orchestra had been announced, creating a completely new context for his recording career.

In Fritz Reiner's last three years at the Metropolitan Opera, Rudolf Bing was general manager. Even in his earliest years, Bing was quite different from Edward Johnson. Viennese-born, Bing had had experience in opera administration in Germany and England. Unlike Johnson, who delegated much of the artistic direction of the company to Frank St. Leger, Bing was his own artistic director, and Max Rudolf served as musical administrator until he went to the Cincinnati Symphony Orchestra in 1958.[33] During the 1949–1950 season, a year of observation inside the Metropolitan, Bing developed his own approach to directing the company. His plans for a new look on the stage of the old Thirty-ninth Street house included four major events—new productions of Verdi's *Don Carlo* and Wagner's *Der fliegende Holländer,* a Broadway-style *Fledermaus,* and the return of Kirsten Flagstad in *Tristan und Isolde* after an absence since

April 1941. For three of these four occasions—the new production of the Johann Strauss operetta and the two Wagner operas—Bing selected Reiner as conductor. Reiner's contract also called for him to conduct *Der Rosenkavalier* and *Don Giovanni*.

On opening night, Fritz Stiedry conducted a new production of *Don Carlo* that immediately defined Bing's artistic style at the Metropolitan. Rolf Gérard's brilliantly executed and beautifully lighted stage design filled the whole of the great proscenium and stage with three-dimensional scenery rather than painted canvas. From Broadway came Margaret Webster to direct an expensive production, financed in large part by a gift from Mrs. John D. Ryan, daughter of Otto Kahn; she sold a Rembrandt painting to raise the money.

For *Fledermaus,* the *Die* dropped for the occasion, Bing again turned to Broadway for Garson Kanin as director, Gérard as designer, and Howard Dietz to adapt the book in idiomatic American English. Bing planned at least twenty performances, partly to release rehearsal time for other productions. Columbia Records made a fifty-thousand-dollar loan to underwrite a national touring company. As part of its five-year contract with the Metropolitan, Columbia would record an "original cast" long-playing album, hoping for once to recoup its annual guarantee to the Metropolitan. In the early planning stage, Reiner was still nominally a Columbia artist, and Bing may well have assumed that Reiner would conduct the recording. Neither Reiner's correspondence nor his diary mention that possibility.

As an observer in 1949–1950, Bing kept in touch with Reiner, planning this production. In a friendly letter on 30 March 1950, Reiner expressed misgivings about a rumored approach to Danny Kaye to play the drunken jailer Frosch. He suggested instead the Broadway comedian Bobby Clark or even Lawrence Tibbett, now retired from opera. He had seen Gérard's scenic work and liked it but thought Dorothy Kirsten better suited to the role of Rosalinda than the Bulgarian Bombshell.[34] Bing had not yet selected Garson Kanin to stage the production, but Reiner cautioned against engaging someone from the theater, recalling the lessons he had learned from nonoperatic stage directors. By early June, however, Reiner was lunching with Kanin, Gérard, and Max Rudolf, deeply involved in planning and casting; unknown to the Metropolitan, he was already committed to RCA-Victor. A week later he signed a contract to conduct thirty-two performances in the 1950–1951 season, including four of *Fledermaus,* for a fee of thirty-two thousand dollars. He stipulated, however, that he would not conduct the operetta on the postseason tour.

Reiner's move to RCA-Victor and the projected recording of excerpts from *Die Fledermaus* created a serious problem for Bing and Columbia Masterworks. Since Columbia could not begin to record the Metropolitan production until after its premiere on 20 December, RCA-Victor would have its abbreviated version in the stores months ahead of Columbia's. Moreover, Reiner and RCA-Victor included in their cast singers whom the Metropolitan needed for its premiere and subsequent Columbia recording. Max Rudolf reviewed these casting problems in a memorandum to Bing that was obviously a summary of previous discussions.[35] At one point, Bing proposed to both record companies that the Metropolitan *Fledermaus* recording be a joint project.[36] Rudolf later recalled a disagreeable meeting between George Marek and Alan Kayes of RCA-Victor and Bing, in which the record company executives boasted that their recording would be more strongly cast than Columbia's.[37] In mid-September Bing wrote to Reiner, referring to a recent conversation, expressing the hope that they were "still on speaking terms," and proposing an early talk to resolve problems. Two weeks later Bing suggested that they proceed with the "original arrangement" for Reiner to prepare and conduct the first performance, with another conductor to direct the Columbia recording.[38] Bing may have been making a genuinely conciliatory effort to keep Reiner at the helm of the important *Fledermaus* project or merely humoring him while seeking a replacement.

Meanwhile, Reiner and Kanin became embroiled over the staging of the operetta. Opera conductors require eye contact with their singers as much as they do with orchestra players, to assure coordination between stage and pit. As Reiner had learned with John Houseman in *The Devil and Daniel Webster,* the relationship can become confrontational if the director lacks musical experience. By the end of October 1950, with Reiner deep in rehearsals for *Der fliegende Holländer,* the conductor wrote Kanin a characteristically blunt refusal to accept certain staging recommendations that he felt impinged on his musical authority.[39] Nine days later Bing wrote to Kanin, upholding Reiner on such matters as conducting the overture facing the audience (Reiner: "Not feasible"), the use of a gypsy band onstage in the second act, and the choice of a waltz for Balanchine's ballet.[40] In his account of the difficulty of working with Reiner, Kanin recalls the conductor's objection to having the chorus lying on pillows during "the orgy scene." "You will sing *standing* and facing the audience and keeping your eyes on *me.* Very hard, this ensemble, to keep together."[41] There is no question in the correspondence that Bing fully backed Reiner in his conflict with Kanin. Despite Kanin's assertion that such disputes over staging resulted in Reiner's replacement as conductor of *Fledermaus,* the recording problem was more critical.

By mid-November Bing had solved his recording problem with Eugene Ormandy. With special permission from the Philadelphia Orchestra, Ormandy accepted what would be his only full-scale operatic engagement. Bing could now take a firm line with Reiner. On 22 November the two had what must have been an acrimonious telephone conversation, followed a day later by a letter from Bing referring to the "unfortunate conversation" in which Reiner "withdrew" from *Fledermaus,* claiming that he was "bored" with the work after recording it, and citing difficulties with the staging.[42]

On 24 November, in a "conciliatory" gesture, Reiner tried to rescind his withdrawal, but Bing advised him with thanks by letter that he had already engaged Ormandy.[43] In his *5000 Nights at the Opera,* Bing does not mention telling Reiner in this letter of Ormandy's engagement but gives an amusing account of "Reiner [raging] about the house trying to find out who his replacement would be before I announced it to the press," while he hid out in a secret office.[44] Bing felt reasonably sure that Reiner would not walk out completely as long as he could look forward to conducting Kirsten Flagstad's return in *Tristan und Isolde* later in the season. Reiner's assistant Tibor Kozma continued the preparation begun by Reiner until Ormandy's arrival a week before the premiere.[45] According to Kanin, Ormandy announced to the company at his first rehearsal, "And for heavens sake, don't look at *me* all the time."[46] Max Rudolf later recalled Reiner's walking into his office, unannounced as usual, to find Ormandy there in conference. "I hear that you are going to conduct *Fledermaus.* Do you know the piece?"[47]

While preparing *Fledermaus,* Reiner was also rehearsing a new production of *Der fliegende Holländer,* which the Metropolitan had not presented since 1940. Hans Hotter made his American debut in the title role. The first of eight performances took place on 9 November, shortly after opening night. The critical reception was mixed, but generally more favorable than for the *Parsifal* of 1949. Even though its staging was, along with *Don Carlo,* a harbinger of the Bing era, this production was never given again. Reiner conducted *Don Giovanni* for a second season in a row, this time in nine performances, with Paul Schoeffler returning on 17 November for the title role. At the opening performance, Nadine Conner, the scheduled Zerlina, was ill, and Roberta Peters made her unscheduled debut with great success. Born in the Bronx, she was twenty years old when she began a distinguished career at the Metropolitan. She was one of Reiner's favorite singers.

Before Kirsten Flagstad's return, Reiner conducted two performances in December of *Tristan und Isolde* with Helen Traubel. Although Kolodin questioned Reiner's tempos, he granted that his performance had authority. Thomson, as usual more sympathetic to Reiner, heard "transparency of sound" and "musical line and substance." All agreed that the production was visually "shabby."[48] On 22 January 1951 Kirsten Flagstad returned to the Metropolitan Opera after a controversial absence of ten years. An Austrian émigré himself,

Bing drew a distinction between such artists as Flagstad and Wilhelm Furt-wängler, whom he viewed as passive toward the Nazis, and such active sym-pathizers as Elisabeth Schwarzkopf and Herbert von Karajan. He never per-suaded his board to allow Furtwängler's engagement before his death, and he engaged Schwarzkopf and Karajan only after a "decent" interval. In 1951, how-ever, there was considerable outcry against Flagstad, enough for Bing to take the precaution of having special police in the auditorium. That measure proved unnecessary, for the audience greeted her at the end of the prelude with pro-longed applause and, after the "Liebestod," called her back for nineteen curtain calls. Originally scheduled for but two performances of *Tristan und Isolde,* Flag-stad returned for a third, postseason appearance. To assuage her resentment over the return of Flagstad, Helen Traubel sang the Marschallin in the first four of seven *Der Rosenkavalier*s that Reiner conducted that season. On the 1951 post-season tour, Reiner conducted *Tristan und Isolde* in Boston and Cleveland and *Don Giovanni* in Cleveland.

Whereas Johnson had generally formalized contractual arrangements a few weeks before opening night, Bing was corresponding with the Hurok office about the 1951–1952 season as early as mid-January 1951. At that stage, he and Reiner had agreed on eight performances of *Le nozze di Figaro,* six of *Salome,* eleven of *Carmen* in a new production, six of *Elektra,* and six performances of either *Die Meistersinger* or *Otello,* including the postseason tour.[49] Opting for Wagner over Verdi, this pattern prevailed for the succeeding season. By mid-June Reiner and Bing had signed a three-page contract, considerably more detailed than the one-page form previously used. It called for a weekly payment of twelve hundred dollars, without compensation for three weeks of prelimi-nary rehearsals, no more than an average of two performances a week, and the Metropolitan's consent for any engagements with symphony orchestras.

Reiner began rehearsals for *Le nozze di Figaro* on 24 October and con-ducted its first performance on 19 November, four days after a new production of *Aida* that opened Bing's second season. The Mozart comedy was essentially the old Herbert Graf production, which Reiner had conducted on tour in 1949 and in three performances in his second season. The nine performances, in-cluding one in Philadelphia, were scattered through the season with many cast changes, including notable appearances by Victoria de los Angeles as the Con-tessa and Cesare Siepi as the Conte.

Reiner again conducted *Salome,* which had become something of a call-ing card for him and was still a drawing card in the box office. Again Ljuba Welitsch sang the title role, this time in all five performances (including one in Philadelphia) between 10 January and 6 February 1952. Elisabeth Hoengen made her Metropolitan debut as Herodias, and Hans Hotter was an impressive

Jokanaan. Set Svanholm sang four of the five Herods, the fifth being taken by Charles Kullman. Reiner had expressed his misgivings about casting Svanholm as Herod in a postcard from the Lido to Max Rudolf the previous summer, suggesting Jan Peerce for the role. Reiner probably recalled that tenor's singing Wagner at Lewisohn Stadium in 1939.

In his five seasons with the Metropolitan Opera, Reiner conducted three new productions. *Carmen* on 31 January 1951 was the most successful of these, artistically and in the box office. It was one of the standard operas badly in need of rehabilitation that Bing intended to offer in new productions; it had not been restaged since 1923. For this new production, Bing turned again to Rolf Gérard for brilliant and sometimes garish decor and, for its staging, to Tyrone Guthrie, another director associated mainly with the legitimate theater. There is no indication that Reiner found him objectionably ignorant of opera. When shortage of money made it impossible to stage the act IV *corrida* in an outdoor setting, Gérard and Guthrie placed the action, not too convincingly, in the Toreador's dressing room.[50] Otherwise, this production served the Metropolitan well for many years, at Thirty-ninth Street and on tour.

For his leading lady, Reiner had Risë Stevens, whom he had known earlier and had advised to go abroad for experience. By the time Reiner arrived at the Metropolitan, she was already an established star, one of the Americans who carried the company through the war years. In the three seasons that he conducted *Der Rosenkavalier,* she sang most of the Octavians, and in the spring of 1951 she recorded excerpts from that opera with Erna Berger. *Carmen* was, of course, a long-time favorite of Reiner. He had not conducted it in the theater since Dresden, although he had recorded it the previous spring with the same leading lady. Despite misgivings about the staging, Virgil Thomson, a great admirer of French music, praised the production highly: "Fritz Reiner's musical handling from the pit is a marvel of clarity and animation. The production is unquestionably a success. . . . I suspect that I shall remember it as the most convincing I ever saw."[51] Although there were only four performances in New York that season, Reiner conducted five *Carmen*s on the postseason tour. After the first performance, Risë Stevens wrote warmly to Reiner of her high regard for his collaboration over many years. *Carmen* was "the greatest thrill of all," thanks to the conductor's responsive understanding.[52]

What Irving Kolodin chronicled as "one of the tautest, most explosive versions of *Elektra* the theater has ever housed" received five performances, the first on 18 February 1952. Olin Downes in the *Times* reported that *Elektra* aroused the most enthusiastic audience reception of any opera in Bing's two years at the Metropolitan.[53] Reiner's searing performance of the orchestral score received the unusual accolade for a conductor at that time of a solo curtain call.

Regina Resnik later recalled how she had been on the receiving end of Reiner's humor during rehearsals for *Elektra*. Long a favorite singer of the conductor, she had endured his teasing during rehearsals for what he insisted was her gaining weight. Actually she was in the early months of a pregnancy that she had not disclosed to anyone at the Metropolitan. At one rehearsal, in Chrysothemis's exchange with Elektra, Resnik came to the younger sister's anguished proclamation, "Kinder will ich haben!" At this Reiner banged his baton on his stand, shouting, "That's it!" He turned to the stage manager: "Somebody get her a chair." A few months later, when Resnik's first child was born, Reiner sent her a dozen roses with a card reading "Kinder sollst du haben." [54]

For a second season, Reiner conducted *Die Meistersinger* in four performances in New York and one on tour in Boston. During the intermission of a Saturday afternoon broadcast of *Parsifal* on 12 April 1952, Reiner participated in the weekly Opera Quiz. Unfortunately this has not been preserved.

In April 1952 Reiner and Bing signed a contract for the coming season, repeating the terms of 1951–1952 except for an increase to fifteen hundred dollars for performances on tour. In what was to be his final season at the Metropolitan Opera, Reiner conducted five operas, four of them repeating productions he had done earlier—*Der Rosenkavalier, Don Giovanni, Carmen,* and *Die Meistersinger*. His fifth assignment, at the request of the composer, was the American premiere of Stravinsky's *The Rake's Progress*.

The Metropolitan had telecast opening night for three seasons as a sustaining program. In 1952 it turned to closed-circuit paid television in the hope of reaping some financial return. On 11 December 1952, shortly after the announcement of Reiner's Chicago engagement, *Carmen* was transmitted to theaters in twenty-two cities. Audience members paid three dollars and up for the dubious privilege of watching a hazy black-and-white image projected on a large screen, accompanied by poor sound. The venture, undertaken by Theater Network Television, was not a success either for the entrepreneur or for the Metropolitan. They dropped plans to offer two more such telecasts.

In 1952–1953 there were six performances of *Die Meistersinger,* one of them in Philadelphia. Irving Kolodin found *Der Rosenkavalier* "orchestrally . . . one of the finest *Der Rosenkavaliers* to Reiner's credit at the Metropolitan, which put it among the best ever." [55]

During his American career, Reiner conducted two operatic world premieres—Menotti's *Amelia al ballo* and Moore's *The Devil and Daniel Webster*—and the American premieres of Milhaud's *Le pauvre matelot, Elektra* in the original German, and Stravinsky's *The Rake's Progress*. For the Metropolitan production of his opera, Stravinsky himself requested Reiner as conductor and George Balanchine as director. For the part of Anne Truelove, the composer would have preferred Elisabeth Schwarzkopf, who had sung the role in the Venice premiere, but Bing rejected her because of her Nazi taint. Hilde Gueden sang instead. Stravinsky would have preferred Eugene Berman as designer, but librettist W. H. Auden objected to him, so Horace Armistead received the commission.[56] For the 14 February 1953 premiere, Reiner began rehearsals with the singers on 24 October and with the chorus and orchestra in December. Eugene Conley was Tom, Mack Harrell was a notably musical Shadow, and Blanche Thebom was Baba, with Paul Franke, Martha Lipton, Lawrence Davidson, and Hugh Thompson in supporting roles. Falling on a Saturday matinee, the first performance was broadcast nationally. In the course of little more than a month there were four more performances, all with the same cast.

Reviewing the American premiere of *The Rake's Progress,* the New York critics split along predictable lines. Olin Downes complained of "this tedious labored artificial score."[57] In keeping with his advocacy of contemporary music and his high regard for both Stravinsky and Reiner, Virgil Thomson waxed rapturous: "A definitive performance . . . especially the orchestra. . . . Words fail me. The impeccable Fritz Reiner, who conducted, and the composer, who knew what he wanted . . . have given us a musico/dramatic production as nearly perfect as any I have heard in my lifetime."[58] Kolodin, in retrospect, took a middle view: "Reiner's meticulous balancing of vocal and instrumental elements did not clarify all the subtleties of the writing—first performances rarely do—but he gave a high gloss to the sound of Stravinsky's evocation of eighteenth-century aria opera."[59]

Following this American premiere, Stravinsky himself conducted a recording of his opera, with the same cast, as a part of Goddard Lieberson's project of documenting the composer as conductor of his own music. In the opera house, Reiner had used a piano for the recitatives and the graveyard scene because he could not trust the sound of a harpsichord to carry in the large auditorium without amplification. In the recording studio, Stravinsky used the prescribed instrument. Reiner was not present at the recording sessions, although Stravinsky obviously benefited from his preparation.[60]

Then and since, there were reports of Stravinsky's dissatisfaction with Reiner's performance. The surviving evidence is contradictory. At the rehearsals Stravinsky admonished Reiner to make the orchestra play more softly and with shorter note values. Given the importance of the occasion, to say nothing of Stravinsky's outspoken aversion to conductors generally, gossip in New York music circles was inevitable. Nor was there any question of distinct differences in their respective performances—Reiner's as documented in off-the-air transcriptions and Stravinsky's own commercial recording for Columbia. At the same time Stravinsky sent Reiner a telegram during the run of performances offering his "heartiest thanks" and expressing his hope for future collaborations.[61]

Several months later Martin Mayer's review of Stravinsky's recording of *The Rake's Progress* in the December 1953 issue of *Esquire* magazine drew responses from both Reiner and Stravinsky. In it Mayer implied that differences between Stravinsky's recording and Reiner's performances reflected the composer's criticism of the conductor, citing in particular Reiner's failure to use the harpsichord. In a letter to *Esquire* Stravinsky explicitly endorsed Reiner's interpretation; he also wrote a "Dear Friend" letter to Reiner, assuring him of his full confidence.[62] Reiner was one of the few conductors Stravinsky consistently respected, since their first encounter in 1925. Responding to an interviewer in Tokyo in 1959, he listed "the three best conductors of my music, Pierre Monteux and Fritz Reiner, who have become lazy, and Robert Craft." His 1966 collaboration with Craft refers to Reiner as one of "the better craftsmen and conscientious musicians . . . who, incidentally, was an effective antidote to the windmill and grandstand schools." This was as high praise as Stravinsky ever bestowed on a profession that he viewed as the natural enemy of composers.[63]

In addition to the five performances in 1953, there were two more of *The Rake's Progress* the following season, with Alberto Erede conducting. Bing had offered them to Reiner as the only production that season that would have fitted into his Chicago schedule, but Reiner declined. After seven performances in two seasons, *The Rake's Progress* disappeared from the Metropolitan repertory, although it has since been performed as much as any other opera of its period both in America and abroad. For his part, Rudolf Bing never passed up an opportunity to declare that *The Rake's Progress* was the "biggest mistake" of his direction of the Metropolitan Opera.

Reiner's last performance at the Metropolitan Opera House on Thirty-ninth Street was of *Carmen* on Saturday evening, 11 April 1953. After the performance, Reiner, Bing, and their wives met in the general manager's office for a private farewell. This was not, however, Reiner's last performance with the company, for he joined it on tour for ten performances in April and May, more than in any other season, of *Carmen, Der Rosenkavalier, Don Giovanni,* and *Die Meistersinger*. His final appearance with the company was on 26 May in Toronto; appropriately, the opera was *Carmen*. The next day in Toronto, Reiner gave a cocktail party for the members of the orchestra before entraining for Rambleside.

Toward the end of the season, Reiner looked back on his American career since 1922. He recalled the "incredible emergence of the American composer" in which he had played a part, and he paid tribute to the quality of American orchestras as "unsurpassed in the world." The orchestra and chorus of the

Metropolitan, he declared, were without equal. Reiner noted further that it was easier to program new music with symphony orchestras than in opera.[64]

However, before taking over the Chicago Symphony Orchestra, Reiner had one more operatic engagement to fulfill in Naples. Instead of the Milhaud *Christophe Colomb* postponed from the previous year, he conducted four performances of *Carmen* in an arena near Naples. To spend as much time as possible at Rambleside preparing for the Chicago season, he limited his trip to a month in Naples, except for several days of holiday with Eva and Werner Bartenstein at Ischia. Sailing on the *Andrea Doria* at the end of July, he began rehearsing *Carmen* on 6 August; the performances were 21, 23, 27, and 28 August. The cast included Giulietta Simionato as Carmen and Galliano Masini as Don José. Reiner's diary shows several social engagements, among them a visit with the Bernasconis. They were a wealthy Neapolitan family whose talented teenage daughter Francesca was later piano soloist with the Chicago Symphony Orchestra.

Returning on the *Andrea Doria,* the Reiners arrived home on 10 September, three weeks before setting out for Chicago.

CHAPTER XI

The Road to Chicago

Fritz Reiner took command of the Chicago Symphony Orchestra in 1953 after more than a decade of turmoil following the death of Frederick Stock in the fall of 1942. Brought from Germany by Theodore Thomas, Stock had served as principal violist and assistant conductor until the orchestra's founder died in 1904. During his thirty-eight-year tenure, the Chicago Symphony Orchestra became a vital force in its own community and one of the most important in America. More than any other conductor of a major American orchestra in his time, Stock was imbued with a strong devotion to his city and to its musical culture. He founded the Chicago Civic Orchestra to train young musicians, inaugurated concerts for young people, and persuaded the Orchestral Association to establish a pension fund for retiring musicians. By making Chicago his home, he won the affection of generations of Chicagoans.[1]

Stock's passing in October 1942 confronted the trustees of the Orchestral Association with finding a successor, a task for which their long dependence on him left them ill fitted. To succeed Stock the trustees selected an amiable Belgian, Désiré Defauw. Steeped in the Gallic style, his music-making was the antithesis of the tradition of Theodore Thomas and Frederick Stock. Meanwhile, manager Henry Vogeli, who had served the orchestra for almost as long as Stock had, died in 1943. To replace him the trustees engaged the assistant manager of the Boston Symphony Orchestra, George A. Kuyper, a former English instructor.

When Defauw proved not up to the task, the trustees quietly asked the United States Department of State in late 1946 to advise them on the status of Wilhelm Furtwängler.[2] When the department responded negatively, they then turned to Artur Rodzinski, a one-time protégé of Arthur Judson. Initially Leopold Stokowski's assistant in Philadelphia, he had served successively as conductor of the Los Angeles Philharmonic, the Cleveland Orchestra, and the New York Philharmonic-Symphony Orchestra. Judson had brought him to New York to succeed John Barbirolli in 1943, where he restored that orchestra's quality and prestige. However, Rodzinski confronted the boards and managers who engaged him with a bewildering mixture of ruthlessness, mysticism, idealism, and callous practicality. After nearly four stormy but artistically distinguished seasons in New York, Rodzinski challenged the Philharmonic board with an ultimatum to choose himself or Judson. When the board supported its manager by summarily firing the conductor in the spring of 1947, Rodzinski publicly aired his grievances against both the board and Judson, arousing considerable sympathy in the press. Rodzinski had actually been negotiating for several months with the Chicago Symphony Orchestra, to whom he had already committed himself. So confident was Rodzinski of success in Chicago that he accepted the post there in 1947 without a contract, merely with a handshake, in keeping with tradition at the Orchestral Association.[3]

Rodzinski soon found himself at odds with the Chicago trustees and Kuyper, not only for his erratic behavior but also for artistic aspirations that clashed with their conception of financial practicality. His ambition to involve the Chicago Symphony Orchestra in opera production led first to a brilliant success with Strauss's *Elektra* in concert. He followed this with an expensive staged production in the Civic Opera House of *Tristan und Isolde* featuring Kirsten Flagstad with the Chicago Symphony Orchestra in the pit. Undeterred by the unprecedented deficit these operatic projects incurred, he went behind the backs of the trustees to explore the possibility of selling Orchestra Hall and renovating Dankmar Adler and Louis Sullivan's Auditorium Theater as a venue for both concerts and opera.[4] When the trustees refused his demand for an unprecedented five-year written contract, Rodzinski took his case to the public through the press, as he had a year earlier in New York.

The trustees turned again, this time publicly, to Furtwängler, reviving the same outrage in American musical circles that the New York Philharmonic-Symphony Orchestra had encountered in 1936 by proposing him as successor to Toscanini. As on that occasion, Furtwängler withdrew his name from consideration. After a year with Eugene Ormandy as musical adviser, the trustees reviewed a short list of possible conductors, including George Szell, William Steinberg, Rafael Kubelik, and Fritz Reiner. They rejected Reiner and Steinberg "for reasons accepted by the trustees" but gave careful consideration to Szell before voting unanimously to engage Kubelik for three years beginning in the fall of 1950. Kubelik was thirty-six years old when he assumed his post, at an annual salary of thirty thousand dollars.[5]

One reason for not offering Szell the Chicago post was the trustees' fear that his selection would aggravate the long-standing antagonism of Claudia

Cassidy, the powerful critic at the Chicago *Tribune*. From 1942 on Cassidy had savagely attacked the trustees of the Orchestral Association, first for appointing Defauw and then for dismissing Rodzinski. Cassidy was not one to confine her coverage of the Chicago Symphony Orchestra to reviews of its musical performance. She also commented editorially on the policies, performance, and personalities of the management, the Orchestral Association, and the trustees.

Born in 1899 in southern Illinois, Claudia Caroline Cassidy graduated from the University of Illinois in journalism at a time when women were still rare in that profession.[6] Except for exposure to music via her mother's phonograph, two courses at the university—a semester each of Development of Modern Drama and of Early French Drama—constituted her formal education in the performance arts. She joined the *Journal of Commerce* in 1923 at first as a secretary and later reviewed theater and music. There Cassidy had ample opportunity to develop her colorful style of alternating invective or enthusiasm. She became influential far beyond the paper's limited circulation of twenty-one thousand. When Colonel Robert McCormick lured her to the Chicago *Tribune* in 1942 to cover music and dance as well as theater, her potential readership grew to over a million, making her a major power in Chicago's cultural affairs.

Cassidy was no mere cantankerous curmudgeon. By training and long experience, she was a thoroughly professional journalist. Despite some legendary musical bloopers, she was a stickler for factual accuracy. Professionals and public alike kept her phone ringing with queries of "Who?" "When?" or "What?" for which she checked her voluminous files and answered with invariable courtesy in an uncommonly sweet voice. She surveyed her domain uncompromisingly, enthusing over what she regarded as quality and castigating what she deemed mediocrity or worse. She was merciless in attacking "road" companies from New York, including the Metropolitan Opera, for foisting mediocrity on Chicago. The revival of first-rate opera, after the long drought since the demise of the Chicago Civic Opera in 1932, was an especially fervent cause. It shared priority with her obsession with the decline of the Chicago Symphony Orchestra after Stock. Artur Rodzinski's eagerness to share with her his ambitions for the orchestra and for opera in Chicago cemented her intense devotion to him.

Some summers she and her husband, William Crawford, traveled to Europe, whence Cassidy's dispatches to the *Tribune* alternated between reports of major music festivals and colorful accounts of travel. Not infrequently, her flair for vivid scenic description spilled over into her music criticism:

In the south of France, by an inlet curve of the sea, you come suddenly and breathtakingly on a black cathedral built of lava thrust formidably high and sheer. It dwarfs the landscape and stuns the eye. It is grim, implacable, beautiful and somewhat jubilant, for it seems to be alive. You know it was born of violence and welded in fire, to which at any epic moment it may return. Odd, how clearly I saw it last night when Rudolf Serkin played Beethoven's "Waldstein" in Orchestra Hall.[7]

Cassidy's rejection of Désiré Defauw and her fervor for Rodzinski brought her into direct confrontation with the trustees of the Orchestral Association and with George Kuyper. She condemned these men for insulting a Chicago public that deserved only the very best and for dishonoring the tradition of Frederick Stock and all that he had meant to Chicago. She regarded the trustees as interlopers who had usurped the "public" that had created the orchestra and supported it with contributions and attendance. She was particularly antagonistic toward aristocratic Edward L. Ryerson, a member of a family that had made major contributions to art, education, and culture in Chicago. A long-time trustee, he had been president of the association since 1938.

When the trustees fired Rodzinski, he took his case to the public through Cassidy, who rose to new heights of invective in the *Tribune*. She was merciless in her attack on what she viewed as Kubelik's mediocrity. Of his performance of *Das Lied von der Erde* she wrote that he was "a lost soul from start to finish, tho he thumbed an occasional ride from an orchestra that had every right to seem embarrassed." Describing his accompaniment of Claudio Arrau in the Liszt A Major Concerto, she reported that "Mr. Kubelik rushed at the concerto with exuberance, flailing arms of such violence that the orchestra gave him precisely what he asked for, a coarse grained performance almost unbelievably loud."[8] Kubelik also alienated the musically conservative element of the community, including the trustees and Cassidy, by introducing novel and contemporary music at his concerts—one work new to Chicago on most programs. He and the orchestra were capable of distinguished performances, as witnessed by the series of recordings they made for the Mercury Olympian label.[9] Needless to say, his contract was not renewed after 1953. At the annual meeting of the Orchestral Association in June 1952, Ryerson resigned from its presidency. His successor was Dr. Eric Oldberg, a nationally renowned neurosurgeon with a strong but conservative commitment to music.

As with Cassidy, the tradition of Frederick Stock also motivated Eric Oldberg. The son of Arne Oldberg, long-time professor of composition at Northwestern University, he grew up in a rich musical environment. Stock was a close friend of the family and an idol for Eric from childhood on. His father's musical friendships from study in Vienna introduced him to such artists as Artur Schnabel, Bruno Walter, and George Szell. Although he pursued a distinguished career as a surgeon, he never lost his devotion to music and his deep-rooted enthusiasms and prejudices. He preferred music from the central German tradition, tolerated other standard repertory, and abominated all but the most conservative contemporary music. His wife, Hilda, was an excellent pianist, who played chamber music with members of the Chicago Symphony Orchestra at the Oldberg home. Eric Oldberg inevitably took an interest in the orchestra, becoming a member by invitation of the socially exclusive and self-perpetuating Orchestral Association in 1940. He was elevated to its board of trustees three years later. Because of the intensity of his devotion to music and his outspoken musical preferences, he carried special authority with his fellow trustees, whose primary role was fiduciary.

Eric Oldberg was one of three major figures who played crucial roles in the fortunes of Fritz Reiner during his decade in Chicago, the others being George Kuyper and Claudia Cassidy. The interplay of these three among themselves and with Reiner had important consequences for his role in Chicago. This was especially the case with the mutual distrust between the president, the manager, and the music director until Kuyper's departure in 1959. Oldberg's lack of rapport with George Kuyper amounted to mutual hostility. Kuyper was in his own way something of a prima donna, vain, manipulative, and opinionated. Impressive of stature with arrestingly craggy features and a shock of wavy gray hair, he was a physically commanding figure. He took keen interest, as a former educator, in the content and presentation of the Young People's Concerts, which had been founded by Stock. Since assistant conductors Tauno Hannikainen and George Schick lacked proficiency in speaking publicly in English, Kuyper designated himself as commentator on the youth programs. One of the best professional American orchestra managers, Kuyper was also executive secretary of the Ravinia Festival. As the employer of the players of the Chicago Symphony Orchestra for six weeks every summer, Ravinia was an important adjunct, though organizationally separate. In the absence of a music director there, Kuyper enjoyed considerable influence over its artistic policy. Nor was the Ravinia Festival the manager's only peripheral activity. He took charge of the radio and television programs of the orchestra, in part as its manager and in part as a paid independent production adviser, an anomalous though lucrative arrangement. The trustees countenanced such arrangements as saving the association salary expense.

Despite financial problems in the orchestra's early years and again in the Depression of the 1930s, the postwar Orchestral Association was one of the most prosperous in America, its net assets totaling over eight million dollars, including real estate (primarily Orchestra Hall) valued at one million and endowment funds in excess of seven million dollars.[10] Less than half of those resources was restricted to such special purposes as education (mainly the Civic Orchestra and Young People's Concerts) and pension and sick funds for the players in the orchestra. During the Reiner era, the annual expenses of the Orchestral Association amounted to around a million dollars. This included both the

Symphony Orchestra and the Civic Orchestra, which Stock had founded as a training group.[11] Earned income from ticket sales covered well over half of the orchestra's expense. If endowment income and annual contributions failed to balance the budget, the association could draw on reserves in its unrestricted endowment, counting on a steady flow of bequests to replenish and increase those funds. Such affluence carried its price, for the strong representation of the business community on the board of trustees placed less emphasis on tapping Chicago's philanthropic resources than it did on the prudent management of existing funds.

Although Reiner had conducted *Der Rosenkavalier* in 1940 and the Chicago Symphony Orchestra at Ravinia for a week during the summer of 1937, there was no indication that he saw any long-range significance in these engagements. In the spring of 1948, during Rodzinski's confrontation with the Chicago trustees, Nora Shea told Reiner of Judson's recommendation of him to the Chicago board.[12] But Judson had little influence with the Chicago trustees or management. All this changed in 1948 when Sol Hurok became Reiner's manager. Because of his promotion of ballet, Hurok was a great favorite with Cassidy. He had no difficulty in arranging for Reiner to meet her in November 1948. Such was the importance of this encounter that his press agent briefed Reiner in a long letter on what he should say to this formidable writer. She advised Reiner to concentrate on opera, especially emphasizing his forthcoming affiliation with the Metropolitan Opera and the endorsement of Richard Strauss.[13] This meeting established a warm friendship between the journalist and both Reiners, especially with Carlotta, who skillfully played up her activity in the theater and her continuing personal friendships there. For her part, Cassidy's reports to the Reiners on the Chicago Symphony Orchestra were even more vitriolic than what she was publishing in the *Tribune*, effectively preparing them before they even reached Chicago.

Reiner's four appearances in Chicago in two years—Ravinia engagements in 1948 and 1949, three weeks in Orchestra Hall, and *Die Meistersinger* with the Metropolitan Opera in 1950—firmly established him as a candidate to lead the Chicago Symphony Orchestra. During these visits, the Reiners met influential supporters of the orchestra and of the Ravinia Festival. Among them was Florence (Mrs. Julius) Lackner, who introduced the Reiners to Eric Oldberg at dinner in the luxurious Imperial House restaurant. Although Reiner's campaign for the orchestra suffered a setback in December 1949 when the trustees engaged Kubelik, it did not deter him or his Chicago friends from continuing their efforts on his behalf. Eric Oldberg's election in 1952 to the presidency of the Orchestral Association signaled a decisive shift in its direction.

An interviewer in 1978 reported Oldberg's recollections: "Resolving to restore the orchestra to its earlier prominence, Oldberg confirmed his remembrances of Fritz Reiner's capabilities through a telephone conversation with George Szell, conductor of the Cleveland Orchestra. Without consulting the orchestral Board, Oldberg traveled to New York City in the fall of 1952 and offered Reiner the conductorship of the Chicago Symphony Orchestra. Reiner accepted Oldberg's proposal and awaited confirmation from the Board."[14]

This laconic account oversimplified the actual process. Given Oldberg's well-known respect for the Cleveland conductor, he probably discussed the position with his friend before agreeing that Cassidy's antipathy toward him would have made his engagement impossible. Rather than approach Reiner directly, Oldberg first did so through Florence Lackner, and Reiner responded through the Hurok office. Meanwhile, in her "On the Aisle" column in the *Tribune* of 9 November—one of her periodic recapitulations of the Rodzinski affair—Claudia Cassidy openly speculated about Reiner. This probably reflected discreet inquiries from Oldberg seeking her advice and support on a replacement for Kubelik. Around this time Oldberg also invited several long-time musicians from the orchestra to his home for an informal supper, at which he explicitly sought their views on possible conductors. Philip Farkas, then first horn in the orchestra, later recalled discussion of Reiner: "He's difficult, but he's good." The musicians suspected that Oldberg had already made up his mind but was seeking their support.[15]

Finally, Oldberg arranged to meet Reiner in his Central Park South apartment at lunch on Sunday, 23 November, for a confidential discussion of a subject not known to his board. At some point Reiner asked his close friend at the Metropolitan Opera, Francis Robinson, to sound out Cassidy directly for her views on his taking the Chicago post. Cassidy later wrote that he had himself asked her, "Shall I come to Chicago?"[16] Meanwhile, Oldberg disclosed his negotiations to the trustees and sought their approval. He returned to New York to meet Reiner on the morning of Sunday, 7 December 1952, when they reached a basic understanding for the conductor's engagement.

Fritz and Carlotta Reiner arrived in Chicago a week before his first rehearsal with his new orchestra. His diary shows meetings with Oldberg at lunch and dinner that may have included friends or, more likely, some of the trustees. Reiner also had the principals of the string sections to his hotel to discuss bowings. He impressed these hardened musicians by playing *Ein Heldenleben* at the piano from memory.[17] At the first rehearsal on 9 October, he took charge of an apprehensive orchestra, actually firing one player: "I don't accept that kind of playing in my orchestra." Philip Farkas recalled: "In a two-hour rehearsal he pulled us apart and put us together again . . . and we needed it, we all knew that.

And when he put it back together and we went straight through *Ein Helden-leben,* it was a revelation. . . . As he went out the door, he was the only calm one. The rest of us were wringing wet. One of our wags in the orchestra, (second violinist) Royal Johnson, said, 'Well, not much of a conductor but an awfully nice fellow.'" [18]

A week later Reiner conducted a program consisting of Berlioz's overture to *Benvenuto Cellini,* the Brahms Second Symphony, and *Ein Heldenleben.* During the next ten weeks, in addition to the regular weekly subscription concerts in Orchestra Hall, he conducted the orchestra in seven other cities in Illinois, Wisconsin, Michigan, Iowa, and Ohio.

Reiner's first Chicago contract was for three years, until the spring of 1956, with renewal to be negotiated a year earlier, when his contract was extended to 1959. These contracts called for him to conduct some sixty concerts during twenty to twenty-two weeks of the twenty-eight-week season, with provision for adjustments in pay for more or fewer weeks or concerts. His initial 1953–1956 salary was forty-five thousand dollars for twenty-two weeks, reduced by two thousand dollars for each week of vacation beyond six. For 1956–1959, the terms were essentially the same, except his annual compensation was increased to over fifty thousand dollars. Reiner spent as little time as possible in Chicago, usually arriving from Rambleside in time to start rehearsals and leaving for home once the postseason recording sessions ended. He took little interest in the other activities of the Orchestral Association: the Civic Orchestra, the Young People's Concerts, and programs in high schools.

Reiner inherited a potentially fine band of musicians, the core of them deeply imbued with a German tradition going back to Theodore Thomas and Frederick Stock. Many of Reiner's players had indeed played under the latter. A symbiotic relation with its training affiliate, the Chicago Civic Orchestra, further reinforced the cohesiveness of the orchestra. Civic instructors were leading players in the symphony, where nearly a quarter were former Civic students. That relationship unquestionably promoted cronyism, in which Civic applicants had an inside track by virtue of their teachers' influence. It also established a strong tradition and esprit de corps in the senior orchestra. Moreover, both Rodzinski and Kubelik had chosen well in filling important principal positions from outside Chicago—Adolph Herseth on trumpet, Arnold Jacobs on tuba, Bert Gaskins on piccolo, Clark Brody on clarinet, and Leonard Sharrow on bassoon. Reiner already knew and liked some of them from guest conducting with other orchestras. In his first two seasons Reiner brought to Chicago principal cellist János Starker and violinist Victor Aitay from the Metropolitan Opera and oboist Ray Still from Baltimore.

The president of Local 10 of the American Federation of Musicians was James C. Petrillo, then at the zenith of his power as head of the AFM. Although local subordinates dealt with Kuyper on day-to-day issues, they cleared important matters with Petrillo at his national office in New York, where Kuyper frequently had to go to discuss Chicago union business with him. Petrillo excluded the members of the orchestra from these negotiations, taking a paternalistic approach: "My boys want this" or "My boys want that." He forbade the formation of a committee representing the orchestra players similar to that in most other professional orchestras. Although the minimum weekly salary for the twenty-eight-week season was under $150 in Reiner's first five years, at least two-thirds of the one hundred players in the orchestra received "overscale" of as much as twice that figure or more. Nor did the contracted weekly salary include telecasts, recordings, or teaching Civic Orchestra students. Once Petrillo and Kuyper had settled on contract terms that each knew his respective colleagues could accept, Petrillo met at lunch with Oldberg for a formal ratification.

Turnover in the personnel of the Chicago Symphony Orchestra under Reiner was relatively modest. In his first two years in Chicago there were sixteen changes in an orchestra personnel of one hundred, several of them by attrition, voluntary or under pressure, and some by direct firing. Oldberg was especially protective of older musicians who had played under Stock and whom he viewed as members of the orchestra's family. By long-standing practice in major orchestras, one of a new conductor's prime prerogatives was the choice of his own concertmaster. When Reiner came to Chicago in 1953, he did not make an immediate change, retaining John Weicher in the position to which Stock had appointed him. Despite Oldberg's friendship with Weicher and his appreciation of the violinist's link to the Stock tradition, Reiner made no secret of looking for a more congenial concertmaster. In this he moved with uncharacteristic caution. He consulted such colleagues as Isaac Stern and Zino Francescatti and listened to a number of qualified violinists. After much consideration, he decided in December 1958 to engage Sidney Harth for the position, moving Weicher to principal second violin and designating him as personnel manager.

During his ten seasons with the Chicago Symphony Orchestra—seven of them full-time and the last three only partial—Fritz Reiner conducted nearly five hundred compositions.[19] He did not rely merely on music he had played earlier but added significantly to his own repertory. More than a third of the music he conducted in Chicago was new to him. Equally important, he introduced sixty compositions not previously heard on Chicago Symphony Orchestra programs. Three hundred and fifty out of five hundred compositions were by composers living when he played them, and forty were by American composers. However, at this point in his career he was not anxious to undertake the kind of exploration of new idioms that he had in Cincinnati and Pittsburgh, especially in the face of the conservatism of both Cassidy and Oldberg.

Reiner programmed the first performances of the suite from Copland's *The Tender Land,* the Divertimento by the Russian composer Alexander Tcherepnin, then a resident of Chicago, and *Souvenirs* by Samuel Barber. The latter occasioned some disagreement between the composer and the conductor, who proposed deleting the "Pas de deux" section. Finally Reiner acceded to Barber in deference to "a father's wishes."[20] Reiner also programmed Barber's *Prayers of Kierkegaard* (with Margaret Hillis's Concert Choir), Virgil Thomson's Cello Concerto (with Pierre Fournier), Lukas Foss's Second Piano Concerto (with the composer), Alan Hovhaness's *Mysterious Mountain* (which Reiner recorded), and works by Alvin Etler, Bernard Heiden, Charles Turner, Wallingford Riegger, Randall Thompson, Arne Oldberg, and Alexei Haieff.

Nor did Reiner neglect music by modern European composers. He gave the American premieres of Milhaud's Symphony no. 7, Rolf Liebermann's Concerto for Jazzband and Symphony Orchestra (recorded), and Malcolm Arnold's Symphony no. 2. From him Chicago heard for the first time Hindemith's Violin Concerto and Cello Concerto, Prokofiev's Cello Concerto, Ginastera's *Variaciones concertantes,* and von Einem's *Capriccio.* For the first time in his career, he programmed music by Anton von Webern, introducing to Chicago the Six Pieces for Orchestra, opus 6, and that composer's orchestration of the Ricercare a 6 from Bach's *Musikalisches Opfer* on successive programs in November 1957. He sought the American premiere of the orchestral version of the "Golden Calf" music from Schoenberg's *Moses und Aron,* but the high price asked by the composer's widow for the performing rights dissuaded him. He offered most of the Bartók orchestral music already in his own repertory, though little of it was new to Chicago. He added to it the Viola Concerto (with principal violist Milton Preves), the Third Piano Concerto (with Géza Anda), and the Music for Strings, Percussion, and Celesta. Anda also played the Second Piano Concerto, and both Yehudi Menuhin and Isaac Stern played the composer's Violin Concerto no. 2. Reiner offered a variety of Stravinsky's music, ranging from *The Firebird* and the suite from *Pulcinella* to the Symphony of Psalms and the arrangement of Bach's chorale *Vom Himmel hoch;* he offered the first Chicago performance of Stravinsky's partly serial ballet score *Agon.* His concert programs also included a few substantial opera excerpts in concert, most notably from *Der Rosenkavalier* with Astrid Varnay and from *Elektra* with Inge Borkh, Martha Lipton, Frances Yeend, Paul Schoeffler, and Julius Patzak. In the Orchestra Hall performances of *Elektra,* Reiner placed the singers on a high platform behind the orchestra and devised an effective enhancement of the shattering conclusion by having the stage lights suddenly dimmed.

With Fritz Reiner conducting twenty or more weeks of its subscription seasons, the Chicago Symphony Orchestra needed to engage few guest conductors. The assistant conductors, George Schick at first and later Walter Hendl, conducted at least one week of subscription concerts. Until his illness in 1960, Reiner played the central role in selecting guests, but his contract required the approval of the trustees. At one point Oldberg had to reassure his fellow trustees that newspaper reports of an invitation to Herbert von Karajan were not definitive and that Reiner would always refer such matters to them. In the fall of 1955, while Reiner was in Vienna, Carlo Maria Giulini began a long association with the Chicago Symphony Orchestra, making his American debut on 3 November. Giulini was uniquely beloved by the musicians and reciprocated with a special affection for them. Igor Stravinsky, Leopold Stokowski, Sir Thomas Beecham, Bruno Walter, and George Szell also appeared as guests with the orchestra. Walter and Szell were Oldberg's houseguests when they came to Chicago. Cassidy's antipathy to Szell limited his Chicago appearances. She once wrote to Carlotta that Szell had come down with a raging fever and his temperature had "shot up to 89." Reiner urged Kuyper to engage Leonard Bernstein on at least one occasion before his former pupil became conductor of the New York Philharmonic. He firmly rejected a lady conductor, who had been pestering him for some years, even for a Saturday night popular concert: "(1) Chicago is not ready for this sort of experimentation; (2) it might create the impression of a 'Sideshow'; (3) there is no future for a female orchestra leader with a male orchestra; (4) she wants to use my invitation to get other engagements; (5) the lady is obnoxious; and (6) she is no Lollabrigida."[21]

Claudia Cassidy and her colleague Seymour Raven at the *Tribune* had waged a relentless campaign against associate conductor George Schick, partly because of his association with Kubelik and partly because they viewed his previous operatic experience as beneath contempt. Nevertheless, Reiner was in no hurry to engage another associate until Schick resigned effective April 1956.[22] For the season following Schick's departure, concertmaster John Weicher took charge of the Civic Orchestra and the Young People's Concerts, with Kuyper continuing as commentator in the latter. Weicher also conducted those Saturday evening programs not assigned to guests engaged by way of audition. In the fall of 1957 Reiner and Kuyper engaged Samuel Antek for several Young People's Concerts. A former violinist in the NBC Symphony Orchestra, Antek was scheduled to make his first appearance as associate conductor at a Saturday evening popular concert in early February 1958 but died suddenly on 23 January.

Reiner then turned to Walter Hendl, one of his pupils at Curtis who had succeeded Leonard Bernstein as Rodzinski's assistant in New York before becoming conductor of the Dallas Symphony Orchestra in 1949. Knowing that Hendl would be leaving Dallas at the end of the 1958 season, Reiner announced his engagement as associate conductor on 22 March 1958. His duties included the Young People's Concerts, most of the Saturday evening concerts, at least one week of subscription concerts, playing piano in the orchestra, and generally assisting Reiner. Weicher continued to direct the Civic Orchestra. Hendl conducted his first Saturday concert on 5 April and took over a Tuesday afternoon subscription concert on the twenty-second when Reiner suffered a shoulder pain.

Although Hendl came to the Chicago Symphony Orchestra as Reiner's protégé, George Kuyper quickly established a close relation with him. In part this was the natural outgrowth of their working together on the Young People's Concerts. Kuyper had relinquished his role as commentator but continued to advise Hendl on programming and presentation. Given the tensions between Kuyper and Reiner—to say nothing of the conductor's suspicious inclinations—Reiner at times viewed Hendl's closeness to the manager as evidence of disloyalty. Reiner took special offense when Hendl told Donal Henahan of the *Daily News* that Jascha Heifetz had specifically requested that he conduct the recording of the Sibelius Violin Concerto scheduled for January 1959. Although Hendl may have been unaware of the actual circumstances, Heifetz had in fact wanted Reiner to conduct this recording session, which fell in the conductor's midseason vacation. (Reiner was also annoyed that Heifetz would not appear in concert, as most other recording soloists did.) To salvage an important recording session, Kuyper and RCA-Victor persuaded Heifetz to accept Hendl as conductor for the session. Henahan's report of Heifetz's "request" offended Reiner by what he took to be disloyalty on Hendl's part.

On the other hand, Reiner appreciated Walter Hendl's admirable service as associate conductor, especially his associations with younger American composers. Reiner could confidently count on him to step in whenever he was indisposed. Hendl conducted other RCA-Victor recording sessions with soloists whom Reiner did not want to accompany. More than most who held such positions with major orchestras, Hendl had significant audience appeal and an ability to build a following with his music-making. Since Reiner took no interest in the Young People's Concerts and little in the popular concerts, his associate had considerable independence. Hendl worked more closely with Kuyper than with Reiner in both areas. In January 1959 Kuyper persuaded the board of the Ravinia Festival Association to engage Hendl as its first artistic director, while Kuyper remained its executive secretary.

One of Reiner's earliest repertory concerns was the inclusion of major choral works. The orchestra had been relying on local amateur groups, which Reiner found wanting. During his first season he used the men from the Northwestern University Choral Union in the Brahms *Alto Rhapsody*. Unwilling to avoid in his second season what he regarded as a necessary part of an orchestra's repertory, he scheduled Samuel Barber's *Prayers of Kierkegaard* and Carl Orff's *Carmina burana* in March 1955 and, in his final concert, the Beethoven Ninth Symphony. Since the Barber and Orff works were difficult, he persuaded the trustees to bring Margaret Hillis's professional Concert Choir from New York during its tour of the Midwest. For the less demanding Beethoven symphony, he called on the Swedish Choral Club. When Hillis's 1956 tour did not materialize, Reiner again turned to a local group for the Stravinsky Symphony of Psalms. The Northwestern University Choral Union proved to be less than satisfactory because of conflicts with the university's academic schedule. The brief chorus at the end of *Elektra* required only a few professionals from the Lyric Theater. Bruno Walter conducted the only major choral work in the 1956–1957 season, Brahms's *Ein deutsches Requiem,* again with the Northwestern University group. Meanwhile, Reiner was planning the Verdi *Requiem* for 1957–1958, intending eventually to record it. Although Reiner had hoped to reengage the Concert Choir for the Verdi, the cost of bringing it to Chicago from New York proved to be prohibitive.

At that point Reiner persuaded Oldberg and the trustees to have Hillis organize a local chorus under the auspices of the Orchestral Association as a permanent choral adjunct. In May 1957 the association announced the establishment of this Chicago Symphony Orchestra Chorus. Initially, it was completely amateur, but there was an understanding both with the choristers themselves and with the American Guild of Musical Artists for a year-by-year professionalization of the group.[23] Reiner planned to call on this new chorus twice in the 1957–1958 season—for *Messiah* in December and for Verdi's *Requiem* in April. However, when Bruno Walter indicated that his January 1958 appearance would be his last in Chicago, Oldberg wanted him to conduct the Mozart *Requiem* with the new chorus at his farewell concerts. It would have been impossible for Hillis to prepare *Messiah* and the Mozart *Requiem* with a new chorus in so short a time. Reiner, at Oldberg's urging, reluctantly relinquished what would have been the first appearance of the new chorus in December and turned to the Apollo Musical Club for *Messiah*. In his visits to the evening rehearsals of the chorus, Reiner was delighted with its progress under Hillis, with whom he developed an extremely cordial working relation, based on her ready understanding of his requirements. Recalling their working association, Hillis called

Reiner a "pussy cat." Founded at Reiner's instigation, the Chicago Symphony Orchestra Chorus became under Margaret Hillis's leadership one of the most distinguished in America; Hillis announced her retirement in 1991.

As so often happened when Reiner scheduled a major "production," the preparation of the Verdi work was a period of mounting tension. The reluctance of soprano Leonie Rysanek to sing out fully in orchestra and choral rehearsals especially annoyed Reiner. To accommodate the daytime work of the choristers, it was necessary to hold their rehearsals with the orchestra in the late afternoon. Because of the musicians' union contract, these rehearsals could not run past seven o'clock. The final afternoon rehearsal of chorus, soloists, and orchestra was stormy: though fully satisfied with the chorus, Reiner was extremely demanding of the orchestra. When the cello section entered a bar early at the end of the "Hostias," Reiner furiously reprimanded its leader, János Starker, breaking his baton on the edge of his music stand. As seven o'clock approached, Reiner, after first ignoring warning signals, finally stormed off the stage in a rage.[24] A few weeks later the cello section gave a party for their leader, who was leaving to teach at Indiana University and to pursue a solo career. Their farewell present was a tie clasp in the form of a broken baton.

Given Reiner's dislike of outdoor summer concerts, it is not surprising that he resisted the blandishments of the Ravinia Festival Association and of George Kuyper to conduct his orchestra at its summer home. They finally succeeded in the summer of 1958, offering Reiner a chance to prepare for the coming tour to the East Coast with a week of four concerts. The Reiners did not like the hotel accommodations in nearby Highland Park and divided their stay between the home of their old friend Florence Lackner in Highland Park and their apartment in downtown Chicago. The concerts were a great success, although the Reiners declined all invitations to social events that were an important part of the Ravinia season. Reiner never again accepted a standing invitation to return to Ravinia.

By the time Reiner arrived in Chicago in 1953, the nagging problem of opera there finally showed signs of resolution. Carol Fox and Lawrence Kelly organized the Lyric Theater of Chicago, offering a three-week season in November 1954 at the Civic Opera House that featured the American debut of Maria Callas in *Norma*. In early planning for the first season, Kelly had approached Reiner about presenting a fully staged *Salome* at the Civic Opera House. Reiner's orchestra would be in the pit, and performances would be included in the orchestra's subscription series.[25] Although Fox repeated Kelly's inquiries later, such a joint venture by the Lyric and the Chicago Symphony Orchestra would have been prohibitively expensive and logistically complicated for both parties. During the second Lyric season Callas severed her relations with the company. When Reiner returned from Vienna in 1955, shortly after Callas's angry confrontation with a process server in her dressing room, he commented to the awaiting press: "It is incredible what a prima donna will not do for publicity. Such bad taste. But it is no surprise to me. I have seen many singers act that way. They can be a problem, especially opera singers. They need a strong hand to keep them disciplined."[26] With Cassidy's support Fox forced Kelly out of the company, renamed the Lyric Opera of Chicago. With the growing success of the new company under Fox's leadership, Cassidy's pressure to involve the Chicago Symphony Orchestra in opera production waned.

During Reiner's years in Chicago, the four daily newspapers dominated the media—the *American*, the *Daily News*, the *Sun-Times*, and the *Tribune*. Arts coverage by radio and television was negligible. Radio station WFMT had started its programming of classical music but seldom carried special news coverage of the orchestra. The orchestra distributed routine press releases by mail to a basic press list. The orchestra's publicity department consisted of approximately one-fourth of one person's time.[27] Partly because of limitations of staff but also because of an institutional reticence, the Chicago Symphony Orchestra actually shunned publicity, other than minimal promotion of concerts. Typical of this policy was the explicit decision not to announce officially the renewal of Fritz Reiner's contract in 1958. Having suffered in previous years from unfavorable press coverage, the trustees regarded such matters as private. Publicity or press conferences would simply invite questions concerning salary and other information that they did not want to disclose, even if this resulted in media speculation quite wide of the facts. The Orchestral Association invited the major media to such ceremonial occasions as its annual meeting, to hear summary reports and confirmation of decisions already settled in private by the trustees. At the first board meeting over which he presided in 1952, Oldberg proposed that he could take care of the press himself, excepting weekly routine announcements of concert programs from the office. He made himself available, selectively, to the press, sometimes off the record, offering what he deemed to be proper information. The trustees were also reluctant to support publicity efforts that might glamorize their music director and create the impression that he was the central figure in the organization. They overlooked the possibility that the quality of his music-making was essential to their institutional image and their fund-raising potential.

This policy satisfied Reiner's obsession with privacy. However, he complained of insufficient promotion of activities in which he was especially interested, such as Margaret Hillis's new chorus. As the leading celebrity in the organization, Reiner should have been the focus of more official publicity than he received, but this was partly Reiner's own fault. Both he and Carlotta were reluctant to give "human interest" interviews, especially with journalists whom they considered musically uninformed. They offered less resistance to interviewers from such national media as weekly news magazines or from such specialized publications as the *Saturday Review* or *High Fidelity,* whose writers Reiner would see in New York or at Rambleside. RCA-Victor persuaded him that such coverage would bolster the sale of recordings and generate royalties. Reiner generally regarded the primary function of public relations personnel as shielding him from the media. Although he claimed, as did many celebrities, that he never read about himself, errors of fact or unfavorable comment in the media brought angry telephone calls from Carlotta to Orchestra Hall.

Each of the four major Chicago daily newspapers employed full-time personnel to cover music, both to report news events and to review performances. At the *Daily News,* Irving Sablosky and later Donal Henahan took a comparatively impersonal and professional approach to their coverage of the Chicago Symphony Orchestra. Roger Dettmer of the *American* first met the Reiners, before they came to Chicago, in the spring of 1953 at a party given by Virgil Thomson in New York. Both Reiners enjoyed his distinctive writing style and sophisticated manner and respected his musical judgment.

At the *Sun-Times,* Felix Borowski carried on the tradition of old-style writing about music until his death in 1956 at the age of eighty-four. Born in England, he had been a major figure in Chicago as composer, teacher, and critic since 1897 and personally knew both Thomas and Stock. For many years the orchestra employed him as program annotator; such a relationship was not uncommon in earlier times, regardless of potential conflict of interest. Despite frequent visits in the Orchestra Hall office, Borowski scrupulously observed the boundaries of propriety and confidentiality. His successor was Robert Charles Marsh, educated in philosophy and mathematics.[28] He was an avid admirer of Arturo Toscanini, Artur Rodzinski, and George Szell, but not, to the same degree at least, of Fritz Reiner. Reiner resisted Marsh's efforts to establish personal contact and came increasingly to dislike him, especially for what he regarded as factual laxity and lack of musical judgment. When Marsh compared his tempos in a Beethoven symphony performance unfavorably with Toscanini's, Reiner grumbled, "Did Toscanini leave him the metronome in his will?" On another occasion, after an unfavorable review of a recording, Carlotta wrote to RCA-Victor asking the company to send no more records to Marsh for review.[29]

None of these journalists wielded the influence and power in the community or with the Orchestral Association that Claudia Cassidy and her associate Seymour Raven at the *Tribune* did. In keeping with the policy established by Oldberg, the management announced all major news "on *Tribune* time." The other journalists resented this favoritism, just as they begrudged Cassidy's access to Oldberg and the Reiners. At the same time, relations between Cassidy and Kuyper remained hostile and mutually distrustful. Cassidy had long disliked Kuyper for what she viewed as his arrogance in defending conductors and policies she did not like. He held her in contempt for her lack of musical knowledge and for her usurpation of decision making at the Orchestral Association. He also resented her direct access to both Oldberg and Reiner, convinced that she was undermining him with them. At the outset at least, Claudia Cassidy was the Reiners' closest friend in Chicago. For their first years in Chicago, his diaries show more entries for "Claudia and Bill" than for all other social engagements in Chicago combined. Well before Reiner and Kuyper became working colleagues, Cassidy had fully acquainted the Reiners with the manager's shortcomings. Though Carlotta occasionally disclosed confidential information about the orchestra, Cassidy never published these confidences. Still, they may have given her "leads" to pursue and enabled her to pry information from others. It especially annoyed Kuyper to receive calls from Cassidy checking on information that could have come only from the Reiners.

Initially Cassidy was a Reiner enthusiast. Although she expressed occasional misgivings about a specific performance as a falling-off from his customary high standard, a Reiner performance that truly moved her could inspire some of her most extravagant prose. At the same time, her enthusiasm for Reiner did not diminish the fervor of her other personal crusades. She and Raven periodically revived charges that a small group of elitists had usurped the Orchestral Association and continued to advocate restoring the Auditorium Theater as the home of the Chicago Symphony Orchestra. As early as the spring of 1953 Raven delivered a lesson on proper public relations in a letter chiding Reiner for discussing with another reporter matters that the *Tribune* writer regarded as "off the record."[30] On some issues, Raven became the *Tribune* point man in criticism of the orchestra; after a Callas benefit concert with the Chicago Symphony Orchestra, he attacked Kuyper for including the players' services, by a technicality in the union contract, in their basic weekly responsibilities instead of paying them extra.[31] On another occasion he posted himself in the balcony of Orchestra Hall, where he could see for himself whether there was a change in woodwind players of which the management had failed to inform the *Tribune*.

Reiner's attitude toward Cassidy was something on which he was uncharacteristically reticent. When Philip Farkas left the orchestra in 1960 to teach at Indiana University, Reiner remarked to him, "Well, at least you won't have to read Claudia Cassidy every morning."[32] Carlotta, however, counted the critic among her closest friends, combining a genuine affection with looking out for her husband's best interests. Reiner, for his part, must have enjoyed Cassidy's company to have spent so much time with her when he was so busy with his work. On the other hand, with friends he could trust, especially away from Chicago, he expressed open contempt for her musical opinions but grudging respect for the power she wielded.

The Reiners did not consider the social obligations of a "resident" conductor in the same light. Their withdrawal from what many supporters of the orchestra viewed as an integral part of a conductor's role was a constant source of resentment in Chicago society. The trustees viewed it as a hindrance to their ability to raise money to support the orchestra. Eric Oldberg was among those who yearned for a return to the tradition of Frederick Stock and the role he had played as a loyal resident Chicagoan. To such criticism Reiner bluntly responded, "They have my music; they cannot have my body."

CHAPTER XII

Chicago Triumph

When Fritz Reiner arrived in the fall of 1953, the Chicago Symphony Orchestra had been broadcasting regularly over radio or television since 1945. Sponsored locally by Chicago Title and Trust over WGN-TV, its one-hour telecasts in 1953 were also carried on the short-lived Dumont network, which distributed kinescope films of the broadcasts to other cities.[1] Although billed as the "Chicago Symphony Orchestra," the program group employed approximately half its personnel in rotation. Some of the trustees regarded this series as beneath the proper dignity of their orchestra, because of both its reduced size and the lighter repertory it played. The additional income for the players tempered these misgivings somewhat, especially because the sponsor paid them, relieving the musicians' pressure in negotiations for the basic seasonal contract. Kuyper strongly supported the telecasts, for, as manager, he recognized their value. He also received additional compensation as production adviser. Thanks to Kuyper's interest in television, the Chicago Symphony Orchestra received more television exposure than any other American orchestra of that era.

To Chicago Title and Trust, the participation of Reiner in the telecasts assumed major importance, despite the extra expense to accommodate the conductor's insistence on a larger orchestra and his higher fee, initially one thousand dollars for each telecast. Since the telecasts fell outside his basic contract, these additional fees were a significant supplement to his forty-five-thousand-dollar salary. However, Reiner became increasingly disenchanted with the telecasts when friends in New York, especially at the Hurok office and RCA-Victor, reacted unfavorably to the quality of both sound and picture of the 1953 broadcasts from the Dumont affiliate in New York.[2]

At the same time the sponsor's marketing advisers discovered that Reiner was not the drawing card they had expected. For the season beginning in the fall of 1957, the sponsor announced "a new and exciting dimension . . . breaking out of the annual pattern of sponsoring the Chicago Symphony Orchestra exclusively, [as a] result of several years' research and planning—in an effort to appeal to a larger and more diversified audience."[3] This season opened with Reiner conducting the Chicago Symphony Orchestra with Alec Templeton as soloist, followed by the Duke Ellington band and an evening of folk music including Richard Dyer Bennett, the Weavers, and Mahalia Jackson. Reiner conducted only the final program of the season in April. His fee for each program was now two thousand dollars. The reduced orchestra appeared on several other programs, with guest conductors and soloists from the subscription season.

In May 1958 Chicago Title and Trust announced the termination of the series after thirteen years on radio and television. Working directly with WGN-TV, Kuyper devised a new weekly series, *Great Music from Chicago,* in which the orchestra would play a major part. The station saw in this project the possibility of selling the series in videotaped syndication to other independent stations throughout the United States and abroad.[4] Again Reiner conducted only the first and last programs. Kuyper assigned four programs to Walter Hendl, more than any other conductor. This series continued through 1963, but Reiner's illness limited his later participation.[5]

The trustees were reluctant to allow radio broadcasting of the public concerts from Orchestra Hall for fear of reducing ticket sales. During the 1957–1958 season, however, they found a radio outlet in New York for these concerts that would not affect the Chicago box office. Louis Schweitzer, Reiner's neighbor in Weston, owned radio station WBAI-FM in New York City. Reiner and Schweitzer proposed that WBAI carry the weekly Thursday evening concerts in New York only. To satisfy the players and their union, Schweitzer made a substantial contribution to the orchestra's pension fund. Reiner, of course, was delighted to obtain exposure for his Chicago orchestra in New York. Stephen F. Temmer, the WBAI producer in charge of these broadcasts, traveled to Chicago each week to supervise them. Using a single-microphone arrangement similar to that employed earlier by Mercury for its recordings, he made excellent audio tapes of some of the finest performances of Reiner and the Chicago Symphony Orchestra.[6]

Beginning in 1916, the Chicago Symphony Orchestra had made occasional phonograph recordings with Stock, Defauw, and Rodzinski.[7] In the three seasons before Reiner's arrival, the orchestra recorded a distinguished Mercury "Olympian" series under Kubelik.[8] Since Mercury's contract ran into 1954, the company was anxious to lure Reiner away from RCA-Victor and continue recording with the orchestra. Although Kuyper suggested at one point that the two companies share the conductor and the orchestra, Reiner and RCA-

Victor were adamant about their exclusive contract.[9] Eventually the orchestra terminated its Mercury contract, after recording four LP sides in January 1954 conducted by Antal Dorati.

With great fanfare at a press conference in December 1953, Reiner, the Orchestral Association, and RCA-Victor signed exclusive contracts, setting in motion the production of a series of recordings that have since attained a unique renown.[10] Like Reiner's own contract with RCA-Victor, the association's called for exclusivity and royalties based on actual sales of recordings, under a complicated formula for sharing the cost of the orchestra personnel by the conductor, the association, and the company. On 6 March 1954 Fritz Reiner and the Chicago Symphony Orchestra taped their first recordings for RCA-Victor, Strauss's *Ein Heldenleben* and the dance from *Salome*. Two days later they recorded *Also sprach Zarathustra*. In April the recording crew returned to Orchestra Hall, where Reiner heard and approved the edited Strauss tapes and recorded the Brahms First Piano Concerto with Artur Rubinstein and two Mozart symphonies.

Despite its acoustic shortcomings for both audience and players in performance, Orchestra Hall proved to be an ideal venue for stereophonic recording. There was no proscenium as such: the walls around the very wide but shallow stage created a flat curve that rose to a concave ceiling, giving the effect of a shallow shell. Although the extreme width of the stage made it difficult for the players to hear one another, it provided a broad soundstage ideal for stereophonic recording. Without an audience, the empty hall produced a warm resonance, well balanced over the frequency range.[11] With few exceptions, the orchestra retained its regular concert seating for recording. The stereophonic versions of these recordings reveal that during his first season Reiner seated the second violin section to his right, an arrangement he abandoned for the rest of his time in Chicago. When Reiner arrived in Chicago, velour drapes covered the wall behind the orchestra and below the chorus risers to reduce sound reflection. When Leopold Stokowski, always an experimenter with acoustics, was guest conductor early in 1958, he had the drapes taken down for his concerts. After discussion with him and some experimentation of his own, Reiner also preferred to have the orchestra play against a bare wall, for both concerts and recordings.[12]

Initially RCA-Victor made two sets of tapes, one monaural and the other experimentally in stereo. Producer Richard Mohr and engineer Lewis Layton worked in one control area in the basement of Orchestra Hall with single-track Ampex machines to produce the tapes from which the monaural recordings would be processed. Meanwhile John Pfeiffer and Leslie Chase, in another room, recorded two-track tapes from another set of microphones. By

1956 RCA-Victor developed three-track taping, as a source for both mono and stereo production masters. Henceforth Mohr and Layton made most of the recordings by Reiner and the Chicago Symphony Orchestra.[13]

Recording sessions generally followed concert performances on Thursday evening and Friday afternoon, usually on Saturday morning and afternoon or on the following Monday. Such scheduling made it possible to pay the musicians at a lower "symphony rate." More important, four or five rehearsals and two performances preceded the recordings. Before the sessions began, Mohr went over the music with Reiner to plan their work and to anticipate problems that he and Layton would encounter in microphone placement, balance, and recording level. Reiner seldom needed to rehearse during a session, which generally began with the orchestra playing a few short passages to guide the technicians.[14] Once these details of balance and dynamics were set, Layton made few adjustments of the controls, only to accommodate exceptionally soft or loud passages to the magnetic limits of recording tape. Mohr and Layton were remarkably adept in avoiding a sense of dynamic compression on the master tape. Transferring this sound to the production of vinyl discs was another matter, involving problems of phase shift, cutting instruments, and the physical characteristics of the lacquer masters and the final vinyl. In an effort to adapt its high-fidelity recording process to the limitations of home reproducing equipment, RCA-Victor at one point introduced some calamitous tampering with the excellent original sound, which fortunately was preserved on the original master tapes.[15]

With Mohr, who had produced most of his recordings since 1950, Reiner enjoyed a close working relation and a warm affection. Both he and Carlotta appreciated the producer's iconoclastic wit and urbane professionalism. Reiner was naive about the recording process, unaware of the editing and technical capabilities of audio tape that Otto Klemperer once characterized as a *Schwindel*. Working in long "takes," Reiner preferred to correct mistakes or secure better playing with longer "inserts" than with short snippets that would have satisfied technical needs. From playbacks in recording sessions or from edited masters, he listened for the musical result, unconcerned with how it was attained. On at least one occasion he was so absorbed in musical detail that he was not aware that the stereo channels were reversed on the playback equipment.

Reiner applied to his recordings even more exacting standards than he set for his concert performances. His recordings sometimes betrayed a caution absent from the more spontaneous performances that preceded them. If balance or ensemble did not satisfy him, he consulted with Mohr on how to achieve what he wanted, preferably from the podium and only as a last resort at the control panel. His consistent tempo and dynamics made Mohr's tape-editing much easier. He sometimes let slips pass in the interest of the overall musical effect. However, when he taped the Beethoven First Symphony in 1961, he was so dissatisfied with the finale at the end of a tiring day that he insisted on calling another session to record less than five minutes of music. The next day he was satisfied after a few minutes of a minimum two-hour call; the result was one of Reiner's most characteristic performances on records.

Determination of the repertory to be recorded involved interminable discussions and correspondence between Reiner and the officials of RCA-Victor. For recordings to follow well-rehearsed performances, Reiner had to fit RCA-Victor's repertory into his concert schedule or, as some claimed, to fit the concert repertory into RCA-Victor's needs. This caused much anguish among the Chicago critics, who complained of RCA-Victor's domination of the repertory offered Orchestra Hall subscribers. On a few occasions Reiner declined the company's suggestions. He removed the Mahler First Symphony from his projected concert repertory and recording schedule until he could make a key change in personnel. Undoubtedly Reiner would have liked to record music that RCA-Victor vetoed, particularly orchestral music of Bartók that he had not recorded. The company had a long tradition of artistic archconservatism. (It would be difficult to substantiate the reputations of Reiner, Stokowski, and Koussevitzky as champions of contemporary music from their recorded repertory for RCA-Victor.) Eric Oldberg's own preferences were equally conservative: he vetoed potentially lucrative recordings of Ferde Grofé's *Grand Canyon* suite and Carl Orff's *Carmina burana* as beneath the dignity of the Chicago orchestra.

In ten years Reiner recorded 122 compositions with the Chicago Symphony Orchestra. RCA-Victor viewed Reiner as a specialist in the music of Richard Strauss and such twentieth-century composers as Rachmaninoff, Ravel, Prokofiev, Stravinsky, and Bartók. Although he recorded Beethoven symphonies throughout his Chicago years, he never completed the full cycle of nine. Despite having Charles Munch and Pierre Monteux on its roster, RCA-Victor allowed Reiner to record a few pieces by Debussy and Ravel; his performances of the latter's music were among his most memorable. Recording, for Reiner, always had its financial motivation, and he preserved a substantial popular repertory, ranging from Rimsky-Korsakov's *Scheherazade* to overtures by Rossini, Mendelssohn, Smetana, and Tchaikovsky. RCA-Victor also extensively documented his mastery of the second beat in three-quarter time in music by the various waltzing Strausses.

A consummate collaborator with instrumental and vocal soloists, Reiner was in great demand to record concertos. He strongly resisted being regarded, as he put it, as RCA-Victor's "house conductor," unless he could anticipate substantial royalties from recording with a popular soloist. Because of his disinclination to share top billing or royalties with others, concerto proposals required protracted negotiations. After a successful recording in the fall of 1955, not preceded by concert appearances, of the Tchaikovsky Piano Concerto no. 1, he later resisted booking Emil Gilels in concert, because of his strong feelings about the Russian suppression of the Hungarian uprising of 1956. (At that time he had conspicuously replaced a Shostakovich symphony with the Bartók Concerto for Orchestra on a concert program.) Under pressure from RCA-Victor, he finally agreed to present Gilels on subscription concerts in the Brahms B-flat Concerto in February 1958, only to learn at the last moment that the soloist had not memorized the work in time. After playing the Tchaikovsky concerto on Thursday and Friday subscription concerts, Gilels, Reiner, and the orchestra recorded the Brahms concerto. This required six and a half hours of short "takes" that challenged Mohr's editing expertise. Gilels was apparently oblivious of Reiner's feelings toward him; a friend reported that photos of only two conductors had a place of honor on the piano in his Moscow home—those of Toscanini and Reiner.

Less successful was RCA-Victor's effort in January 1956 to record four concerted works with Artur Rubinstein. Reiner and Rubinstein's collaboration in the Brahms D Minor Concerto in April 1954 had been a major success artistically and financially for all concerned. To include all four pieces in concert performances, Rubinstein spent a week in Chicago, playing in four concerts the Rachmaninoff C Minor Concerto and Rhapsody on a Theme of Paganini and the Liszt E-flat and Grieg concertos. Obviously, the pressure of so many recordings, rehearsals, and concerts strained the endurance and patience of two elderly and temperamental musicians. Rubinstein resented Reiner's sarcastic remarks about his mistakes and walked off the stage. All of Mohr's diplomatic skill was required to persuade him to finish taping the Rachmaninoff works. The Grieg and Liszt were recorded later in New York with another conductor. Rubinstein did not appear again with the Chicago Symphony Orchestra during Reiner's lifetime. His imitations with a long Upmann cigar of a certain Hungarian conductor became regular after-dinner entertainment. In 1962, when Art Buchwald interviewed Rubinstein at his home in Paris, the pianist described Reiner as "the only [conductor] I never really liked." Carlotta wrote Buchwald that her husband had always admired Rubinstein but suggested that he may have offended the pianist by maintaining that Chopin was not really a Polish composer but rather French.[16]

Reiner's recorded repertory with vocal soloists included only one operatic project, excerpts from *Elektra* with Inge Borkh, Frances Yeend, and Paul Schoeffler in April 1956. Had RCA-Victor been willing, Reiner would probably have programmed the entire opera in concert and subsequently recorded it. For the *Elektra* excerpts Reiner had the soloists sing from a special platform at the rear of the orchestra at both the concerts and the recording sessions. Despite the singers' objections, this placement produced an extraordinary aural perspective. His two Mahler tapings also called for vocalists, Lisa della Casa in the Fourth Symphony and, in 1959, Maureen Forrester and Richard Lewis in *Das Lied von der Erde*.

Reiner's participation in the November 1955 reopening of the Vienna State Opera led to concerts and recording sessions with the Vienna Philharmonic, not directly for RCA-Victor but through the American company's arrangement with British Decca.[17] Discussions between Reiner, RCA-Victor, and Decca began early in 1955, with a proposal for Decca to record the dress rehearsals and two performances of *Die Meistersinger* in Vienna.[18] In order to record abroad, Reiner needed the permission of Petrillo's American Federation of Musicians. The union did not want conductors of American orchestras to make recordings abroad rather than with their own orchestras, which were more expensive than foreign groups. Reiner's first sessions with the Vienna Philharmonic in September 1956 included stereo versions of two Richard Strauss tone poems, *Till Eulenspiegels lustige Streiche* and *Tod und Verklärung,* that he had recorded monaurally six years earlier in New York. Commenting on the "bewildering inconsistency" of the Vienna Philharmonic, Decca's recording producer John Culshaw noted that "some sessions under Fritz Reiner in September of that year had been a revelation."[19] Further discussions with Decca included the possibility of Reiner's recording *Die Walküre* or *Siegfried* with the London Symphony Orchestra, but Reiner viewed those operatic projects skeptically because they did not include sufficient rehearsal time.

In earlier years Reiner rejected European offers unless they enhanced his prestige. He was not prepared to commute to and from Europe by air, as many of his contemporaries were increasingly inclined to do. Once appointed to the Chicago post, he received more prestigious invitations, but his schedule in Chicago prevented his accepting a Strauss *Capriccio* in Munich, a *Don Giovanni* in Venice, and a *Parsifal* at La Scala with Maria Callas as Kundry. In 1956 he turned down a *Ring* in Venice, to be staged by Wolfgang Wagner, suggesting to his Italian agent that Wagner should invite him to Bayreuth in the summer when his Chicago schedule permitted. There was one invitation he could not refuse—to conduct a new production during the reopening of the Vienna State Opera in November 1955. This invitation was handled by Lacy Hermann, husband of the Viennese soprano Hilde Gueden, who had sung with Reiner at the Metropolitan. Although he spelled his first name "Lacy" on his New York letterhead, the Reiners addressed him as "Laci," a Hungarian nickname for László. In December 1954 Hermann wrote Reiner, referring to previous conversations and letters, about the possibility of his inviting Karl Böhm to make his American debut in Chicago. Böhm, as director of the Vienna State Opera, would reciprocate by inviting Reiner to conduct *Die Meistersinger* during the gala reopening of the opera house in November 1955. Since the Austrian conductor had enjoyed the favor of the Nazi government, having replaced Fritz Busch in Dresden in 1934, his American debut was a matter of some delicacy. Hermann expressed concern to Reiner about Claudia Cassidy's reaction to Böhm, who had heard that the critic could ruin a musician's American career. Carlotta replied that Cassidy had liked an *Ariadne auf Naxos* that Böhm had conducted in Salzburg.[20] Böhm made his American debut in Chicago in February 1956.

Sailing in mid-August on the *Queen Mary,* the Reiners went by rail from Cherbourg to Vienna via Zurich, where they visited Eva and her family. Shortly after they reached Vienna, Tuśy arrived from Ljubljana for a surprise visit with her twelve-year-old son, Vovček, whom Carlotta found "enchanting." The Reiners also attended a party for the New York Philharmonic-Symphony and Dimitri Mitropoulos, in Vienna during a European tour. Following two weeks of rehearsals, the Reiners returned to Rambleside briefly in late September before proceeding to Chicago to open the orchestra's season. They flew to Zurich from New York on 6 November and then on to Vienna. For their first transatlantic flight, Claudia Cassidy enlisted the help of a friend at Swissair to arrange for their every comfort, including two lower berths in the sleeper section of the plane. They arrived in Vienna in time for the opening of the restored opera house and for five days of final rehearsals. Reiner conducted *Die Meistersinger* on 14 November and again on the twentieth. His old colleague Herbert Graf was responsible for the staging, and Robert Kautsky designed sets and costumes in the style of Dürer's Nuremberg.

Reiner's *Meistersinger* received mixed reviews, more cordial from the Viennese press than from some foreign visitors. The *Neues Österreich* found Reiner's interpretation faithful to the score in its detail, his tempos in the Bayreuth tradition. The *Weltpresse* took satisfaction that the spotlight was on the music rather than on the conductor and praised Reiner's unity of conception, his light but sure hand, and the clarity of his authentic interpretation.[21] On the other hand, in *Opera* Peter Heyworth found *Die Meistersinger* "the worst of the five productions" and compared Reiner unfavorably with Böhm, whom he had heard conduct the same opera eighteen months earlier at the Theater an der Wien. He observed that Reiner had come "with certain fixed and transatlantic notions of how an orchestra should sound and proceed[ed] to impose his tastes on a body with quite different characteristics and traditions." He declared it "a fundamentally misconceived affair, lacking any of the humanity, warmth, and tenderness that should irradiate the music."[22] Equally devastating was the terse verdict of Henry de la Grange in the New York *Times: "Die Meistersinger* proved disappointing mainly because of Fritz Reiner's conducting."[23] In letters to Lacy Hermann in Vienna and to Martin Feinstein in Hurok's office, Carlotta was indignant that the only appearance of an American-based conductor in so important an international musical event should be dismissed in such a cavalier fashion. Hermann replied that de la Grange was a part-time correspondent for the *Times* and a friend of Menotti, "which explains why he doesn't like Reiner."[24] By the time the restored opera house opened, Böhm was under heavy attack in Vienna. His perceived quid pro quo with Reiner was but one of the complaints against him that led, a few months later, to his replacement by Herbert von Karajan.

Between performances of *Die Meistersinger,* Reiner found time on 17 November for a concert with the chorus of the Gesellschaft der Musikfreunde and the Vienna Symphony Orchestra. The program included the Stravinsky Symphony of Psalms and Orff's *Carmina burana.* Eva Bartenstein was in Vienna and attended the rehearsals for the choral concert. She recalled that her father worked the chorus so hard that its chairman protested that his choristers were tired from standing so long. Reiner replied, "I have been on my feet also." The Viennese press praised Reiner's command of the contemporary idiom. Returning to Chicago after an absence of four weeks, he told of receiving invitations to bring his American orchestra to Europe.

This Vienna appearance led to further engagements in Europe that met Reiner's requirement for major exposure. Thanks to these contacts, Reiner arranged a busy summer in Europe in 1956. Crossing to Genoa on the *Andrea Doria* in late July, the Reiners were driven to Montecatini Terme, where they spent two weeks "taking the cure." Carlotta found the climate oppressive and preferred spas in Switzerland and Austria. From Montecatini their Venetian chauffeur drove them to Cortina, where they visited Cassidy's friends William and Edith Mason Ragland. En route they stopped at Pontecchio, where an old caretaker recognized Reiner. From Cortina they went to Salzburg, arriving four days before Reiner's concert with the Vienna Philharmonic on 22 August. He conducted Berlioz's overture *Le carnaval romain,* Beethoven's "Emperor" Concerto with Claudio Arrau, and Strauss's *Also sprach Zarathustra.*[25] From Salzburg, the Reiners' driver took them to Zurich and Lucerne via Ulm and Munich.

During his visits with Eva in Zurich, Reiner had met Walter Schulthess, an important Swiss impresario. He arranged for Reiner to conduct in 1956 at the annual summer festival in Lucerne. For his first appearance there on 1 September 1956 Reiner led the Philharmonia Orchestra from London in a program that included the *Carnaval romain* overture and *Also sprach Zarathustra*. Walter Gieseking played the Beethoven Fourth Piano Concerto, a few weeks before his death. Following this appearance in Lucerne, the Reiners flew from Zurich to Vienna for the conductor's first recordings with the Vienna Philharmonic.

Returning to open the Chicago season on 3–4 October, Reiner again reported European interest in a tour by the Chicago Symphony Orchestra. In 1958 Schulthess brought Reiner back to the Lucerne Festival to conduct the Berlin Philharmonic Orchestra, with Rudolf Serkin as soloist. Following Reiner's Ravinia week, he and Carlotta sailed to Naples on the *Cristoforo Colombo*. Among their fellow passengers were Igor and Vera Stravinsky, whose company they enjoyed. Reiner later sent to Cassidy a copy of a photograph taken of the two musicians.[26] This time Reiner turned down recording sessions in Vienna, preferring not to interrupt his vacation with anything but the Lucerne concert. The Reiners proceeded by car on a five-day tour through Burgundy, the Loire Valley, and Normandy before embarking on the *United States* at Le Havre on 11 September. They rested for two weeks at Rambleside before returning to Chicago to prepare for the orchestra's tour to the East Coast.

The previous spring Reiner had made his first guest appearance with another American orchestra since taking his post in Chicago. For one week in March 1958 Reiner exchanged podiums with Eugene Ormandy. It was Reiner's first appearance with this orchestra in the Academy of Music in its winter subscription series in twenty-two years. His concerts were in Philadelphia on 7, 8, and 10 March 1958 and in Carnegie Hall on the eleventh. The program included the Berlioz overture to *Béatrice et Bénédict,* Mozart's "Linz" Symphony, Ravel's *Rapsodie espagnole,* and the Prokofiev Fifth Symphony. According to Carlotta, the Philadelphia Orchestra welcomed Reiner warmly and played superbly.[27] In both Philadelphia and New York, Reiner received glowing reviews. Of the Carnegie Hall concert, Ross Parmenter wrote: "Those whose interest was primarily musical must have been fascinated, as this listener was, by hearing a musician of such penetrating intelligence manipulating an ensemble of such subtlety and refinement as the Philadelphia to carry out his individual and always interesting musical ideas."[28]

Dorothy ("Buffie") Chandler had been trying for several years to lure Reiner to the Los Angeles Philharmonic, as a part of her effort to raise that orchestra to first rank. By early 1959 she was well on her way, with Eduard Van Beinum as music director of the orchestra. She herself headed a campaign to build a new home for the orchestra as an alternative to Philharmonic Auditorium. To the Reiners she extended the kind of hospitality that they seldom experienced elsewhere: a chauffeured limousine was at their disposal, and they had the finest suite in the Town House Hotel. Reiner conducted two subscription pairs in Los Angeles in January 1959. His programs included the Prokofiev Fifth Symphony and Stravinsky's Divertimento from *The Fairy's Kiss*. Despite some misgivings about the quality of the orchestra at that time, Reiner accepted Chandler's invitation to return to Los Angeles in 1961; his intervening illness prevented his filling that engagement.

Carlotta Reiner invariably declined social engagements in Chicago because of her husband's busy schedule of work.[29] During twenty or more weeks a year, Reiner conducted an average of three concerts a week, entailing four or five rehearsals. In addition, he conducted television broadcasts and recording sessions. His administrative responsibilities involved almost daily consultations with Oldberg and Kuyper and frequent dealings with New York managements and RCA-Victor by letter or telephone. Although his contract called for the association to provide a secretary for him, Carlotta usually filled that role. As she explained, it would take too much time for him to go down to the office, where he would have to share Kuyper's already overburdened secretary, Ruth Hughes Carroll. Reiner rarely used the grim office set aside for him at Orchestra Hall, except to rehearse with soloists at the piano. Other than his direct contact with Oldberg, Kuyper, and the musicians, Carlotta was the channel through whom Reiner routinely communicated. Even with Kuyper, she frequently conveyed inquiries and instructions on behalf of her husband by telephone: "Doctor wishes . . ." or "Doctor wants to know . . ." Only with Eric Oldberg did she not routinely act as her husband's intermediary, although she typed his letters to the association president. Nor was she ever involved in Reiner's work with the musicians of the orchestra directly or through the management. Backstage, after concerts, she screened friends, fans, and strangers who lined up outside the conductor's dressing room, controlling their access to him.

For their first five seasons in Chicago the Reiners lived modestly at the Whitehall Hotel on Delaware Street. They leased two adjoining suites, one of them set aside as Reiner's private working studio. They paid rent year-round on one suite and seasonally on the other. They took most of their meals at the hotel, in its dining room or in their rooms. On Sundays, when the hotel dining room was closed, Carlotta cooked her husband's Hungarian and German favorites. In May 1958 the Reiners leased a spacious and comfortable furnished duplex at 1320 North State Parkway, their Chicago pied-à-terre for the next three years. In the days before such perquisites for celebrity conductors as association-leased limousines, Reiner rode to and from Orchestra Hall in public taxis, except when a member of the staff or orchestra picked him up on the way to work. After the conductor had finished his work at Orchestra Hall, the stage librarian accompanied him out to the Michigan Avenue sidewalk, carrying his briefcase, to hail a taxi for him. Only for an occasional soloist or guest conductor of exceptional importance did the Orchestral Association or RCA-Victor arrange for a hired limousine to collect the celebrity from his hotel and return him there. Oldberg personally made such arrangements for Bruno Walter and George Szell when they were his houseguests.

Because the Reiners spent less than half a year in Chicago and did not regard it as their legal residence, they sought to list as many as possible of their Chicago expenses as business deductions on their income tax returns. By this time Barton G. Hocker, whom Reiner had first met as an associate of James A. Davidson, had become his trusted accountant and business adviser. After protracted negotiation by "Bud" Hocker and Reiner's Connecticut lawyer, the Internal Revenue Service ruled that the Reiners could deduct only one-fourth of their Chicago expenses. Carlotta therefore kept a detailed record of all expenses connected with their Chicago stay, for she resented every penny paid in taxes. When Kuyper drew up the schedule for each season, Reiner checked with Hocker to ensure the most favorable tax impact.[30]

Aside from Claudia Cassidy and her husband, William Crawford, the Reiners had few friends in Chicago. During their first years there they met several times for lunch or dinner with Reiner's old friend and colleague Claire Dux Swift von der Marwitz. She and her husband were in Salzburg in 1956 when Reiner conducted there. Her failing health limited her social activities, although she remained a faithful patron of Reiner's concerts. When Herbert von Karajan conducted the Berlin Philharmonic on tour in Chicago in October 1956, he joined the Reiners for dinner with Elisabeth Schwarzkopf and Walter Legge. The Reiners were also frequent guests of RCA-Victor at expensive restaurants in connection with recording sessions. They dined occasionally with the Oldbergs, usually at the Casino Club. In May 1955 the Oldbergs honored the Reiners with a cocktail party at the Casino Club to celebrate the twenty-fifth anniversary of their marriage. At Christmas 1955, when Reiner was still in Chicago for concerts, the Oldbergs entertained the Reiners in their home. However, socializing between the Oldbergs and Reiners became less frequent in 1956, and it almost ceased after Hilda Oldberg suffered serious injuries in an automobile accident in the fall of 1957.

By that time relations between Reiner and Oldberg had cooled markedly. The president did not hesitate to express his musical opinions to Reiner, offering detailed criticism of Reiner's plans for a season's repertory. He ended one long letter of detailed critique by explaining his role as that of a "musical adviser." Eric Oldberg was proud of his father's position in the community and at Northwestern University as a composer. Although Reiner had programmed Arne Oldberg's *St. Francis of Assisi,* with Louis Sudler as baritone soloist, in October 1955, Eric felt that Reiner should do more. Reluctant to press Reiner directly, he urged Kuyper to suggest performing another of the elder Oldberg's compositions. In the spring of 1958 Kuyper happily reported to Eric that Reiner would include Arne's *Paolo and Francesca* in the first half of a program featuring *Ein Heldenleben* and Isaac Stern's performance of the Prokofiev Second Violin Concerto. Oldberg responded angrily to the placement of the music on the program. Kuyper reported to Reiner that Oldberg suggested dropping his father's music entirely.[31] In any event, Reiner's program on 30–31 October was as he had originally proposed: Rossini's overture to *La scala di seta,* the Oldberg *Paolo and Francesca,* the Prokofiev concerto, and *Ein Heldenleben.*

Reiner had earlier lent the letters he had received from Béla Bartók to the Hungarian-American musicologist Otto Gombosi, for his work on a projected biography of the composer. Apparently Gombosi supplied copies of the letters to János Demény for his 1954 collection of Bartók's correspondence. Victor Bator, the composer's executor and the curator of the Bartók Archives in New York, protested the inclusion of letters in Reiner's possession without his permission. Reiner ignored Bator's request that all documents, or copies, concerning the composer be sent him for the archives.

With the growing fame of the Chicago Symphony Orchestra under Reiner, both the Hurok office and the orchestra management sought national publicity for their achievement, especially in anticipation of possible tours within the United States and to Europe. *Time* commissioned Boris Chaliapin to paint an oil portrait of Reiner for eventual use on a cover of the magazine. Chaliapin, whose father Reiner had known, came to lunch at Rambleside in August 1957 and returned the following January for a series of sittings that lasted until early summer.[32] *Time* did not use the portrait for a cover, probably because of the cancellation of the 1959 tour to Russia. Chaliapin loaned the portrait to the Reiners, who hung it in their Rambleside living room. After Reiner's death, Carlotta turned down Chaliapin's offer to sell her the painting, and the artist reclaimed it.[33]

During these years the Reiners enjoyed the housekeeping at Rambleside of the totally devoted Ann Gaito, the only servant who stayed with them any length of time. She combined extraordinary competence and total devotion with the ability to stand up to Carlotta's exacting demands. While the Reiners were in Chicago, Ann visited Rambleside regularly, checking on its condition and passing on detailed instructions from Carlotta to the gardener and repairmen. She and Carlotta exchanged an extensive correspondence about Rambleside and Ann's regular visits to Amelia Irwin, Carlotta's mother, for whom the Reiners were financially responsible. Mrs. Irwin had been living in a Bridgeport apartment, but she suffered a stroke in 1956, at the age of eighty-nine. She moved to a nursing home in Norwalk, where Ann Gaito visited her regularly.

While the Reiners led an austere social life in Chicago, Rambleside more than ever became a haven from the pressures of work in Chicago. Many visitors to Rambleside, for lunch or for a weekend, combined business with pleasure in a relaxed and congenial atmosphere. Most were professional or business colleagues—Hurok, Kuyper, and George Marek, Alan Kayes, and Richard Mohr from RCA-Victor. Francis Robinson, from the Metropolitan Opera, was a regular visitor and one of the few whom the Reiners visited in New York for dinner and a performance at the opera. Reiner could be seriously absorbed in business for a time and then, once he had settled it, become a charming and solicitous host. Carlotta worked her magic in the kitchen, either supervising Ann or preparing her own specialties. Meals at the Rambleside dining table were leisurely and genial occasions. Reiner loved good wines, his special favorites being those of the Rhineland and Bordeaux. He ordered these regularly from the Chicago wine importing firm headed by Paul Fromm, who was then just beginning his involvement in underwriting contemporary music.

In 1954 both Reiners prepared and signed new wills. Fritz Reiner also signed over to Carlotta, by quitclaim deed in 1956, his interest in the Rambleside property and improvements.[34] Although this might reflect concern about Reiner's health, it is more likely that it represented prudent planning, given the twelve-year difference in the couple's ages. Carlotta's attitude toward health and the practice of medicine was a mélange of prejudices and misconceptions. Her own Christian Science upbringing and her obsessive concern for her husband's well-being colored her accounts of both their ailments. By turns vague or detailed, they embraced rabid denunciations of specific doctors and the medical profession generally. Reiner's most persistent physical problem was muscular strain, especially in his shoulders and back, which he had treated by various osteopaths and chiropractors.[35] Despite his renowned economy of gesture, it appears that his conducting involved muscular tension not apparent to the audience. On at least one occasion muscular spasms in his shoulder were so painful in the middle of a concert that Walter Hendl had to finish the program. In Chicago, unfortunately, he did not have the therapeutic benefit of the Rambleside swimming pool, which he used daily when weather permitted.

In March 1956 Reiner saw Dr. Wright Adams at Billings Hospital in Chicago for a checkup that revealed an elevated white corpuscle count that Dr. Ellrich, his regular doctor in Bridgeport, had not observed previously. A few weeks after his visit to Dr. Adams, Reiner noted in his diary that he had given up smoking. This was by no means unusual, for he did so periodically, only to resume the habit. A heavy cigarette smoker, Reiner kept a pipe rack and canister of tobacco on his work desk and enjoyed a fine Cuban cigar after a good meal. In 1958 Reiner made a note of a phone conversation: "Ellrich-Aorta little hardening, Card. normal - Sediment normal - Blood count normal - X-ray lungs OK - urine +1 albumen."[36]

On 5 December 1956, excavation for the foundation of the Borg-Warner Building, on the site of the old Pullman Building, threatened the structure of Orchestra Hall, to the south. The Orchestra Hall building actually tilted northward. The city of Chicago and the Orchestral Association closed the building to the public while engineers examined it. Although the offices continued in use, Kuyper moved rehearsals and all public events to the Civic Opera House on Wacker Drive or, when that was booked, to the Medinah Temple. These structural problems gave Cassidy and Raven at the *Tribune* an opportunity to belabor one of their favorite topics, the restoration of the Auditorium Theater as a home for the Chicago Symphony Orchestra. Cassidy had written to the Reiners two years earlier predicting that the demolition of the Pullman Building would create problems for the orchestra. In the fall of 1956 Cassidy and Raven revived in the *Tribune* their doubts about Orchestra Hall, recalling Rodzinski's efforts to replace Orchestra Hall with a renovated Auditorium. An adjoining column quoted Frank Lloyd Wright in support of restoring the architectural masterpiece of Dankmar Adler and Louis Sullivan.

Although Reiner refrained from volunteering his views either on the crisis at Orchestra Hall or on its long-range solution, Carlotta had no such reticence in her letters to Cassidy. She agreed that the Auditorium would be the "best choice."[37] Three weeks after Orchestra Hall closed, Carlotta wrote from Rambleside to her friend at the *Tribune*, there was still no word from Eric Oldberg about the Hall problem. A mutual friend wrote that Hilda Oldberg had remarked how much her husband enjoyed having George Szell as a houseguest with whom he could discuss the problem of Orchestra Hall. Carlotta replied that it was "nice that Eric has Mr. Szell in the house to discuss plans for the new Orchestra Hall. Maybe he will get around to consulting Fritz—seeing that he has two more years to conduct in the building."[38]

The city and various insurance companies completed a thorough inspection of the building and ordered changes in the excavation next door. Undamaged, Orchestra Hall reopened with a Young People's Concert on 17 January 1957. Bruno Walter conducted a pair of subscription concerts on the nineteenth and twentieth. Oldberg, especially anxious that Walter appear in Orchestra Hall, used every contact he and other trustees had with the city government to secure permission to reopen the hall in time for Walter's rehearsals and concerts. For nearly two years the problem of Orchestra Hall preoccupied trustees of the Orchestral Association, who reviewed several proposals, including one recommending construction of a new building on another site.[39] While the trustees deliberated the future of Orchestra Hall, Kuyper urged Reiner to express his views to Oldberg on performance needs. To judge from an undated memo in Reiner's handwriting, he limited his comment to the stage, dressing rooms, and basement facilities.[40] Both Al Pulley and Alan Kayes at RCA-Victor declared that Orchestra Hall was acoustically the best in the country for recording and urged the provision of a special room for the permanent installation of recording equipment.

The *Tribune* reported without comment Eric Oldberg's announcement that the orchestra would remain in Orchestra Hall but that the trustees would continue to plan its renovation. However, Cassidy wrote to Carlotta that there would be no new hall, no Auditorium, because "a little group of men" had wrested control of the Orchestral Association from the Chicagoans who had originally financed it.[41] In these discussions Reiner acted with unwonted circumspection, while Carlotta made no secret of her agreement with Cassidy's advocacy of the Auditorium Theater and her criticism of the trustees. Despite her views, of which he certainly heard a great deal at home, Reiner kept his own counsel. Much as Reiner may have valued Cassidy's support, he was not prepared to become her ally in this particular crusade. The lesson of Rodzinski was not lost on him.

By the mid-1950s the Chicago Symphony Orchestra was the only important American orchestra not to have toured extensively in its own country or abroad, despite its growing fame under Reiner through recordings. Tours by American and European orchestras were viewed as indispensable to an orchestra's and a conductor's prestige. Orchestras also regarded touring as essential in the promotion of their recordings, which, with the advent of the long-playing record, were assuming increased importance in orchestral finances. Foreign countries, and eventually the United States as well, gave substantial financial support to overseas tours as a showcase of national culture.

Nevertheless, the "touring" of the Chicago Symphony Orchestra consisted of ten concerts a year in the dilapidated Pabst Theater in Milwaukee and, once a season, a three-day tour to Michigan, Ohio, Indiana, or downstate Illinois. The annual union contract covered all these services. Reiner conducted no more than half the Milwaukee concerts, which he and Carlotta viewed as a burdensome imposition. He also conducted the three-day tours, for which he received an extra fee.

In mid-1956 Reiner, Kuyper, and Hurok discussed with RCA-Victor the possibility of a transcontinental tour in the summer of 1957. They went so far as to consider a second conductor. For this Reiner recommended Leonard Bernstein, not yet committed to the New York Philharmonic, as "the most gifted of the younger conductors . . . and he is an American!"[42] However, the trustees rejected the project as financially unfeasible. Kuyper and Hurok did not press the issue further once they learned that the Philadelphia Orchestra was booking a similar five-week tour with support from Columbia Records.

The following spring, Oldberg briefed his fellow trustees on possible "grand" tours for 1958–1959. Although the orchestra had received several invitations from Europe, such a tour, he conjectured, would cost at least $150,000 and bring little prestige. A tour to the West Coast would cost $50,000 and bring no prestige. Oldberg preferred a tour to the Atlantic seaboard, if RCA-Victor would guarantee an increase of at least $10,000 in record royalties. Such a tour would cost the association $25,000.[43] Kuyper and Hurok visited Rambleside in June 1957 to prepare an announcement, to be released simultaneously in Chicago and New York, that the Chicago Symphony Orchestra would make a two-week tour, booked by Hurok, to the East Coast in October 1958. Carlotta wrote to Cassidy: "Let us hope that our president doesn't throw a gear in the works. He seems to be a champion gear thrower."[44] The trustees approved the concept of the tour in July, providing that Reiner would conduct ten concerts and that RCA-Victor would help. The announcement, though prepared in June, finally appeared in December 1957, long after rumors had fully anticipated its impact.

After a week of preparatory rehearsals at Orchestra Hall, this tour began at the University of Michigan in Ann Arbor on 6 October 1958 and continued to Cleveland; Rochester; Syracuse; the University of Vermont, Burlington; Boston; New York; Philadelphia; Rutgers University, New Brunswick, New Jersey; and Washington, D.C. The repertory for the ten programs, which varied from city to city, included *Ein Heldenleben,* the Brahms Third Symphony, the Bartók Suite no. 1, Stravinsky's Divertimento from *The Fairy's Kiss,* two excerpts from *Götterdämmerung,* and the *Corsaire* overture by Berlioz. It was a comfortable tour for all—ten concerts in fourteen days, traveling mostly daytimes by train. There was eager anticipation of the trip to Europe and Russia that had been recently announced for the coming summer. At the Cleveland concert, George and Helen Szell visited the Reiners backstage during the intermission but, as Reiner observed later, did not stay for *Ein Heldenleben.* The high point of the tour was the concert on 14 October in Boston's acoustically extraordinary Symphony Hall. Following the Berlioz overture, Reiner's face was all smiles: "For the first time I have really heard my orchestra!" For many years afterward, musicians who played that concert recalled their performance of *Ein Heldenleben* as the most perfect they had ever experienced. The acoustics of Symphony Hall made it possible for them to hear one another and to share the mounting tension of a flawless performance. As one player remarked afterward, it was like a baseball pitcher producing a perfect game, with the players gradually realizing, from inning to inning, as it were, that something extraordinary was happening. Backstage after the concert, Arthur Fiedler complimented several Chicago players: "You're not men—you're gods!" Reiner always recalled that concert in Boston as the finest he had ever conducted.

The audience in Carnegie Hall the next evening included a host of Reiner's old friends and colleagues who had come to hear for themselves what he had wrought in Chicago. One member of the audience remarked on the large representation of conductors who had come there "for a lesson." Paul Henry Lang of the *Herald-Tribune* especially appreciated Reiner's "truly memorable interpretation" of the Brahms Third Symphony: "Mr. Reiner gave an amazing demonstration of his powers of musical concentration, for whether in the treble, the bass, or the middle, as the principal theme or as mere ornament, the motif was always brought out, yet never lost its proper role in the context. The symphony, which reaches its culmination in the last movement, was re-created before us, step by step, and it grew like a cleansing tide sweeping away the debris left on the stage of Carnegie Hall by the smart, smooth, and sentimental performances so often heard there."[45]

It was a happy conductor and orchestra that arrived from Washington at the LaSalle Street Station on the morning of 20 October. The Reiners were among the last to disembark onto the station platform, where Carlotta performed her customary ritual of counting the luggage—all fifteen pieces. While she dealt with the porters, Reiner, a squat figure in a long coat and a wide-brimmed black felt hat, walked deliberately down the platform to the taxi stand. He carried a dripping package of iced caviar, a gift from Karl Bauer of Associated Music Publishers. Beside him, carrying the briefcase of scores, was Walter Hendl, who shared a taxi with the Reiners for the ride to the State Street apartment. A member of the staff followed in another cab with the luggage. Although notified in advance of the arrival, the Chicago press did not send reporters or photographers to record the orchestra's return from its triumphal tour. To cover the tour itself, the Chicago newspapers sent no critics of their own but arranged to republish the reviews from the New York press. Nor were any trustees or other major supporters of the orchestra present anywhere on the trip.

There were no official plans for public observance of Fritz Reiner's seventieth birthday on 19 December 1958. It was the players themselves who spontaneously saluted their leader with a brassy "Happy Birthday" as he came onstage for the Friday matinee concert. Reiner responded, in one of his rare speeches from the stage: "At the threshold of my middle age, I am deeply moved by this demonstration of your friendship and loyalty—and even more I am deeply moved by this marvelous birthday gift by my orchestra. There is no more precious gift than last night's and this afternoon's concerts by my orchestra."[46] He continued with the hope that there would be many more such occasions. The following Saturday evening, Eric Oldberg and the trustees honored Reiner with a formal dinner at the Casino Club. At this festive occasion Oldberg presented to the Reiners a piece of fine Georgian silver. Privately several trustees grumbled over the fifty thousand dollars spent on the eastern tour for the conductor's glorification and expressed apprehension about what the European tour the next summer might cost. The Reiners remained in Chicago until New Year's Day, for recordings of Bartók's Music for Strings, Percussion, and Celesta and the Hungarian Sketches. Then they entrained for Rambleside for a brief rest before filling the engagement with the Los Angeles Philharmonic.

The eastern tour and the celebration of his seventieth birthday marked the apogee of Fritz Reiner's tenure in Chicago and, in many ways, the culmination of his career. In five and a half years he had made the Chicago Symphony Orchestra his own instrument, one of the finest anywhere. Nonetheless, Chicago offered Reiner its share of frustrations. He had to resist pressure to reduce the size of the orchestra and avoid extra pay for important players. Kuyper reported Oldberg's complaints at carrying the load of the orchestra "with little help from the music director" and at being the buffer between the conductor and the trustees.[47] When Oldberg brought up the renewal of Reiner's contract in the summer of 1955, the trustees urged delaying consideration. In what appeared to be notes for a conference with Oldberg in 1957, Reiner gave vent to some frustrations: publicity on the formation of the chorus was too little and too late, poor rehearsal facilities were provided for the new chorus, Kuyper failed to keep him advised on Antek's first Young People's Concert, he was not consulted on Orchestra Hall plans, and there was inadequate publicity on his role in the European tour.[48]

But a deeper cancer was eating at the stability of the Orchestral Association. Reiner's future role was uncertain. When some trustees complained at the Casino Club party of the cost of the October tour, they were voicing a theme that ran through their deliberations concerning Reiner for over five seasons. In their minutes one finds little hint of appreciation for his musical achievement or for his restoration of the stature of the orchestra locally and nationally. Instead they voiced constant anxiety about his cost to the Orchestral Association. Through all their concern for living within their financial means, they gave no thought to capitalizing on widespread enthusiasm and pride in Chicago for Reiner's achievement in restoring the orchestra's glory.

The trustees were quite content to husband their existing endowment with little thought of building a broad base of philanthropic support in Chicago for the rejuvenated orchestra. In 1958–1959, the season of the triumphant tour to the East Coast and of planning for a European tour, only 1,591 contributed to the Chicago Symphony Orchestra. In that same season, the Cincinnati Symphony Orchestra had over 17,000 contributors (albeit through the Institute of Fine Arts), and the New York Philharmonic-Symphony Orchestra had nearly 14,000.[49] Nor did the trustees, in contemplating the possibility of building another hall, consider exploiting Reiner's revitalization of the orchestra that was, as much as real estate or trust investment, their raison d'être. How little the trustees appreciated their music director is evidenced by Oldberg's negotiation early in 1958 of a new contract with Reiner for two instead of three years. This scarcely represented a vote of confidence in Reiner and his accomplishment. Despite press rumors of this new contract, neither Oldberg nor the trustees authorized an official announcement of its conclusion.

For this Fritz Reiner was unquestionably partly to blame, for he made no effort to reach out to the community; his nonresident status was in sharp contrast to Stock's commitment. At the seventieth birthday party the Reiners were virtual strangers to many of the trustees and their wives. Within the organization he worked for, there was no one he could regard as a friend. Ironically, his closest confidant, other than his wife, was a journalist. Cassidy must have recognized the weakness of Reiner's position, if only from her contact with Oldberg. Instead of coming to his defense, she began using a carping tone not previously evident in her coverage of Reiner's concerts. Beneath that criticism unquestionably lay Cassidy's realization that all was not well in planning the orchestra's European tour.

Yet, despite frustrations and aggravations with Oldberg, the trustees, and Kuyper, Fritz Reiner could take satisfaction in the creation of a great orchestra, the culmination of his career. Such successes did not come easily, and they owed more than a little to a previously absent willingness to accommodate. But problems were developing that quite exceeded Reiner's ability to adjust himself to broader realities.

CHAPTER XIII

Reiner's Music

As a musical intellect, as an incomparable technician, as the possessor of an ear virtually unparalleled in his field, Fritz Reiner held a unique spot in 20th-century musical life and thought.

—Harold C. Schonberg, New York *Times,* 24 November 1963

Fritz Reiner regarded the conductor as "the living conscience of the orchestra."[1] A pervading characteristic of his own performances, whether in concert, opera, or recordings, was their thorough honesty and integrity. His notion of "conscience" was both practical and ethical. He implemented that notion with his autocratic control of the performance of a hundred musicians. Moreover, he had a deep sense of responsibility, ethical and technical, to the art. Despite his sensitivity to criticism or to applause from an audience, Reiner seldom planned his performances to gain approval from his listeners, although he occasionally gave in to management and board pressure in his programming and to financial considerations with recordings. Reiner approached his task supremely confident that he was right in every detail, that he *knew* the music he was rehearsing or presenting. He expected the same dedication from everyone else. With him, music was something that he had to control completely through his innate talent, his training, and his hard work. A musical performance was something he had fixed in his mind through intense study, and he had a special ability to realize that concept in performance. Music was the part of his life that he could control, unlike the "real world" in which he found so much frustration.

In his lifetime, Fritz Reiner was regarded as the greatest living baton technician. He liked to say that a student who had completed his course of instruction could rehearse and perform a complicated piece of music solely by his gestures and without any verbal instructions to the players. The audience, who saw only the back of his stocky figure and the economical gestures with which he controlled a performance, missed Reiner's communication with his performers. The listener-viewer who expected choreographic gymnastics on the podium left the hall disappointed. On the other hand, the musicians who faced Reiner in rehearsal and performance experienced something quite different—the communication of a musical concept through richly varied body language of which the famous "vest-pocket beat" was but one element. Although he occasionally spread his arms exuberantly, he usually presented to his players a compact figure: players could take in his eyes and facial expression while following his beat. Impassive as Reiner may have appeared from behind, he was to the musicians in front of him the living embodiment of the music in which he was completely absorbed. Recalling Richard Strauss's well-known dictum, "It is the public that should get warm, not the conductor," Reiner wrote: "Someone once asked me how it is that I do not perspire after conducting 'Salome.' Well, I do, of course; but I try to hold my own excitement in check. I know quite well that excitement in me will not excite my co-workers; it may simply make them uneasy. They must feel that they are under my *self-controlled* control."[2]

Although he sometimes contended that a conductor's facial expression was irrelevant to his communication, his own included a penetrating hawklike gaze. With what many have described as the "hooded" eyes of a falcon (his eyesight was just as sharp), he fixed every one of a hundred players with a hypnotic stare. His expressive face immediately communicated rage or pleasure; even his way of puffing out his cheeks or pursing his lips conveyed a message. Philip Farkas, principal horn with the Chicago Symphony Orchestra during Reiner's first years there, recalled the versatility of his body language:

He conducted with everything he had, not only with his hands. I recall he'd be looking at the first violins, so we'd get only a profile. A big brass entrance would come in. He'd suddenly turn his head and, still directing his hands toward the violins, would look at us and puff out his cheeks right on the beat, which was a real demonstration of when the winds should come in. Then, if we'd had that attack he gave with his cheeks, if he wanted a crescendo, his eyebrows would go slowly higher. While still working with the first violins, he might kick out in back of him and bring in the violas with his foot.[3]

Harold C. Schonberg described Reiner as "a short man who used a big baton and a tiny beat."[4] But the beat of that long baton conveyed an expressive message of extraordinary eloquence, variety, precision, and musical energy. By holding the bulbous end of his long baton with the tips of his fingers, he achieved an extraordinary flexibility in his beat. Although he sometimes admonished his students, "Don't subdivide," the movement of his fingers or the flexing of his wrist produced within his beat subsidiary pulses that gave special life to his music. Cellist János Starker and violinist Victor Aitay came to the United States after World War II from Budapest, where they had studied under Reiner's oldest and closest friend, Leo Weiner. He was, as Reiner often stated, a poor conductor but a great teacher. Starker recalled that, on first encountering Reiner's music-making in this country, he found Weiner's teachings realized in performance. Both Aitay and Starker cited "agogics" as central to Weiner's teaching. "The general pulse never changes," said Aitay. "Agogics—that's what he was teaching . . . those little agogics *in between* the general pulsation." Starker described this as "*disciplined* freedom . . . the freedom of rubato within the bar." In a paragraph that Reiner deleted from the handwritten text of his "Outline for Course in Conducting" when he had it typed, he wrote: "The tone has the following qualities: height, strength, duration, color, character, intensity. All these shadings can be conducted and synchronized on the same tone in the orchestra."[5]

Another musician's account casts further light on Reiner's phrasing. One day at lunch, Sebastian Caratelli, flutist in the Pittsburgh Symphony Orchestra, asked Reiner about his ability to make every note or phrase an integral part of an organic totality. Reiner replied without hesitation: "Rhythm. . . . Structural unity, we know, holds a central place in the desiderata of all art. Rhythm (meter, pace, accents, and so forth) is not only the propelling force of music, but also the common relator of musical motion. Structural unity, therefore, depends in large measure on the understanding of the interrelationship and judicious organization of the various elements of rhythm." In reporting this conversation, Caratelli unfortunately did not include Reiner's musical examples illustrating his views, but he did recall his own efforts to apply Reiner's precepts in practice. During a rehearsal of *Petrushka* following the conversation at lunch, Reiner turned to the flutist after a cadenza and remarked wryly, "Tomorrow, when we play it again, show me that you understand what we discussed this afternoon." That evening Caratelli pored over the passage in question, working out a precise formula for counting beats for phrases, groups of sixteenth notes, and rests, "tempered by a slight *rubato* in the groups of sixteenth notes." When he played the passage at rehearsal the next morning, Reiner beamed, "You understood, you understood."[6] Reiner's idea of rhythm in this context encompassed Aitay's and Starker's agogics and rubato, as well as Caratelli's recognition of the underlying organic unity of a Reiner performance.

Tibor Kozma, Reiner's assistant at the Metropolitan Opera for five seasons, confirmed his "knack for establishing exact mathematical relationships, 'common denominators' between two tempos." Beyond such technicalities, Kozma perceived in Reiner "an artistic personality based on the precarious equilibrium between an explosive, almost menacing elemental temperament and a strong, mature, immensely disciplined intellect which exerts a constant effort to keep that temperament in check. Without this smoldering tension . . . Reiner would not be himself."[7]

Beyond such fragmentary testimony one must go to Reiner's performance itself to appreciate the qualities of his musicianship. Agogics, rubato, and dynamic shading were not necessarily confined in the bounds of bar lines, for he would carry them through larger phrases and entire musical "paragraphs." These gave rhythmic articulation not only to the basic pulse and shape of a phrase but also, in the larger movement of the music, to the organic coherence that so impressed Caratelli, "the interrelationship and judicious organization of the various elements of rhythm." The figure appearing first in the seventeenth bar of the prelude to *Tristan und Isolde* pervades the prelude in a succession of transformations and elaborations. Reiner's articulation of the repetitions of this phrase produced expressive variety and coherence simultaneously. Paul Henry Lang recognized this in his review of the 1958 Carnegie Hall performance of the Brahms Third Symphony, when he wrote of Reiner's "powers of musical concentration, for whether in the treble, the bass, or the middle, as the principal theme or as a mere ornament, the motif was always brought out."[8]

According to Kozma, one element in Reiner's greatness was his "uncanny sense for form and proportion":

Whenever I listen to Reiner conducting one of those long acts of Wagner's or Strauss's operas, I always have the impression that he has planned every tempo and every transition from one tempo to another to fit logically into the entire structure that evolved between the rising and falling of the curtain. Try to imagine what it means to know exactly at the beginning of, say, "Elektra," how you will organize the climaxes that come in the music an hour later (while making music of the most complicated technical difficulties all the time) and you *might* get an idea of what a long breath your imagination needs, what intellectual and emotional discipline, what knowledge of the score it takes to achieve it. This structural depth and breadth of Reiner's music-making, this "long breath" of his musical vision is, to my mind, the only interpretive solution of the formal problems presented by works that are indeed somewhat over-extended; but this solution is also infinitely harder to achieve than the inspired emotionalism with which these problems are generally approached.[9]

Reiner was also a master of syncopation, not merely the juxtaposition of two rhythms but also balancing them and articulating them into a larger structure. It was to such organic coherence that Reiner applied the term *rhythm* in a broader sense. George Gaber, a percussionist in the Pittsburgh Symphony Orchestra, recalled: "Every gesture had a relationship to everything that happened in the orchestra . . . whether it's a threatening attack for a syncopated downbeat or . . . raising the eyebrows or puffing the cheeks. Or wagging his tongue for a tremolo. Or giving his elbow in three while he's conducting a straight two with his left hand."[10]

An impressive example of this flexibility within a larger beat was Reiner's performance of the slow movement of Prokofiev's Fifth Symphony, with its rhythmic variety in a unified whole. Players in his orchestras frequently commented on his uncanny ability to bring a succession of changing pulses into rhythmic coherence with the simplest beat. Clarinetist Clark Brody recalled that Reiner achieved his rubato less by subdividing the beat than through a "unanimity of feeling." "He just let the players play."[11] In the last very slow section of *Das Lied von der Erde,* Reiner scrupulously followed Mahler's admonition to "beat in one," while projecting the succession of differing meters in the scoring. On the other hand, to control rhythmic flow better, he did not hesitate to change the barring of a score, especially when, as in Stravinsky's *Mavra,* he found the composer's writing unclear. This also happened in Pittsburgh, as double-bass player Murray Grodner recollected: "Many times he would change the score in the way it could be beat versus the way it was meant to be beat. He would take, for instance, some measures that were not symmetrical and put them together to form one big 4/4 bar, which would *completely* solve an orchestral problem."[12] Farkas also spoke of Reiner's rehearsing the Rolf Liebermann Concerto for Jazzband and Symphony Orchestra: "One of the sections . . . was a series of eighth-note measures, a 3/8 followed by a 4/8, by a 5/8, and finally ended up with a 7/8. And he literally picked his teeth while he did that—so blasé about the whole thing—just flipping his hands in a nonchalant appearing way, but it was absolutely correct." Gaber also cited Reiner's conducting of Gershwin: "When he had to do *I Got Plenty o' Nothin'* . . . it was incredible: the man had an instinct to swing."[13]

A critical challenge to a conductor's rhythmic control is in transition—from one tempo to another or from one type of phrase to another. In the finale of Beethoven's First Symphony, Reiner's transition from the slow introduction to the allegro anticipated the faster rhythm. Equally impressive were his tempo changes in the third movement of the Beethoven Ninth. There he clearly defined the contrasting themes and tempos but still realized Beethoven's organic idea. Whether Reiner had in his mind some mathematical formula for relating these tempos one to another, as Caratelli did with the *Petrushka* cadenza, is beside the point. By the time he conducted them, the relations had become intuitive. Reiner applied the same rhythmic coherence to such larger musical expanses as *Also sprach Zarathustra,* in which he (and Strauss, to be sure) held together a sprawling succession of musical ideas. Here coherence was not so much a matter of a sequence of "sections" or "movements" as the manner in which rhythm and phrasing permeated the unity of the work. However, it was the mature music dramas of Wagner that evoked Reiner's extraordinary demonstration of his mastery of transition, producing the kind of "endless melody" so characteristic of the composer. Here, as elsewhere, Reiner projected not only the "upper" melody but also a vibrant counterpoint of rhythm and harmony in the lower and inner voices to achieve a coherent flow of music.

An underlying principle of much of his rhythmic sense was vocal line. As a teacher, Reiner used Mozart operatic recitatives to instill a sense of controlled freedom in vocal phrasing. He could extend similar control over long passages in the music dramas of Wagner as tightly as he could pull together the alternating recitatives and arias/ensembles of *Le nozze di Figaro* or *Don Giovanni*. Opera singers recalled the extraordinary firmness of his orchestral support of the vocal line, not only in dynamics but also in the instrumental reflection of the vocal phrasing. He often admonished singers he trusted, "Don't wait for me. Go ahead. I'll be there with you." His "accompaniment" of Lauritz Melchior in act III of *Tristan und Isolde* at Covent Garden in 1936 matched the great tenor's extraordinarily expressive declamation. He treated the principal players in the Chicago Symphony Orchestra similarly. In rehearsal, he would turn to a player and ask, "Are you comfortable?" He would then adjust his beat to a player's breathing or individual phrasing.

Reiner's sense of rhythm and the importance he ascribed to it may well have reflected the Magyar music that Bartók and Kodály were bringing to the attention of the younger generation of Hungarian musicians when Reiner was a student. Elisabeth Schwarzkopf, when asked to suggest a list of "desert island" recordings, included a Johann Strauss waltz as conducted by Reiner, "the perfect mixture of Hungarian dash, military exactitude, and charm."[14] That sense of swing pervaded his mastery of rhythmically complex scores by Stravinsky, Richard Strauss, Shostakovich, and Bartók, as much as it did a Beethoven scherzo or a Haydn finale.

To his underlying sense of rhythm Reiner added a keen feeling for orchestral tone color and sonority. He was a master of complicated scoring, elucidated with almost Mozartean clarity. The prodigious deluge of sound in a work like Bartók's *Miraculous Mandarin,* with its barbaric rhythms and complex textures, found in Reiner a consummate master. Equally impressive was his control of the subtle shadings of Ravel's *Rapsodie espagnole*. Strong, clear colors generally dominated his tonal palette, unless style dictated otherwise; his sonority was rooted in the cellos, basses, and horns. By his Chicago years, his dynamics were more subtle than the extremes of which he boasted in Cincinnati. He blended timbres less for piquant effect than to reveal the implications of harmony, whether at any one moment or, more important, in modulation, to enhance movement through time.

"It must be clean!" was his frequent and exasperated admonition to his players. He demanded precise attack and release, correct intonation, and instrumental balance to produce the appropriate sonority. To a bass section's efforts, he once reacted angrily, "I ask for a C, and you give me a dull thud." He was especially exacting with the percussion section, demanding rhythmic precision—not just playing in time—and a command of timbre and sonority that challenged the potential of the instruments and their players. Even with the notorious acoustics of Orchestra Hall in Chicago, Reiner mastered the difficulties of orchestral balance, especially controlling the tendency of the brass to play too loudly. He evoked this balanced sonority economically—with a frown aimed at a too-loud section, with a coaxing glance at a player, or with gestures of restraint or encouragement with his left hand. Since the players had such difficulty hearing one another clearly on the Orchestra Hall stage, they had to rely on the conductor's control.

Musicians all agreed that Reiner came to rehearsals completely prepared, with definite ideas of what he wanted to do and how he wanted to do it. "His criticism always seemed to come because he heard what he wanted in his head and he was trying to get it out of the orchestra." [15] Although Reiner must have been a quick study in his youth in Dresden and Cincinnati to have prepared so much music, he later insisted on ample seclusion for the intensive study of his scores. In the summer of 1963 he spent months restudying the score of *Götterdämmerung,* finally announcing at lunch one day that it was ready. Occasionally he canceled a work because, after thorough study, he decided that it was not worth performing or that it would not fit into his program scheme.

His ability to delight composers was legendary. Because of his reputation for playing new music, composers and publishers inundated him with new scores. Some of these he studied closely; others less deserving received cursory review. He did not use rehearsals to read a score he was considering: he had made up his mind before putting the music on the players' stands. He occasionally used recordings as a shortcut in making programming decisions. Although some of his collection consisted of his own recordings, he also had a miscellaneous selection, some sent by publishers or composers. He ordered records to "audition" a work he did not know or a soloist under consideration. However, he never used recordings to learn a piece of music or to investigate the interpretation of another conductor. Although he sometimes suggested that his pupils practice before a mirror after they knew a work, it is hard to imagine his doing this himself in his maturity.

Reiner often played the piano to rehearse concerto soloists and singers and occasionally read new scores at the piano. He insisted that his students at Curtis be able to sight-read complicated scores at the piano. It was through intensive mental study, however, that he fixed in his mind how the music would sound in performance and decided how to achieve that sound. This was as true of music he had played previously and knew well as it was of completely new scores. He marked his scores mercilessly, frequently with heavy black or colored crayon. Such marks were apparently reminders of what to do in rehearsal, reflecting practical means of realizing his mental picture. This crude scrawling in scores—exclamation points, a symbolic eye to capture his attention, an arrow to indicate an important cue, or refinements of dynamics—was vividly expressive. Although these markings for himself were crude, he entered his occasional rescoring of instrumentation in meticulous red ink for the librarian to copy into the orchestral parts. Reiner's "retouching" of the Schumann Second Symphony would merit study by young conductors.[16]

In a few scores Reiner wrote descriptive verbal comments, which Roger Dettmer discovered during a visit to Rambleside some years after Reiner's death. The conductor had annotated a study score of the Brahms Second Symphony in detail, in German and in English, suggesting that these notes probably date from the Cincinnati years.[17] These fanciful "programmatic" comments were more like Bernstein's account of Koussevitzky than Reiner. More characteristic of him is the story of his preparing the Beethoven Fourth Symphony: after a long and agonizing rehearsal of the first three movements, he admonished the exhausted players in the finale: "Everybody must be happy!"

Since Reiner knew precisely what he wanted, he seldom experimented in rehearsal and then only with a clear purpose. In Orchestra Hall, such experiments were more often to check the acoustics. Given the force of his mental idea of the music, it is not surprising that he became furious when his players did not execute it. According to János Starker: "His rehearsing was, first and foremost, to get what's written, to play the right notes, to play the right time and to observe the right values and to produce something which we can only describe as professionalism at its highest. . . . From then on, his job was to put it together and unify the concept which was his. And that concept was guided by the highest respect for the composer. Beyond that, obviously his greatest strength was . . . the *balancing*. It was creating structures, he was *creating buildings*."[18]

With a work new to himself or to the orchestra, Reiner proceeded according to what he sensed the music required. Sometimes he began by reading long passages without pause, occasionally a whole work or movement. With his eyes fixed on the score, beating time economically, he made few corrections, as if to orient the players in the new music. Then he would start again at the beginning, working in detail. With other new works, he would conduct a first reading in detail, insisting on minute adjustments as he went along. At this point, his beat could become extremely precise, smaller and smaller to concentrate the players' attention. It was no wonder that Chicago players, thirty years later, retained an indelible memory of Reiner's performance of certain music, no matter how often they played it afterward under other conductors. Although he worked with separate sections of the orchestra in Cincinnati and Pittsburgh, he did so rarely in Chicago, possibly because section rehearsals required special union permission. However, when he programmed the *Elektra* excerpts in 1956, the union allowed such preparation as overtime only in the week preceding the performances.

Even with a traditional work, Reiner often began by "taking everything apart," before "putting it back together." Although he might eventually play through a familiar movement or symphony in its entirety, sometimes he would omit such a run-through on the day of the concert, especially if a soloist or a more demanding piece was on the program. On the other hand, when preparing music to be recorded, no matter how familiar, he worked on the score as if it were new. Then the tension could pervade Orchestra Hall for a week. Though he conducted the initial performances of an opera with precise and tense gestures, he became more relaxed in later readings. In fact, as Starker and others have pointed out, Reiner sometimes became bored with a work that he had rehearsed or played too often. In Friday afternoon repetitions in Chicago of the previous night's program for an audience of socialites, his leadership could become as perfunctory as the response of the patrons. On one such occasion, a Chicago violinist turned to his partner and whispered, "Do you think we will ever see our loved ones again?" Nevertheless, when he repeated a limited repertory during the two-week tour in October 1958, there was no trace of boredom in his performances of *Ein Heldenleben* or the Brahms Third Symphony. Each concert on this tour was a new challenge for him and the orchestra.

Reiner liked to tell players, "People say that I hate musicians. That is not true. I only hate B-A-D musicians." Nor did he wait for a player's weaknesses to emerge gradually. Adolph Herseth, principal trumpet of the Chicago Symphony Orchestra, had a term for Reiner's testing a player, "spending one's time in the barrel." Reiner expected mature professionalism of his players: "I am not here to teach you how to play." He seldom spent time fussing with bowings during rehearsals but turned to his section leaders to "fix it." He relied on these principals to make many decisions on bowing, although he was always available for discussion. He could be sarcastic when string players used bowings marked in their scores for other conductors. Reiner often came to work with a list of details to be attended to in rehearsals, but he seldom bothered his players with last-minute instructions backstage before a concert.

Auditioning new players for his orchestras, he listened for intonation, rhythmic security, and tone, and for the ability to sight-read. Sight-reading, he said, was the most important qualification, and the best way for a musician to learn sight-reading was to play chamber music.[19] He would ask to hear not only the standard audition pieces but also music the player had never seen before.

Still, Reiner could not always fully assess a player in audition, and sometimes he made poor choices. As he looked for the external qualities of musicianship, he seemed oblivious to the personality of the player he was listening to—his resilience, his leadership ability, and his character as formed by professional experience. Reiner's criteria were too impersonal, too heedless of the human element. He was incapable of accepting gracefully the consequences of his choice, but he continued to make life miserable for a player until he was rid of him. Consequently he was more secure in hiring a player he had known and admired elsewhere or who came recommended by someone he trusted. Nor could he have worked under the more recent system of auditioning behind a screen, with a heavy rug on the floor to make sure that the conductor cannot guess gender from the sound of footsteps. In his reliance on New York contractors, Reiner frequently ran afoul of local union regulations in ways that would not have been tolerated a few years later.

Visiting soloists regarded Reiner as one of the great accompanists of his time, as long as he respected them. "In accompanying there was nobody better. . . . Many times he would just take the orchestra spots that were difficult and not even go through the whole concerto before the soloist came, because he wanted to let the soloist shape the performance, and not his idea of what it should be."[20] In personality and temperament, no two musicians could have differed more than Fritz Reiner and Rudolf Serkin—the one saturnine and contained, the other outgoing in warmth and musicality. For more than twenty years, though, they were superb collaborators. Each contributed his individuality to a joint creation in which neither dominated nor relinquished any of his artistic integrity; it was a synergy in which the total was greater than the sum of the parts. Soloists like Yehudi Menuhin, Isaac Stern, and Géza Anda sought performances of Bartók's concertos with Reiner as part of their own artistic experience.

The efforts of RCA-Victor to record soloists with Reiner, both renowned and untested, created problems with Reiner and with the Chicago critics, who complained when the company chose soloists for the subscription concerts. If Reiner liked a soloist, as he did such young Americans as William Kapell, Byron Janis, Eugene Istomin, and Van Cliburn, the collaboration was a happy one. On the other hand, Chicago flutist Donald Peck recalled a recording session with the young Russian pianist André Tchaikowsky: "They were getting along great, and Reiner used to take an interest in young people. He and Cliburn were like grandfather and grandson. Reiner liked Tchaikowsky. And Tchaikowsky was bouncing around and buttering up to Reiner. . . . But during the middle of the recording session [of Mozart's Concerto in C, K. 503], Tchaikowsky said, 'You know, Dr. Reiner, I've never played this concerto before.' . . . Reiner said, 'WHAT? You've never played this, and you dare to come here and record this with me and my orchestra?' After that, Tchaikowsky couldn't do anything right."[21] A celebrity like Heifetz or Horowitz could place some restraint on a barely willing Reiner. Heifetz taxed Reiner's patience by his insistence on repeating passages until they met his satisfaction, but Reiner also respected the violinist's perfectionism. That patience vanished when he encountered the technical shortcomings of Rubinstein.

With singers Reiner expected the same reliability he sought from instrumentalists. For opera, he auditioned singers not only in the roles for which he was considering them but also in actual performance of other repertory. When Reiner first scheduled Mahler's *Das Lied von der Erde* in Chicago in February 1958, he engaged the then relatively unknown Christa Ludwig on the recommendation of Elisabeth Schwarzkopf and Walter Legge. As the singer later recalled, it was not a happy occasion: "He was exaggerating things I didn't know."[22] Despite his frequent aspersion of vocalists generally, he enjoyed productive collaboration with such singers as Elisabeth Rethberg, Kirsten Flagstad, Regina Resnik, Risë Stevens, Leontyne Price, and Alexander Kipnis.

Fritz Reiner's renown as a superlative technician in his lifetime tended to obscure the breadth and depth of his musicianship. His perception of musical style was shaped by the Austro-German symphonic tradition and the music dramas of Wagner. As early as his Dresden years, and especially in Cincinnati, he broadened his range to include the Russian, Italian, and French traditions. His characteristic musicianship and technique were admirably suited to provide a bridge between the tradition of his musical upbringing and his exploration of contemporary music. His restraint of sentiment and the forthrightness of his approach were sympathetic to music composed after the First World War, and his penetrating technique and musicianship brought the new idioms to life in performance, with the same approach that he applied to music of the past. In this Reiner was in the forefront of a generation of musicians who accorded greater respect to the creators of music than to its interpreters.

However, Richard Taruskin went too far in suggesting that Reiner saw the music of the past in terms of his modernism. Taruskin described Reiner as a stylistic "authenticist" on the isolated evidence of Reiner's Columbia recording of the Fifth Brandenburg Concerto.[23] He contended that Reiner's tempo in the first movement betrayed a "geometric" tendency, as opposed to the "vitalist" style of German tradition. He found in Reiner's Bach "a specifically twentieth-century style of performance that is often linked with a certain invention of

Mr. Elias Howe."[24] Where, asked Taruskin, did Reiner get such "modern ideas" about Baroque style? Not from Arnold Dolmetsch's writings, for he was in Dresden, "hobnobbing with Nikisch, Muck, Mahler, and Strauss, vitalists to a man."[25] Unaware of the possibility of Reiner's acquaintance with Riemann's Collegium Musicum in Leipzig, Taruskin speculated that the source of Reiner's view of Baroque was the music of his own time, specifically the music and ideas of Igor Stravinsky. "I believe it was Stravinsky who taught Reiner—and the rest of us—about Bach the geometrist as it must have been Landowska . . . who taught Stravinsky."[26]

Actually, Reiner was unsympathetic to Stravinsky's "neoclassical" style, despite his being a superlative interpreter of the composer's music. There is ample evidence of Reiner's rejection of neoclassicism both by explicit statement and in musical practice. One need only compare Reiner's and Stravinsky's commercial recordings of the Divertimento from *The Fairy's Kiss*. Reiner's longer lyric phrases and rhythmic articulation are a far cry from the composer's angular melody and concentration on isolated beats and figures. "Stravinsky made a god of the eighth note, but I don't," Reiner told Adele Addison when they were preparing *Mavra* in Chicago.[27] A more comprehensive example of these differences can be heard in comparing Stravinsky's Columbia recordings of *The Rake's Progress* with an off-the-air transcription of Reiner's 1953 broadcast from the Metropolitan Opera. Despite the angularity of Stravinsky's vocal line and rhythm as written, Reiner found in much of this score something of the lyricism of Handel and Mozart.

One must also question Taruskin's description of Reiner's Baroque style as "geometric" in the Brandenburg Concerto recordings. The geometric approach emphasizes the beat and the short figure, rather than the phrase, as the major rhythmic element. Such an emphasis leads to a rhythmic inflexibility and to a monotony of dynamic inflection, antithetical to Reiner's own style.[28] Nor did Reiner cultivate the "detached" articulation that authenticists of a later generation would regard as a sine qua non of early eighteenth century–style performance.

Reiner experimented restlessly with the Baroque. After performing a Handel concerto grosso in Dresden with two klaviers (probably harpsichords) as continuo, he used a harpsichord in a 1923 Cincinnati performance of the Bach B Minor Suite. But in his Pittsburgh recording, he added a lower octave to the bass to secure a more "symphonic" nineteenth-century sonority. In the Columbia Brandenburgs and the later Bach suites for RCA-Victor, the bass was lighter. One can, with effort, detect the harpsichord sound in the continuo. In the Brandenburgs of 1949 he employed two players to a part. The dry acoustics of the recording studio heightened this spare effect. Listeners of that time found the sound austere, despite the marked vibrato of the string players, who of course used modern instruments. The later RCA-Victor recordings of the four suites benefited from the warmer acoustics of Manhattan Center.

Reiner was never satisfied with the keyboard continuo in the concert hall or opera house. At the Metropolitan, he used a piano for the recitatives in Mozart and Stravinsky because a harpsichord would not carry in the large theater; in some Mozart operas, he played the piano himself. In Chicago he experimented with amplification of the harpsichord and with a "prepared" piano that Seymour Raven in the *Tribune* dubbed a "perhapsichord." In Reiner's performance of the Fourth Brandenburg Concerto on a 1956 WGN telecast, one heard a small group in a rendition that in sonority might well have passed for an "authenticist" reading of three decades later, except for the warmer sound of the string vibrato. Reiner was apparently seeking *Werktreue,* a realization of an ideal in his mind, possibly reflecting an encounter with the Collegium Musicum in Leipzig. This scarcely implied a lack of conviction on his part. In Chicago he once engaged for a Bach keyboard concerto a pianist who made much of playing Bach in an authentic style, "as Bach intended." After their rehearsal an exasperated Reiner exploded privately, "If that is how Bach intended his music to be played, *Bach* was wrong!"

Reiner played very little of the sacred music that was so central to Bach's overall repertory, which might have given him a deeper practical insight into the style. In one of the joint appearances with the Toronto Mendelssohn Choir, he conducted two choral excerpts from the B Minor Mass. Except for three Handel oratorios in Chicago, Reiner avoided Baroque choral music entirely. Nor did he program any of the masses of Haydn, Mozart, and Schubert, although he had planned the Beethoven *Missa solemnis* when he became ill in 1960. This may have reflected a lack of professional choruses available to him until 1958 in Chicago. From later historical periods, he offered Brahms's *Ein deutsches Requiem* and the Verdi *Requiem,* symphonic works of sacred import. As his recording of the Verdi *Requiem* showed, his approach was distinctly secular and operatic. It is not unreasonable to suggest that Reiner's lack of religious orientation in his music could be traced back to an ambivalence stemming from his conversion from Judaism to Roman Catholicism.

"Mozart first, Mozart second, and Mozart third."[29] For all his fame as an interpreter of Wagner, Richard Strauss, and contemporaries, Reiner repeatedly asserted that Mozart was his favorite composer. More than the technical importance of teaching his students to conduct the recitatives of *Le nozze di Figaro* and *Don Giovanni,* there was something in Mozart's personal language that especially appealed to him. It may well have been that, with Mozart, Reiner was seeking something that he himself lacked in emotional candor as he responded to the summons described by H. C. Robbins Landon: Mozart "invites us to share his emotional world, he takes us by the hand, as it were, and leads us, ultimately requiring us to follow wherever he goes."[30] Mozart's mastery of vocal line—the lyricism of his arias and the cadence of speech in his recitatives—found a special response in Reiner's musicianship. For Reiner the music of Mozart, Haydn, and Beethoven defined a classical style that permeated instrumental music through the symphonies of Brahms. Although he recognized the intensified expression and vastly expanded structures of Beethoven, he approached that composer's music from its roots in the immediate past. The same was true of his performances of Schubert. The "Great" C Major Symphony under his direction was not an evocation of epic grandeur, but rather a coolly chiseled classic statement. In the music of these Viennese masters, Reiner, like other conductors of his time, seldom played the repeats in sonata-form movements. Nor did he reduce the strings as much as later "authenticists" would prescribe; however, he never allowed the strings to obscure the wind detail. (The Chicago recordings of Mozart symphonies in 1955 were with a string distribution of 13-12-8-6-4, or 23 fewer players than the orchestra's usual string section.) Late in his Chicago years, he failed to persuade RCA-Victor to record the nine Beethoven symphonies with a reduced orchestra, quantitatively reflecting the usage of the composer's time.

The Romantic self-expression of Schumann and Mendelssohn evoked less sympathy from Reiner. On the other hand, the music of Brahms had a classic solidity combined with a flexibility of phrase and rhythm. The music dramas of Wagner and the operas and symphonic poems of Richard Strauss were widely recognized as specialties of Reiner. He achieved a remarkable balance between the symphonic and the vocal in the operas of both composers. Even with such music, the influence of Mozart on Reiner was seldom absent. This may explain the disappointment expressed by some critics in his performances of Wagner's operas, for he avoided the rhetorical excess that often passed for grandeur in this music.

Berlioz was for Reiner more the author of a treatise on orchestration than a self-indulgent Romantic. Although Reiner projected the instrumental mastery of Mahler with precision and excitement, he shunned as much as possible that composer's neurasthenia. Similarly, his readings of the symphonies and symphonic poems of Tchaikovsky projected that composer's emotional expression without allowing it to descend into maudlin bathos. With other Russian music, Reiner responded to its characteristic national melody and color and to its rhythmic vitality. He was equally responsive to the distinctive idiom of such

French composers as Debussy and Ravel. In Reiner the immaculate precision of Ravel found an outstanding champion.

Throughout his career Reiner acknowledged two major influences on his youthful development as a conductor—Arthur Nikisch and Richard Strauss. To someone acquainted with the modest recorded legacy of these two musicians, this may seem rather strange. Although Nikisch's recordings confirm Boult's characterization of him as "wayward" and "impulsive" interpretively, there can be no question of his technical mastery. It is quite possible that the younger Hungarian was mesmerized by the older master. Both Strauss's assiduously cultivated reputation for restraint of gesture and his pioneering devotion to Mozart must have enhanced his appeal to Reiner.[31] Unfortunately, there is no documentation of Reiner's work in Cincinnati with which to judge the impact of these two influences on him in his youth, but his boasting in Cincinnati of ranging dynamically from the "most delicate whisperings" to "a dazzling forte" is ominous, especially as confirmed by various reviewers. On the other hand, even the fragmentary evidence of the 1931–1932 Bell Laboratories recordings of the Philadelphia Orchestra show a quite different control of sonority. These and Reiner's earliest substantial recordings from Covent Garden in 1936 and 1937 fully anticipated the mastery of his later years.[32] Certainly the 1938 New York *Post* recordings of Wagner and Debussy sound like the Reiner of later years, quite different from earlier descriptions of his performances. Recalling Reiner's comment that Nikisch was a combination of Toscanini and Reiner, one might suggest that actually it was Reiner who was Nikisch and Toscanini mixed together. Baton mannerism aside, Reiner tempered Nikisch's impetuous irregularities with his Italian colleague's greater musical discipline. In their time, Nikisch and Mahler represented opposite poles of style, much as Toscanini and Mahler's disciple Mengelberg did for a later generation. Reiner had little use for Mahler as a conductor in his youth or for Mengelberg later.

Joseph Horowitz, while enlarging on what he viewed as the pernicious influence of Toscanini, dismissed Reiner (with George Szell) as one of the "Toscanini beneficiaries and admirers, [who] mainly contributed to a symphonic climate seizing and amplifying aspects of the all-purpose formula: objectivity, precision, linear tension."[33] If Reiner was a "beneficiary" of Toscanini's influence, he could have scarcely encountered that conductor before his own musicality had been shaped by his Budapest training and by the examples of Nikisch and Strauss. Moreover, the Toscanini whom Reiner encountered in Italy and New York in the 1920s was different from the later object of Horowitz's animadversion. Reiner was certainly guilty of precision: all agree on the importance he accorded, though not slavishly, to playing the music as written. But such precision did not preclude an empathetic response to the expressive force underlying what was written. Like Nikisch, Reiner conducted in phrases, not bar lines. No one could listen to Reiner's performances—from Mozart to Bartók, from Haydn to Wagner and Strauss—and fail to experience his emotional involvement in his best music-making. As for "linear tension," if Horowitz had in mind the arching rhythmic articulation that was a hallmark of Reiner at his best, the conductor would have had to plead guilty. But that articulation had its moments of repose, relaxation, and variation, hardly evidence of an "all-purpose formula."

Horowitz seemed to think of Reiner's musicianship as rejection of expressivity in favor of objectivity or, in Taruskin's terms, the "geometric." To deny this is not to suggest that Reiner necessarily indulged in expressive excess or that he used music to exploit personal emotion at variance with the music. János Starker, a perceptive observer of Reiner at the Metropolitan Opera and in Chicago, drew a distinction between sentimentality and emotion: "Reiner was not a sentimental musician, he was an emotional musician, and the emotions that he expressed in his music were higher than anybody else ever."[34] Sometimes his reluctance to give himself over to expressive involvement modified his musical impact—his limited response to the music of such composers as Schumann and Mahler, for example. On the other hand, where his characteristic musicianship and emotional temperament responded to expressive balance, he could produce such inspiring performances as his recordings of the Beethoven "Pastoral" and the Brahms Fourth.

Nevertheless, at times an element of that balance was an underlying reserve—*self-controlled* control—as if Reiner were too emotionally inhibited to give himself over completely to accept with all his heart such an invitation as Mozart's. There was in Reiner the musician a disinclination to commit himself emotionally and a tendency to retreat to technical musicianship, dazzling as it might be in the music of Haydn, Strauss, or Ravel. Ultimately this was a manifestation of Fritz Reiner the man—the man who was incapable of a happy relationship with his elder daughter, who found it more difficult to control the real world than a hundred disciplined musicians from the podium. It was in this inner struggle that Fritz Reiner the man and Fritz Reiner the artist confronted one another and did not always achieve a happy resolution. But that very conflict contributed to Fritz Reiner's greatness as an interpreter of music.

THE CINCINNATI SYMPHONY ORCHESTRA
Outline for
MEMORANDUM

From ___ *Course of Conducting* ___ Date ___

Technic of conducting must be learned and practiced before conducting actually an orchestra. Pupils must be capable of conducting an important work clearly and musically —— without previous rehearsing with orchestra

General-Studies

1) If possible play an orchestra instrument preferably a string instrument and assist at rehearsals actively at the percussion section.

2) Study orchestration (Berlioz - Strauss Instrumentationslehre) (translated?) with scores of Strauss, Berlioz Strawinski, Hindemith.

3) Sing in a chorus & if possible conduct a chorus (to help technical knowledge, equipment)

4) Analise masterworks harmonically & structurally. (knowledge of harmony. counterpoint, musical forms, and is obligatory)

assist in orchestra rehearsal
sing in chorus
accompanyment
orchestration
Harmony counterpoint, form

First page of Reiner's draft of Outline for Course in Conducting, *1931.*

Mary Louise Curtis Bok and Reiner at dress rehearsal in Philadelphia Academy of Music for the premiere of Gian Carlo Menotti's Amelia Goes to the Ball, *1937.*

Reiner with Lauritz Melchior and Kirsten Flagstad, San Francisco Opera, October 1936.

Reiner and Edward Specter, manager of the Pittsburgh Symphony Orchestra, 1938.

Béla Bartók and Reiner at Rambleside, c. 1943, photographed by Reiner with self-timer.

Ljuba Welitsch as Salome, general manager Edward Johnson, and Reiner at the Metropolitan Opera, February 1949.

Reiner with Goddard Lieberson and Edward Wallerstein of Columbia Records publicizing the introduction of the long-playing phonograph record, 1949.

Richard Mohr, Reiner, Robert Shaw, Risë Stevens, Licia Albanese, and Jan Peerce listening to recording playback of Carmen, *Manhattan Center, May/June 1951.*

Reiner rehearsing soloists, orchestra, and chorus of the Metropolitan Opera for the American premiere of The Rake's Progress. *Shown at rear right, Hilde Gueden, Blanche Thebom, and Giulio Gari seated behind Mack Harrell and Norman Scott; with chorus master Kurt Adler beside Igor Stravinsky lower right.*

Reiner and Dr. Eric Oldberg, president of The Orchestral Association, Chicago 1954.

Claudia Cassidy at her Chicago Tribune *desk.*

*Artur Rubinstein and Reiner listening to playback of
Brahms D Minor Piano Concerto recording,
Orchestra Hall, April 1954.*

Boris Chaliapin portrait of Reiner commissioned by Time, *1958.*

Carlotta and Fritz Reiner at Rambleside, summer 1962.

Reiner conducting rehearsal of Götterdämmerung *at the Metropolitan Opera, November 1963.*

"Unfeasible"

The euphoria generated by the Chicago Symphony Orchestra's East Coast tour in October 1958 and by the observance of Fritz Reiner's seventieth birthday in December was rudely extinguished in February 1959 when Reiner himself canceled the orchestra's projected tour of Europe, the Near East, and Russia. Such was the reaction of the orchestra's players, the trustees, the press, and the public at large that one writer later described Mrs. O'Leary's cow as "a saint by comparison."[1] Reiner's action had important consequences for all concerned, not least for himself, as he was toppled from the pedestal that he had attained in his previous five and one-half seasons in Chicago.

Reiner himself had initially pressed for an overseas tour by reporting, when he returned from Europe in 1955 and 1956, that he had been "invited" to take his orchestra to Europe.[2] George Kuyper enthusiastically embraced the notion of a European tour. He joined Reiner in seeking to overcome the reluctance of Oldberg and the trustees to commit the Orchestral Association's financial resources and fund-raising potential to such a tour. Reiner and Kuyper were in touch with two managers overseas—Wilfrid Van Wyck in London and Walter Schulthess in Zurich, both of whom had seen Reiner in Vienna in 1955. When Van Wyck proposed a European tour in 1959 based on the Edinburgh and Salzburg festivals, Reiner had to respond that the trustees "had no intention" of providing funds for such a tour.[3] Schulthess was in a position to offer the Chicago Symphony Orchestra three concerts at the Lucerne Festival during a week in early September 1959. This would have been an anchor for a tour including the Salzburg and Edinburgh festivals.

At that time an American orchestra needed financial support for a European tour from the President's Cultural Presentations Program in the U.S. State Department. This agency contracted with the American National Theater and Academy (ANTA) for advice and implementation of the program. Primarily interested in promoting the American theater, ANTA was a nonprofit organization that administered overseas performance programs. Once its advisory panel approved a project, ANTA acted as liaison between the organization and the State Department in planning a tour abroad. Meanwhile, the State Department advised its various embassies and consulates to develop goodwill and create optimum exposure for American culture. Although the touring organization valued its participation for the prestige accruing to itself, ANTA and the State Department had other foreign policy objectives. The touring organization thus had to work with several layers of bureaucracy, each with its own agenda—ANTA as agent for the State Department, the department itself, the overseas booking agent, and, once on tour, the local embassy and consular officials.

Such friends of Reiner as Virgil Thomson and Paul Henry Lang on the ANTA music advisory panel kept him informed of their support of the Chicago orchestra. It was from Thomson that Reiner first heard early in 1957 that the panel had recommended including the Chicago Symphony Orchestra in an elaborate American cultural showcase at the Brussels Fair in the summer of 1958, along with the orchestras of Boston, New York, and Philadelphia.[4] Carlotta Reiner wrote to Claudia Cassidy, "confidentially," that ANTA was interested in the orchestra's appearing abroad. The Orchestral Association would have to cover part of the expense, and the rest would come from State Department funds. She added that Reiner had told Oldberg: "I really don't see how our Board can afford to see the Chicago Orchestra treated like a stepchild, sort of the forgotten orchestra in the U.S.A."[5] The trustees had already dismissed a European tour in April 1957, when they approved the East Coast tour. In October 1957 they reacted coolly to ANTA's official invitation to the Brussels Fair, agreeing to accept only if Mayor Richard J. Daley would commit the city of Chicago to underwriting the trip.[6] When Oldberg wrote Daley to this effect, the mayor replied that the city had no funds for such a project. Oldberg therefore declined the invitation to Brussels: the association could not raise the necessary eighty-five thousand dollars even if the federal government were to pay thirty thousand dollars and cover one-third of the transportation cost.[7]

Thanks to the continued efforts of Reiner and Kuyper, ANTA early in 1958 again recommended the Chicago Symphony Orchestra for a major European tour in 1959. It would be the first American orchestra to visit Russia and other Iron Curtain countries as a part of growing cultural contacts with that area. The tour would also include the Middle East. In May 1958 Reiner joined Kuyper in New York to meet with Robert F. Schnitzer, the ANTA official in charge of the overseas program. Schnitzer then wrote Kuyper confirming the general arrangements for a six-week tour. It would begin either in May 1959 to permit the orchestra to return in time for the Ravinia season or in August after Ravinia. The State Department allocated $316,000 for the tour, with preference for performing in Iron Curtain countries. Schnitzer also acknowledged that appearances in the major capitals and festivals of Western Europe would be a "necessary" part of the tour. He expressed pleasure at Reiner's offer to include an American work on every program and, wherever possible, to play music by a composer from the country visited. Although Schnitzer's basic proposal was for a six-week tour, he mentioned the possibility of extending it to as many as eight weeks. Judging from experience with other American orchestras, Schnitzer estimated that there would be an average of five or six concerts a week.[8] Oldberg announced to the press on 29 May 1958 that the orchestra had been invited to tour Russia, Eastern Europe, and major capitals in Western Europe for six weeks in the late summer and early fall of 1959 and that the orchestra would perform at the Lucerne Festival in September 1959. On 20 June, at a meeting of the Orchestral Association, Oldberg hailed the tour as a major achievement in building the international renown of the Chicago Symphony Orchestra.

Reiner placed great importance on the Lucerne Festival, where the orchestra would play three concerts during a week in September. Oldberg thought that Reiner should conduct two of the three concerts, but Reiner wanted guest conductors for two concerts, allowing him time to record with the Vienna Philharmonic. Despite considerable discussion, Reiner, Oldberg, Kuyper, and Schulthess never reached a final decision on the guest conductors for Lucerne. Herbert von Karajan, Otto Klemperer, Carlo Maria Giulini, Pierre Monteux, and Rafael Kubelik were among those mentioned, with general agreement that Karajan should be the first choice. Reiner also favored Schulthess as agent for booking the rest of the tour, except for Gosconcert in Russia. However, ANTA had never worked with Schulthess and preferred Antoine Heller in Paris, who had arranged tours of the Philadelphia and Cleveland orchestras. At one point Kuyper considered working with both agents, but he eventually settled on Heller under pressure from Schnitzer.[9]

Kuyper arranged to go to Lucerne while Reiner was there conducting the Berlin Philharmonic. He planned to meet with him and Schulthess and then to proceed to Brussels for a meeting with Heller. At the last minute he cabled Reiner in Lucerne that Schnitzer had advised him to cancel his trip.[10] Kuyper then left for a vacation in California, leaving it to his secretary to explain to Reiner by letter that a new State Department official had advised Schnitzer of a change in policy.[11] The new official in charge of the Cultural Presentations Program was James F. Magdanz, who promptly vetoed the Lucerne Festival appearance in September 1959. The department could not afford to pay for a full week of but three concerts, and for foreign policy reasons, the orchestra would have to be elsewhere at that time.

Returning to Rambleside from Lucerne, Reiner spoke at length by telephone with Schnitzer, who reviewed the conversation in a letter to Kuyper.[12] Schnitzer explained that the Lucerne engagement and Reiner's absence in Vienna were contrary to State Department policy. Because of responses from embassies and consulates, the tour would probably begin in mid-August at Baalbek, Lebanon, and proceed northward via Greece through Iron Curtain countries, eliminating appearances in Edinburgh and Salzburg. From Schnitzer, Reiner learned that the tour would be expanded to eight weeks and that it might not be possible to visit the major centers in Western Europe. At this point Schnitzer probably knew, but did not tell Reiner, of the likelihood of an even longer tour, of as much as eleven or twelve weeks, because of responses from Eastern Europe. In any event, Kuyper knew of this possibility in the early fall of 1958, before the East Coast tour. Sensing the need for close communication at this crucial juncture, Schnitzer suggested to Kuyper that they both keep Reiner informed by sending him copies of their correspondence at Rambleside.[13] According to Carlotta, Schnitzer stopped sending these copies once Reiner arrived in Chicago in early October, assuming that the manager would share their correspondence with the conductor.

During the orchestra's East Coast tour, Kuyper met with Schnitzer in New York; it is not clear whether Reiner was at this meeting. Kuyper finally went to Paris in November to confer with Heller on booking arrangements. While he was there, he received a cable from Reiner stating that he could not accept more than five concerts a week for eight weeks. His penciled draft of that cablegram reads:

AFTER CAREFUL CONSIDERATION HAVE DECIDED THAT 8 WEEKS WITH FIVE CONCERTS IS THE MAXIMUM I AM ABLE TO CONDUCT. 12 IS TOO MUCH FOR (1) MY PERSONAL STAMINA. I HAVE A GREAT OBLIGATION TO FULFILL TO CHICAGO AS LONG AS I AM MUSICAL DIRECTOR AND EVEN IN THE FACE OF GOVERNMENTAL PLANNING CHICAGO MUST COME FIRST. (2) WE DONT NEED TO SATURATE EUROPE WITH CHICAGO CONCERTS OF PROPAGANDA PURPOSES. EIGHT WEEKS OR EVEN SIX WEEKS SERVE THE SAME PURPOSE FOR THE U S GOVERNMENT. (3) FOR CHICAGO PROPAGANDA—AGAIN 6–8 WEEKS CAN DO THE JOB AS WELL AS 12—EVEN BETTER BECAUSE THE PUBLIC CAN BE SATURATED WITH TOO MUCH OF US ABROAD. (4) THE CREAM OF GENERAL AMERICAN PUBLICITY IS ALREADY TAKEN OFF BY PHILADELPHIA, BOSTON, AND NEW YORK—WE ARE JUST MOPPING UP THE CREAM. (5) THE ORIGINAL OBJECTION IS STILL THE MOST IMPORTANT—HEALTH—HEALTH—HEALTH. IT WOULD TAKE TOO LONG FOR A "PICK UP" BEFORE CHICAGO SEASON—60 CONCERTS— AND COULD EVEN JEOPARDIZE IT. SEPT AND OCT IN THE RAINY SEASON WITH INADEQUATE ACCOMMODATIONS CAN MAKE A LOT OF TROUBLE—BOTH FOR ME AND FOR THE MEN.[14]

It would appear that Kuyper was unable or disinclined to represent Reiner's position in his arrangements with Heller, ANTA, and the State Department. Reiner later contended that Kuyper never fully informed him how extensively he had committed him and the orchestra.

Not surprisingly, the Chicago press took up the cause of the prospective tour as a cultural showcase that would counteract the city's reputation as "hog butcher to the world." Given the paucity of official information from Orchestra Hall, the four music editors indulged in rumor, speculation, and gossip. Cassidy of course had the benefit of direct contact with the Reiners, but professional ethics prevented her from disclosing such information from Carlotta as the cancellation of the Lucerne Festival. Instead, she had her travel agent ask for hotel reservations in Lucerne during the visit of the Chicago Symphony Orchestra. Learning from that source that the orchestra would not appear, she could report what she already knew from the Reiners.[15] But Cassidy neglected to reveal what the *Tribune*'s Washington bureau had learned at the State Department, probably from Magdanz. Having indicated on 13 January that the tour would include "no major European capitals," the department stated on 26 January that the tour would be "the richest yet offered to any American orchestra." Although Cassidy had published her news of the Lucerne cancellation, she failed to carry the State Department reports at a time when their publication might have had a serious impact, nor did the *Tribune* press the department to clarify its vagueness. Instead Cassidy delayed reporting the department's January statements until March, after the storm had broken over Reiner's cancellation.[16]

Robert Marsh in the *Sun-Times* expressed doubt whether the tour would actually occur because it had been "common knowledge" during Reiner's years at the Metropolitan Opera that he had a "cardiac problem." This drew a heated denial from Reiner himself, by registered mail to publisher Marshall Field, Jr., and equally indignant letters from Oldberg and Hurok, which Marsh briefly mentioned in a later sidebar. Marsh also reported that a *Sun-Times* Paris correspondent had talked with Heller, who projected a twelve-week tour in twenty countries. According to Heller, Reiner would have to accept diplomatic social engagements. The Paris agent also noted that Oldberg had vetoed guest conductors and that because Walter Hendl was not known in Europe, the burden would fall on Reiner.[17] Twenty-five years later, after the announcement of Carlotta's bequest to Columbia University, Marsh renewed and elaborated on his earlier assertion: "In his seasons at the Metropolitan Opera, just before coming to Chicago, [Reiner] had used his heart condition to get out of numerous assignments that he didn't want. But this time Reiner had a fit. He had been examined recently, and had 'the heart of a 17-year-old.' He threatened to sue. I stuck by my story. If he went to court, the Sun-Times would have the right to have him examined by independent medical experts. That ended all talk of a lawsuit."[18] There is no indication in Reiner's files that he threatened to sue, nor any indication in publisher Marshall Field's reply that the *Sun-Times* would require a medical examination; Field's response was simply a perfunctory expression of confidence in its critic.[19] None of Reiner's colleagues in New York recalled any knowledge or suspicion of a heart condition, or of Reiner's evading "numerous assignments" at the Metropolitan Opera.[20]

Early in February 1959 Donal Henahan wrote an article in the *Daily News* based on a phone conversation with Schnitzer, confirming that the tour would begin in August and last for ten or eleven weeks, that Reiner had proposed Hendl to Schnitzer as a second conductor, and that there would be no time to rehearse other conductors. The Chicago Symphony Orchestra, he promised, would enjoy the same support as was given the orchestras of New York, Philadelphia, and Boston.[21]

Despite his earlier miscalculation of the prestige that might accrue to the Chicago Symphony Orchestra from a European tour, Eric Oldberg had become deeply committed to it. The civic and social circles in which the trustees and their families moved enthusiastically hailed the prospective tour as a brilliant coup for Chicago. If Oldberg was a new convert to the cause, George Kuyper was an old believer: for him, this European tour was to be the crowning achievement of his professional career. Neither Oldberg nor Kuyper fully recognized the depth of Reiner's misgivings in the fall of 1958 after the cancellation of Lucerne and his conversation with Schnitzer, and they also seem to have ignored Reiner's November cable to Kuyper in Paris. To Oldberg and Kuyper it was inconceivable that the Chicago Symphony Orchestra's European tour might not take place. They clearly conveyed this conviction to Schnitzer, as each assured the other that he could "handle" Reiner, who had, after all, initiated the idea.

Ultimately, it was Antoine Heller in Paris who precipitated the inevitable confrontation, by asking Kuyper for Reiner's tour programs, including one of contemporary music for the Venice Bienniale. In response, Reiner wired his colleague in Chicago:

MR HELLER MUST UNDERSTAND THAT PROGRAMS ARE SUBJECT TO BOOKINGS AND BOOKINGS ARE SUBJECT TO OUR APPROVAL. THEREFORE AS LONG AS TOUR IS UNDECIDED I HAVE NOT YET PLANNED ANY STANDARD PROGRAMS. THE CONTEMPORARY PROGRAM REQUEST FOR THE BIENNIALE ENGAGEMENT IS UNREALISTIC IN VIEW OF LACK OF TIME FOR PREPARATION BECAUSE OF RECORDING AND SOLOIST COMMITMENTS DURING REMAINING WEEKS OF OUR SEASON AND FURTHERMORE ITS USEFULNESS IS QUESTIONABLE FOR OTHER EVENTUAL BOOKINGS. GREETINGS.[22]

The same day Carlotta wrote to Cassidy: "The affaire European Tour gets curiouser and curiouser. The latest is that they want programs for those mythical dates—at least I assume they are mythical because we don't know any of them (except for Mr Marsh's article). . . . The whole thing reminds me of Alice in Wonderland, Verdict first, Testimony afterwards."[23]

Kuyper responded to Reiner's telegram on 4 February with a rambling letter, "I am in the middle of much confusion about the whole question." He accused Reiner of placing obstacles in his path and, for the first time, asked him for an unequivocal answer, "Do you intend to go through with the tour?"[24] Reiner telephoned both Kuyper and Oldberg, repeating his arguments of the previous November. He urged postponing the tour to May 1960, asserting that Oldberg agreed with him.[25] By the time Reiner returned to Chicago from Rambleside on the weekend of 15 February, Schnitzer had rejected any notion of postponement because the tour had been "publicized and booked throughout Europe." Reiner contemptuously replied that Heller had yet to provide any definite schedule.[26] Finally, Schnitzer flew out to Chicago to meet with Oldberg, Kuyper, and Reiner at the Chicago Club on 24 February. Faced with Reiner's adamant refusal, Oldberg insisted that he assume full responsibility publicly for the cancellation and that he refrain from any public comment or wider explanation; Oldberg did not want any Rodzinski-like airing of dirty linen in the media.

Reiner announced the cancellation of the European tour to the stunned orchestra players at the beginning of their rehearsal on 26 February. He spoke extemporaneously, referring to the "awful tour" as "unfeasible" and to rainy weather in Moscow. Some of the players responded with hissing. Later that day some players found an old dress suit and spread it on the floor of the musicians' dressing room with a sign, which some recalled read "Farewell, European Tour—Thanks, Fritz"; others recalled a sign reading "Unfeasible = rain in Moscow." The suit lay on the floor with dusty footprints on it.[27] This was the only support to later reports that the players hanged Reiner in effigy.

Meanwhile, on the sixth floor of Orchestra Hall, the staff prepared a brief press announcement, minutely reviewed and revised by Oldberg, who deleted all mention of his agreeing with Reiner's decision. The text was not submitted to Reiner for his comment or approval.[28]

Dr. Eric Oldberg, President of the Orchestral Association, announced today that the Chicago Symphony Orchestra's projected European tour, in the late summer and early fall of 1959, has been deferred as a result of a decision by Dr. Fritz Reiner, conductor and musical director of the Orchestra, that he would be unable to fulfill the engagement at this time. It was mutually agreed by the Orchestral Association and the American National Theater and Academy (ANTA), which administers for the State Department the President's Special

International Program for Cultural Presentations, that the tour should be postponed, with the hope that it may be reinstated at some future time.

The day after the Chicago announcement, Leonard Bernstein told the cheering musicians of the New York Philharmonic that they would replace the Chicago Symphony Orchestra on the tour. So prompt an announcement indicates that Schnitzer and the State Department had anticipated Reiner's withdrawal for some time. The New York Philharmonic played fifty concerts in sixty-seven days, of which Leonard Bernstein conducted thirty-six, an average of less than four a week; Thomas Schippers conducted thirteen concerts, and Seymour Lipkin one.[29]

Two days after Reiner's announcement at rehearsal, the players in the Chicago Symphony Orchestra met and elected their first representative committee. This reflected not only indignation over Reiner's cancellation of the European tour but also unhappiness with the progress of Ravinia negotiations for the summer of 1959. They resented having been kept in the dark on arrangements for the tour almost as much as they did Reiner's cancellation of it. The combination of these two issues accounted for their defying Petrillo and the local union in forming the long-forbidden representation of the players. Disagreement among the players was evident in a letter to Reiner from "Members of the Chicago Symphony Orchestra," who deplored the conductor's unilateral cancellation of the tour but disassociated themselves from any discourtesy to the conductor.[30] It was not clear whether this unsigned letter came from the new committee or an unofficial group of individuals. There is no question, however, that the handling of the tour by Reiner, management, and the trustees accelerated the deterioration of labor relations at Orchestra Hall.

At Oldberg's insistence, neither Kuyper or Reiner nor anyone on the staff was allowed to elaborate on the brief press release. When Hurok offered to send Martin Feinstein to Chicago to assist in damage control, Oldberg and Kuyper rejected anything that might be viewed as a defense of Reiner. As usual when Orchestra Hall surrounded itself with a stone wall, the press indulged in an orgy of speculation. The media interviewed Schnitzer and Magdanz, both of whom angrily placed the blame squarely on Fritz Reiner. For several weeks the local writers reviewed Reiner's affront to Chicago in detail, not always factually. They invented various figures—ranging from seventy thousand to one hundred fifty thousand dollars—as Reiner's annual salary. Calling the cancellation "an intolerable business," Roger Dettmer in the *American* accused Reiner of callousness toward the players, who each lost the two thousand dollars he had counted on from the tour, and of being "thoughtless about the city of Chicago." Marsh in the *Sun-Times* was more evenhanded toward Reiner. He criticized the "answer no questions policy . . . [that] has had Orchestra Hall officials acting as if the first man who talked would be out of a job." He pointed out that, beginning with the Ravinia season in June 1959, followed by a twelve-week tour and then the twenty-eight-week subscription season, the orchestra would have been scheduled for forty-six consecutive weeks of work.[31]

Claudia Cassidy bluntly attacked Reiner. After referring to "a few brilliant seasons" in the past, she returned bitterly to what she perceived as domination by RCA-Victor of Reiner's programming: "We have listened to junk galore because it was being recorded and we of the audience were hearing it rehearsed." She blamed the withdrawal by Chicago Title and Trust from the television program on "Reiner's price per concert [as] too rich for the sponsor's blood." When ANTA and the State Department and the Orchestral Association refused "to take the rap, . . . it came to rest with Reiner, because that was where it belonged. . . . It would be assuring at about this point, if Chicago and one of its distinguished musicians in residence, Fritz Reiner, woke up and stayed up."[32] Nine months later, looking back on the major events of the 1950s, Cassidy returned to the attack: "Somewhat preoccupied with record-making of late, Mr. Reiner's concerts have not retained the magnetic brilliance that packed Orchestra hall at the start of his regime, and it has been a serious disappointment that [1] he declined to take the orchestra on a spectacular European tour [brilliantly pinch-hit by Leonard Bernstein and the New York Philharmonic] and [2] that he does not make Chicago his home, and so takes off at the holidays, leaving the town absurdly orphaned at the Christmas and New Year's concerts."[33] (In fairness to Reiner, it should be noted that, from 1953 through 1958, he in fact conducted concerts during the holidays in five of six years.) Not surprisingly, Reiner viewed Cassidy's turning against him as personal disloyalty. Although Carlotta continued to write her and pay her such personal courtesies as sending her flowers, the relationship cooled.

True to his promise to Oldberg, Reiner refrained from voicing his views to the local media. However, when Ross Parmenter, in the New York *Times,* reported the Chicago orchestra's cancellation and the New York orchestra's acceptance of the tour, he mentioned that the Chicago players had hissed at their conductor. Unwilling to allow such a statement to stand unchallenged in New York, Reiner responded. After reviewing the heavy schedule such a tour would involve, he denied that his players had hissed or booed his announcement of the cancellation of the tour.[34] Parmenter published what was apparently a portion of a longer statement that appeared later that spring in the *Musical Courier:*

Our Chicago season contains a heavy schedule of rehearsals, concerts and recordings—every day but Sunday has its claims. A 10 to 12-week tour coming before the season is not feasible. After a trip of such duration it is not possible to guarantee the usual high standard of performances for the Chicago audience, who have the right to expect their orchestra and their conductor to be in top form. ANTA refused to shorten this tour—to the length of previous trips made by Boston and Philadelphia, which were five to eight weeks. I have suggested a tour in the Spring of 1960—after our season.

The innuendoes of the Press regarding my health are not true, thank God, and the same goes for the behavior of my orchestra. There was no hissing or booing when I gave them the announcement. I realize that the news was disappointing, particularly to the younger men who have never been to Europe; but the majority recognize the inescapable fact that a tour of such duration is not a sightseeing pleasure trip.[35]

While refraining from other public comment, both Reiners spoke about it in conversation and wrote about it in letters to friends and family. To her mother, Eva, and Tuśy, Carlotta wrote of the "intolerable burden" such a tour would have placed on her husband in the midst of a heavy schedule of concerts in Chicago. Describing the State Department as completely unreasonable in its demands, she portrayed Schnitzer as having "a Barnum complex with Napoleonic overtones." To her mother she wrote, "In this world one has to PAY for everything one wants; and to be spared the certain heavy physical endurance test that such a tour means—then we must stand up to the blame without fussing—but it isn't pleasant."[36]

Neither Oldberg nor Kuyper forgave Reiner. Deeply depressed by the collapse of the culmination of his career, George Kuyper was outspoken in his burning aversion toward Reiner and in his resentment of Oldberg's inability to control the conductor as promised. In a few months he would abruptly leave the orchestra he had served since 1943. For Oldberg, Reiner's cancellation of the European tour was an equally devastating blow to his standing as president of the association and to his deep devotion to the orchestra. For all his earlier doubts about the prestige value of such a tour, he now assumed the role of a Chicagoan betrayed by an outsider. He voiced his complaints against Reiner in terms almost identical with Cassidy's: "a few brilliant concerts" in earlier years, the influence of recordings on the orchestra's repertory, the formation of the orchestra committee, the cancellation of the television sponsorship, and, most of all, Reiner's failure to join the orchestra "family" as a Chicago resident. Following the first concert after the cancellation of the tour, he wrote a bitter letter to Reiner criticizing the playing and the hiring of a blond percussionist to play one bar on the cymbals in the "second-rate" overture to Kabalevsky's *Colas Breugnon*. He was confident that Reiner would appreciate his frankness, he wrote, motivated as it was by his "unswerving" support and high regard.[37]

Despite Reiner's willingness to assume full public responsibility for the tour fiasco, it is obvious from the facts now available that none of the principals involved were free of blame and that the alacrity with which Oldberg and Kuyper made Reiner the scapegoat was unseemly at best. If Oldberg's initial coolness toward touring abroad reflected a lack of understanding of the musical world beyond Chicago, his later resentment of Reiner for his betrayal of Chicago was equally provincial. Once Reiner and Kuyper had persuaded Oldberg of the importance of such a project, none of them had a clear understanding of its total impact on the orchestra or of the necessity to mobilize the community. There was no evidence that the trustees had made any plans to raise the money in Chicago to pay the association's share of the cost, nor was there any sign that they saw such an effort as a stepping-stone toward widening the base of financial support for the orchestra. Oldberg's almost casual exchange of letters with Mayor Daley in 1957 regarding the Brussels Fair betrays a naïveté typical of the trustees. Kuyper was equally shortsighted in preparing for the tour. No one on his staff, including himself, had any experience with a major orchestra tour. With his characteristic penchant for secrecy, he failed to keep Oldberg and Reiner informed of all he knew. Frank three-way discussion between these top officials of the orchestra was rare: it was impossible for these three proud and egotistical men to meet face to face and iron out their differences, especially in view of their intense personal dislike for one another. Had they done so after the cancellation of the Lucerne Festival, they might have devised a unified approach to ANTA and the State Department based on the more limited tour anticipated by Schnitzer in May 1958. They might even have saved the Lucerne engagement, if that were the price of assuring Reiner's support.

Both ANTA and the State Department contributed to the disaster by progressively extending the tour and reducing the importance of major cities in Western Europe. Reiner had every right to recall Schnitzer's original proposal of a six-week tour. Magdanz's sudden cancellation of Lucerne may have reflected higher department policy, but Reiner viewed it as the arbitrary decision of an officious bureaucrat. Nor was the department's omission of Western European cities and festivals consistent with earlier promises to Reiner.

A major share of the blame must devolve on Fritz Reiner himself, as original instigator of the European tour and, ultimately, as its destroyer. He failed from the beginning to view such a tour realistically. With his myopic concentration on the week in Lucerne and his absurd notion of recording with the Vienna Philharmonic, he seemed not to have realized that a European tour, especially its Iron Curtain segment, could not be planned for his personal convenience. He failed to keep his promise to plan suitable programs, putting off that decision until other priorities intruded.

The European tour fiasco may thus be regarded as a paradigm of Fritz Reiner's handling of the practicalities of his career. Though he could command absolute authority over a hundred musicians in an orchestra, he failed to comprehend that he could not exercise equal control off the podium. Sealed off from the world at Rambleside, with Carlotta protectively aggravating his worst impulses, Reiner was incapable of flexibility. It was impossible for him to understand that the extraordinary skill he brought to communicating a musical conception to an orchestra, and through that orchestra to a public, had no counterpart outside performance. He could no more accept that reality than he could tolerate an inferior or badly prepared player in his orchestra, and he reacted as he would on the podium—with jejeune ill temper and intransigence. Consequently, he suffered a defeat that cast a cloud over the last years of his life.

Despite the scandal, Reiner and the orchestra continued the subscription season into April 1959, punctuated by a heavy schedule of recording. Reiner's most notable purely orchestral offerings in the spring of 1959 were the Bruckner Third Symphony, which was new to his repertory, and the orchestra's first performance of the Bartók Viola Concerto with Milton Preves as soloist. Reiner relaxed his anti-Russian feelings sufficiently to offer the Shostakovich Sixth Symphony, probably a remnant of his tour planning. George London appeared with distinction in an all-Wagner program, always a highlight of a Reiner season. The most innovative programming was Handel's *Judas Maccabaeus* with the orchestra's chorus and Maria Stader, John McCollum, Russell Oberlin, and Kenneth Smith as soloists. In a characteristically theatrical gesture, Reiner had the boys' choir of the First Unitarian Church, dressed in red robes and carrying palm branches, enter from either side of the stage to join in "See the Mighty Hero Comes. Sound the Trumpets." In preparing this oratorio, as with others of Handel, Reiner sought the musicological advice of Paul Henry Lang. Although he scarcely went the whole distance in pursuit of "authenticity," he included a harpsichord in the reduced orchestra and engaged the countertenor Russell Oberlin to sing the alto part. As George Kuyper pointed out, these programs, planned during Reiner's midseason holiday, betrayed little consideration of repertory suitable for the European tour.

In the fall of 1959 Reiner included in his preholiday sequence of programs six works new to Chicago and to his own repertory. To open the season in October, Reiner broke with the tradition of purely orchestral programs and offered Berlioz's dramatic symphony *Roméo et Juliette* with the orchestra's chorus. The following week brought Stravinsky's one-act opera *Mavra*. As with previous opera-in-concert presentations, the soloists sang from a platform at the rear of the orchestra. Since the opera's plot revolved around the tenor suitor's appearing in disguise, Reiner had his cast wear costumes borrowed from the Lyric Opera. On the same program with this lighthearted masquerade, Reiner conducted both of Respighi's most popular orchestral suites, *I pini di Roma* and *Fontane di Roma,* obviously in preparation for recording them.

Continuing with new repertory, Reiner programmed *Landscapes* by the Chinese-American Chou Wen-Chung in early November. This he followed a week later with Stravinsky's arrangement of Bach's chorale variations on *Vom Himmel hoch da komm' ich her,* on the same program with the local premiere of Ned Rorem's *Design for Orchestra.* With the chorus now established under Margaret Hillis, Reiner could schedule it regularly in shorter works: a week after the Bach-Stravinsky variations, the women from the chorus participated in a complete performance of Mendelssohn's incidental music for *A Midsummer Night's Dream.* December brought Virgil Thomson's orchestration of eight Chorale Preludes by Brahms, followed by Stravinsky's *Agon,* one of Reiner's rare performances of serial music. For this performance the orchestra engaged an outside mandolin player, who gave Reiner considerable trouble in rehearsal with missed entrances. At the final session an exasperated Reiner instructed the orchestra to make a cut that included the most troublesome passage for the harried mandolinist. At the concert that night, however, the mandolinist played into the deleted passage, and it took all of Reiner's fabled control to bring the whole orchestra together again. The player's problem was obviously his terror of Reiner, for, when the New York City Ballet appeared the following summer at Ravinia, he played his part perfectly in several performances under Robert Irving's direction. (Irving overcame his reluctance to program *Agon* at Ravinia once he learned that the orchestra had played it under Reiner.)

Since Reiner had reduced his 1959–1960 schedule to eighteen weeks, the remaining ten were filled by Walter Hendl, Alfred Wallenstein, Igor Markevitch, John Barbirolli, and the eighty-one-year-old Thomas Beecham, on his final American tour. Markevitch's appearances early in 1960 stirred rumors of Reiner's possible retirement from Chicago. The players in the orchestra were divided in their estimation of the guest's ability. At the first of his three subscription pairs Markevitch created an excellent impression on the press, audience, and many players. Speculation spread of the possibility of Markevitch's replacing Reiner and even of a "letter of intent" from the trustees offering him the music directorship.[38]

Rudolf Serkin had long been one of Reiner's favorite soloists, as a colleague on the Curtis faculty and a collaborator in Pittsburgh and in the summer broadcasts of the New York Philharmonic-Symphony. Serkin appeared with Reiner more than any other soloist, including six seasons out of ten in Chicago. They frequently expressed regret that their respective contracts prevented their recording together after the Brahms D Minor Concerto in Pittsburgh. In 1959 Serkin suggested playing something the next season outside his traditional repertory. Reiner proposed the Bartók First Piano Concerto, which had not been played by a major orchestra in the United States since he and the composer had introduced it in New York and Cincinnati more than thirty years earlier. Serkin welcomed the suggestion, especially the prospect of sharing Reiner's special knowledge of the music. They played the concerto at a pair of subscription concerts in Chicago in late February 1960 and repeated it in New York in mid-March.

As with orchestral repertory, RCA-Victor influenced the choice of some important soloists, despite Reiner's resentment of being used as the label's "house conductor." In the spring of 1960 he began an important recording collaboration with Van Cliburn, who had won the 1958 Tchaikovsky Competition in Moscow. Cliburn came under Hurok's management and signed a recording contract with RCA-Victor. Reiner and the young Texan made an oddly contrasting couple physically—the squat, laconic Hungarian with the gangling, curly-haired Texan towering over him. Reiner assumed a grandfatherly attitude toward Cliburn, who valued the older musician's artistic guidance. It was not the first time that Reiner had established a cordial relation with a young American. His bond with William Kapell was notably warm, and the Cliburn relationship interrupted a similar one with Byron Janis, whom RCA-Victor dropped in favor of the glamorous Texan. Cliburn first appeared in April 1960 with the Chicago Symphony Orchestra in the Schumann Concerto and the Brahms B-flat. He immediately recorded the former, leaving the Brahms to a later, and more fully studied, taping a year later. He also recorded the MacDowell Concerto and the Prokofiev Third with Walter Hendl conducting the orchestra.

Recordings had by now assumed importance with the Chicago Symphony Orchestra; as the association's share of expenses was paid off, net royalties began to add significantly to the orchestra's income. During Reiner's last two full seasons, from the fall of 1958 to the summer of 1960, he and the orchestra recorded fifty-five compositions for RCA-Victor in Chicago. During eleven weeks after his return in February 1959, recording sessions following six Thursday-Friday subscription pairs drew on repertory rehearsed and presented in concert. These included several short "marketable" selections—Tchaikovsky's *Marche slave,* the *Colas Breugnon* overture of Kabalevsky, and the march from *Prince Igor,* for instance—that provoked the anger of Oldberg and Cassidy when they had to be "rehearsed" in the weekly subscription programs. RCA-Victor's collections of such repertory, in spectacular performances and sound, proved to be money-makers for the company, for the orchestra itself, and, by no means least, for the conductor. Among Reiner's specialties were orchestral excerpts from *Die Meistersinger* and *Götterdämmerung,* Reiner's only recording of Wagner in Chicago. The spring of 1959 also produced Prokofiev's cantata

Alexander Nevsky, in which the Chicago Symphony Orchestra Chorus made its first recording with all members being paid union scale; Rosalind Elias was the mezzo-soprano soloist.

The following season brought more sessions for such major repertory as Respighi's two most popular Roman suites, Mahler's *Das Lied von der Erde* with Maureen Forrester and Richard Lewis, Reiner's third recorded version of *Don Juan,* the Fifth and Eighth symphonies of Schubert, Debussy's *La mer,* and the Haydn Eighty-eighth Symphony in G. For the "market" Reiner conducted music by the Viennese Strausses and a stunning performance of Rimsky-Korsakov's *Scheherazade,* featuring some of the orchestra's solo players in a context of ensemble brilliance. Recording considerations also dictated the inclusion of an extensive portion of Tchaikovsky's ballet score for *The Nutcracker* on the subscription programs.

Another problem created by recording considerations was the tendency of RCA-Victor executives to change their minds. Since Reiner planned his programs in anticipation of recordings, cancellations often required changes, sometimes dropping important repertory. Reiner postponed a projected *The Rite of Spring* because of RCA-Victor; his illness prevented his performing it in 1960–1961. It was one of the few major twentieth-century works he never played. Reiner was also anxious to record all the Beethoven symphonies, but RCA-Victor kept postponing completion of the series. Reiner and his orchestra recorded only six of them in nine years.

Meanwhile, the arrangement between RCA-Victor and British Decca involved Reiner in plans for more recording abroad. RCA-Victor had rejected recording the Verdi *Requiem* in Chicago because of the cost of the chorus and the number of sessions needed. At one point Decca considered recording it during the summer of 1959 in Florence, then with the Vienna Philharmonic while Reiner took time off from the Chicago Symphony Orchestra's European tour. Finally, the *Requiem* was set for the late spring of 1960 in Vienna, to be followed by sessions in Rome devoted to Verdi's *Otello* with Leonie Rysanek, Jon Vickers, and Tito Gobbi. Reiner applied to the American Federation of Musicians for permission to record the *Requiem* in Vienna and *Otello* in Rome but received permission only for the *Requiem.* [39]

Difficulties beset the *Requiem* sessions in Vienna, which occupied Reiner from 28 May to 26 June. Leonie Rysanek, who had given Reiner problems in Chicago in 1958, delighted Reiner at "a wonderful session" with the chorus but then failed to return, writing to Reiner that the dry and dusty air of Vienna hurt her throat. Carlotta observed that she was singing in *Un ballo in maschera* at the opera and had given a recital. Reiner was delighted with her replacement, Leontyne Price, who was in Vienna to sing in the *Requiem* with Giulini. When

Giulietta Simionato failed to appear, Rosalind Elias replaced her. Jussi Bjoerling confirmed his reputation for late appearances; these were his last recording sessions before his death the following fall. Only Giorgio Tozzi of the soloists was on hand when needed. Although it was possible to rearrange some of the schedule with the chorus, four orchestral sessions were devoted to Dvořák Slavonic Dances and Brahms Hungarian Dances.[40]

The 1959–1960 season of WGN-TV telecasts followed the pattern of the preceding year, as the *Tribune*-owned station continued to compile a series of programs as *Great Music from Chicago* for syndication. In both 1958–1959 and 1959–1960, Reiner opened and closed the series. He had by this time lost interest in the television activities of the orchestra. The quality of sound fell far short of what he considered appropriate. Added to a weekly stint of eight rehearsals or concerts, to say nothing of increased recording activity, the three-hour session on Sunday evenings with merely part of his orchestra became an appreciable burden as he grew older.

Within a year of becoming music director of the New York Philharmonic, Leonard Bernstein invited his old teacher to guest conduct his orchestra for two weeks of subscription concerts in March 1960. This was Reiner's first appearance in that orchestra's subscription season since 1943. It was old friends whom he greeted at his first rehearsal with an expression of his pleasure at conducting the orchestra of "my old pupil." As he had seventeen years earlier, Reiner offered music by Béla Bartók, this time on both programs. It was no longer the cacophonous horror it had been in the 1920s with the Cincinnati Symphony Orchestra. Bartók's music was now entering the mainstream of the symphonic repertory, thanks in large measure to Reiner's advocacy. Reiner celebrated the occasion by offering the suite from *The Miraculous Mandarin* and, with Serkin as soloist, the same First Piano Concerto that Mengelberg and the Philharmonic had not played in 1927.[41] Reiner received an enthusiastic welcome from the players in the orchestra, the Carnegie Hall audience, and the press, a triumph in a setting that he had long coveted. Bernstein and the Philharmonic management immediately arranged for Reiner's return the following season. When illness prevented that, they continued their efforts to bring the ailing conductor back to New York, hoping to include him in the dedicatory concerts at Lincoln Center.

CHAPTER XV

Finale

In the summer of 1959 the trustees of Northwestern University conferred on Reiner an honorary degree of Doctor of Fine Arts. Before the formal announcement from the university, Seymour Raven at the *Tribune* inquired of Reiner for his other academic honors. Reiner's reply listed his 1909 diploma from the Academy of Music in Budapest; Doctor of Music, University of Pennsylvania, June 1940; and Doctor of Music, *honoris causa,* University of Pittsburgh, June 1941. He added that he had also studied law at the university in Budapest, but not long enough to earn a diploma.[1] Since Northwestern would not confer a degree in absentia, the Reiners made a special three-day trip to Evanston to attend the commencement ceremonies in June. Two years later Loyola University in Chicago conferred on him an honorary degree of Doctor of Laws, but poor health prevented his personal appearance.

Life at Rambleside continued as before, with frequent entertaining of small groups of guests, most of them with business connections in recording or management. Carlotta's mother, Amelia Irwin, continued to be a concern: now in her nineties, she depended on the Reiners for her care in a nursing home in Norwalk. In April 1959 Reiner set up a trust fund for her to save taxes and ensure her future care, which cost him around four thousand dollars a year. Shortly before leaving for Chicago in October 1960, Reiner noted in his diary the death of his oldest and closest friend, Leo Weiner.

A more nagging concern was the welfare of Tuśy in Ljubljana, who now lived with her mother and her son, Vovček. Both Tuśy and her mother wrote to Reiner complaining of his neglect and lack of understanding. He responded, usually via Carlotta, with characteristic exasperation. One source of Tuśy's resentment was that the Reiners visited Eva in Zurich but had not visited Ljubljana since the summer of 1952. In 1960, after the Verdi *Requiem* sessions in Vienna, it was Eva, not Tuśy, whom the Reiners invited to join them at the Hotel Astoria in Albisola, a seaside resort. This was to be their last visit to continental Europe.

George Kuyper's disappointment at Reiner's cancellation of the European tour assumed such obsessive proportions that he sought another position. After failing in the spring of 1959 to obtain a post as manager of the Philadelphia Orchestra, he accepted an offer from the Southern California Symphony Association in November 1959 to manage the Los Angeles Philharmonic Orchestra and the summer activities of the Hollywood Bowl.[2] When Kuyper met with Oldberg on the morning of Friday, 6 November, to plan the agenda for a trustees' monthly luncheon meeting later that day, he told the president that he had agreed to assume the Los Angeles position in three weeks.[3] Following the trustees' meeting, Kuyper returned to Orchestra Hall thoroughly shaken, for Oldberg had not reported the manager's resignation to the other trustees. The Chicago press reported Kuyper's departure on Monday the ninth as a dispatch from Los Angeles.

Eric Oldberg immediately offered the position to Seymour Raven, Claudia Cassidy's colleague at the Chicago *Tribune*. A native of Chicago, Raven had a master's degree in music from Northwestern University. He had at one time played in the percussion section and studied conducting with the Chicago Civic Orchestra. Since 1947 he had been Cassidy's loyal associate at the *Tribune,* and she was deeply devoted to him. In engaging Raven, Oldberg explicitly sought to firm up her support, which he regarded as essential to his hope of replacing Reiner at the helm of the Chicago Symphony Orchestra. Despite his dedication and knowledge of the public aspect of a symphony orchestra, Raven was initially inexperienced in management. His was on-the-job training, under the guidance of Eric Oldberg and in consultation with his former associate at the *Tribune*. The caustic critic, who had castigated the social elite for "usurping" the Orchestral Association, now found himself its surrogate, while Cassidy was co-opted in her long-standing confrontation with Orchestra Hall. Raven got on well with Reiner. The tour fiasco had a chastening effect on the conductor, and the two men established a firm mutual respect. Nor could Reiner ignore how effectively Oldberg had outmaneuvered him vis-à-vis Cassidy. Even in disagreements, Reiner readily excused Raven as the agent of the trustees.

Appointing Seymour Raven as manager was Oldberg's first step in easing Reiner out of the Chicago Symphony Orchestra. His complaints, voiced privately but passionately, centered on Reiner's failure to become a part of the "Chicago family." With his almost obsessive nostalgia for the days of Frederick Stock, Oldberg blamed Reiner for the breakdown of the once happy relations between the players, the management, and the trustees. Oldberg fondly recalled the time when the wives of trustees knitted garments for the newborn babies of the musicians' wives. The conductor's fee demands had, in Oldberg's opinion, caused the cancellation of Chicago Title and Trust's sponsorship of the weekly television program. He blamed Reiner for the organization of the players' committee, convinced that the conductor's harsh treatment of the players had fueled the opposition of "a few trouble-makers" to the well-meaning efforts of the trustees and the generous community they represented.[4]

As early as January 1960 Robert Marsh reported "rumors in New York" that Reiner was planning to leave his post in Chicago.[5] In April Roger Dettmer raised the question of Reiner's position under the headline "Is Fritz Reiner to Be Eased Out?" citing hearsay that the conductor's contract, which would expire in 1961, had not yet been renewed. He warned the trustees of the possible consequences to the orchestra of losing Reiner.[6] Briefed regularly by Raven on the progress of Oldberg's negotiations for the renewal of Reiner's contract, Cassidy withheld comment until mid-May, when she asserted that "all is not rosy at Orchestra Hall." There were, she wrote, "too many off nights" while the conductor "used the podium for his own convenience." She again belabored the canceled European tour, the influence of RCA-Victor, and Reiner's failure to make Chicago his home.[7]

From entries in Reiner's diary it appears that contract discussions were under way in April 1960, when Raven telephoned him to convey Oldberg's offer of a one-year extension to 1962. This would renew the terms of his existing contract, except to reduce the conductor's schedule from eighteen to sixteen weeks with a corresponding reduction in pay—forty concerts at the rate of one thousand dollars each that had prevailed throughout Reiner's tenure so far. Reiner responded with a counteroffer of forty concerts for forty thousand dollars for each of two years, to the spring of 1963, with out-of-town concerts at fifteen hundred dollars each.[8] At some point Reiner appears to have considered resigning his post, according to an undated note typed by Carlotta indicating that his desire for an easier workload would make it impossible for him to fulfill his responsibilities as music director of the orchestra.[9] There is no indication in his own files or in the trustees' minutes that Reiner ever sent such a letter. He may have had in mind following the example of such other elder conductors as Pierre Monteux and Bruno Walter, who guest conducted in the United States and abroad without the administrative responsibilities of being a music director under contract to one orchestra. The interest of the New York Philharmonic in his return the next season may have encouraged such thoughts. His establishment as a major recording artist made Reiner financially independent of an increasingly arduous full season at modest compensation. His recording royalties were approaching his salary from the Orchestral Association.

At the end of April Oldberg informed the trustees of the proposed renewal of Reiner's contract for one year, through the 1961–1962 season.[10] On 10 May, after the Reiners had returned to Rambleside before leaving for Vienna, Oldberg wrote the conductor outlining the new agreement and setting forty concerts for 1961–1962. He was apparently sufficiently certain of a settlement to instruct Raven to call Reiner to discuss a press announcement. Reiner did not sign this new contract until 23 September; there was no public announcement. Two weeks later, after he had resumed rehearsals in Chicago, the entire question of contract became moot when Reiner suffered a serious heart attack.

Despite Marsh's reports in early 1959, Fritz Reiner apparently enjoyed normal health until late in his seventy-second year. He was, to be sure, a resolute hypochondriac, abetted by Carlotta's overprotectiveness. Those who knew and worked with Reiner could have easily attributed his and Carlotta's constant complaints about his workload to poor health. To judge from entries in his diary, his principal afflictions were dental and muscular. The rigid physical control of his conducting style apparently created considerable muscular tension, especially in his shoulders and back, requiring frequent recourse to massage. During summers at Rambleside, he had the excellent therapy of his own swimming pool. On vacations abroad, the Reiners often visited seaside resorts or spas where they could swim regularly. In August 1959, during a summer spent entirely at Rambleside, he noted in his diary that he had talked by phone with his doctor: "Thank God, negative!" He did not indicate the source of his concern.[11]

Reiner's willingness in the spring of 1960 to reduce his duties in Chicago undoubtedly indicates weariness on his part, not surprising in a man of nearly seventy-two. Nor was his reluctance to conduct more than five concerts a week for eight weeks in Europe unreasonable. Carlotta's attitude toward health generally and medicine especially was ambivalent and mercurial. The daughter of a devout Christian Scientist, she rejected that aspect of her upbringing to the point of trying to dissuade her mother from the practice. Although she could inveigh vehemently against the medical profession and complain about specific doctors, she did not hesitate to call on them in the middle of the night at the slightest indication of her husband's discomfort. Reiner saw his doctor frequently enough to have had warning of cardiac trouble, had there been evidence of it before October 1960. Given his hypochondria, he certainly would have modified his life-style accordingly.

After his return from Italy in July 1960, Reiner enjoyed a relaxed summer at Rambleside, setting out on 29 September, by train as usual, for Chicago and the apartment on North State Parkway. For his opening concert on Thursday, 13 October, he planned three of his specialties—the prelude to *Die Meistersinger*, the Schumann Second Symphony, and the Prokofiev Fifth. Through Hurok, the orchestra had scheduled the American debut of the Russian pianist Sviatoslav Richter at a special benefit concert on Saturday evening, the fifteenth, to be followed by a recording of the Brahms B-flat Concerto. Following a restful weekend after his arrival in Chicago, Reiner began rehearsals on Monday, 3 October. On the fourth he attended a cocktail party given in his honor by RCA-Victor at the Ambassador Hotel. On the sixth he discussed dates for a second New York Philharmonic appearance the following season.

Early in the morning of Friday, 7 October, Reiner experienced agonizing chest pains and was rushed to St. Luke's Hospital, suffering from what was eventually diagnosed as a blockage of the coronary artery. Later the orchestra announced that Reiner had suffered what Oldberg described as "a congestive condition." Although Reiner's disease had nothing to do with his specialty of neurosurgery, Eric Oldberg as a prominent member of the staff at St. Luke's Hospital in effect took charge of his care. Both he and Carlotta were reluctant at this point to reveal Reiner's condition publicly as a heart attack. Raven secured the services of Erich Leinsdorf, a favorite of RCA-Victor, to conduct the Richter concert and recording. Walter Hendl took over Reiner's program for the opening subscription pair.[12]

After seven weeks at St. Luke's, Reiner returned to the apartment on North State Parkway. At the hospital and at home, he discussed orchestra business with Oldberg and Raven, while Carlotta scrupulously screened all communications from friends. The Reiners went to Rambleside on 19 December and did not return to Orchestra Hall until the end of March, for five final weeks of subscription concerts. On the evening of 30 March, he walked slowly onto the stage of Orchestra Hall and mounted a three-sided enclosed podium surrounding a high chair, modeled on the one that Frederick Stock had used in his last years. It had been eleven months since Fritz Reiner had conducted his orchestra in a concert, and both the orchestra and the audience welcomed him with a standing ovation at the beginning and end of a program consisting of Mozart's Symphony no. 39 in E-flat, Wagner's *Siegfried Idyll,* and the Beethoven "Pastoral" Symphony. His instrumental soloists during the following weeks included Leonard Pennario, Eugene Istomin, and Isaac Stern, the latter in the Second Violin Concerto of Bartók, on the same program as the Pastorale, Fantasy, and Fugue of Leo Weiner. An all-Beethoven concert closed the season with the First and Ninth symphonies, both of which RCA-Victor recorded a few days later.

The Reiners gave up their leased apartment at the end of April and stayed at the Blackstone Hotel during two weeks of recording before returning to Rambleside. They had considered visiting Europe that summer, going so far as to make reservations on the *Queen Mary* for 12 July. However, while lunching at the St. Regis Hotel in New York during a break in recording playbacks, Reiner suffered another attack. After a three-week stay at Doctors' Hospital in New York, he needed a nurse for three more weeks at home. Despite that convalescence, he suffered another setback and was in Norwalk Hospital for another week. During much of this time, Reiner was out of touch with Raven and Oldberg, who had by now taken over planning the coming season with only occasional input from the ailing music director. Reiner's own Chicago schedule repeatedly changed with the ups and downs of his health, creating major problems for Raven in his efforts to engage and reschedule guest conductors as Reiner's plans changed.

Carlotta Reiner later recalled the frequency of her husband's "attacks" in numbers varying from eight to thirteen. Many of these appear to have been episodes of pain and distress, requiring a short rest. Later developments in heart surgery might have prolonged Reiner's useful life significantly, but in the early 1960s, medication and rest were the only therapy available, and these offered uncertain prognosis. Reiner gave up smoking on his doctors' orders and ate a more modest diet, eschewing rich food and heavy sauces. Carlotta and Ann Gaito showed great ingenuity in making plain food interesting to him. In airports or railway stations, he used a wheelchair; otherwise he walked even more deliberately than he had before. For Carlotta, her husband's illness became her consuming preoccupation, intensifying her protective solicitude. Although she discussed his condition explicitly with his doctors, she avoided specifics with their friends, alternating between expressions of hope for his recovery and elaborate descriptions of his weakness. When Reiner was feeling well, he and Carlotta had friends in for lunch. Overnight guests were out of the question, since Reiner had moved into the guest room in the studio wing to avoid climbing the stairs to his regular bedroom. Most of the visitors were professional or business friends, who became accustomed to receiving last-minute calls from Carlotta, canceling a visit if necessary. Several of her notations in the diaries of Reiner's middle-of-the-night distress followed days when they entertained visitors. They celebrated Reiner's seventy-third birthday in December 1961 with friends, including Francis Robinson, Dorle and Dario Soria, and Richard Mohr.

Although Reiner was unable to visit his daughters in Europe, he was in touch with them regularly by letter. Following visits to her sister in Ljubljana, Eva confirmed Tuśy's reports of poor health and straitened finances, for which her former husband took no responsibility. According to the younger sister, Tuśy was bringing her drinking problem under control. To Tuśy's appeals for money, Reiner responded grudgingly with one hundred dollars to help pay her debts. He sent another one hundred dollars to outfit Vovček with what Carlotta called his "trousseau" when he joined the Yugoslav army. Finally, Reiner committed himself early in 1962 to sending Tuśy twenty-five dollars a month via Eva; later, after the death of Carlotta's mother in November at the age of ninety-seven, he raised the monthly stipend to fifty dollars.

Reiner returned to Chicago early in 1962 for six weeks of concerts, never scheduling them in more than two successive weeks. His programs included music by Richard Strauss—the *Sinfonia domestica, Also sprach Zarathustra,* and excerpts from *Salome.* Rudolf Serkin played the Beethoven "Emperor" Concerto, a last collaboration with Reiner. Van Cliburn returned in the Rachmaninoff Second Concerto in March, and the season closed on 26–27 April 1962 with *Israel in Egypt,* Reiner's last performances as music director of the Chicago Symphony Orchestra. On 23 April Orchestra Hall obliquely announced Reiner's retirement as music director, a decision recorded several days earlier in the trustees' minutes:

> Fritz Reiner, Music Director of the Chicago Symphony Orchestra for the past nine seasons, will serve as Musical Adviser for the season of 1962–1963. He will highlight his tenth year of distinguished service by conducting several weeks of subscription concerts in Orchestra Hall.
> The announcement was made by Dr. Eric Oldberg, President of The Orchestral Association, after the Board of Trustees was notified of Dr. Reiner's desire for a relaxation of his responsibilities.
> Following an illness in October, 1960, Dr. Reiner reduced his activities during the 1960–61 and 1961–62 seasons upon the advice of his physicians. "I have since determined," said Dr. Reiner, "that with evenly spaced appearances, and without the burden of administrative responsibility, I can look forward to much fruitful activity."
> "This expectation is shared by all of us," said Dr. Oldberg, "and we hope to have many years of great Reiner concerts in Chicago. With this in mind, we have made a standing invitation to Fritz Reiner."[13]

There was no mention of the fact that the contract settled before the conductor's heart attack in October 1960 had in fact expired in April 1962.

At the final concerts of the season on 26 and 27 April, the audience greeted Reiner with vociferous warmth. On Thursday evening, he responded, "Thank you a thousand times for your support and appreciation. I have only three words—I will be back." No ceremony marked the conclusion of Reiner's direction of the Chicago Symphony Orchestra, no tribute spoken from the stage, no presentation of suitably engraved silver to add to the collection of memorabilia at Rambleside, no special concert to honor the departing leader. In her review Claudia Cassidy expressed regret that Reiner ended his reign with a Handel oratorio that featured the chorus in such "singularly undramatic" music rather than with "Reiner and Reiner's orchestra at their zenith."[14] The next week, the trustees announced that the French conductor Jean Martinon would become music director of the Chicago Symphony Orchestra in the fall of 1963. The newly designated musical adviser had played no part in that choice. Carlotta maintained in later years that had Oldberg or Raven consulted her husband, he would have urged the engagement of Karl Böhm.

Eric Oldberg had actually set in motion the choice of a successor to Fritz Reiner some time previously, certainly as early as George Kuyper's resignation in November 1959. At that time, well before Reiner's illness, he confided to associates that Reiner would be the next to go. After Reiner's heart attack, Oldberg hoped to persuade his friend George Szell to move from Cleveland to Chicago, but Szell would not leave Cleveland and strongly urged retaining Reiner for as long as he was able to serve.[15] Raven went to Grand Rapids, Michigan, early in 1961 to hear Igor Markevitch conduct a French orchestra on tour there. He reported an unfavorable impression of that conductor's command of the standard classics. In the spring of 1961 Oldberg and Raven traveled to Dallas to meet with Georg Solti, who had recently parted from the Los Angeles Philharmonic over Mrs. Chandler's and George Kuyper's handling of the engagement of Zubin Mehta as associate conductor. In a meeting with Solti and his manager, Siegfried Hearst, Oldberg and Raven discussed the Chicago position with Solti but insisted that he conduct at least twenty weeks each season and make Chicago his residence. Solti, who had just accepted the musical direction of the Royal Opera at Covent Garden, would not agree to such terms.[16]

Meanwhile Jean Martinon had made a successful American debut at Ravinia in the summer of 1960. Raven engaged him to conduct at Orchestra Hall for three weeks during the winter season of 1961–1962. At their meeting in March 1962 the trustees approved a five-year contract with Martinon beginning in the fall of 1963. It provided that the conductor would make his home in Chicago and would agree not to conduct anywhere for at least four weeks of his midseason vacations.[17]

Fritz Reiner was not the only problem facing Oldberg and Raven after the latter became manager of the orchestra early in 1960. Seymour Raven inherited potentially explosive relations with the players and with their union. The organization of the players' committee a few days after Reiner's cancellation of the European tour was the culmination of simmering discontent with working conditions generally and with the "cozy" relations between the union and association that excluded the musicians. Although Reiner's action triggered the formation of the committee, its roots went back to Petrillo's long-standing ban on such a committee as an invasion of the prerogatives of the union as its members' sole bargaining representative. In dealing with the Orchestral Association's first serious labor problems, Oldberg and Raven counted on Petrillo's opposition to the players' organizing their own committee. They believed that he would support the association in its effort to stamp out a perceived conspiracy of a few troublemakers. Neither Oldberg nor Raven recognized the Chicago players' growing militancy as part of a larger movement in the labor relations of all of the major symphony orchestras in the United States. These players, sensing that their unions did not represent them adequately, were taking matters into their own hands.[18] This miscalculation cost the Chicago Symphony Orchestra dearly in the summer and fall of 1962.

In the spring of 1961 Raven gave the required one-year notice to five players in the orchestra that their contracts would not be renewed in 1962. He assumed that Petrillo would not support the players, who were regarded as ringleaders in opposition to both the association and the union leadership. Confronted by a group of musicians from the orchestra, Reiner, as music director, disclaimed any knowledge of Raven's action and made it clear that he did not support it on artistic grounds.[19] Petrillo ultimately persuaded Oldberg to withdraw these termination notices, as a personal favor, which Oldberg assumed would be reciprocated.[20]

This tension culminated in the summer of 1962 in an acrimonious confrontation between the players and the Orchestral Association during negotiations of a new union contract, which in the past had been settled confidentially between the union and association leadership. This time the players forced Petrillo to allow their committee's participation in the negotiations as "observers." In a ten-page review in April 1962 of his role in the association's growing labor difficulties, Eric Oldberg did not hesitate to place on Reiner a major share of blame for the deterioration of the "family" relationship between the association and the musicians. Although he cited other problems, including bad faith on the part of Petrillo and the players' committee, Oldberg recapitulated in angry detail his long-harbored resentment of Reiner. He sent a copy to Reiner four days before Reiner's designation by the trustees as musical adviser.[21]

The musicians tried to draw Reiner into the controversy. Having reached an impasse with the association in September, they telegraphed their former music director at his Rambleside home, "requesting [his] participation in a mediatory capacity." Despite press reports, Reiner had no intention of acting in this role, and he wired the players' spokesman accordingly. In another telegram, he assured Raven of his best wishes for an amicable settlement.[22] In due course, this bitter dispute was resolved following the intervention of Mayor Daley. At a special meeting of the Orchestral Association in the fall of 1962, Eric Oldberg distributed a five-page memorandum that Carlotta's friend Rebecca Lowry described as an "apologia pro vita sua."[23] Oldberg stepped down as president of the association and resigned as trustee at the association's next annual meeting.

He was deeply embittered, not least by what he perceived as the betrayal by the orchestra musicians and the end of the Chicago Symphony Orchestra as he revered it. For this outcome he held Fritz Reiner largely responsible.

While the Chicago Symphony Orchestra awaited the arrival of its new music director, it announced a season of guest conductors, including seven weeks with Reiner. His programs generally repeated his long-established repertory, but there were a few important innovations. He introduced the *Deux images* of Bartók to the Chicago audience and offered the world premiere of a symphony that his friend Robert Russell Bennett dedicated to him. Having delighted Reiner with her contribution to his recording of the Verdi *Requiem* in Vienna, Leontyne Price joined him and the Chicago orchestra in Berlioz's *Les nuits d'été* and Falla's *El amor brujo*. Reiner conducted the Chicago Symphony Orchestra for the last time, now as a guest, on 18, 19, and 20 April 1963 in a program consisting of Rossini's overture to *Semiramide,* the Brahms Second Symphony, and the Beethoven G Major Concerto with Cliburn. He was too ill to conduct on 2–3 May as originally scheduled.

From time to time Reiner had turned down various conductors, some of them with prestigious posts, who wanted to study privately with him. He maintained that training conductors required an institutional setting. After his retirement as music director of the Chicago Symphony Orchestra, several schools approached him regarding conductor training. The University of Florida, where Dohnányi had been in residence at the end of his life, invited Reiner to supervise instruction in conducting, but such a post would have kept him away from Rambleside. He responded more positively to an invitation from Peter Mennin to participate in a program, sponsored by the Ford Foundation, of auditioning young conductors at the Peabody Institute. Although Mennin had moved to the presidency of Juilliard, he was still in charge of the Peabody program, in which a panel of distinguished conductors auditioned and advised applicants. By letter and in phone conversations, Reiner and Mennin discussed audition procedures and repertory in anticipation of Reiner's joining the jury, but he withdrew from what he came to view as a responsibility that would conflict with other commitments. However, the seriousness with which he took Mennin's project is evidence of a continuing interest in training conductors.

Reiner's illness sharply curtailed his recording activity: in three years he recorded only fifteen compositions, twelve of them in Chicago. In the spring of 1961, his first sessions after his illness, he recorded three Beethoven symphonies—the First, Sixth, and Ninth. The following year he re-recorded *Also sprach Zarathustra*. Otherwise his Chicago recordings were collaborations with two soloists for whom RCA-Victor planned intensive promotion. Van Cliburn and Reiner recorded the Beethoven "Emperor" Concerto and the Brahms B-flat Concerto in 1961, the Rachmaninoff Second Concerto in 1962, and the Beethoven G Major Concerto in 1963. The latter was Reiner's last recording with the Chicago Symphony Orchestra. With Leontyne Price he recorded Falla's *El amor brujo* and the Berlioz *Les nuits d'été* in March 1963. When Reiner stepped down as music director of the orchestra in 1962, RCA-Victor notified Raven that henceforth any recordings with the Chicago Symphony Orchestra would be on a "date basis." Without Reiner there was no longer a continuing contract with the orchestra. At the same time the company negotiated a new contract with Reiner that permitted him to record with any orchestra that he and RCA-Victor agreed on. Their discussions included possibilities of opera recordings in Europe that never materialized. In late 1962 Reiner was in touch with the Vienna Philharmonic concerning the possibility of recording music by Bartók, Weiner, Kodály, and Prokofiev.

RCA-Victor had recently arranged with *Reader's Digest* to make special recordings of standard orchestral music to be sold by the magazine through mail-order promotion. Most of these recordings were with the Royal Philharmonic Orchestra in London. The repertory was selected according to a poll by the magazine of its readers' preferences. In late September 1962 the Reiners flew to London for recordings of the Brahms Fourth Symphony and the Tchaikovsky Fifth for this *Reader's Digest* series. RCA-Victor paid Reiner a flat fee of four thousand dollars for each symphony, plus travel expenses. Eva Bartenstein came to London from Zurich to join the Reiners at the Westbury Hotel. The hotel manager turned out to be a music lover, a member of the Berlioz Society, who gave his distinguished guest special attention. After completing the Brahms Fourth on 5 October, Reiner suffered chest pains in the middle of the night and was taken to a London hospital. Though he had to cancel the Tchaikovsky recording, Reiner was well enough to fly back to the United States a week later. At Rambleside his doctor examined him and reported no damage from the London trip.[24]

Reiner made his last recordings a year later in New York with handpicked players. The musicians were identified on the record label as "Fritz Reiner and His Orchestra." Recruited by Felix Eyle, personnel manager of the Metropolitan Opera orchestra, these old Reiner hands dated back to his days at Curtis: flutist Julius Baker, oboist Robert Bloom, and violist Walter Trampler, among others. The only player from Chicago was violinist Victor Aitay, who came from Hungary in 1946 to join the Pittsburgh Symphony Orchestra, played under Reiner at the Metropolitan Opera, and came to Chicago in 1954 as assistant concertmaster. Reiner originally planned to record the 95th and 101st symphonies of Haydn and Mozart's Divertimento in B-flat for Thirteen Winds, but he decided in June to drop the divertimento. RCA-Victor recorded the two Haydn symphonies at Manhattan Center in widely spaced sessions in September.[25] As with most of Reiner's recording sessions, Richard Mohr was the producer, and Lewis Layton the engineer.

Now that Reiner was no longer committed to the Chicago Symphony Orchestra, he could accept invitations to conduct both the New York Philharmonic and the Cleveland Orchestra. Rudolf Bing invited him to return to the Metropolitan Opera early in the 1963–1964 season.[26] Reiner jokingly referred to his discussions with Bing as planning "a little opera," which was in fact *Götterdämmerung*, for the Wagnerian repertory was the general manager's main interest in engaging Reiner.[27] When asked why he had accepted, of all operas, one of the longest and most demanding in the entire repertory, Reiner brushed off such concerns quite casually, even when Robert Marsh in Chicago suggested that it might well be *Reinerdämmerung*. Despite Carlotta's deep concern, Reiner seemed quite at ease with his decision, spending months engrossed in the score that he had not conducted since 1936 in San Francisco. Although he seldom discussed music he was studying, he was anxious to share his thoughts about *Götterdämmerung* with friends. He talked of his preliminary impressions of singers new to him and the cuts he was making in the performance to meet the Metropolitan's time limits. He even went to his study to fetch the big score to illustrate his observations.

It seemed as if, after months of coddling his failing health, Fritz Reiner was intent on giving this effort all the energy and concentration that he could summon, without worrying about the consequences. It is possible that he had come to believe that, if he was to go, it would be in a blaze of Wagnerian glory. He enjoyed working with Birgit Nilsson, whom he found "rock solid." The cast also included, as Waltraute, Irene Dalis, whose early rehearsals so impressed Reiner that he regretted the cuts in her scene. The first performance of *Götterdämmerung* was set for Thursday, 14 November. Reiner was to conduct five performances of the opera, the last on 14 December, after which he planned to go to Chicago for rehearsals and concerts to celebrate his seventy-fifth birthday.

On 20 October the Reiners left Rambleside to take up residence in a suite at the Essex House in New York. Except for a three-day weekend at home, Reiner began a daily schedule of piano, orchestra, and stage rehearsals, which the Met staff spaced at comfortable intervals out of consideration for his health. At the dress rehearsal for the prologue and act I on Friday, 8 November, Reiner was so frail that he had difficulty holding his baton high enough for the singers and orchestra to see his beat. Felix Eyle, the orchestra manager, adjusted the light on Reiner's stand and shifted some players to improve his visibility. For the ailing conductor, the orchestra and singers poured forth the vibrant Wagnerian sound typical of Reiner. During breaks in this long session, Carlotta brought hot broth and sandwiches to her husband, who remained in his chair at the podium.[28] Reiner spent a restful weekend in the hotel. A typical New York autumn rain was falling, with a penetrating dampness and chill. On the evening of Monday the eleventh, after rehearsing act II, Reiner came down with a cold, which, given his weakened condition, quickly developed into pneumonia. He was moved from the hotel to Mt. Sinai Hospital. Josef Rosenstock took over the final rehearsal and the performances.

Knowing that the end was near, Carlotta regretted that her Fritz could not die at Rambleside. As the news of Reiner's death came over the radio on the afternoon and evening of 15 November, friends and colleagues gathered at the Essex House to console Carlotta. Dorle Jarmel Soria, who had first known Reiner when she was press representative for the Judson office in the 1930s, was a tower of strength, doing her best to dilute Carlotta's refreshment and keeping order in a room full of sympathetic friends. Walter Legge, who had been with HMV during Reiner's Covent Garden seasons, sat on the floor, holding Carlotta's hand. Van Cliburn called from wherever he was on tour, offering to cancel engagements to return to New York to play at Reiner's funeral. Hurok was out of the country, but his colleague Walter Prude was there with his wife, Agnes de Mille. Arthur Judson came to pay his respects to a musician whose career had once been close to him. Rudolf Bing, after a performance of *La bohème,* stopped by on his way to his own suite in the same hotel. By midnight the room was empty but for Dorle Jarmel Soria, who stayed with Carlotta through the night. The next morning Ann Gaito arrived from Connecticut to relieve her, while the Hockers and a few friends joined Carlotta to plan her husband's funeral. William Schuman, then president of Lincoln Center, agreed to speak. Reluctant to carry the full burden of the occasion, he suggested that the Juilliard String Quartet play some appropriate music. Although Reiner had never met them, he had admired their recordings of the Bartók string quartets. Carlotta and Schuman were delighted with their choice of the finale of the Sixth Bartók Quartet.

People whom the *Times* described as "Notables of the Musical World" gathered on the eighteenth at the Campbell Funeral Home on Madison Avenue to honor the memory of their great colleague. Conspicuously absent was anyone from Chicago, officially or unofficially. The program book for the orchestra's concerts of 21 and 22 November announced that the scheduled performances the following week of Mozart's Requiem and Stravinsky's Symphony of Psalms would be dedicated to Fritz Reiner's memory. When President John F. Kennedy was assassinated in Dallas, the Mozart and Stravinsky works were dedicated jointly to his memory and to Reiner's. The one orchestra to give special recognition to Reiner was the New York Philharmonic. Prior to Reiner's death, Leonard Bernstein had taped a *Tribute to Teachers* telecast in which he spoke of his great mentor as "the one man, among those still living, who was most influential in shaping [my] career." The program aired on national television in December.[29]

William Schuman delivered the final tribute to Reiner at the funeral.

"Example," according to Albert Schweitzer, "is everything." "Example is everything." Nowhere in the myriad activities of man is example so clearly the all-embracing criterion as in teaching. All great artists by the very nature of their functioning are teachers. Teachers because their role is to interpret, to reveal, to illumine. Yet it is rare indeed that we think of the artist of superb gifts as other than a virtuoso performer. Fritz Reiner, to be sure, was a virtuoso performer. But he was ever the teacher. He taught not in the classroom alone. He taught all who performed in his orchestras—all who heard him—all who saw him. Fritz was the teacher of all of us through every facet of his astonishing mastery of the art he practiced.

Yet these demonstrable attributes were the end result of the true example of his life in art: a complete and total commitment of self—of all his intellectual and emotional resources to the art that was his life. Example, indeed, is overwhelming.

Can the qualities of a man ever fully be revealed in words? I think not. But key words come to mind when one thinks of Fritz Reiner. The first is respect. This master enjoyed the respect of all. He won it through a lifelong work of thought and action. Respect for his superb craftsmanship was the most obvious: that revolutionary conducting technique with its economy of means—the turn of the wrist—the direction of the eye—the sound elicited through gestures contained within the modest proportions of the body sphere. Respect, too, for the cool objectivity which enabled him to stand aside and evaluate—an objectivity of such high discipline that it was at his beck and call to serve subjective conditions. Cool objectivity, yes—but as the tool to insure the warm result so deeply felt. Respect for his dedication to the new music of his time, especially to that of his own generation. Respect for his programs over the years which included virtually all the major works new to our century. Respect for his scholarship and his true sense of music's history. Respect for his constant awareness of music's constant need for nourishment at the source and his response to the composers of his day.

Another key word is courage. Always the courage of his convictions in standards of performance, in choice of repertory and in his personal beliefs. And to the end the physical courage to go on—knowing that it might take its toll. Let us not be deceived—beneath that cool objectivity, which we have noted, was a deep passion for making music, and for him making music was life.

And a third word is devotion: the devotion of the artist to his art; the devotion his dedication evoked in others. And for Fritz, the strains of professional life were eased by his personal life enriched beyond measure by the devotion of his wife, Carlotta, truly his helpmate for more than thirty years.

"It is not the critic," said Theodore Roosevelt, "who counts, not the man who points out how the strong man stumbled, or where the doer of deeds could have done them better. The credit belongs to the man who is actually in the arena . . . who strives valiantly . . . knows the great enthusiasms, the great devotions, and spends himself in a worthy cause, who . . . knows in the end the triumph of high achievement; so that his place shall never be with those cold and timid souls who know neither victory nor defeat."

Words of Shakespeare and Learned Hand:

> "Fear no more the heat o' the sun,
> Nor the furious winter's rages;
> Thou thy worldly task has done,
> Home art gone, and ta'en thy wages."

"That is the nature of all things: though, little as we may like to acknowledge it, it is irrelevant to their value and their significance; for permanence as such has neither value nor significance. All that will then matter will be all that matters now; and what matters now is what are the wages we do take home. Those are what we choose to make them; we can fix our pay; the splendor and the tragedy of life lie just in that. Values are ultimate, they admit of no reduction below themselves."

Our tribute today is one of affection and gratitude. We are grateful for his full and productive life; grateful for the privilege of our association with so pre-eminent an artist. And for us, his friends and colleagues—his pupils—his example will endure. His unassailable standards will ever guide all of us. As the years unfold, he will be with us through that special wonder of human life— "the immortality of continuing influence."[30]

Carlotta Reiner lived at Rambleside until her death in January 1983, devoted to the home that meant so much to her and to her husband. The urn containing Reiner's ashes remained for some time on the piano in his study, before she moved it to his darkroom in the basement.

In the first years after his death, Carlotta ventured occasionally into New York City to visit old friends in the theater and music worlds. She was an honored guest at the opening of Philharmonic Hall in September 1964, an occasion in which Leonard Bernstein and the New York Philharmonic had hoped for Reiner's active participation. When the new Metropolitan Opera House was finished at Lincoln Center in 1966, she joined Rudolf Bing in placing bronze markers in memory of Fritz Reiner on seats as close as possible to the conductor's podium. For a time Carlotta was active in the Metropolitan Opera Guild, serving on committees for special benefits, but she soon found that her companions in that work were more interested in current opera affairs than in the past in which she was so absorbed. She also visited Chicago, where the Oldbergs, Cassidy, and a few other friends received her warmly, but discovered that they too had moved on beyond Fritz Reiner. When a fellow guest at a concert commented what an occasion it was to have her visiting Orchestra Hall, she replied that *every* night her husband conducted there was an occasion. In November 1973, while the Chicago Symphony Orchestra was in New York for a pair of Carnegie Hall concerts, Robert Sherman at WQXR arranged a program to mark the tenth anniversary of Reiner's death. He interviewed Carlotta and several Chicago musicians, who reminisced about Fritz Reiner. She enjoyed the occasion and often played a tape recording of the program for visitors at Rambleside. A few years after Reiner's death, Carlotta traveled to Europe to visit the Bartenstein family in Zurich and Tuśy and Vovček in Ljubljana, presenting them with a new electric refrigerator. For several years she sought relief from the rigors of Connecticut winters in the Caribbean, usually at St. Vincent, where some Davis Hill neighbors also spent the winter.

As time passed Carlotta left Rambleside and Westport rarely, expecting her friends to visit her. A few friends remained loyal to her: the totally devoted Hockers, on whom she relied for business advice; several nearby neighbors; a new friend from New York City, Betty Stillman, who spent many weekends at Rambleside; and Roger Dettmer, no longer a Chicago critic but always a welcome visitor. Despite her efforts to retire, Ann Gaito had to return to the house periodically when Carlotta found a succession of replacements unacceptpable. When Reiner's granddaughter, Monika Bartenstein, came from Switzerland to visit Carlotta at Rambleside in 1976, she was shocked to find the house so run down, scarcely what she expected from her mother's reports of her visits while Reiner was living.

Without the restraining discipline of her husband and the responsibility of caring for him, Carlotta sought solace and escape from her loneliness in alcohol. Her irascibility and contentiousness became a sore trial to her friends. With her obsessive loyalty to her husband's memory, she was unable to tolerate any praise of other musicians, especially of the younger generation. In her recollections of Reiner, she created an exaggerated fantasy of his perfection, proclaiming how much he loved his players and how much they loved him. She became infuriated at any suggestion that he had not been the kindest and most beloved of conductors and replied angrily to any description of Reiner as one of the most despotic martinets of his generation.

Carlotta often discussed with her friends establishing a suitable memorial to her husband, to which she would leave her own by no means modest estate as an endowment. Initially she talked of endowing at a conservatory or university a program of conductor training that would embody Reiner's pedagogical and musical ideals. An essential adjunct to that training would be a research archive containing Reiner's scores, library, and papers. In the mid-1960s she discussed this with several educators and musicians, especially Peter Mennin, president of the Juilliard School of Music. He proposed incorporating her plans in the new Juilliard Building at Lincoln Center for the Performing Arts. A major obstacle was Carlotta's insistence that the Reiner archive be housed in a special room in the new building, reproducing the conductor's study at Rambleside. The scores and library would have to be kept completely separate from the school's general collection and to be restricted to specially qualified students. These conditions were not acceptable to Mennin, who hoped eventually to receive from Carlotta an endowment for Juilliard's conducting curriculum free of such restrictions.[1]

Meanwhile, President Roscoe Miller of Northwestern University, some trustees, and George Howerton of the university's music school made several visits to Rambleside. They hoped to persuade Carlotta to establish a memorial to Reiner at Northwestern, close to the scene of his greatest triumphs. Thanks to the Tax Reform Act of 1969, Carlotta and Barton Hocker saw a tax advantage in her making a gift to Northwestern that year. It was then still possible for her to take a substantial tax deduction for her gift and still retain physical possession of it for her lifetime, a device that the new legislation would abolish after 1969. In December Northwestern announced that it would receive a collection of Reiner's papers, his scores, his library, and the furnishings of his study at Rambleside, to be installed in a special Fritz Reiner Memorial Room, "as soon as the university's proposed Fine and Performing Arts Center is complete." Thomas Willis, Claudia Cassidy's successor at the *Tribune,* visited Carlotta at Rambleside and later described the projected Reiner studio:

> There, amid the pictures, furniture, mementos, students and scholars will attempt to take the measure of one of their illustrious forebears. Although an exact inventory has not yet been worked out, Mrs. Reiner wants to preserve as much as possible.
> "The most important point is that everything should be together, small scores, large scores, records, tapes, pictures, instruments, and the rest. I turned down one library because they wanted to break things up—put Fritz's Beethoven scores with all the other Beethoven scores, the letters in one place, and the pictures in another. This way no one will have to put the pieces back together."[2]

Carlotta still pursued her desire to endow conductor training in memory of her husband. She doubted whether any one school could establish the kind of program she had in mind as worthy of her husband's standards. Her thoughts turned to an independent foundation that would make grants to conducting students individually. With this in mind, she talked of requiring the trustees of her proposed foundation to consult with the presidents of Juilliard and the Peabody Institute and the head of the Henry Street Settlement House in selecting conductors to receive support.

Actually, although Carlotta talked of it as her own idea of a memorial to him, Reiner's own will had specified conductor training in some detail. In that will, executed in 1962, Reiner divided his estate into two equal portions. One portion passed outright to Carlotta, and the other half he left to a trust from which Carlotta enjoyed the income for life. As appraised for tax purposes, Reiner's estate was valued at $502,554. This was a modest figure: Reiner's library of scores and books was valued at five hundred dollars, his record collection at seventy-five dollars, and the rare Chrysler Town and Country sedan at one hundred dollars. The most important assets were market securities and the capitalization of Reiner's record royalties. His estate did not include the valuable Rambleside property; Reiner had deeded his share to Carlotta in 1956.

In his will, Reiner described in some detail the Fritz and Carlotta Reiner Memorial Fund that would become operative on Carlotta's death. After payment of ten-thousand-dollar bequests to each of his daughters, he directed that the income from the remainder of the trust be paid to

deserving musicians and students of music. . . . Preference shall be given to assistant orchestra leaders and those studying to be orchestra leaders as hereinafter defined.

.   .   .   .

The term "musicians and students of music" is intended to cover (i) those persons who play or are studying one or more musical instrument, (ii) those persons who are studying to be composers or teachers of musical instruments (not teachers of voice) and (iii) those persons who are assistant orchestra leaders. It is intended that benefits shall be conferred not only on those who are studying music as above stated, but also on those persons, such as assistant orchestra leaders who, because of lack of opportunity to gain experience in this country, accept or seek work abroad to enhance their talent, which work does not or will not pay sufficient remuneration adequately to provide for them. In such cases, however, benefits from this fund shall not cover the requirements of any member of such musician's family, only the musician.

The beneficiary or beneficiaries are to be determined each year by majority vote of the presidents or other heads of the Juilliard School, the Peabody Institute and the Henry Street Settlement, who are also to suggest to the Trustees the amount to be paid to each during the ensuing year. . . . If my wife shall leave a Will under which a similar trust is set up for the benefit of musicians and students of music, the trust fund of this Will is to be combined with the trust fund under my wife's Will so that there will be one trust of our combined funds to effectuate the aforesaid purposes.[3]

He appointed as executors of his will, as well as trustees of the fund, Carlotta, Barton Hocker, and the Chase bank in New York. Reiner effusively expressed his full confidence in Hocker as executor and trustee.

These very specific directions were never carried out. The trust itself was never established, although the designation of Carlotta as a trustee would suggest that Reiner assumed that she would establish it in her lifetime and would add to it in her will. Instead, the executors implemented a "marital" provision in Reiner's will that enabled them to invade the trust if necessary to maintain Carlotta's standard of living or to provide for her care in case of serious illness. On 22 April 1981, when Carlotta's care at Rambleside required full-time nurses, the executors—Carlotta herself, Hocker, and the Chase Manhattan Bank—petitioned the probate court in Westport to dissolve the marital trust and turn over all its assets outright to Carlotta for her care. In effect this also revoked Reiner's bequests to Eva, who was still living, and to Tuśy, who had died in 1973. More important, the dissolution of Reiner's trust relieved the executors from establishing the memorial fund he called for in his will and from carrying out his plan for educating conductors.

Carlotta, Hocker, and the trustees of Columbia University created a new trust on 11 May 1981. Three days later she signed her own will, leaving the bulk of her estate to the new Columbia trust.[4] This new trust, of which Carlotta,

Hocker, and the trustees of Columbia University were trustees, established a Fritz Reiner Center for Contemporary Music at Columbia.[5] Its terms were disclosed, only in a general way, in announcements to the press by Columbia president Michael J. Sovern and by Schuyler G. Chapin, then dean of the School of the Arts. The university's press release covering Sovern's announcement to the Chicago alumni on 24 October 1984 stated:

The Reiner center will further Columbia's long tradition of involvement with composition and the study and dissemination of contemporary music. Activities envisioned for the center include the sponsorship of conferences, lectures, concerts, publications and recordings. An archive for contemporary music at the center will serve as a repository for the letters and photographs to the conductor from many composers who were his friends, among them Béla Bartók, Igor Stravinsky, Arnold Schoenberg and Darius Milhaud. The University has appointed the composer and scholar Chou Wen-chung to be the center's director and the Fritz Reiner Professor of Musical Composition.[6]

In New York Schuyler G. Chapin responded to a reporter's question, "Why Columbia?"

It came about through curious circumstances. Carlotta wanted to set her affairs in order a few years ago, and she told me, "I hate lawyers, I hate wills, and I'm mad at Northwestern University. I hear you have a pretty good school. Come tell me about it." It seems she had given most of Reiner's scores to Northwestern, and they hadn't done much about it. So I went and, after a certain amount of backing-and-forthing, she signed a will making Columbia her beneficiary, with a cover letter signed by her, me and the president to keep the money out of general operating funds and set it aside only for this.

Chapin added that Reiner's record royalties amounted to between fifty and sixty thousand dollars annually and could increase with the transfer of his Chicago Symphony Orchestra recordings to compact discs.[7]

In addition to the Columbia bequest, Carlotta gave to the Curtis Institute of Music in Philadelphia Reiner's personal record collection, several videotapes, his piano, three music stands, the various gifts, decorations, and honors he had received during his career, and a eighteenth-century Maria Theresa breakfront cabinet for their display. Her will also gave to Curtis Reiner's correspondence with Leonard Bernstein and other documents concerning him. Among several personal bequests were ten thousand dollars to Eva Bartenstein, but nothing to Tusy's son, Vovček Assejew; ten thousand to Ann Gaito; and twenty thousand to Betty Stillman.[8] She appointed Hocker sole executor of her will, left him and his wife the furnishings of Rambleside, automobiles, letters and photographs, and jewelry, "with the request that he dispose of said property in the manner which he believes to be in accordance with my wishes." Finally, she made a cash gift of one hundred thousand dollars personally to Hocker, in addition to his fee as executor. For tax purposes, Carlotta's estate was appraised at $1,697,849.63. When distributed by Hocker as executor, Columbia University received real estate valued at $700,000, autographed photos and letters worth $15,000, recording contracts valued at $148,053.37, and cash on hand and from an Internal Revenue Service refund of $93,000, a total of approximately $956,000. When the university later sold the Rambleside property to a Westport developer, the reported price was $1.2 million, which brought the value of Carlotta's bequest closer to $1.5 million.[9]

There can be no question that the encouragement of contemporary music was a cause consistent with Reiner's own ideals, but among the alternatives he must have considered, contemporary music was not the one he had himself chosen as his memorial. Nor was his choice capricious; in defining it so precisely, he must have discussed it with Carlotta and, very likely, with Hocker as well. In appointing her as one of the trustees, he anticipated that she and Hocker would establish his trust during her lifetime. He must also have expected, with Carlotta's and Hocker's knowledge, that she would, in her will, add funds and real estate that would make his own modest trust viable. Carlotta's almost obsessive anxiety over the conducting scheme, while carefully concealing her husband's explicit intent, suggests that she was by no means at ease with the idea. As time passed, she became disenchanted with Northwestern University, which had to postpone and alter its earlier plan to build the comprehensive arts center on which Carlotta counted. Contrary to what Carlotta told Chapin, Northwestern could scarcely have "done much" about a gift that she retained during her lifetime. After Northwestern moved its Music Library into its traditional Deering Library, the university failed to convince Carlotta of its intention to honor Reiner properly. She never considered it seriously as an appropriate center for conductor training.

Nor was Columbia University prepared to establish such a curriculum, for its music program was more academic than practical. However, Schuyler Chapin was an old friend of the Reiners. He had worked in the Judson division of Columbia Artist Management, for Columbia Records, for Leonard Bernstein's Amberson Productions, for Lincoln Center, and as general manager of the Metropolitan Opera, before joining Columbia University. Given Carlotta's reluctance to carry out Fritz's intended conductor training, she embraced Chapin's proposal. It was easy for her and Hocker to devise a legal means of bypassing Reiner's own wishes. The dissolution, rather than the invasion, of the marital trust in Reiner's will, on grounds of Carlotta's obvious needs in her final illness, led her and Hocker to create a new intermediate trust, a common device to avoid placing the details of a bequest in the public probate records.

In the last years before her death in 1983, Carlotta made sporadic efforts to extract the composer correspondence from the papers already committed to Northwestern. A young woman from Westport, Gina Pia Bandini, came regularly to Rambleside to do secretarial work toward the end of Carlotta's life. She helped her locate some of the composer correspondence to be set aside for Columbia. They succeeded only partially, for Northwestern has a significant number of such letters.

Neither Hocker nor Columbia has offered additional information on their trust, and Columbia has not responded to my repeated inquiries concerning the composer correspondence and other materials of biographical interest.[10] These materials, as of 1993, remain in the School of the Arts. Nor has Columbia disclosed either the terms of the trust or its plans to implement Carlotta's bequest. The Fritz Reiner Center for Contemporary Music has supported an occasional performance of contemporary music but has not announced details of the sort of comprehensive program projected by Sovern in his 1984 announcement.[11] Both Curtis and Northwestern received documentation of Reiner's telecasts: Curtis received videotapes of several late programs, and Northwestern has a few early kinescope films, which were transferred to tape for preservation. By exchange between the two libraries, each now has a complete set of eight videotapes.

During the summer of 1983 the Hockers sold at an auction in Portland, Maine, the Rambleside furnishings they received from Carlotta. This sale included at least two lots of materials that could have been part of the 1969 gift to Northwestern. One carton of scores, mostly of contemporary music, some with Reiner's performance markings and some inscribed to the conductor by composers, eventually reached the Bagaduce Music Library in Blue Hill, Maine.[12] A used book dealer in Maine purchased for two thousand dollars a lot of two thousand items, including scores (some inscribed), autographed photographs, letters (including one from Leonard Bernstein), and books from the Rambleside library.[13] Of greater concern has been the loss of an undetermined number of Reiner's working orchestral scores, which never reached Northwestern. These include, for instance, symphonies of Beethoven and Brahms, some missing from Rambleside even during Carlotta's lifetime.

After Carlotta's death, Robert Marsh wrote two articles in the Chicago *Sun-Times* reviewing the stormy relations between the conductor and the Chicago community and expressing regret that Reiner had so completely bypassed the Chicago Symphony Orchestra in his will.[14] In fact it was Carlotta who had ultimately passed over the orchestra in her bequest to Columbia, though Reiner himself would surely have agreed, given his feelings about Chicago toward the end of his life.

The developer who purchased Rambleside from Columbia University subdivided it into eleven expensive residential sites. The property was criss-crossed with roads blasted from the rock and bulldozed through the meadows and woods. Reiner's ashes, together with those of Carlotta and her mother, finally came to rest in the Willowbrook Cemetery plot Carlotta had purchased a few years before her death.

It is impossible not to sense the irony of the frustration of Fritz Reiner's final aspirations expressed in his will. It was, in many respects, the most altruistic gesture of an otherwise self-centered man. In life he had displayed a distinct ineptitude in controlling the real world as completely as he did the practice of his art. Having on so many occasions in his life sought unsuccessfully to shape his own destiny, he must certainly have expected his Last Will and Testament to be the most inviolable of his innermost designs. His will reflected both careful consideration and characteristic prejudices, as indicated by his specific exclusion of teachers of singing as possible beneficiaries. Yet he suffered his share of dis-appointments in his professional career, and his final ambitions were ultimately thwarted posthumously by those he trusted most.

My greatest debt is to Northwestern University and to Don L. Roberts, Debbie Campana, and the staff at the Music Library, for the special courtesies and warm friendship extended to me during many visits to the Fritz Reiner Library.

Eva Reiner Bartenstein, Reiner's daughter in Zurich, and Vladimir ("Vovček") Assejew, his grandson in Ljubljana, have supported my work by sharing their memories and such family and personal documents as they regarded to be of biographical interest.

Early in my research on Reiner, Dr. Elizabeth ("Erzi") Klinger's colorful reminiscences of him as her piano teacher in Budapest and later as a friend in America contributed to my understanding of my subject.

In addition to the individuals and institutions listed in the bibliography, I am deeply grateful to a number of men and women who extended special courtesies: Dr. János Karpáti, librarian at the Liszt Academy of Music in Budapest; Frank Rainer Krupicka of Wolfsheim, Germany; Dr. Wolfgang Reich of the Saxon State Library; Eberhard Steindorf of the Dresden State Orchestra; Ingeborg Pahlitzsch of the Dresden Opera Library; Elizabeth Walker, librarian at the Curtis Institute of Music; Jean Bowen and her staff at the Library of the Performing Arts of the New York Public Library at Lincoln Center; Wayne Shirley and Samuel Brylawsky at the Library of Congress; Diana Haskell and others at the Newberry Library; Barbara Haws, archivist of the New York Philharmonic; Stephen Monder and his staff at the Cincinnati Symphony Orchestra; Gideon Toeplitz and Bruce Carr at the Pittsburgh Symphony Orchestra and Sadie Cohen, a former staff member; Robert Tuggle at the Metropolitan Opera Archives; Henry Fogel, Brenda Nelson-Strauss, Evelyn Meine, and Marilyn Arrado at the Chicago Symphony Orchestra; John von Rhein at the Chicago *Tribune* and Thomas Willis, formerly on its staff and now on the music faculty at Northwestern University; Roger Dettmer, former music critic of the Chicago *American,* who also read an early version of chapters III and IV as a former Cincinnatian; Richard Mohr and John Pfeiffer, producers of

Reiner's RCA-Victor recordings; at the Voice of America, Michael H. Gray; Don Tait; and Gina Pia Bandini Cooper. I am especially grateful to Henry Fogel for allowing me to review the minutes of meetings of the Board of Trustees of the Orchestral Association.

Many Reiner colleagues shared their reminiscences with me and offered encouragement, including Victor Aitay, Schuyler G. Chapin, Adrian Daprato, John Di Janni, Edward and Dorothy Druzinsky, John S. Edwards, Donald and Margaret Evans, Boris Goldovsky, Morton Gould, Adolph Herseth, Margaret Hillis, Arthur Judson, Paul Henry Lang, Goddard Lieberson, Edgar Muenzer, Gordon Peters, Edna Phillips, Milton Preves, Max Rudolf, Lionel Sayers, Sol Schoenbach, Marjorie Garrigue Smith, Dorle J. Soria, János Starker, and Samuel Thavieu.

The Fritz Reiner Society, its president, Stephen C. Hillyer, and members Arthur J. Helmbrecht, Jr., and Albert Schlachtmeyer have generously shared a variety of materials on Reiner. The society's newsletter and semiannual *Podium* documented an impressive series of important interviews and discussions.

David Hamilton has advised and assisted me in many areas of research.

To William Schuman I owe special thanks for his encouragement, advice, and help.

Permissions

Previously unpublished letters, drafts, diary entries, and other writings of Fritz Reiner, Carlotta Reiner, and Berta Reiner Assejew from the Fritz Reiner Library in the Music Library at Northwestern University are published by permission.

Previously unpublished letters from Leonard Bernstein to Fritz Reiner are published by permission of the Estate of Leonard Bernstein and Northwestern University.

Illustration Credits

Vladimir Assejew. Reiner with his grandson Vladimir Assejew.
Eva Reiner Bartenstein. The young huntsman.
BMG Classics and the respective estates of Fritz Reiner and Artur Rubinstein.
    Artur Rubinstein and Reiner.
Chicago *Tribune*. Reiner and Dr. Eric Oldberg; Claudia Cassidy.
Cincinnati Historical Society. Anna Sinton Taft.
Culver Pictures. Reiner, George Gershwin, Deems Taylor, and Robert Russell
    Bennett at All-American concert, Lewisohn Stadium, New York, 10 August 1931.

Curtis Institute of Music. Mary Louise Curtis Bok and Reiner; Reiner with Lauritz Melchior and Kirsten Flagstad.

Dorothy Siegel Druzinsky. Carlotta and Fritz Reiner at Rambleside, summer 1962.

Metropolitan Opera Association. Ljuba Welitsch, Edward Johnson, and Reiner (Louis Melançon photo); Reiner rehearsing *The Rake's Progress* (Sedge LeBlang photo).

National Portrait Gallery, The Smithsonian Institution. Boris Chaliapin portrait of Reiner commissioned by *Time,* 1958.

Billy Rose Theater Collection, New York Public Library for the Performing Arts; Astor, Lenox and Tilden Foundations. Carlotta Irwin.

Music Division, New York Public Library for the Performing Arts; Astor, Lenox and Tilden Foundations. Burkard caricature of Arthur Nikisch; Herbert Graf, Arthur Judson, and Reiner; Reiner with Goddard Lieberson and Edward Wallerstein.

Fritz Reiner Library at the Music Library, Northwestern University. Reiner Frigyes with his mother, Irma; Friderick Reiner with Angela (Elca) Jelacin; conductor at the Saxon State Opera; Reiner and Berta Gerster-Gardini; Reiner's daughters Eva and Berta; Kossuth portrait; first page of *Outline for Course in Conducting;* Reiner and Edward Specter; Béla Bartók and Reiner at Rambleside; *Carmen* recording playback.

The Podium. Reiner conducting rehearsal of *Götterdämmerung;* action photo of Reiner (on jacket).

Carlotta Reiner. Arturo Toscanini and Reiner.

Robert Tuggle. Richard Strauss.

Abbreviations Used

Diary   Red-bound volumes labeled "Diary, 1931–1963," in Fritz Reiner Library, Music Library, Northwestern University

MOA   Archives of the Metropolitan Opera Association

NU   Northwestern University Music Library, Fritz Reiner Library

NYP   New York Philharmonic Archives

NYPL   New York Public Library, Library of the Performing Arts at Lincoln Center

OA   The Orchestral Association (Chicago), Minutes of meetings of the Board of Trustees

TU   Temple University, Urban Archives Center

UP   University of Pittsburgh, Hillman Library, Archives of Industrial Society

I: Reiner Frigyes

1.   These various names can be found in such sources as Reiner's Laibach wedding certificate of 1911, directories of the Franz Liszt Academy of Music, newspaper clippings in the scrapbooks of the Cincinnati Symphony Orchestra at the Cincinnati Historical Society, and materials in NU.

2.   Photos of Reiner's parents from the Rambleside studio have disappeared, but other early family photos are in NU. Reiner's Laibach wedding certificate, 25 October 1911, also in NU, identifies Ignácz as *Kaufman,* or merchant.

3.   Fritz Reiner, interview with Gertrude Guthrie-Treadway, Cincinnati *Enquirer,* 25 September 1925. See also Hope Stoddard, *Symphony Conductors of the U.S.A.* (New York: Thomas Y. Crowell Company, 1957), 171–181. A copy of Carlotta's account is in NU. When Edward Downes interviewed Reiner at Rambleside on 13 March 1963, the conductor recalled more details of his youth; the interview was broadcast during the intermission in a Metropolitan Opera performance on 23 March.

4.   From an undated booklet on Wagner issued by Columbia Masterworks, in NU.

5.   The certificate is in NU. Eva Reiner Bartenstein, interview with me, Zurich, Switzerland, October 1984.

6.   For an account of Budapest during Reiner's youth, see John Lukacs, *Budapest, 1900* (New York: Weidenfeld and Nicholson, 1988).

7. Reiner to Francis Robinson, 29 November 1957, copy in NU.

8. One of Reiner's student compositions, a movement for string quartet, was performed at Northwestern University in October 1988.

9. Reiner's enrollment from 1903 to 1909 is recorded in the annual directories of the Franz Liszt Academy of Music.

10. This diploma, bearing the signatures of Reiner's instructors, hung for many years in the hallway outside his studio at Rambleside, but it disappeared after Carlotta Reiner's death.

11. Fritz Reiner, "Reiner Discusses the Making of a Conductor," *Musical America*, 25 October 1941.

12. "Erzi" studied with Reiner from 1908 until his departure for Dresden in 1914. She eventually abandoned her musical studies for medicine. She moved to the United States in 1927, where, as Dr. Elizabeth Klinger, she renewed her friendship with Reiner. For many years she and her husband were surgeons in New York and Wisconsin, remaining friends of Reiner's until his death. In July 1984 I visited Erzi Klinger at her home in Vancouver, British Columbia, and heard firsthand her recollections of him.

13. In later interviews and conversations, Reiner usually referred to the Vigopera and Népopera as *Volksoper* or comic opera companies, although most of his activity was in "grand" opera.

14. Reiner interview with Guthrie-Treadway.

15. Ferenc Bónis, "Reiner Frigyes," in *Zenei lexicon*, ed. Denes Barthes (Budapest, 1965), gives 1909 as the date of Reiner's debut as conductor at the Vigopera; 1908 was the date usually cited by Reiner himself. Carlotta Reiner's memorandum to Claudia Cassidy (copy in NU) also gives 1908.

16. *Répertoar Slovenskih Gledalisc, 1867–1967* (Ljubljana, 1967). I am grateful to Edward Engelking of Warsaw for sending me copies of relevant extracts from this book. Other information on Reiner's activity in Laibach is from my interview with his grandson Vladimir Assejew in Ljubljana in October 1984.

17. The original wedding certificate is in NU. Although her name given on the certificate is Angela, Reiner usually referred to her as Elca, pronounced "Elsa."

18. Photos in NU.

19. Elca's younger daughter, Eva Bartenstein, told me something of her mother during our talks in Zurich in October 1984. Erzi Klinger also recalled her as a young woman in Budapest.

20. Reiner's five-year contract with the Népopera, dated 1910, is in NU. An incomplete collection of Népopera playbills in the theater division of the Hungarian National Library starts only in the fall of 1912. Nóra Wellmann of the National Opera archives has provided additional information on Reiner's repertory at the Népopera, going back to December 1911.

21. See Lucy Beckett, *Richard Wagner, Parsifal* (Cambridge: Cambridge University Press, 1981), 94.

22. Reiner to Pierre Monteux, 14 February 1955, copy in NU; Vera Stravinsky and Robert Craft, *Stravinsky in Pictures and Documents* (New York: Simon and Schuster, 1978), 93.

23. Nóra Wellmann to me, 10 March 1992.

24. Stoddard, *Symphony Conductors*, 175.

1. Although some reports refer to Reiner as "Nachfolger Schuchs," Schuch's successor, neither Reiner nor anyone else was general music director in Dresden between Schuch's death in 1914 and Fritz Busch's appointment to that post in 1922.

2. The Saxon Court/State Opera playbills, press clippings, and other documentation for this period survived the 1945 bombing thanks to their storage in the lowest cellar of the Semper Theater. Bound volumes of the daily playbills (complete with cast changes) and Tagebücher of the theaters provided most of the information here on Reiner's work in Dresden.

3. Contract in NU.

4. Cesar Saerchinger, "Fritz Reiner: Perpetual Prodigy," *Saturday Review,* 31 May 1952. Saerchinger's statement was probably based on Reiner's account.

5. See Howard Mayer Brown, "Pedantry or Liberation? A Sketch of the Historical Performance Movement," in *Authenticity and Early Music,* ed. Nicholas Kenyon (Oxford: Oxford University Press, 1988), 34. Established by Hugo Riemann in 1908 at the University of Leipzig, the Collegium Musicum was more concerned with preparing modern performance editions of "early" music than with practical performance.

6. Reiner quoted in Harold C. Schonberg, *The Great Conductors* (New York: Simon and Schuster, 1967), 335.

7. Sir Adrian Boult, *Boult on Music* (London: Toccata Press, 1983), 39.

8. Rodney Philip, "Reiner, Fritz," in *The New Grove Dictionary of Music and Musicians,* ed. Stanley Sadie, vol. 15 (London: Macmillan, 1980). This entry was subsequently corrected, at my suggestion, in H. Wiley Hitchcock and Stanley Sadie, eds., *The New Grove Dictionary of American Music,* vol. 4 (New York: Macmillan, 1986).

9. Reported to me in conversations with János Starker.

10. Schonberg, *Great Conductors,* 206–214.

11. Boult, *Boult on Music.* Although Toscanini admired Nikisch, he is said to have declared later that Nikisch's famous recording of the Beethoven Fifth Symphony did not represent what he recalled hearing in concert.

12. Schonberg, *Great Conductors,* 17.

13. Fritz Reiner, "The Technique of Conducting," *Étude,* October 1951.

14. Ingeborg Pahlitszch at the Saxon State Opera library reviewed a mass of ancient press clippings, marking every mention of Reiner.

15. Eva Bartenstein recalled her mother's accounts of Richard Strauss's visits during interviews with me in Zurich in October 1984.

16. Eva Bartenstein quoted in Rollin R. Potter, "Fritz Reiner: Conductor, Teacher, Musical Innovator," Ph.D. dissertation, Northwestern University, 1980, p. 17.

17. Elca's suspicions and spying were reported to me during interviews in Zurich in October 1984 with Eva Bartenstein, who could only have heard of them from her mother.

18. I learned of Reiner's affair with Charlotte Benedict from their grandson, Frank Rainer Krupicka of Wolfsheim, Germany, both by telephone and during a three-day visit in Santa Fe in July 1992. Krupicka had a copy of his mother's Dresden birth certificate, which omitted the father's name, old press clippings from Chicago

found among his grandmother's belongings by relatives, and copies of photographs of Charlotte and Erika. His account, though circumstantial, in no way conflicts with other information about Reiner's years in Dresden.

19. Eva Bartenstein letter to me, 25 June 1992.

20. German army pass in NU, compared with Reiner's performance schedule in the playbills in Dresden Opera archives.

21. Obituary of Berta Gerster-Gardini in New York *Times*, 8 August 1951; Tagebücher and German opera singer directories in the library of the Dresden Opera in 1984.

22. *Musical America*, 25 November 1911, had a reproduction of an oil portrait of her.

23. Information on Berta Gerster-Gardini from my interview with her Cincinnati accompanist, Marjorie Garrigue Smith, October 1986, at her home in Elizabethtown, New York.

24. Various publicity folders in the University of Cincinnati Music Library mention recitals by Gerster-Gardini in Berlin, Dresden, Danzig, and Cassel, but no operatic activity.

25. Eva Bartenstein letter to me, 29 August 1992. The woman holding the child resembles known photographs of Berta Gerster-Gardini. This photograph was reproduced in *Podium*, Fall/Winter 1988, 13.

26. The breakup of Reiner's first marriage is described in incomplete and one-sided detail in Reiner's correspondence with lawyers in Dresden, Ljubljana, and Budapest (in NU).

27. The Saxon Theater Tagebücher, still in the Dresden Opera library, include the home addresses of such important personnel as the conductors.

28. Copy of the lease, dated 20 April 1920, in NU.

29. There are a number of letters between Reiner and his Dresden lawyer, Dr. Langerhan, in NU.

30. The final divorce documents have not survived, but these arrangements can be inferred from correspondence in NU.

31. Eva Bartenstein, in Zurich interviews and later correspondence with me, recalled this trip to Dresden and having had the photo taken with Berta.

32. Tagebücher at Dresden Opera. Reiner-Kutzschbach letter, 3 January 1921, copy in NU.

33. Reiner correspondence at NU. My correspondence with Hamburg Philharmonic. Dr. János Karpáti, librarian at the Franz Liszt Academy, found mention of an application for the Budapest post in Géza Staud, *A Budapest Opera Ház 100 Éve* (Budapest, 1984), a history of the first hundred years of the Budapest Opera.

34. Joseph Szigeti, *With Strings Attached* (New York: Alfred A. Knopf, 1967), 105.

35. Reiner letter, 16 September 1920, copy in NU.

36. Saerchinger, "Fritz Reiner."

37. Correspondence in NU.

38. Adela Rocha of the Gran Teatre del Liceu to me, 12 April 1991.

III: Orchestra Builder

1. On Theodore Thomas's important role in the history of music in Cincinnati, see Theodore Thomas, *A Musical Autobiography,* ed. G. P. Upton (Chicago: McClurg,

1905); Ezra Schabas, *Theodore Thomas* (Urbana: University of Illinois Press, 1989); Charles E. Russell, *The American Orchestra and Theodore Thomas* (Garden City, N.Y.: Doubleday, 1927); Rose Fay Thomas, *Memoirs of Theodore Thomas* (New York: Moffat, Yard and Company, 1911); and Philip Hart, *Orpheus in the New World: The Symphony Orchestra as an American Cultural Institution* (New York: W. W. Norton and Company, 1974), 23–25.

2. See Louis Russell Thomas, "A History of the Cincinnati Symphony Orchestra to 1931," Ph.d. dissertation, University of Cincinnati, 1972. Major sources for that history were the scrapbooks of press clippings from the Cincinnati Symphony Orchestra, now at the Cincinnati Historical Society, as well as minutes of the orchestra's executive committee and trustees' meetings. Although I have thoroughly reviewed the scrapbooks, I rely on Thomas's "History" for the minutes. Since the Reiner correspondence files in NU are incomplete for the Cincinnati period, Thomas's account and the clippings have been especially valuable sources.

3. Thomas, "History," 647n. It is impossible to estimate the total dollar amount of the Tafts' support of the Cincinnati Symphony Orchestra; Anna Taft, especially, made many personal gifts to musicians or to special projects that were not recorded in the association's accounting.

4. See Hart, *Orpheus*, 71–95.

5. Thomas, "History," 500. Reiner's copy of the contract is in NU.

6. Cincinnati *Enquirer*, 29 September 1922; Cincinnati *Times-Star*, 29 September 1922.

7. The score with Reiner's notes is in NU.

8. Cincinnati *Enquirer*, 28 October 1922. All repertory information is from the bound volumes of the Cincinnati Symphony Orchestra programs in NU.

9. New York *World* as reprinted in the Cincinnati *Times-Star*, 3 February 1923.

10. Thomas, "History," 507–509.

11. Ibid., 513–514.

12. New York *Times*, 4 May 1923.

13. *Musical America*, 6 October 1923.

14. Thomas, "History," 516–517.

15. Of the Dresden furniture, only Reiner's desk and chair remain. They are now in NU.

16. Thomas, "History," 542–544.

17. Extensive Reiner and Judson correspondence in NU.

18. Jay Harrison in New York *Herald-Tribune*, 24 November 1963.

19. From Roger Dettmer's taped interviews with Herbert Tiemeyer and Herbert Silbersack.

20. Repertory information from bound volumes of Cincinnati Symphony Orchestra programs.

21. Correspondence with Copland and Sessions in NU.

22. Igor Stravinsky, *Autobiography* (New York: Simon and Schuster, 1936), 191–192.

23. V. Stravinsky and Craft, *Stravinsky in Pictures*, 302, without specific reference to source.

24. New York *Times*, 7 January 1926.

25. Cincinnati *Times-Star*, 14 January 1926.

26. New York *Times*, 27 February 1927.

27. Cincinnati *Times-Star*, 12 February 1927.

28. Cincinnati *Times-Star,* 20 February 1928; also Reiner's personal reminiscences.

29. Béla Bartók, *Béla Bartók Letters,* ed. János Demény (New York: St. Martin's Press, 1971), no. 139 in the English language edition, 29 October 1928. Reiner had loaned his correspondence with Bartók to the musicologist Otto Gombosi, who provided it to Demény and translated it for the English edition, which erroneously gives Reiner's address as Westport, Connecticut. The letter and its envelope, correctly addressed to Cincinnati, are in NU.

30. Béla Bartók to Reiner, 29 October 1928.

31. Reiner and Eugene Ormandy correspondence, 14 and 19 February 1925, in NU.

IV: An Expanding Career

1. Thomas, "History," 514n.

2. This description of the household is from correspondence and a November 1986 interview with Marjorie Garrigue Smith at her home in Elizabethtown, New York. As Berta's studio pianist, she was a frequent visitor in the home and one of Berta's closest confidantes.

3. Thomas, "History," 561.

4. Correspondence and bank vouchers in NU.

5. I have been unable to document this engagement further, beyond mention in the Cincinnati press.

6. Serge Prokofiev, *Autobiography* (Moscow: Foreign Languages Publishing House, n.d.), 64; Szigeti, *With Strings Attached,* 105; Nicolas Slonimsky, *Music since 1900,* 4th ed. (New York: Charles Scribner's Sons, 1971), 393.

7. Nóra Wellmann to me, 10 March 1992.

8. There are many clippings in NU from the Buenos Aires press—in Spanish, Italian, and German—covering Reiner's performances.

9. Although the press clippings in NU include voluminous coverage of the Buenos Aires engagement and less extensive documentation of other appearances, there is nothing on London, Vienna, or Russia. In fact, there is no indication that Reiner ever conducted in Germany after he left Dresden.

10. Giampiero Tintori, *Cronologia: Opera, balletti, concerti, 1778–1977* (Milan: Teatro alla Scala, 1978) includes Reiner's concerts with the La Scala orchestra in 1929, 1931, and 1949, but none earlier, nor concerts in Venice. However, there is clear mention of a 1927 appearance in press clippings and in correspondence in NU.

11. Judson interviews with me at his home in Harrison, New York, 1969–1970.

12. For a brief account of the founding of the Stadium Concerts, see Howard Shanet, *Philharmonic: A History of New York's Orchestra* (Garden City, N.Y.: Doubleday, 1975), 236–240.

13. Repertory for the Lewisohn Stadium concerts in NYPO and from correspondence in NU.

14. Correspondence in NU; program information from the Los Angeles Philharmonic; audience estimate from New York *Times,* 24 July 1924.

15. Programs in NYP; John Erskine, *The Philharmonic-Symphony Society of New York* (New York: Macmillan, 1943), 97; correspondence in NU. Thomas, "History," 556n,

also mentions appearances with the "Buffalo Symphony" that I have been unable to verify.

16. Philadelphia *Evening Ledger,* 8 and 21 February 1927, in TU.

17. Judson to Reiner, 23 September 1927, in NU; unidentified press clipping in TU.

18. Unidentified press clipping in TU. Herbert Kupferberg, *Those Fabulous Philadelphians* (New York: Charles Scribner's Sons, 1969), 71–72.

19. Although there are other accounts of the origins of CBS, I heard Judson's own version during interviews in 1970. See also Sally Bedell Smith, *In All His Glory: The Life of William Paley* (New York: Simon and Schuster, 1990).

20. New York *Times,* 8 September 1927.

21. Correspondence and royalty statement in NU. The 1927 Welte-Mignon catalog in NYPL lists most of these player-piano rolls.

22. Reiner to Louis T. More, 7 January 1927, copy in NU; Thomas, "History," 586.

23. Reiner to Judson, 18 January 1928, copy in NU.

24. Cincinnati *Times-Star,* 15 May 1927.

25. Thomas, "History," 576–581, 603–613. For the long-range impact of the institute on the Cincinnati Symphony Orchestra, see Hart, *Orpheus,* 240–290.

26. Thomas, "History," quoting trustees' minutes, 27 May 1929.

27. Thomas, "History," 646–648, and numerous clippings from the Cincinnati press.

28. Correspondence in NU; clippings at Cincinnati Historical Society.

29. Tušy's son, Vladimir Assejew, in Ljubljana has a yearbook of the academy for 1929. Correspondence regarding Tušy's schools and summer camps in NU.

30. Tušy's letters in NU.

31. Copy of Carlotta Reiner undated letter to Tušy Assejew following Reiner's death in NU; also Carlotta's reminiscences to me.

32. Eva Bartenstein, interview with me, October 1984.

33. Carlotta Reiner letters to Claudia Cassidy, August 1953, copies in NU. The Theater Collection of NYPL has information on Carlotta Irwin and extensive material on Stuart Walker and his activities. The account here also includes my recollection of Carlotta's later reminiscences.

34. Marjorie Garrigue Smith, interview with me, November 1986.

35. Correspondence, 17 November 1927, in NU.

36. Berta Gerster-Gardini to Marjorie Garrigue Smith, 14 August 1929, shown me by Mrs. Smith, November 1986.

37. Press clippings at Cincinnati Historical Society.

38. The account of meeting Strauss was one of Carlotta's favorites in later years.

39. Cincinnati *Times-Star,* 7 October 1930, clipping in NU, with a penciled notation in Carlotta's handwriting: "I wrote this!"

40. Thomas, "History," 632–633.

41. Carlotta's later reminiscences. Reiner's refusal to withdraw was reported at a trustees' meeting on 11 August 1930.

42. Thomas, "History," 644.

1. Reiner to Miss Weiss at Curtis, 3 April 1931, copy in NU.
2. Tintori, *Cronologia,* gives this date for a concert including Bossi's Theme and Variations, opus 131; the Mozart A Major and Brahms D Major violin concertos, with Adolf Busch; and Respighi's orchestration of the Bach C Minor Passacaglia.
3. Harvey Sachs, *Toscanini* (Philadelphia: J. B. Lippincott Company, 1978), 208–215, gives a comprehensive account of the Bologna incident and its aftermath, mentioning Reiner's visit. See also Harvey Sachs, *Music in Fascist Italy* (New York: W. W. Norton and Company, 1987); idem, *Reflections on Toscanini* (New York: Grove Weidenfeld, 1991); and Richard Taruskin, "The Dark Side of Modern Music," *New Republic,* 5 September 1988.
4. New York *Times,* 4 June 1931.
5. Undated pencil draft in 1931 file in NU. Before she mastered the typewriter, Carlotta kept pencil copies of important correspondence.
6. Philadelphia *Bulletin,* 19 February 1932, clipping in TU.
7. See Taruskin, "Dark Side."
8. Correspondence and leases in NU.
9. Eliza Ann Viles, "Mary Louise Curtis Bok Zimbalist; Founder of the Curtis Institute of Music and Patron of American Arts," Ph.d. dissertation, Bryn Mawr College, 1983. Mrs. Bok was in the tradition of Jeannette Meyers Thurber with the National Conservatory of Music and American Opera Company, Anna Sinton Taft in Cincinnati, Elizabeth Sprague Coolidge in Washington, and, in more recent years, Martha Baird Rockefeller and Alice Tully in New York.
10. Correspondence and most of Reiner's Curtis contracts in NU.
11. Correspondence in NU.
12. Boris Goldovsky, *My Road to Opera* (Boston: Houghton Mifflin Company, 1979), 138–139, 154. Goldovsky's book is invaluable for its firsthand recollections of Reiner conducting opera in Philadelphia and teaching at Curtis. During the summer of 1985 Goldovsky added details to this account during an interview with me in Santa Fe.
13. Program information in the library of the Curtis Institute of Music.
14. Transcriptions of some of these CBS broadcasts are at the Library of Congress. Bound volumes of all recital and radio programs by Curtis students and faculty, including the radio broadcasts conducted by Reiner and his students, are in the library of the Curtis Institute of Music.
15. Morton Gould, interview with me, San Francisco, July 1985.
16. Both the manuscript and typed copies are in NU. Neither is dated, but the handwritten copy is on Cincinnati Symphony Orchestra stationery, indicating an early date.
17. Goldovsky, *My Road to Opera,* 155; Goldovsky interview in Santa Fe in the summer of 1985. Lukas Foss's more general comments at Conductors' Guild meeting at Columbia University in January 1988, transcribed as "Conductors' Guild Holds 'Reiner Retrospective,'" in *Podium,* Spring/Summer 1988.
18. Reiner, "Technique of Conducting."
19. Leonard Bernstein's letter of 27 August 1940 and subsequent undated letter to Reiner in NU. Reproduced by permission of the Estate of Leonard Bernstein.

20. Randall Thompson to Reiner, 15 October 1940, in NU.

21. Peter Rosen, *Reflections,* quoted in Joan Peyser, *Bernstein: A Biography* (New York: Birch Tree Books, William Morrow, 1987), 83.

22. Vladimir Assejew, interview with me, October 1984.

23. Philadelphia *Bulletin,* 25 March 1935, clipping in TU.

24. Correspondence with Mrs. Bok and others in NU.

25. Mrs. Bok to Reiner, 7 February 1941, and copy of Reiner's reply, 8 February 1941, in NU.

VI: Opera and the Philadelphia Orchestra

1. Boris Goldovsky *(My Road to Opera,* 163) overlooks this performance and identifies *Elektra* a week later as Reiner's debut. Programs and cast listings for the 1931–1932 season of the Philadelphia Grand Opera are in the library of the Curtis Institute of Music.

2. Richard Strauss to Reiner, as quoted in New York *Times,* 9 August 1931. The original letters, possibly at Columbia University, are not available. The "good news" probably refers to Reiner's hopes with the Philadelphia Orchestra.

3. New York *Times,* 30 October 1931.

4. In conversations with me in 1970, Arthur Judson gave a comprehensive account of the Philadelphia Orchestra's operatic venture. Nothing he told me was at variance with Kupferberg's *Fabulous Philadelphians* or with Oliver Daniel's *Stokowski: A Counterpoint of View* (New York: Dodd, Mead, 1982), but his account was more detailed than any found in other sources. Boris Goldovsky's *My Road to Opera* offers important information from his perspective.

5. Shanet, *Philharmonic,* 268–269; Sachs, *Toscanini,* 234.

6. Daniel, *Stokowski,* 321.

7. Louis Biancolli, *The Flagstad Manuscript* (New York: Putnam, 1952), 62.

8. *Lady Macbeth of the Mzensk District* was an international scandal at its first performance in Leningrad in January 1934. Artur Rodzinski's performance a year later in Cleveland preceded the one in Philadelphia.

9. Goldovsky, *My Road to Opera,* 212.

10. Reiner to Alexander Archipenko, 17 August 1934, copy in NU.

11. Philadelphia *Public Ledger,* 9 October 1932, clipping in NU.

12. Despite conjecture, there was no discussion of Reiner in the official records of the Philadelphia Orchestra.

13. Reiner to Arthur See, 14 December 1935, copy in NU.

14. Programs from the Philadelphia Orchestra; Edna Phillips interview.

15. Philadelphia *Public Ledger,* 25 January 1936, clipping in NU.

16. This story has been told, with variations, by several writers, notably Kupferberg, *Fabulous Philadelphians,* and Daniel, *Stokowski.* My account also draws on my interviews with Judson in 1970.

17. Philadelphia *Inquirer,* 2 January 1933, clipping in NU.

1. Claire Dux Swift to Carlotta Reiner, 24 October 1932, in NU.

2. Correspondence and undated draft in NU. There is no indication the petition was circulated.

3. Eva Bartenstein, interview with me, October 1984.

4. Aaron Copland and Roger Sessions letters to Reiner, in NU.

5. Judson to Reiner, 4 December 1937, in NU.

6. Shanet, *Philharmonic,* 234–257.

7. Milton Goldin, *The Music Merchants* (New York: W. W. Norton and Company, 1969), 164–172. Under pressure from the United States Justice Department, the two conglomerates separated from the radio networks in 1940 and gradually relaxed their control of the national concert scene. Changes of corporate names reflected these legal adjustments, ultimately resulting in Columbia Artists Management, Inc. (CAMI) and National Concert and Artists Corporation (NCAC). By the 1960s the latter went through a series of ownerships resulting in its demise, leaving the Columbia group, minus its original organizer, still a formidable manager of concert musicians.

8. New York *Times,* 3 November 1932.

9. Program from New York *Times,* 1 January 1933. I have been unable to locate any other reference to Reiner's substitution for Stokowski.

10. New York *Times,* 20 July 1934, with editorial, 23 July; Philadelphia *Bulletin* clipping in TU; and correspondence in NU.

11. See Daniel, *Stokowski,* 305–314; and Bert Whyte, "The Roots of High Fidelity Sound," *Audio,* June 1981.

12. Maxfield and other correspondence in NU. In 1979 and 1980 the Bell Laboratories issued two long-playing records of Stokowski's performances, with some technical information. Stephen C. Hillyer, "FRS Centenary Tape Features Reiner's Earliest Recordings," *Podium,* Spring/Summer 1988, quotes Mark A. Obert-Thorn's report that some of the original vertical-cut discs, lasting approximately eight and a half minutes at 33⅓ rpm, were transcribed on tape by Ward Marston. The Fritz Reiner Society in 1988 offered its members fragments from Reiner's Wagner and Russian programs on cassette tapes from restoration by Ward Marston and Obert-Thorn. The fragments of the Horowitz performance and the Philadelphia Grand Opera *Lohengrin* have not been transcribed.

13. Reiner to lawyer Maurice Speiser, 20 September 1935, copy in NU.

14. Extensive correspondence with Speiser in NU. Stampers of these records may still exist at the RCA-Victor division of Bertelsmann Music Group. Some of Reiner's performances have also been included in a 1991 compact disc collection honoring the sesquicentennial of the New York Philharmonic(-Symphony) Orchestra.

15. An exception was made for Sergei Rachmaninoff to conduct recordings of his own music.

16. Because Reiner's entries in his diary were incomplete and there was little correspondence concerning this activity, it is impossible to document his participation more precisely.

17. Voluminous correspondence in NU. The Detroit Symphony Orchestra has pro-

vided copies of Reiner's Ford Sunday Evening Hour programs through 1941. The Detroit Public Library has supplied additional information, notably on the resumption in 1946. Recorded excerpts from some programs, especially from 1946, are at the Library of Congress. Reiner had at least one program recorded on lacquer discs, which are probably at Curtis.

18. Though well documented elsewhere, this concert is not listed in Tintori's *Cronologia*.

19. Edward Jablonski, *Gershwin* (Garden City, N.Y.: Doubleday, 1987), 278.

20. Slonimsky, *Music since 1900,* entry for 8 September 1932, p. 553.

21. Except for a 15 May 1933 performance of *Tannhäuser* at the Royal Hungarian Opera in Budapest and concert performances with the Budapest Philharmonic in 1935 and 1936, engagements mentioned in passing in various correspondence cannot be verified.

22. H. Baré to Reiner, 3 July 1937, in NU.

23. Telegram from Hans Tessmer to Reiner, 22 December 1931, in NU.

24. New York *Times,* 2 March 1932.

25. Correspondence with Karl Ebert in NU.

26. Correspondence with Vilma Reiner in Budapest and with Hans Heinsheimer of Universal Edition in Vienna in NU.

27. Beecham cable to Reiner, 25 March 1936, in NU; programs from Royal Opera House. See also Harold Rosenthal, *Two Centuries of Opera at Covent Garden* (London: Putnam, 1958), 506.

28. Unidentified clipping, 25 April 1936, at Curtis Institute of Music.

29. Fred Gaisberg to Reiner, 26 May and 20 July 1936, and subsequent correspondence between Carlotta Reiner and "Kleinchen" Melchior, also Reiner to Judson, 17 July 1936, all in NU. In 1991 HMV's successor, EMI, released a set of compact discs of a *Tristan und Isolde* attributed to Sir Thomas Beecham in 1937 of which more than half was actually conducted by Reiner in 1936. Although several "underground" LPs and the EMI compact discs give May 1936 as the date of Reiner's recorded *Tristan und Isolde,* it is more likely that it originated from several of the four performances from which Gaisberg proposed to extract act II for commercial release after the Vienna sessions were canceled. See my letter to the editor in *Gramophone,* March 1992. See also David Hamilton, *"Tristan* in the Thirties," *Musical Newsletter* (Fall 1976): 23–24, and (Spring 1977): 7. More recently Hamilton has studied the underground LP recordings, the EMI compact discs of the 1936 and 1937 performances, and the VAI compact discs of the 1936 test recordings to identify, more precisely than EMI's garbled "documentation," the respective contributions of each conductor to the 1991 compact disc releases. See *Opera Quarterly* 9, no. 3 (Spring 1993): 162.

30. Correspondence in NU.

31. Rosenthal, *Two Centuries,* 526.

32. Unidentified clipping, 8 June 1937, in Curtis Institute of Music.

33. Charles Reid, *Thomas Beecham* (New York: E. P. Dutton, 1962), 192.

34. Leaflet in NU.

35. Arthur Bloomfield, *50 Years of the San Francisco Opera* (San Francisco: San Francisco Book Company, 1972), is a standard authority.

36. Extensive correspondence concerning Bodanzky, the tubas, and other preliminaries to Reiner's San Francisco engagement in NU.

37. Merola later told me of this episode and of other demands by Reiner during his three seasons in San Francisco.

38. A recent compact disc concludes with what appears to be a spurious completion of the act, without Davenport's concluding remarks.

39. An underground recording of act II from the 1937 *Tristan und Isolde* probably originated from the Los Angeles performance: acoustically it is quite different from recordings made in the War Memorial Opera House in San Francisco.

VIII: Pittsburgh Challenge

1. Deeds and other legal documents regarding the Rambleside property were recorded in the office of the Weston town clerk. Although these records show conclusion of legal purchase in 1939, the Reiners began planning their house a year earlier.

2. Unfortunately there is no trace of most of the thousands of photo negatives and prints of the images that this indefatigable photographer took at Rambleside and on his travels. He was very proud of his professionalism, and his letters frequently referred to photos he sent to friends and colleagues. A very few of his black-and-white photo prints and some relatively late 35-mm color slides are in NU, but the whereabouts of the bulk of the collection, known to have been still stored in the Rambleside basement in Carlotta's last years, remains a mystery.

3. See Frederick Dorian and Judith Meibach, "A Short History of the Pittsburgh Symphony Orchestra," *Carnegie Magazine,* January–February and March–April 1986; and two unpublished studies in UP: Kathleen Butera, "The History of the Pittsburgh Symphony," and Alexis Francos, "To Research a Symphony: Some Resources and Tools Available on the History of the Pittsburgh Symphony Orchestra."

4. Private communication to me from Peter Heyworth, biographer of Otto Klemperer, 13 October 1987.

5. Correspondence and Diary in NU.

6. Reiner to Judson, 4 April 1940 and 1 May 1941, copies in NU.

7. Extensive correspondence between Reiner and Specter in manila file folders in NU.

8. Figures are based on an analysis of personnel listed in the printed programs of the Pittsburgh Symphony Orchestra.

9. John Edwards, interview with me, Chicago, 1984; also interview with Jim Unrath for WFMT in September 1977, transcribed in *Podium,* Spring/Summer 1985.

10. These comments are based on a survey of Pittsburgh Symphony Orchestra program books. In general, contemporary music is regarded as a work first programmed by Reiner while the composer was alive. Similarly, Americans are those either born in the United States or active there for most of their careers. Admittedly this creates problems: Bartók's Music for Strings, Percussion, and Celesta was not "contemporary" when Reiner first played it in 1958, because the composer was no longer living, although the later Concerto for Orchestra qualifies. Bloch and Menotti are regarded as Americans, though born abroad, but Stravinsky and Hindemith are not, despite Reiner's having programmed music they composed in America.

11. Reiner's marked conducting score of the Schumann Second Symphony is in NU.

12. New York *Herald-Tribune,* 12 October 1947.

13. Specter to Reiner, 22 August 1946, and copy of Reiner's reply, both in NU.

14. Although Carlotta Reiner promised Columbia University the correspondence between Reiner and composers, a large quantity reached NU along with the bulk of his papers. Columbia is said to have received approximately eighty letters to or from Reiner. This small but very important portion of the correspondence has not been available to me.

15. Schoenberg typed this letter himself, apparently responding to a letter from Reiner, which cannot be located. Despite his handwritten request, "Please return this letter to me," Reiner filed it in his correspondence; the original is in NU. The letter has been published in Arnold Schoenberg, *Arnold Schoenberg Letters,* ed. Erwin Stein (New York: St. Martin's Press, 1965), no. 195, pp. 221–222. Other Reiner-Schoenberg letters are in the Schoenberg collection at the Library of Congress, and some may be at Columbia University.

16. Koussevitzky correspondence at the Library of Congress.

17. Correspondence with Ernest Hutcheson and the Zimbalists in NU.

18. Morton Gould, interview with me, San Francisco, June 1984.

19. New York *Herald-Tribune,* 23 December 1946.

20. See Roland Gelatt, *The Fabulous Phonograph* (Philadelphia: J. B. Lippincott Company, 1955); and Smith, *In All His Glory,* 148–150.

21. Moses Smith to Edward Wallerstein, 9 July 1939, copy to Reiner in NU.

22. Extensive correspondence between Reiner and Columbia Records personnel in NU. Although information on the Reiner's Pittsburgh recordings is included in Helmbrecht, *Discography,* Columbia Masterworks "lab sheets" contain valuable entries made at the time of recording. I am indebted to Michael H. Gray for sharing this information with me.

23. See Hart, *Orpheus;* Gelatt, *Fabulous Phonograph;* and Robert D. Leiter, *The Musicians and Petrillo* (New York: Bookman, 1953).

24. See Hart, *Orpheus,* chap. V.

25. Kupferberg, *Fabulous Philadelphians,* 138–139.

IX: New Directions

1. Diary in NU; press clippings in UP. This advantageous touring was shortly terminated by increases in transportation costs and musicians' union restrictions.

2. Draft in Reiner's handwriting, not dated but in 1946 file at NU; the notation "not sent" was by Carlotta.

3. John Edwards, interview with me, 1984.

4. Schedule from Diary in NU and press clippings in UP; Edwards's reminiscences to me.

5. Reiner listed only a few of his programs for this tour in his Diary, and sources in UP are not complete.

6. Clipping from the Dallas *News,* 19 January 1947, in NU.

7. May Valentine was custodian of a large library of performance materials from the defunct Chicago Civic Opera.

8. Roland L. Davis, *Opera in Chicago* (New York: Appleton Century, 1966), 210–217.

9. See Shanet, *Philharmonic,* 279–329.

10. Cited in Igor Stravinsky, *Selected Stravinsky Correspondence,* ed. Robert Craft, vol. 2 (New York: Alfred A. Knopf, 1982), 218; this letter, not in NU, may be at Columbia University.

11. Broadcast transcriptions of a portion of Reiner's programs in Boston and Cleveland are at the Library of Congress, along with some material from the Pittsburgh Symphony Orchestra.

12. Sachs, *Toscanini,* 274–275.

13. Boris Morros was also an undercover FBI agent who testified before congressional committees on Communist activity in the motion picture capital.

14. Call sheet and page of script in NU; *Variety* clipping in NU. For Agee's comment, see Richard Schickel and Michael Walsh, *Carnegie Hall: The First One Hundred Years* (New York: Henry N. Abrams, 1987), 141.

15. Correspondence with Eva Bartenstein and Tuśy Assejew in NU. Carlotta kept carbon copies of Reiner's letters to Tuśy, but he wrote to Eva by hand and kept no copies. Eva Bartenstein has preferred to retain these as "too personal."

16. Dana Hawthorne to Ralph S. Thorn, 16 January 1945, copy in NU.

17. Diary for 1946 in NU.

18. Nora Shea undated letter to Carlotta Reiner in NU.

19. Reiner to Bruno Zirato, 20 and 21 April 1946, copies in NU.

20. Extensive correspondence and Diary entries in NU.

21. Specter to Reiner, 8 October 1946, in NU.

22. Edwards's account to me in 1984.

23. James A. Davidson to Specter, 20 February 1948, copy to Reiner in NU.

24. Press clippings at UP.

25. New York *Times,* 24 February 1948.

26. Pittsburgh *Sun Telegraph,* 26 February 1948, clipping in UP.

X: The Metropolitan Opera

1. Correspondence and Diary in NU; also NYP.

2. Correspondence and Diary in NU.

3. There is no documentation in NU of Reiner's working routine at the Metropolitan Opera comparable to that of his posts earlier in Pittsburgh and later in Chicago. It was uncharacteristic of Reiner not to have kept written records, especially during the off-season months. This group of files, probably in manila folders, was misplaced. Correspondence in the file boxes in NU deals mainly with non-Metropolitan activities. The Diary helps to determine dates and gives some notion of whom Reiner was seeing. MOA contains some Reiner correspondence and other information, including contracts and extensive press clippings on microfilm. Gerald Fitzgerald, ed., *Annals of the Metropolitan Opera* (Boston: G. K. Hall and Company, 1989), is the current authority for casts and dates. It supersedes William H. Seltsam, *Metropolitan Opera Annals: First Supplement, 1947–1957* (New York: H. W. Wilson Company, 1957). I have also relied on such secondary sources as Rudolf Bing, *5000 Nights at the Opera* (Garden City, N.Y.: Doubleday and Company, 1972); idem, *A Knight at the Opera* (New York: J. P. Putnam's Sons, 1981); Irving Kolodin, *The Metropolitan Opera* (New

York: Alfred A. Knopf, 1966); and Martin Mayer, *The Met: One Hundred Years of Grand Opera* (New York: Simon and Schuster, 1983).

4. Bruno Zirato to Reiner, 14 January 1946, in NU.

5. Mayer, *The Met,* 237. Richard Strauss's telegram, cited frequently in Reiner's publicity, may be at Columbia University, which has not made its Reiner materials available to me.

6. Diaries and correspondence in NU; contract in MOA.

7. Regina Resnik at Conductors' Guild's Reiner Retrospective, Columbia University, 9 January 1988, transcript in *Podium,* Spring/Summer 1988.

8. Mayer, *The Met,* 225.

9. Kolodin, *Metropolitan Opera,* 478. When describing performances in his book that he had previously covered in the daily or weekly press, Kolodin frequently paraphrased his earlier reviews.

10. New York *Times,* 5 February 1949.

11. New York *Herald-Tribune,* 5 February 1949.

12. New York *Herald-Tribune,* 28 February 1949.

13. New York *Times,* 28 February 1949.

14. Press clippings, 22 November 1949.

15. My correspondence with Gunther Schuller, 29 August 1987, and subsequent telephone conversations.

16. Diary and a printed brochure for this orchestra's subscription season. Another source of information for this trip is correspondence between the Reiners and an enthusiastic young critic, Peggy Muñoz, in NU.

17. Diary in NU.

18. New York *Times,* 8 August 1951.

19. Reiner correspondence with Eva Bartenstein in NU.

20. Reiner correspondence with Eva Bartenstein and Diary in NU.

21. Reiner correspondence with Hurok office and Diary in NU; programs in NYP.

22. Diary in NU.

23. Diary in NU; Chicago Symphony Orchestra program books in NU.

24. Program information from the Philadelphia Orchestra; press clipping in TU.

25. In the absence of authoritative documentation by NBC, it is necessary to reconstruct information on Reiner's NBC Symphony Orchestra broadcasts from press announcements, from his Diary and correspondence in NU, and from files at the Library of Congress.

26. Transcriptions of Reiner's NBC Symphony Orchestra broadcasts are in the Library of Congress. A few selections from them have appeared on underground CD recordings. Several of Reiner's Metropolitan broadcasts have been similarly available, though the opera association vigorously resists quasi-commercial distribution in the United States.

27. See Gelatt, *Fabulous Phonograph,* 290–304.

28. Diary for 1952 in NU.

29. See Bing, *5000 Nights,* 163.

30. Diary in NU.

31. For *Fledermaus* plans, see Bing, *5000 Nights,* 163. Recording dates from Diary in NU, and from Helmbrecht, *Discography.*

32. Diary in NU.

33. Reiner respected Max Rudolf highly and on several occasions recommended his book *The Grammar of Conducting* (New York: G. Schirmer, 1950).

34. Reiner to Bing, 30 March 1950, in MOA.

35. Max Rudolf undated memorandum, probably midsummer 1950, to Bing, copy in MOA.

36. Bing, *5000 Nights,* 163.

37. Max Rudolf, interview with me, Philadelphia, January 1988.

38. Bing to Reiner, 16 and 29 September 1950, copies in MOA.

39. Reiner to Garson Kanin, 31 October 1950, copy in NU; also quoted in Bing, *5000 Nights,* 164.

40. Bing to Kanin, 9 November 1950, in MOA.

41. Kanin's preface to Bing, *Knight at the Opera,* 13.

42. Bing to Reiner, 23 November 1950, copy in MOA.

43. Bing to Reiner, 24 November 1950, copy in MOA.

44. Bing, *5000 Nights,* 165.

45. Mayer, *The Met,* 249.

46. Kanin's preface to Bing, *Knight at the Opera,* 14.

47. Max Rudolf, interview with me.

48. Press clippings, 2 December 1950, in MOA.

49. Correspondence in NU.

50. Kolodin, *Metropolitan Opera,* 521.

51. Thomson quoted in Seltsam, *Metropolitan Opera Annals: First Supplement,* 50.

52. Risë Stevens to Reiner, 3 February 1952, in NU.

53. New York *Times,* 19 February 1952.

54. Regina Resnik's reminiscences at Conductors' Guild's Reiner Retrospective.

55. Kolodin, *Metropolitan Opera,* 533.

56. Ibid., 527; Mayer, *The Met,* 250.

57. Downes as quoted in Kolodin, *Metropolitan Opera,* 529.

58. New York *Herald-Tribune,* 22 February 1953.

59. Kolodin, *Metropolitan Opera,* 527.

60. There have been conflicting reports about Reiner's presence at the Stravinsky recording sessions. Given Reiner's defection to RCA-Victor, Goddard Lieberson probably would not have invited him to the Columbia sessions. Max Rudolf clearly recalled that Reiner was not there: "There was no reason for him to be there." Nor do members of the orchestra recall Reiner's presence.

61. Igor Stravinsky telegram to Reiner, 16 March 1953, in NU.

62. Clipping of Martin Mayer's review; clipping of Stravinsky's letter to *Esquire;* and his letter to Reiner, all in NU.

63. Igor Stravinsky and Robert Craft, *Themes and Episodes* (New York: Alfred A. Knopf, 1966), 148; V. Stravinsky and Craft, *Stravinsky in Pictures,* 480.

64. New York *Times,* 22 March 1953.

1. Philo Adams Otis, *The Chicago Symphony Orchestra: Its Organization, Growth, and Development, 1891–1924* (Chicago: Clayton Summy, 1925), remains the standard account of the Chicago Symphony Orchestra's early history. Thomas Willis is preparing a history of the orchestra. See also Hart, *Orpheus*, chap. II, for an overview of Theodore Thomas and his efforts in Chicago. Throughout this chapter and those that follow, I rely on personal recollections from my association with the Chicago Symphony Orchestra between 1955 and 1961, but I have included only those facts that are documented elsewhere. Copious material on Reiner's Chicago years is in NU. Microfilms of the orchestra's press clippings from 1891 on are in the Newberry Library and NU.

2. OA, 9 January 1947. Although Furtwängler had been cleared by the Allied military authorities in Austria as early as March 1946, his clearance in Germany was delayed until December of that year.

3. For Chicago trustee deliberations, see OA. For Judson's version of his problems with Rodzinski in New York, see Hart, *Orpheus*, 90.

4. Opened in 1889, the Auditorium Theater was a remarkable architectural achievement by Louis Sullivan and Dankmar Adler, noted as much for the acoustics of its large hall as for its innovative design. The Chicago Symphony Orchestra played there for its first thirteen seasons but found the theater's large capacity an actual disadvantage in building a subscription audience. At Theodore Thomas's insistence, the Orchestral Association built Orchestra Hall, completed in 1904. With the opening of the Civic Opera House in 1929, the Auditorium was no longer the central site for opera and concerts in Chicago. It suffered neglect and was, during World War II, a USO center containing bowling alleys. Later purchased by Roosevelt University, it has been substantially restored and is once again home to performances.

5. OA, 8 October 1948, 29 December 1948, and 6 December 1949.

6. Bernard Asbell, "Claudia Cassidy: The Queen of Culture and Her Reign of Terror," *Chicago*, June 1956, remains one of the few published accounts of the career of this extraordinarily private woman. Since Cassidy declined my requests for an interview for this biography, I have relied chiefly on Asbell's account.

7. Chicago *Tribune*, 3 December 1952.

8. Chicago *Tribune*, 2 November 1951 and 6 April 1951.

9. Beginning in 1966, Kubelik returned to Chicago as guest conductor. He enjoyed great success in nine seasons and participated in the orchestra's centennial concert in October 1991.

10. The Orchestral Association published a summary balance sheet each year in the program for the opening concerts.

11. The Orchestral Association also received income from office tenants and from the rental of Orchestra Hall to churches and presenters of concerts and other public events; the net income from this meant that the orchestra's priority use of the building was essentially rent-free.

12. Nora Shea to Reiner, 26 March 1948, in NU.

13. Friede Rothe to Reiner, 8 November 1948, in NU.

14. Potter, "Fritz Reiner," 86.

15. Philip Farkas at Reiner Symposium in Bloomington, 11 March 1978, in *Podium,* 1978–1979.

16. Claudia Cassidy, "Farewell to Reiner," Chicago *Tribune,* 24 November 1963.

17. Recollection of violist Milton Preves, in conversations with me.

18. Farkas at Bloomington symposium.

19. Chicago Symphony Orchestra programs, 1953–1963, bound volumes in NU and the Newberry Library.

20. Samuel Barber letters to and from Reiner, September 1953, in NU.

21. Cassidy to Carlotta, undated, in NU; Reiner to Kuyper, 4 May 1954; copies in NU.

22. After leaving Chicago, George Schick first joined the staff of the NBC opera program. Later, at the Metropolitan Opera, he was conductor and music administrator. From 1969 until 1976 he was president of the Manhattan School of Music.

23. Margaret Hillis's visits to Rambleside, summer of 1954, in Diary. Reiner and Kuyper correspondence in NU. I worked with Margaret Hillis in organizing the Chicago Symphony Chorus.

24. I attended this rehearsal, witnessed Reiner's behavior, and had the unpleasant task of notifying him of the end of the rehearsal.

25. Lawrence Kelly to Reiner, 5 May 1954, in NU.

26. Chicago *Tribune,* 27 Nov. 1955.

27. I served in that capacity for five and a half years.

28. At present writing (1994), Marsh is still at the *Sun-Times* but has relinquished his role as "dean" of Chicago music critics.

29. Carlotta to Alan Kayes, 30 October 1958, copy in NU.

30. Seymour Raven to Reiner, with copy to Eric Oldberg, 23 May 1953, in NU.

31. Chicago *Tribune,* February 1958.

32. Farkas at Bloomington symposium.

XII: Chicago Triumph

1. Because of the loss of a considerable portion of the Chicago Symphony Orchestra archives in 1966, information on these radio and television projects is incomplete. For pre-1953 information, the principal source is internal promotional material from Chicago Title and Trust, supplied by Evelyn Meine and Brenda Nelson-Strauss of the orchestra's revived archival efforts. W. J. T. Hyer, of Television Airshows, has also provided important information. From his research on the history of the orchestra's radio and television activity, Steven Smolian has shared information on the Reiner era.

2. Reiner correspondence with Alan Kayes and Martin Feinstein, in NU.

3. Chicago Title and Trust promotional brochure and press release, fall 1957.

4. Although this syndication effort failed, several programs in this series reportedly appeared on Japanese television.

5. Several kinescopes from the Dumont broadcasts in 1953–1954 and some videotapes from *Great Music from Chicago,* with Reiner conducting, are in NU. These provide rare visual documentation of Reiner's conducting.

6. In 1985 Stephen F. Temmer made copies of these tapes for the Chicago Symphony

Orchestra archives and for the Northwestern University Music Library. Approximately four hours of the orchestra's performance under Reiner, all of it repertory not available on commercial recordings, were released on LP or CD recordings for fund-raising benefits. These collections of recordings include some Reiner radio performances: *Chicago Symphony Orchestra—From the Archives, The Reiner Era* (CSO 86/2); *Chicago Symphony Orchestra—From the Archives, Volume III* (CSO 88/2); *Chicago Symphony Orchestra—The First 100 Years* (CSO 90/12); and *Mozart* (CSO CD 91/2). All include annotations of historical interest. Roger Dettmer's "jacket" notes for CSO 86/2 reviewed the circumstances of the WBAI-FM broadcasts, from which the recordings were made. I have also verified and expanded this information by letter and telephone with Temmer. The notes by Henry Fogel and Philip Huscher for CSO 90/12 also offer important historical information.

7. Frederick Stock's recordings for Columbia in May 1916 were the first by any American symphony orchestra under its own name.

8. Don Tait's discography of the Chicago Symphony Orchestra is scheduled for publication in 1994 by Greenwood Press in Westport, Conn. Richard Oldberg's unpublished manuscript "The Oldberg Discography of the Chicago Symphony Orchestra" provides similar documentation. Helmbrecht's discography also covers Reiner's Chicago recordings.

9. Alan Kayes to Reiner, 6 February 1953; Reiner to Oldberg, 21 March 1953; Kayes to Oldberg, 17 June 1953; all in NU.

10. RCA-Victor's Chicago announcement followed shortly the company's demonstration at a professional meeting in New York of its new stereo recording process. This had already been tested, at sessions in New York, where Leopold Stokowski conducted a free-lance orchestra. The Chicago recordings in March 1954 were the first tapings to lead to the publication of stereophonic LPs, open-reel and cassette tapes, and eventually to compact discs.

11. Renovations of Orchestra Hall in 1966 and 1981 seriously impaired its acoustics for recording.

12. Michael Gray, "Recording Reiner," *Absolute Sound*, no. 49 (Fall 1987): 45–63, gives an account of the choice and placement of microphones and other technical details for Reiner's recordings with the Chicago Symphony Orchestra. This article also explains matrix numbering and other matters of interest to audiophiles, including the significance of the "shaded dog" label. See also Jonathan Valin, *The RCA Bible* (Cincinnati: The Music Lovers Press, 1993). Though an extreme example of "audiophilia," this book reprints Gray's article and describes the RCA-Victor "Living Presence" recording process in authentic detail. In addition to inaccuracies concerning Fritz Reiner, its musical judgments are clouded by an obsession with audio criteria.

13. Although the early performances were initially released only monaurally, some appeared later in stereo LP format. Other recordings appeared in stereo on compact discs many years later. The three Strauss performances also appeared on 45-rpm discs, to which RCA-Victor clung stubbornly. It would soon abandon these, however, for classical repertory. Some of these early recordings were also published on two-track open-reel tape; eventually most of the later Chicago performances appeared in a four-track version of that format.

14. Rare exceptions to this procedure occurred only when a soloist recorded music

that had not been played in concert. On such occasions the union's more expensive "studio rate" prevailed.

15. The development and promotion of "Dynagroove" resulted in a drastic deterioration of the sound from LP discs. Though some of Reiner's Chicago recordings were later issued in this form, all were originally issued with the "shaded dog" labels so highly prized by later record collectors. These modifications of frequency and dynamic range in the processing were later corrected by independent technicians (Mobile Fidelity, Chessky) or by RCA-Victor itself (compact discs). They have restored the exceptional quality of the original Mohr-Layton achievement.

16. Carlotta to Art Buchwald, 12 June 1962, copy in NU.

17. In the postwar realignment of international recording affiliations, RCA-Victor lost its longtime relationship with HMV and needed a source for less expensive European recordings.

18. Reiner to Hurok, 10 March 1955, copy in NU.

19. John Culshaw, *The Ring Resounding* (New York: Viking Press, 1967), 60.

20. Extensive correspondence between Reiner and Lacy Hermann in NU.

21. Clippings in NU.

22. *Opera*, January 1956.

23. Henry de la Grange, "Reopening in Vienna," New York *Times,* 27 November 1955. (As Henry-Louis de la Grange, this critic later wrote a highly regarded biography of Gustav Mahler.)

24. Hermann to Reiner, 7 December 1955, in NU.

25. Itinerary from copies of Carlotta's letters to Cassidy and Diary in NU.

26. Carlotta to Cassidy, 4 October 1958, in NU. The photograph, taken by the ship's photographer, is in the *Tribune* photo files.

27. Carlotta to Edith Mason Ragland, 18 March 1958, copy in NU.

28. New York *Times,* 12 March 1958.

29. Carlotta's letters to her mother, Amelia Irwin, and her housekeeper, Ann Gaito, in Connecticut, copies in NU, describe in great detail the Reiner routine in Chicago.

30. Carlotta to Barton G. Hocker, 28 January 1957, and others, copies in NU.

31. Kuyper to Reiner, 10 June 1958, in NU.

32. Diary, 11 August 1957, 3 January 1958 through 22 May 1958, in NU.

33. The Boris Chaliapin portrait of Fritz Reiner is now at the National Portrait Gallery of the Smithsonian Institution.

34. The Weston town clerk's office has a full record of the Reiners' transactions regarding the Rambleside property.

35. Reiner's diary had many entries for massage as well as doctors' appointments for himself and Carlotta.

36. Dr. Wright Adams to Reiner, 20 March 1956; note in Diary, 27 May 1958, both in NU.

37. Cassidy to Carlotta and copy of Carlotta to Cassidy, 27 January 1957, in NU.

38. Carlotta to Cassidy, 23 December 1956, and to Rebecca Lowry, 29 December 1956, copies in NU.

39. According to OA, for the rest of 1957 and through most of 1958, scarcely a trustees' meeting did not include some discussion of Orchestra Hall or some long-range plan for relocating it.

40. Handwritten notes in 1958 file in NU.

41. Cassidy to Carlotta, 18 June 1957, in NU.

42. Reiner to Kuyper, 25 September 1956, copy in NU.

43. OA, 26 April 1957.

44. Carlotta to Cassidy, 8 June 1957, copy in NU.

45. New York *Herald-Tribune,* 17 October 1958.

46. As quoted in Chicago *Tribune,* 20 December 1958.

47. Kuyper to Reiner, 6 July 1955, and Reiner's handwritten notes of telephone conversation with Kuyper, in NU.

48. Reiner's entry for 31 December 1957, Diary in NU.

49. Donal Henahan, in Chicago *Daily News,* August 1963.

XIII: Reiner's Music

1. Reiner, "Outline for Course in Conducting," in NU.

2. Reiner, "Technique of Conducting."

3. Farkas at Bloomington symposium.

4. New York *Times,* 24 November 1963.

5. János Starker, interview with Bruce Welleck, "János Starker Speaks about His Reiner Years," *Podium* 1, no. 2 (1977), and 2, no. 1 (1978); "An Interview with Victor Aitay," *Podium,* Fall/Winter 1986; Reiner, "Outline."

6. Sebastian Caratelli, *A Musician's Odyssey* (New York: Vantage Press, 1983), 89–91.

7. Tibor Kozma, "Ave Atque Vale: Fritz Reiner," *Opera News,* 6 April 1953.

8. New York *Herald-Tribune,* 17 October 1958.

9. Kozma, "Ave Atque Vale."

10. George Gaber at Bloomington symposium.

11. Clark Brody, interview with me, Northwestern University, January 1987.

12. Murray Grodner at Bloomington symposium.

13. Farkas and Gaber at Bloomington symposium.

14. Elisabeth Schwarzkopf, interview with Rudolf Sabor, *Records and Recording,* May 1980.

15. Grodner at Bloomington symposium.

16. Reiner's score is in NU.

17. Roger Dettmer, "Kaviar fürs Volk," *Podium,* Spring 1981, p. 18. The score did not reach NU after Carlotta Reiner's death.

18. Starker, interview with Welleck.

19. Reiner to Max Aronoff, 12 June 1959, copy in NU.

20. Grodner at Bloomington symposium.

21. "An Interview with Donald Peck," *Podium* 3 (1979).

22. Christa Ludwig, interview with Andy Karzas, broadcast June 1985 on WFMT, quoted in *Podium,* Spring/Summer 1985.

23. Richard Taruskin, "The Pastness of the Present and the Presence of the Past," in *Authenticity and Early Music,* ed. Nicholas Kenyon (Oxford: Oxford University Press, 1988), 163.

24. Ibid., 169.

25. Ibid., 166, apparently relying on inaccurate information from the "authoritative" *New Grove* of 1980.

26. Ibid., 166–167.

27. Remarks by Adele Addison at Conductors' Guild's Reiner Retrospective.

28. Taruskin, "Pastness of the Present," 166–184. Taruskin's argument involves references to the theories of Edward Cone, to the Bach D Minor Clavier Concerto, to Stravinsky's Concerto for Piano and Winds, and to Stravinsky's own performances (with his son) of music by Mozart and himself.

29. New York *Times*, 22 March 1953.

30. H. C. Robbins Landon, *Mozart's Last Year* (New York: Schirmer Books, 1988), 10.

31. Recent compact disc reissues of recordings by both Nikisch and Strauss, dimly reproduced and, in Strauss's case, with inferior orchestras, make it difficult to analyze the influence of these two conductors on Reiner.

32. These include portions of *Parsifal* and *Der fliegende Holländer* and the complete *Tristan und Isolde* on underground LPs and the latter on compact discs.

33. Joseph Horowitz, *Understanding Toscanini* (New York: Alfred A. Knopf, 1987), 277.

34. Starker, interview with Welleck.

XIV: "Unfeasible"

1. Jay Harrison in the New York *Herald-Tribune*, 24 November 1963.

2. "Reiner Invited to Take Orchestra to Europe," Chicago *Tribune*, 25 November 1955.

3. Wilfrid Van Wyck correspondence with Reiner and Kuyper, 21 September 1956, 13 December 1956, 2 May 1957, 18 June 1957, and 25 June 1957, in NU. Carlotta filed much of the correspondence on the European tour in a special manila folder, which she labeled "Chicago Gems."

4. Reiner to Kuyper, 12 January 1957, copy in NU.

5. Carlotta to Cassidy, 12 January 1957, copy in NU.

6. OA, 26 April and 10 October 1957.

7. Oldberg to Howard S. Cullman, 21 October 1957, Reiner's copy in NU.

8. Robert F. Schnitzer to Kuyper, 12 May 1958, Reiner's copy in NU.

9. Kuyper to Antoine Heller, 23 June 1958, Reiner's copy in NU.

10. Kuyper cable to Reiner, 2 September 1958, in NU.

11. Ruth H. Carroll to Reiner, 2 September 1958, in NU.

12. Schnitzer to Kuyper, 23 September 1958, Reiner's copy in NU.

13. Schnitzer to Kuyper, 23 September 1958, Reiner's copy in NU. Because of increased use of the long-distance telephone, it is not always possible to document details of these negotiations. Although Kuyper frequently recorded telephone conversations for future reference, he did not keep written notes on them.

14. Undated handwritten draft in NU. I recall that Reiner did in fact cable Kuyper in Paris to this effect.

15. Chicago *Tribune*, 13 January 1959.

16. Cassidy did not report the *Tribune* contacts of 13 and 26 January with the State Department until 8 March 1959.

17. Chicago *Sun-Times*, 18 and 30 January 1959.

18. Robert C. Marsh, "Fritz Reiner's Legacy Comes Home," Chicago *Sun-Times*, 19 February 1984.

19. Marshall Field, Jr., to Reiner, 24 February 1959, responding to Reiner's letter of 21 February, in NU.

20. None of Reiner's colleagues at the Metropolitan Opera recalled any indication of health problems that caused cancellation of rehearsals or other obligations. In later correspondence and in personal conversation with me in Chicago in October 1988, Marsh could no longer suggest any sources in New York to clarify his allegations.

21. Chicago *Daily News,* 10 February 1959.

22. Pencil draft, 2 February 1959, in NU. I recall Kuyper's receiving a telegram to this effect.

23. Carlotta to Cassidy, 2 February 1959, copy in NU.

24. Kuyper to Reiner, showing copy to Oldberg, 4 February 1959, in NU.

25. As reported by Kuyper to Schnitzer, 11 February 1959, Reiner's copy in NU.

26. Schnitzer telegram to Kuyper, 16 February 1959, in NU; Reiner's comments, as typed by Carlotta, 17 February 1959, in NU.

27. I saw the suit, without a sign, in this condition on the floor of the dressing room.

28. I drafted the announcement, incorporating Oldberg's and Kuyper's detailed revisions, and sent it by messenger to the four newspapers and by mail to the rest of the press list.

29. Shanet, *Philharmonic,* 631.

30. Unsigned letter to Reiner, 10 March 1959, in NU.

31. Chicago *American;* Chicago *Sun Times,* 15 March 1959.

32. Chicago *Tribune,* 8 March 1959.

33. Chicago *Tribune,* 27 December 1959.

34. New York *Times,* 26 February and 12 March 1959.

35. *Musical Courier,* April 1959.

36. Carlotta to Amelia Irwin, Eva Bartenstein, and Edith Ragland, March 1959, copies in NU.

37. Oldberg to Reiner, 27 February 1959, in NU.

38. Roger Dettmer recalled rumors of Reiner's replacement in "Reiner Remembered," Chicago *Tribune,* 27 November 1988. OA did not mention a "letter of intent."

39. Henry Zaccardi to Reiner, 29 February 1960, in NU.

40. Carlotta to Richard Mohr, 7 May 1960, copy in NU.

41. For Reiner's programs, see Shanet, *Philharmonic,* 626–629. Recordings of Kodály's "Peacock" Variations and Bartók's Piano Concerto and Suite from the *Miraculous Mandarin* from these programs have been issued on an Italian compact disc.

XV: Finale

1. Reiner to Seymour Raven, 10 May 1959, copy in NU.

2. See Wardwell Howell to Reiner, 10 July 1959, in NU. Howell was a management consultant retained by the southern California group to conduct an executive search. After he contacted Kuyper for recommendations of younger prospects, Kuyper independently applied for the job.

3. Kuyper's hasty departure was possible because the Orchestral Association had not signed a contract with him since he joined the Chicago Symphony Orchestra as manager in 1943.

4. Although Eric Oldberg's views were well known to his associates at the time, he later documented them comprehensively in a long letter in which he resigned as president. Oldberg to trustee secretary Merrill Shepard, 16 April 1962, Reiner's copy in NU.

5. Chicago *Sun-Times*, 31 January 1960.

6. Chicago *American*, 24 April 1960.

7. Chicago *Tribune*, 15 May 1960.

8. Diary, 29 April 1960.

9. Typed but undated draft, with Reiner's handwritten corrections, in letter file for 1960 in NU.

10. OA, 29 April 1960.

11. Diary, 3 August 1959.

12. Chicago Symphony Orchestra program book and clippings in NU. The Diary (now often in Carlotta's entries) and correspondence in NU covered details of Reiner's illness and convalescence.

13. Undated press release, signed by Reiner and Raven, copy in NU. OA reported the trustee decision on 20 April. The story appeared in the Chicago press on 23 April.

14. Cassidy review, Chicago *Tribune*, 27 April 1962.

15. I was present at a trustees' meeting on 7 February 1961 when Oldberg made this report.

16. I heard substantially identical reports of this meeting from Seymour Raven at the time and in 1962 from Siegfried Hearst in New York.

17. OA, 16 March 1962, and clippings, 6 May 1962. After warmly greeting the choice of Jean Martinon, Claudia Cassidy eventually turned against him as savagely as she had against Defauw, Kubelik, and Reiner.

18. See Hart, *Orpheus,* chap. V, esp. 112–113.

19. Potter, "Fritz Reiner," 100, quoting Sam Denov, 8 July 1978. Denov's statement coincides with my own recollection.

20. Oldberg to Reiner, 15 September 1961, in NU.

21. Oldberg to Merrill Shepard, 16 April 1962, Reiner's copy in NU.

22. Telegrams to and from Reiner, 9 September 1962, in NU.

23. Rebecca Lowry to Carlotta, 14 September 1962, in NU.

24. Carlotta to Eva Bartenstein, 21 October 1962, copy in NU.

25. Haydn's Symphony no. 101 was rehearsed and recorded on 13 and 16 September; no. 95 on 18 and 20 September.

26. Rudolf Bing to Walter Prude, 4 June 1963, Reiner's copy in NU, confirming dates at a fee of fifteen hundred dollars for each performance, plus one thousand dollars for expenses.

27. Although Robert Herman and Paul Jaretzky of Rudolf Bing's staff, in telephone conversations with me in 1989, recalled that Bing's interest was primarily in the Wagner opera, Bing's letter to Walter Prude allowed for a substitution of another opera by mutual consent.

28. I attended most of this rehearsal.

29. A videotape of this program will be included in a series of Leonard Bernstein's telecasts to be published in 1994.

30. Text for publication in *Podium,* Spring/Summer 1988, supplied by William Schuman.

1. Both Carlotta and Mennin discussed such a gift with me when I was on the Juilliard staff.
2. Chicago *Tribune,* 28 December 1969.
3. "Last Will and Testament of Fritz Reiner," dated 27 September 1962, in the office of the probate judge, Westport, Connecticut.
4. The dissolution of Reiner's trust and Carlotta's will are in the office of the Westport probate judge. Columbia University has declined to disclose the terms of its trust.
5. "Last Will and Testament of Carlotta Reiner," dated 14 May 1981, in the office of the probate judge, Westport, Connecticut.
6. Office of Public Information, Columbia University, for release 24 October [1984].
7. Will Crutchfield, "Columbia to House a Reiner Archive," New York *Times,* 25 October 1984.
8. When I visited him in Ljubljana in October 1984, Tuśy's son, Vladimir ("Vovček") Assejew, could not understand why he had not received Reiner's ten-thousand-dollar bequest to his mother. He knew nothing of the dissolution of the trust because Hocker failed to answer his letters.
9. "Last Will and Testament of Carlotta Reiner" and other documents in the office of the probate judge, Westport.
10. President Michael J. Sovern has referred my inquiries to subordinates. Peter Smith, Chapin's successor as dean of the School of the Arts, failed to supply promised copies of material. Chou Wen-chung, who held the Fritz Reiner chair, never answered any of my letters,; nor has his successor, Mario Davidowsky.
11. Columbia University has ignored my specific requests to be included on the mailing list for announcements of concerts underwritten by the Reiner center, although several friends have sent me copies of such mailings that they have received.
12. The Bagaduce Library in Blue Hill, Maine, supplied NU with a list of these scores.
13. I learned of this purchase only in 1990, too late to trace more than one or two items through queries in *Opera News* and the New York *Times Book Review.*
14. "Fritz Reiner's Legacy Comes Home" and "Fritz Reiner's Parting Shot," Chicago *Sun-Times,* 19 February 1984 and 4 November 1984.

Fritz Reiner's Recordings

This list includes all of Fritz Reiner's published recordings: commercial recordings which Reiner made and approved; "underground" recordings from broadcasts, issued for sale or to members of the Fritz Reiner Society; and off-the-air recordings sold for fund-raising by the Chicago Symphony Orchestra and the Metropolitan Opera Association. Recordings not approved by Reiner are listed in brackets.

Although all commercial phonograph recordings prior to 1950, mostly Columbia Masterworks (COL), were issued on 78-rpm shellac discs (78), many were reissued on long-playing vinyl discs at 33⅓ rpm (LP). A few Reiner recordings for RCA-Victor (RCA) may be found on red 45 rpm vinyl discs, but nearly all of his performances for this company were on LPS. Most of Reiner's Chicago recordings have subsequently appeared on compact discs (CD); in the following list, many prefixes and suffixes used by RCA-Victor are omitted. It has been impractical to list all of RCA's LP and CD reissues and different couplings of Reiner performances; nor are the various tape—open-reel and cassette—formats included here. With a few exceptions, this list gives the catalog number of the initial release of each format—78, 45, LP, and CD.

Since Reiner's death many opera and orchestra performances have appeared on LP and CD from transcriptions of radio broadcasts; these vary greatly in quality and of course lacked his approval. Of special importance are LP and CD commemorative issues by the Chicago Symphony Orchestra. Although the Metropolitan Opera has published an LP set of Richard Strauss's *Salome* and *Elektra*, other Metropolitan performances circulated in the "underground" have not been authorized by that organization. The same is true of material from broadcasts with the NBC Symphony Orchestra, the New York Philharmonic, and other groups. For several years, the Fritz Reiner Society (FRS) issued to its members cassette or open-reel tape copies from various broadcast sources; some of this material has been subsequently duplicated in releases of wider distribution.

The Welte player-piano rolls "conducted" and in some cases performed by Reiner are included here for completeness, despite their great rarity.

An explanation of abbreviations used here can be found at the end of this list.

I owe special thanks to *Fritz Reiner: The Comprehensive Discography of His Recordings,* by Arthur J. Helmbrecht, Jr., archivist of the Fritz Reiner Society; to Richard Oldberg, "The Oldberg Discography of the Chicago Symphony Orchestra"; to Michael H. Gray for sharing copies of Columbia Masterworks "lab sheets"; and to Don Tait, for page proofs of his forthcoming Chicago Symphony Orchestra discography.

Albéniz, Isaac (arr. Arbos). *Iberia,* "Fête-Dieu à Seville."

    CSO, 26 April 1958. RCA: LP LM/LSC-2230; CD 5404. CHESSKY: LP RC9.

(arr. Arbos). *Iberia,* "Triana."

    CSO, 26 April 1958. RCA: LP LM/LSC-2230; CD 5404. CHESSKY: LP RC9.

(arr. Arbos). *Navarra.*

    CSO, 26 April 1958. RCA: LP LM/LSC-2230; CD 5404. CHESSKY: LP RC9.

Bach, Johann Sebastian. Brandenburg Concerto no. 1 in F Major, BWV 1046.

    Chamber Ensemble, 28 October 1949. COL: 78 M/MM-902; LP ML-4281.

Brandenburg Concerto no. 2 in F Major, BWV 1047.

    Chamber Ensemble, 2 December 1949. COL: 78 M/MM-902; LP ML-4281.

Brandenburg Concerto no. 3 in G Major, BWV 1048.

    Chamber Ensemble, 26 October 1949. COL: 78 M/MM-902; LP ML-4282.

Brandenburg Concerto no. 4 in G Major, BWV 1049.

    Chamber Ensemble, 21 October, 3 November 1949. COL: 78 M/MM-903; LP ML-4282.

    [CSO (WGN-TV), 14 November 1956. FRS: ORT/Cass no. 7.]

Brandenburg Concerto no. 5 in D Major, BWV 1050.

    Chamber Ensemble (S. Marlowe, J. Baker, F. Eyle), 3 November 1949. COL: 78 M/MM-903; LP ML-4283.

Brandenburg Concerto no. 6 in B-flat Major, BWV 1051.

    Chamber Ensemble, 27 October 1949. COL: 78 M/MM-903; LP ML-4283.

Concerto for Piano no. 5 in F Minor, BWV 1056.

    [CSO (A. Tchaikowsky), 15 February 1958. RCA: LP DPM1-0444.] Note: RCA-Victor at one point planned to include this recording on LM/LSC-2287; this change may have reflected Reiner's disapproval.

(arr. Cailliet). Fugue in G Minor ("Little"), BWV 578.

    PSO, 4 February 1946. COL: 78 M/MM-695, 12907D.

    [CSO (WGN-TV), 27 November 1957. FRS: ORT/Cass no. 7.]

(arr. Stock). Prelude and Fugue in E-flat Major, "St. Anne," BWV 552.

    [CSO, 17 October 1957. FRS: ORT/Cass no. 7.]

Suite no. 1 in C Major, BWV 1066.

    RCA-V SO, 23 October 1952. RCA: LM-6012.

Suite no. 2 in B Minor, BWV 1067.

    PSO (S. Caratelli), 4 February 1946. COL: 78 M/MM-695; LP ML-4156.

    RCA-V SO (J. Baker), 5 January 1953. RCA: LP LM-6012.

Suite no. 3 in D Major, BWV 1068.

    RCA-V SO, 30 October 1952. RCA: LP LM-6012.

Suite no. 4 in D Major, BWV 1069.

    RCA-V SO, 23 October 1952. RCA: LP LM-6012.

Bartók, Béla. Concerto for Orchestra.

    PSO, 4–5 February 1946. COL: 78 M/MM-793; LP ML-4102.

    CSO, 22 October 1955. RCA: LP LM/LSC-1934; CD 5604.

Concerto for Piano no. 1.

    [NYPO (R. Serkin), 19 March 1960. FRS: ORT/Cass no. 5; AS: CD 526.]

Concerto for Piano no. 3.

[CSO (G. Anda), 20 March 1958. FRS: ORT/Cass no. 5.]

Divertimento for Strings.

[CSO (WGN-TV), 20 February 1957. FRS: LP FRS-1.]

Hungarian Sketches.

CSO, 29 December 1958. RCA: LP LM/LSC-2374; CD 60206.

The Miraculous Mandarin, Suite.

[NBC SO, 15 December 1946. FRS: ORT/Cass no. 2.]

[NYPO, March 1960. AS: CD 526.]

Music for Strings, Percussion, and Celesta.

CSO, 28, 29 December 1958. RCA: LP LM/LSC-2374; CD 5604.

(arr. Weiner). Two Rumanian Dances.

[NBC SO, 19 January 1952. M&A: CD 292.]

Beethoven, Ludwig van. Concerto for Piano no. 4 in G Major, op. 58.

CSO (V. Cliburn), 22, 23 April 1963. RCA: LP LM/LSC-2680; CD 7943.

Concerto for Piano no. 5 in E-flat Major, op. 73.

RCA-V SO (V. Horowitz), 26 April 1952. RCA: LP LM-1718; 45 WDM-1718; CD 7992.

CSO (V. Cliburn), 4, 12 May 1961. RCA: LP LM/LSC-2562; CD 7943.

Coriolan, Overture, op. 62.

CSO, 5 May 1959. RCA: LP LM/LSC-2343; CD 5403.

Fidelio, op. 72, Overture.

CSO, 12 December 1955. RCA: LP LM/LSC-1991; CD 5403.

Symphony no. 1 in C Major, op. 21.

Singer and Reichmann (four-hand piano), date? Welte: Player-Piano Rolls C7595/98.

CSO, 8 May 1961. RCA: LP LM/LSC-6069; CD 60002.

Symphony no. 2 in D Major, op. 36.

PSO, 27 March 1945. COL: 78 M/MM-597; LP ML-4085.

Symphony no. 3 in E-flat Major, op. 55.

CSO, 4 December 1954. RCA: LP LM-1899; CD 60962.

Symphony no 4 in B-flat Major, op. 60.

[CSO (WBAI), 17 April 1958. CSO: LP/CD 88/2.]

Symphony no. 5 in C Minor, op. 67.

Singer and Reichmann (four-hand piano), date? Welte: Player-Piano Rolls 7527/30.

CSO, 4 May 1959. RCA: LP LM/LSC-2343; CD 5403.

Symphony no. 6 in F Major, op. 68.

Reiner and Singer (four-hand piano), date? Welte: Player-Piano Rolls not released?

CSO, 8, 10 April 1961. RCA: LP LM/LSC-2614; CD 60002.

Symphony no. 7 in A Major, op. 92.

CSO, 24 October 1955. RCA: LP LM/LSC-1991; CD 6376.

Symphony no. 8 in F Major, op. 93.

[CSO, 6 February 1958. FRS: ORT/Cass no. 1.]

Symphony no. 9 in D Minor, op. 125.

CSO (P. Curtin, F. Kopleff, D. Lloyd, D. Gramm, CSO Cho.), 1, 2 May 1961. RCA: LP LM/LSC-6069, LSC-3316; CD 6532.

Berlioz, Hector. *Benvenuto Cellini,* op. 23, Overture.

    [CSO, 5 December 1957. CSO: LP 86/2.]

    Le carnaval romain Overture, op. 9.

        [CBS SO, 9 February 1945. FRS: ORT/Cass no. 9.]

        [CSO (WBAI), 5 December 1957. CSO: LP/CD 88/2.]

    Le damnation de Faust, op. 24, Marche hongroise.

        PSO, 1 May 41. COL: 78 M/MM-491, 12906-D.

    Les nuits d'été, op. 7.

        CSO (L. Price), 4 March 1963. RCA: LP LM/LSC-2695; CD 61234.

Bizet, Georges. *Carmen.*

    RCA-V SO (R. Stevens, J. Peerce, L. Albanese, R. Merrill, Shaw Cho.), March, June 1951. RCA: LP LM-6102; 45 WDM-1556; CD 7881.

    Carmen, Excerpts from above.

        MET: CD 114.

    Di Stefano: CD GDS CD 2203.

Borodin, Alexander. *Prince Igor,* Polovtsi March.

    CSO, 14 March 1959. RCA: LP LM/LSC-2423; CD 5602.

Brahms, Johannes. *Academische Festouvertüre,* op. 80.

    Curtis SO, 28 November 1937. Desmar: LP IPA-5001/2. VAI: CD 1020.

    Alto Rhapsody, op. 53.

        RCA-V SO (M. Anderson, Shaw Cho.), 20 October 1950. RCA: LP LM-1146; 45 WDM-1532.

    Concerto for Piano no. 1 in D Minor, op. 15.

        PSO (R. Serkin) 2 February 1946. COL: 78 M/MM-652; LP ML-4100.

        CSO (A. Rubinstein), 17 April 1954. RCA: LP LM-1831; 45 ERD-1831; CD 5668.

    Concerto for Piano no. 2 in B-flat Major, op. 83.

        CSO (E. Gilels), 8 February 1958. RCA: LP LM/LSC-2219; CD 5406.

        CSO (V. Cliburn), 9, 10, 12 May 1961. RCA: LP LM/LSC-2581; CD 7942.

    Concerto for Violin in D Major, op. 77.

        CSO (J. Heifetz) 21, 22 February 1955. RCA: LP LM/LSC-1903; CD 5402.

    Concerto for Violin and Violoncello in A Minor, op. 102.

        RHD SO (N. Milstein, G. Piatigorsky), 29 June 1951. RCA: LP LM-1191; 45 WDM-1609; CD 61485.

    Hungarian Dance no. 1 in G Minor; no. 5 in G Minor; no. 6 in D Major; no. 7 in A Major; no. 12 in D Minor; no. 13 in D Major; no. 19 in B Minor; no. 21 in E Minor.

        PSO, 2, 5 February 1946. COL: 78 X/MX-309; LP ML-4116.

        VP, June 1960. LON: LP CM-9267, CS-6198; CD 417 696.

    Symphony no. 2 in D Major, op. 73.

        [NYPO, 12 March 1960. FRS: ORT/Cass no. 4.]

    Symphony no. 3 in F Major, op. 90.

        CSO, 14 December 1957. RCA: LP LM/LSC-2209; CD 61793 (1995 release).

    Symphony no. 4 in E Minor, op. 98.

        RPO, 2, 3, 5 October 1962. Reader's Digest: LP RD15-4. Quintessence: LP PMC-7182. RCA: LP AGL1-1961. CHESSKY: LP CR6; CD CD6.

Tragische Ouvertüre, op. 81.

    CSO, 14 December 1957. RCA: LP LM/LSC-2209; CD 5406.

Variations on a Theme by Haydn, op. 56a.

    [CSO (WGN-TV), 30 December 1953. FRS: ORT/Cass no. 4.]

Copland, Aaron. Concerto for Clarinet.

    [NBC SO (B. Goodman), 11 June 1951. AS: CD 628.]

The Tender Land, Suite.

    [CSO (WBAI), 10 April 1958. CSO: CD 90/12.]

Debussy, Claude. (arr. Ravel). *Danse.*

    PSO, 1 April 1947. COL: 78 X/MX-296.

Images, "Ibéria."

    PSO, 15 November 1941. COL: 78 M/MM-491; LP ML-4021.

    CSO, 4 March 1957. RCA: LP LM/LSC-2222; CD 5720.

La mer.

    CSO, 27 February 1960. RCA: LP LM/LSC-2462; CD 7018.

Nocturnes, "Nuages," "Fêtes."

    [NYPSO, 22 November 1938. World's Greatest Music: 78 SR-19; PEARL: CD CDS 9922.]

    [CSO (WGN-TV), 13 March 1957. FRS: ORT/Cass no. 6.]

(arr. Busser). *Petite Suite.*

    [NBC SO, 19 January 1952. M&A: CD 292.]

    NBC SO, 21 January 1952. RCA: LP LM-1724; 45 WDM-1724.

Prélude à l'après-midi d'un faune.

    [NYPSO, 22 November 1938. World's Greatest Music: 78 SR-19.]

Delius, Frederick. *Irmelin,* Prelude.

    [CSO (WGN-TV). 10 February 1954. FRS: ORT/Cass no. 10.]

Dvořák, Antonin. *Carnaval* Overture, op. 92.

    CSO, 7 January 1956. RCA: LP LM-1999; CD 5606.

Slavonic Dances in C major, op. 46, no. 1; A-flat Major, op. 46, no. 3; in G Minor, op. 46, no. 8; in B Major, op. 72, no. 1; in E Minor, op. 72, no. 2.

    VP, June 1960. LON: LP CM-9267, CS-6198; CD 417 696-2.

Symphony no. 9 in E Minor, op. 95.

    Robinson and Singer (four-hand piano), date? Welte: Player-Piano Rolls 7864, 67, 71, 75.

    CSO, 9 November 1957. RCA: LP LM/LSC-2214; CD 5606.

Falla, Manuel de. *El amor brujo.*

    PSO (C. Brice), 5 February 1946. COL: 78 M/MM-633; LP ML-2006.

    CSO (L. Price), 4 March 1963. RCA: LP LM/LSC-2695; CD 5404.

El sombrero de tres picos, Three Dances.

    CSO, 26 April 1958. RCA: LP LM/LSC-2230; CD 5404. CHESSKY: LP RC9.

La vida breve, Interlude and Dance.

    CSO, 26 April 1958. RCA: LP LM/LSC-2230; CD 5404. CHESSKY: LP RC9.

Franck, César. Symphony in D Minor.

    Reiner? and Singer. Welte: Player-Piano Rolls 7708/11.

Gershwin, George (arr. Bennett). *A Symphonic Picture of Porgy and Bess.*

    PSO, 27 March 1945. COL: 78 M/MM-572; LP ML-2019.

Glinka, Mikhail. *Kamarinskaya.*

    PSO, 2 February 1946. COL: 78 12715D.

    Ruslan and Ludmila, Overture.

    CSO, 14 March 1959. RCA: LP LM/LSC-2423; CD 5605.

Gluck, Christoph W. *Orfeo ed Euridice,* Minuet and Dance of the Blessed Spirits.

    RCA-V SO, 16 June 1953. RCA: LP LM-2141; 45 ERA-215.

    Orfeo ed Euridice, "Che farò senza Euridice."

    RCA-V SO (R. Stevens), 21 March 1951. RCA: 45 ERA-138; LP LM-9010; 45 WDM-9010.

    Orfeo ed Euridice, "Che puro ciel."

    RCA-V SO (R. Stevens), 21 March 1951. RCA: LP LM-9010; 45 WDM-9010.

Granados, Enrique. *Goyescas,* Intermezzo.

    CSO, 26 April 1958. RCA: LP LM/LSC-2230; CD 5404. CHESSKY: LP RC9.

Haydn, Franz Joseph. Symphony no. 88 in G Major.

    CSO, 6 February 1960. RCA: LP LM/LSC-6087; CD 60729.

    Symphony no. 94 in G Major.

    Singer and Reichmann (four-hand piano), date? Welte: Player-Piano Rolls 7545/48.

    Symphony no. 95 in C Minor.

    "His" SO, 18, 20 September 1963. RCA: LP LM/LSC-2742; CD 60729.

    Symphony no. 101 in D Major.

    "His" SO, 13, 16 September 1963. RCA: LP LM/LSC-2742; CD 60729.

    Symphony no. 104 in D Major.

    [CSO (WBAI), 28 November 1957. CSO: LP/CD 88/2.]

Hindemith, Paul. Concerto for Violoncello.

    [CSO (J. Starker) (WBAI), 6 December 1957. CSO: LP/CD 88/2.]

Hofmann, Josef. *Chromaticon.*

    [Curtis SO (J. Hoffman), 28 November 1937. Desmar: LP IPA-5001/2; VAI: CD 1020]

Honegger, Arthur. Concertino for Piano.

    Col SO (O. Levant), 6 July 1949. COL: LP ML-2156.

Hovhaness, Alan. Symphony no. 2, "Mysterious Mountain."

    CSO, 28 April 1958. RCA: LP LM/LSC-2251; CD 5733.

Humperdinck, Engelbert. *Hänsel und Gretel,* Dream Pantomime.

    RCA-V SO, 19 October 1950. RCA: 45 49-3442; CD 61792.

Kabalevsky, Dmitri. *Colas Breugnon,* Overture.

    PSO, 26 March 1945. COL: 78 M/MM-585, 12906D.

    CSO, 14 March 1959. RCA: LP LM/LSC-2423; CD 5602.

Kodály, Zoltán. Galánta Dances.

> [CSO (WGN-TV), 10 February 1954. CSO: CD 90/12.]

Variations on a Hungarian Folksong, "Peacock Variations."

> [NYPO 12 March 1960. AS: CD 526. FRS: ORT/Cass no. 10.]

Liebermann, Rolf. Concerto for Jazzband and Symphony Orchestra.

> CSO (Sauter-Finnegan Band), 6 December 1954. RCA: LP LM-1888.

Liszt, Franz. *Mephisto* Waltz no. 1.

> CSO, 10 December 1955. RCA: 45 SEP-13; LP LM-1999.

Totentanz.

> RCA-V SO (A. Brailowsky), 6 March 1951. RCA: LP LM-1195; 45 WDM-1615.

> CSO (B. Janis), 23 February 1959. RCA: LP LM/LSC-2127; CD 61250.

Mahler, Gustav. *Das Lied von der Erde.*

> CSO (M. Forrester, R. Lewis), 7, 9 November 1959. RCA: LP LM/LSC-6087; CD 5248.

Lieder eines fahrendes Gesellen.

> PSO (C. Brice), 5 February 1946. COL: 78 X/MX-267; LP ML-4108.

Symphony no. 4 in G Major.

> CSO (L. Della Casa), 6, 8 December 1958. RCA: LP LM/LSC-2364; CD 5722.

Mendelssohn-Bartholdy, Felix. *The Hebrides* ("Fingal's Cave") Overture, op. 26.

> CSO, 7 January 1956. RCA: LP LM-2071; CD 61793 (1995 release).

A Midsummer Night's Dream, op. 61. Overture, Scherzo, Intermezzo, Nocturne, Wedding March.

> RHD SO, 30 June 1951. RCA: LP LM-41, LM-1724; 45 WDM-1724.

Symphony no. 4 in A Major, op. 90.

> [CSO (WGN-TV), 10 February 1954. FRS: LP no. 1.]

Mozart, Wolfgang Amadeus. Concerto for Bassoon in B-flat Major, K. 191.

> [CSO (WGN-TV) (L. Sharrow), 14 November 1956. FRS: ORT/Cass no. 3.]

Concerto for Piano no. 25 in C Major, K. 503.

> CSO (A. Tchaikowsky), 15 February 1958. RCA: LP LM/LSC-2287.

Divertimento no. 11 in D Major, K. 251.

> NBC SO, 21, 22 September 1954. RCA: LP LM-1952.

Divertimento no. 17 in D Major, K. 334.

> CSO, 23, 26 April 1955. RCA: LP LM-1966.

Don Giovanni, K. 527, Overture.

> CSO, 14 March 1959. RCA: LP LM/LSC-2287; CD 6521.

Don Giovanni, K. 527, "Ah, del padre in periglio"; "Fuggi, crudele, fuggi!" "Don Ottavio, son morta!" "Or sai chi l'onore"; "Calmativi, idol mio"; "Non mi dir."

> [MetOp (L. Welitsch, E. Conley), 6 January 1951. MEL: LP 27042(?); MRF: LP 1.]

Don Giovanni, K. 527, "Crudele? Ah no, mio bene!"; "Non mi dir."

> MetOpO (L. Welitsch) 10 February 1950. COL: 78 X/MX-340; LP ML-2118.

Don Giovanni, "Ah, chi mi dice mai," "Mi tradì quell'alma ingrata."

> [San Francisco Opera (Elisabeth Rethberg), October 1938. UORC: LP 105.]

Don Giovanni, K. 527, "Don Ottavio, son morta!" "Or sai chi l'onore."

> MetOpO (L. Welitsch, A. De Paolis), 10 February 1950. COL: 78 X/MX-340; LP ML-2118.

Ein musikalischer Spass, K. 522.

    NBC SO, 16/17 September 1954. RCA: LP LM-1952.

Le nozze di Figaro, K. 492.

    [MetOpera (V. de los Angeles, N. Conner, C. Siepi, G. Valdengo), 1 March 1952. Robin Hood Records: LP RHR-514. AS: CD 1108/9.]

Le nozze di Figaro, K. 492, Overture.

    [CSO, 3 March 1963. FRS: ORT/Cass no. 3.]

Le nozze di Figaro, K. 492, "Non so più cosa son."

    RCA-V SO (R. Stevens), 21 March 1951. RCA: 45 WDM-9010; LP LM-9010.

Le nozze di Figaro, K. 492, "Voi che sapete."

    RCA-V SO (R. Stevens), 21 March 1951. RCA: 45 WDM-9010; LP LM-9010. MET: CD 114.

Serenade no. 9 in D Major, K. 320.

    [CSO (WGN-TV), 28 November 1956. FRS: ORT/Cass no. 3.]

Serenade no. 13 in G Major, K. 525.

    CSO, 4 December 1954. RCA: LP LM-1966.

Symphony no. 31 in D Major, K. 297.

    [CSO (WGN-TV), 15 April 1961. CSO: CD 91/2.]

Symphony no. 35 in D Major, K. 385.

    PSO, 2 February 1946. COL: 78 M/MM-836; LP ML-4156.

Symphony no. 36 in C Major, K. 425.

    CSO, 26 April 1954. RCA: LP LM-6035.

Symphony no. 39 in E-flat Major, K. 543.

    CSO, 23 April 1954. RCA: LP LM-6035.

Symphony no. 40 in G Minor, K. 550.

    Singer and Reichmann (four-hand piano), date? Welte: Piano Rolls, not released?

    PSO, 1 April 1947. COL: 78 M/MM-727; LP ML-2008.

    CSO, 25 April 1954. RCA: LP LM-6035.

Symphony no. 41 in C Major, K. 551.

    Reiner and Singer (four-hand piano), date? Welte: Player-Piano Rolls not released?

    CSO, 26 April 1954. RCA: LP LM-6035, VICS-1366; CD 6376.

Mussorgsky, Modest (arr. Shostakovich). *Boris Godunov,* Monologue, Hallucination Scene, Farewell.

    [NYPSO (A. Kipnis), 23 July 1944. Discocorp: LP 210. AS: CD 628.]

(arr. Rimsky-Korsakov). *A Night on Bare Mountain.*

    PSO, 26 March 1945. COL: 78 12470D.

    CSO, 14 March 1959. RCA: LP LM/LSC-2423; CD 5602.

(arr. Ravel). *Pictures at an Exhibition.*

    CSO, 7 December 1957. RCA: LP LM/LSC-220; CD 5407.

Prokofiev, Serge. *Alexander Nevsky,* op. 78.

    CSO (R. Elias, CSO Cho.), 7 March 1959. RCA: LP LM/LSC-2395; CD 5605.

Lieutenant Kijé, Suite, op. 60.

    CSO, 2 March 1957. RCA: LP LM/LSC-2150; CD 5605. CHESSKY: LP RC10.

Peter and the Wolf, op. 67.

    [NBC SO (L. Melchior), 19 June 1949. Legato: Cass ALD 1818.]

Symphony no. 5 in B-flat Major, op. 100.

[CSO, 1 April 1958. CSO: CD 90/12; FRS: ORT/Cass no. 2.]

Rachmaninoff, Sergei. Concerto for Piano no. 1 in F-sharp Minor, op. 1.

CSO (B. Janis), 2 March 1957. RCA: LP LM/LSC-2127.

Concerto for Piano no. 2 in C Minor, op. 18.

CSO (A. Rubinstein), 9, 16 January 1956. RCA: LP LM-6039, LM/LSC-2068; CD 4934.

CSO (V. Cliburn), 31 March, 2 April 1962. RCA: LP LM/LSC-2601; CD 5912.

Concerto for Piano no. 3 in D Minor, op. 30.

RCA-V SO (V. Horowitz), 4 June 1951. RCA: LP LM-1178; 45 WDM-1575; CD 7754.

The Isle of the Dead.

CSO, 13 April 1957. RCA: LP LM/LSC-2183; CD 61250. CHESSKY: LP RC11.

Rhapsody on a Theme of Paganini, op. 43.

RHD SO (W. Kapell), 27 June 1951. RCA: LP LM-126, LM-9026; 45 WDM-1576.

CSO (A. Rubinstein), 9, 16 January 1956. RCA: LP LM/LSC-6035; CD 4934.

Ravel, Maurice. *Alborada del gracioso.*

CSO, 13 April 1957. RCA: LP LM/LSC-2222; CD 5720.

Daphnis et Chloé, Suite no. 2.

[NBC SO, 2 September 1945. FRS: ORT/Cass no. 6.]

Pavane pour une infante défunte.

CSO, 2 March 1957. RCA: LP LM/LSC-2183; CD 5720. CHESSKY: LP RC11.

Rapsodie espagnole.

CSO, 3 November 1956. RCA: LP LM/LSC-2183; CD 5720. CHESSKY: LP RC11.

Le tombeau de Couperin.

[NBC SO, 19 January 1952. M&A: CD 292]

NBC SO, 21 January 1952. RCA: LP LM-1724; 45 WDM-1724.

La valse.

PSO, 1 April 1947. COL: 78 X/MX-296; LP ML-4021.

[CSO, 25 March 1960. CSO: CD 90/12. FRS: ORT/Cass no. 6.]

Valses nobles et sentimentales.

CSO, 15 April 1957. RCA: LP LM/LSC-2222; CD 5720.

Respighi, Ottorino. *Fontane di Roma.*

CSO, 24 October 1959. RCA: LP LM/LSC-2436; CD 5407. CHESSKY: LP RC5.

I Pini di Roma.

CSO, 24 October 1959. RCA: LP LM/LSC-2436; CD 5407. CHESSKY: LP RC5.

Rimsky-Korsakov, Nikolai. *Sheherazade,* op. 35.

CSO, 8 February 1960. RCA: LP LM/LSC-2446; CD 7018. CHESSKY: LP RC4.

Rodgers, Richard (arr. Walker). *Carousel,* Waltz.

PSO, 4 February 1946. COL: 78 12322-D.

Rossini, Gioacchino. *Il barbiere di Siviglia,* Overture.

CSO, 22 November 1959. RCA: LP LM/LSC-2318; CD 60387.

La Cenerentola, Overture.

CSO, 22 November 1959. RCA: LP LM/LSC-2318; CD 60387.

La gazza ladra, Overture.

    CSO, 22 November 1959. RCA: LP LM/LSC-2318; CD 60387.

Guillaume Tell, Overture.

    CSO, 22 November 1959. RCA: LP LM/LSC-2318; CD 60387.

L'Italiana in Algeri, Overture.

    CSO, 22 November 1959. RCA: LP LM/LSC-2318; CD 60387.

La scala di seta, Overture.

    CSO, 22 November 1959. RCA: LP LM/LSC-2318; CD 60387.

Il Signor Bruschino, Overture.

    PSO, 2 February 1946. COL: 78 M/MM-836.

    CSO, 22 November 1959. RCA: LP LM/LSC-2318; CD 60387.

Rubinstein, Anton. Concerto for Piano no. 4 in D Minor, op. 70.

    [Curtis SO (J. Hofmann), 28 November 1937. Desmar: LP IPA-5001/2. VAI: CD 1020.]

Saint-Saëns, Camille. Concerto for Violoncello in A Minor, op. 33.

    RCA-V SO (G. Piatigorsky), 7 December 1950. RCA: LP LM-1187; 45 WDM-1538.

Satie, Erik (arr. Debussy). *Gymnopédies* nos. 1, 3.

    [CSO, 25 March 1960. CSO: CD 90/12. FRS: ORT/Cass no. 6.]

Scarlatti, Domenico (arr. Tommasini). *Le donne di buon umore,* Ballet Suite.

    [CSO (WGN-TV), 31 March 1954. FRS: ORT/Cass no. 7.]

Schubert, Franz. Symphony no. 5 in B-flat Major, D. 485.

    CSO, 27 April 1960. RCA: LP LM/LSC-2516; CD 61793 (1995 release).

Symphony no. 8 in B Minor, D. 759.

    Singer and Reichmann, date? Welte: Player-Piano Rolls C7549/50.

    CSO, 26 March 1960. RCA: LP LM/LSC-2516; CD 5403.

Schumann, Robert. Concerto for Piano in A Minor, op. 54.

    CSO (B. Janis), 21 February 1959. RCA: LP ARP1-4668.

    CSO (V. Cliburn), 16 April 1960. RCA: LP LM/LSC-2455; CD 60420.

Symphony no. 2 in C Major, op. 61.

    [CSO (WBAI), 31 October 1957. CSO: LP 86/2.]

Shostakovich, Dmitri. Symphony no. 6 in B Minor, op. 54.

    [NYPSO, 15 August 1943. AS: CD 628.]

    PSO, 26 March 1945. COL: 78 M/MM-585; LP ML-4249.

Schoenberg, Arnold. *Verklärte Nacht.*

    [CSO (WBAI), 7 November 1957. CSO: LP 86/2.]

Smetana, Bedřich. *The Bartered Bride,* Overture.

    CSO, 12 December 1955. RCA: LP LM/LSC-1999; CD 5606.

Smith, John Stafford. *The Star-Spangled Banner.*

    CSO, 9 November 1957. RCA: LP AHF-1003 (distributed by American Heritage Foundation through schools).

Strauss, Johann (The Younger). Waltz, *An dem schönem blauen Donau,* op. 314.

    CSO, 15 April 1960. RCA: LP LM/LSC-2500; CD 5405.

Die Fledermaus, excerpts (in English).

    RCA-V SO (P. Munsel, R. Resnik, R. Stevens, J. Peerce, J. Melton, R. Merrill, Shaw Cho.), 6–26 September 1950. RCA: 78 DM-1457; 45 WDM-1457; LP LM-1114.

Kaiser-Walzer, op. 437.

    CSO, 15 April 1960. RCA: LP LM/LSC-2500; CD 5405.

Waltz, *Kunstlerleben,* op. 316.

    CSO, 25 April 1960. RCA: LP LM/LSC-2500; CD 5405.

Waltz, *Morgenblätter,* op. 279.

    CSO, 16 April 1960. RCA: LP LM/LSC-2500; CD 5405.

Waltz, *Rosen aus der Süden,* op. 388.

    PSO, 4 February 1946. COL: 78 12941D; LP ML-4116.

    CSO, 25, 26 April 1960. RCA: LP LM/LSC-2500; CD 5405.

Schatzwalzer, op. 418.

    PSO, 15 November 1941. COL: 78 11800D; LP ML-4116.

    CSO, 26 April 1960. RCA: LP LM/LSC-2500; CD 5405.

Polka, *Unter Donner und Blitz,* op. 324.

    CSO, 26 April 1960. RCA: LP LM/LSC-2500; CD 5405.

Waltz, *Wiener Blut,* op. 354.

    PSO, 9 January 1941. COL: 78 11579D; LP ML-4116.

    CSO, 26 April 1960. RCA: LP LM/LSC-2500; CD 5405.

Strauss, Joseph. Waltz, *Dorfschwalben aus Österreich,* op. 164.

    CSO, 15 April 1957. RCA: LP LM/LSC-2112; CD 5405.

Waltz, *Mein Lebenslauf ist Lieb und Lust,* op. 263.

    CSO, 25 April 1960. RCA: LP LM/LSC-2500; CD 5405.

Strauss, Richard. *Also sprach Zarathustra,* op. 30.

    CSO, 8 March 1954. RCA: LP LM/LBO 1800, 45 ERA-1806; CD 5721.

    CSO, 30 April, 1 May 1962. RCA: LP LM/LSC-2609; CD 6722. Mobile Fidelity: LP MFSL 1-322.

Le bourgeois gentilhomme, op. 60, Suite.

    PSO, 4 February 1946. COL: 78 M/MM-693; LP ML-2062, ML-4800. (NOTE: ML-2062 includes all nine nos.; ML-4800 omits "Menuet of Lully" and "Courante.")

    CSO, 17, 18 April 1956 (7 nos., omitting "Menuet of Lully" and "Courante") RCA: LP LM/LSC-6047; CD 5721.

Burleske for Piano and Orchestra.

    CSO (B. Janis), 4 March 1957. RCA: LM/LSC-2127; CD 5734.

Don Juan, op. 20.

    PSO, 9 January 1941. COL: 78 X/MX-190; LP ML-2079.

    CSO, 6 December 1954. RCA: LP LM/LSC-1888; CD 5722.

    CSO, 6 February 1960. RCA: LP LM/LSC-2462; CD 5408.

Don Quixote, op. 35.

    PSO (G. Piatigorsky), 15 November 1941. COL: 78 M/MM-506; LP RL-3027.

    [CSO (J. Starker), 20 March 1958. FRS: ORT/Cass no. 8.]

    CSO (A. Janigro) 11 April 1959. RCA: LP LD/LDS-2384; CD 5734.

Elektra, op. 58.

    [MetOp (A. Varnay, E. Hoengen, H. Hotter, S. Svanholm), 23 February 1952. MET: LP MET 9. LP SJS-7045.

Elektra, "Allein"; "Was willst du, fremder Mensch?"

"Elektra, Schwester."

CSO (I. Borkh, F. Yeend, P. Schoeffler), 14, 16 April 1956. RCA: LP LM/LSC-6047; CD 5603.

Ein Heldenleben, op. 40.

PSO, 10 November 1947. COL: 78 M/MM-748; LP ML-4138

CSO, 6 March 1954. RCA: LP LM/LSC-1807; 45 ERD-1807; CD 5408.

Der Rosenkavalier, op. 53.

[MetOp (A. Varnay, R. Stevens, N. Conner, E. Koreh), 28 February 1953. MEL LP 41.]

Der Rosenkavalier, "Mir ist die Ehre," "Ist ein Traum . . . Spür' nur dich."

RCA-V SO (R. Stevens, E. Berger), 5 April 1951. RCA: LP LM-9010; 45 WDM-9010. MET: CD 114.

(arr. Reiner). *Der Rosenkavalier,* Waltzes.

CSO, 15 April 1957. RCA: LP LM/LSC-2112; CD 5721.

Salome, op. 54.

[MetOp (L. Welitsch, K. Thorborg, H. Janssen, F. Jagel), 12 March 1949. EJS: LP 178. MRF: LP 1; BJR: LP 156. MEL: LP 039; CD 27042.]

[MetOp (L. Welitsch, E. Hoengen, H. Hotter, S. Svanholm), 19 January 1952. MET: LP 9.]

Salome, Dance.

CSO, 6 March 1954. RCA: LP LM-1806; 45 ERD-1806; CD 5603.

Salome, "Ach, du wolltest mich nicht deinen Mund küssen lassen."

MetOpO (L. Welitsch), 14 March 1949. COL: 78 X/MX-316; LP ML-2048.

CSO (I. Borkh) 10 December 1955. RCA: LP LM/LSC-6047; CD 5603.

Sinfonia domestica, op. 53.

CSO, 5 November 1956. RCA: LP LM/LSC-2103; CD 60388.

Till Eulenspiegels lustige Streiche, op. 28.

RCA-V SO, 26 Sept. 1950. RCA: LP LM-1180; 45 WDM-1579

[NBC SO, 19 January 1952. M&A: CD CD 292.]

[CSO (WGN-TV), 31 February 1957. FRS: ORT/Cass no. 8.]

VP, 7 Sept. 1956. RCA: LP LM/LSC-2077; 45 ERA-2077. LON: LP STS-15582.

Tod und Verklärung, op. 24.

RCA-V SO, 27 Sept. 1950. RCA: LP LM-1180; 45 WDM-1580; CD 60388.

VP, 7 Sept. 1956. RCA: LP LM/LSC-2077. LON: LP STS-15582.

Stravinsky, Igor. Divertimento (arr. from *The Fairy's Kiss*).

CSO, 28 April 1958. RCA: LP LM/LSC-2251; CD 5733.

The Song of the Nightingale.

CSO, 3 November 1956. RCA: LP LM/LSC-2150; CD 5733. CHESSKY: LP RCIO.

Tchaikovsky, Peter. Concerto for Piano in B-flat Minor, op. 23.

CSO (E. Gilels), 29 October 1955. RCA: LP LM-1969; 45 ERC-1969.

Concerto for Violin in D Major, op. 35.

CSO (J. Heifetz), 19 April 1957. RCA: LP LM/LSC-2129; CD 1011.

Concerto for Violin in D Major, op. 35, abbreviated.

Orchestra (J. Heifetz), Sept. 1946, in *Carnegie Hall* film, excerpted in 1991 television program *Carnegie Hall at 100.* RCA: VHS videotape 60883-G. (Note: This brief sequence is the only commercially available video of Reiner talking and conducting.)

1812 Overture, op. 49.

CSO, 7 January 1956. RCA: LP LM-1999, LM/LSC-2241; 45 ERA-291; CD 5642.

Eugene Onegin, Waltz.

RCA-V SO, 20 Sept. 1950. RCA: LP LM-103; 45 WDM-1539.

Francesca da Rimini, op. 32.

[CSO (WGN-TV), 4 November 1953. FRS: ORT/Cass no. 10.]

Marche slave, op. 31.

CSO, 14 March 1959. RCA: LP LM/LSC-2423; CD 5642.

The Nutcracker, op. 71, excerpts.

CSO, 30 March 1959. RCA: LP LM/LSC-2328, CD 5642.

The Nutcracker, Waltz.

RCA-V SO, 22 Sept. 1950. RCA: LP LM-103; 45 WDM-1539.

The Sleeping Beauty, op. 66, Waltz.

RCA/V SO, 22 Sept. 1950. RCA: LP LM-103; 45 WDM-1539.

Suite no. 1 in D Major, op. 43, "Marche miniature."

CSO, 14 March 1959. RCA: LP LM/LSC-2423; CD 5602.

Swan Lake, op. 20, Waltz.

RCA-V SO, 22 Sept. 1950. RCA: LP LM-103; 45 WDM-1539.

Symphony no. 4 in F Minor, op. 36.

[CSO (WBAI), 21 November 1957. FRS: ORT/Cass no. 9.]

Symphony no. 5 in E minor, op. 64.

Bacon and Robinson (four-hand piano), date? Welte: Player-Piano Rolls, released?

Symphony no. 5 in E Minor, op. 64, Waltz.

RCA-V SO, 22 Sept. 1950. RCA: LP LM-103; 45 WDM 1539.

Symphony no. 6 in B Minor, op. 74.

Bacon and Robinson (four-hand piano), date? Welte: Player-Piano Rolls C7563/67.

CSO, 16, 17 April 1957. RCA: LP LM/LSC-2216; CD 5602.

Vaughan Williams, Ralph. Fantasy on a Theme of Thomas Tallis.

[CSO (WBAI), 28 November 1957. CSO: LP 86/2.]

Verdi, Giuseppe. *Falstaff.*

[MetOp (L. Albanese, R. Resnik, C. Elmo, L. Warren, G. Valdengo, G. di Stefano), 26 February 1949. EJS: LP 250.]

Messa da Requiem.

[CSO (L. Rysanek, R. Resnik, D. Lloyd, G. Tozzi, CSO Cho.), 3 April 1958. Melodram: LP 238. (Incorrectly labeled "Orchestra e coro: Chicago Lyric Opera.")]

VP (L. Price, R. Elias, J. Bjoerling, G. Tozzi, Gesellschaft der Musikfreunde Cho.), 28 May–26 June 1960. RCA: LP LD/LDS-6091. LON: LP OSA-1294; CD 421608.

Wagner, Richard. *Der fliegende Holländer.*

[MetOp (A. Varnay, H. Hotter, S. Svanholm, R. Nilsson), 30 December 1950. UORC: LP 149.]

Der fliegende Holländer, Excerpts.

[CG (K. Flagstad, H. Janssen), 7 June 1937. EJS: LP 514–15. SRO: CD 808-2 (omits some material from LP).]

Götterdämmerung, Prologue, Siegfried's Rhine Journey.

    CSO, 18 April 1959. RCA: LP LM/LSC-2441; CD 4738.

Götterdämmerung, Prologue, Dawn, Duet, Rhine Journey, and Waltraute Scene.

    [NYPSO, Lewisohn Stadium (F. Easton, K. Meisle, P. Althouse), 22 July 1937. ANNA: LP 1008. EJS: LP 166/67 (omits Prologue).]

Götterdämmerung, Act III, Siegfried's Funeral Music.

    CSO, 18 April 1959. RCA: LP LM/LSC-2441; CD 4738.

Lohengrin, Prelude.

    PSO, 15 November 1941. COL: 78 M/MM-549; LP ML-4054.

Lohengrin, fragments of Prelude.

    [Philadelphia Orchestra, 18 February 1932. FRS: ORT/Cass no. 11, experimental, from Bell Labs.]

Lohengrin, Introduction to Act III.

    PSO, 9 January 1941. COL: 78 M/MM-549; LP ML-4054.

    RCA-V SO, 19 October 1950. RCA: 45 ERA-185; CD 61792.

Die Meistersinger von Nürnberg.

    [Vienna State Opera (I. Seefried, R. Anday, H. Beirer, P. Schoeffler, G. Frick, M. Dickie, E. Kunz), 14 November 1955. MEL: CD CDM 47083.]

Die Meistersinger von Nürnberg, Prelude.

    [NYPSO, 22 November 1938. World's Greatest Music: 78 SR 12.]

    PSO, 9 January 1941. COL: 78 M/MM-549; LP ML-4054.

    CSO, 18 April 1959. RCA: LP LM/LSC-2441; CD 4738.

Die Meistersinger von Nürnberg, Act II, fragment of Watchman's Call.

    [Philadelphia Orchestra, 28 November 1931. FRS: ORT/Cass no. 11, experimental, from Bell Labs.]

Die Meistersinger von Nürnberg, Prelude to Act III.

    PSO, 15 November 1941. COL: 78 X/MX-218.

    CSO, 18 April 1959. RCA: LP LM/LSC-2441; CD 4738.

Die Meistersinger von Nürnberg, fragment of Prelude to Act III.

    [Philadelphia Orchestra, 27 November 1931. FRS: ORT/Cass no. 11, experimental, from Bell Labs.]

Die Meistersinger von Nürnberg, Act III, Dance of the Apprentices.

    PSO, 15 November 1941. COL: 78 X/MX-218.

    CSO, 18 April 1959. RCA: LP LM/LSC-2441; CD 4738.

Die Meistersinger von Nürnberg, Act III, Procession of the Master Singers.

    PSO, 15 November 1941. COL: 78 X/MX-218.

    CSO, 18 April 1959. RCA: LP LM/LSC-2441; CD 4738.

Parsifal, Acts I and III, excerpts.

    [CG (T. Ralf, H. Janssen, L. Weber, Cho.), 27 April 1937. UORC: LP 130.]

Parsifal, Prelude.

    [NYPSO, 22 November 1938. World's Greatest Music: 78 SR-12. PEARL: CD CDS 9922.]

Parsifal, Act I, fragment of Transformation.

    [Philadelphia Orchestra, 28 November 1931. FRS: ORT/Cass no. 11, experimental, from Bell Labs.]

Parsifal, Act II, fragment of Klingsor's Castle.

    [Philadelphia Orchestra, 27 November 1931. FRS: ORT/Cass no. 11, experimental from Bell Labs.]

Parsifal, Act III, "Good Friday Spell."

> [CSO (WBAI), 27 March 1958. CSO: LP 88/2; CD 88/2.]

Parsifal, Act III, fragment of "Good Friday Spell."

> [Philadelphia Orchestra, 27 November 1931. FRS: ORT/Cass no. 11, experimental, from Bell Labs.]

Rienzi, Overture.

> [CSO, 27 March 1958. CSO: LP 86/2.]

Siegfried, Act II, "Forest Murmurs."

> PSO, 9 January 1941. COL: 78 M/MM-549; LP ML-4054.

Tannhäuser, Act I, Venusberg Music.

> PSO, 9 January 1941. COL: 78 X/MX-193.

Tannhäuser, Act II, "Festmarsch."

> RCA-V SO, 19 October 1950. RCA: 45 ERA-185; CD 61792.

Tristan und Isolde.

> [CG (K. Flagstad, S. Kalter, L. Melchior, H. Janssen), May–June 1936. EJS: LP 465. VAI: CD 1004.] (Note: Issued in 1991 as a recording of Sir Thomas Beecham's 1937 performance, EMI CHS7-64077-2 actually includes most of acts I and III from Reiner's 1936 performances.)

Tristan und Isolde, Prelude and "Lovedeath."

> [CSO (WBAI), 27 March 1958. CSO: LP/CD 88/2.]

Tristan und Isolde, Act II.

> [San Francisco Opera (K. Flagstad, L. Melchior, K. Meisle), 14 November 1937, Shrine Auditorium, Los Angeles. Legato: Cass ALD 1576; CD LCD-145.

Tristan und Isolde, Act III, fragments of "Tristan's Vision and Death."

> [Philadelphia Orchestra, 27 November 1931. FRS: ORT/Cass no. 11, experimental, from Bell Labs.]

Die Walküre, Act II (nearly complete).

> [San Francisco Opera (K. Flagstad, L. Lehmann, K. Meisle, L. Melchior, F. Schorr), 13 November 1936. EJS: LP 234. Discocorp: LP RR-426. Legato: CD LCD-133-1 (ending by others).]

Die Walküre, Act III, "The Ride of the Valkyries."

> PSO, 14 March 1940. COL: 78 M/MM-549; LP ML-4054.

Weber, Carl Maria von. *Abu Hassan,* Overture.

> [CSO (WGN-TV), 28 November 1956. FRS: ORT/Cass no. 10.]

(arr. Berlioz). *Aufforderung zum Tanz.*

> CSO, 15 April 1957. RCA: LP LM/LSC-2112. CD 61250.

Weinberger, Jaromir. *Schwanda,* Polka and Fugue.

> CSO, 7 January 1956. RCA: LP LM/LSC-1999; CD 5606.

Abbreviations

PERFORMERS

CG	Royal Opera House, Covent Garden, London
Col SO	Columbia Symphony Orchestra
CSO	Chicago Symphony Orchestra
CSO (WBAI)	From broadcast by WBAI, New York

CSO (WGN-TV)	From audio of WGN-TV, Chicago
CSO Cho.	Chicago Symphony Orchestra Chorus
Curtis SO	Curtis Institute of Music Symphony Orchestra
MetOp	Metropolitan Opera
MetOpO	Metropolitan Opera Orchestra (studio recording)
NBC SO	NBC Symphony Orchestra
NYPO	New York Philharmonic Orchestra
NYPSO	New York Philharmonic-Symphony Orchestra
PSO	Pittsburgh Symphony Orchestra
RCA-V SO	RCA Victor Symphony Orchestra
RHD SO	Robin Hood Dell Symphony Orchestra (Philadelphia Orchestra)
RPO	Royal Philharmonic Orchestra, London
Shaw Cho.	Robert Shaw Chorale
VP	Vienna Philharmonic
VSO	Vienna State Opera

PUBLISHERS

AS	AS Disk, Italy (CD)
CHESSKY	Chessky Records, Inc. (LP and CD)
COL	Columbia Masterworks (78 and LP)
CSO	Chicago Symphony Orchestra (LP and CD)
Desmar	Distributor for International Piano Library (LP)
EJS	Edward J. Smith Golden Age of Opera (LP)
EMA	Educational Media Associates (LP)
FRS	Fritz Reiner Society (open-reel tape, cassette, and LP)
Legato	Legato Classics (CD)
LON	London Records, USA, from Decca, UK (LP, cassette, CD)
M&A	Music and Arts Programs of America (LP and CD)
MEL	Melodram, Milan (CD)
MET	Metropolitan Opera (LP and CD)
MRF	M. R. Fugette (LP)
PEARL	Pearl Records, Ltd. (CD)
Quintessence	International Arts, Inc., Minneapolis (LP)
RCA	RCA Victor (45, LP, CD)
Readers' Digest	Readers' Digest recordings, made by RCA (LP)
SRO	Standing Room Only (CD)
UORC	Unique Opera Recordings (LP)
VAI	Video Artists International (CD)
Welte	Welte-Mignon licensee player-piano rolls
World's Greatest Music	"Anonymous" 78 recordings with members of New York Philharmonic-Symphony Orchestra

Fritz Reiner's Repertory

The principal sources for Fritz Reiner's repertory are the printed programs and advertisements of the sponsors of performances he conducted. Less important are his diary and correspondence, which do not always include changes in his plans. Excerpts from larger works are not included when the entire work was in Reiner's repertory. Given the variability of the sources, it has been impossible to verify some titles.

Achron, Joseph. *Golem.*

Albéniz, Isaac. *Catalonia,* Suite no. 1 for Orchestra; (arr. Arbos) *Iberia,* "El Puerto"; (arr. Arbos) *Iberia,* "Fête-Dieu à Seville"; (arr. Arbos) *Iberia,* "Triana"; (arr. Arbos) *Navarra.*

Albert, Eugène d'. Concerto for Violoncello; *Die toten Augen.*

Andrae, Volkmar. *Kleine Suite,* op. 27.

Arensky, Anton. *Romance.*

Arnold, Malcolm. *Beckus the Dandipratt,* Overture. Symphony no. 2.

Auber, Daniel-François-Esprit. *Fra Diavolo; Masaniello, ou La muette de Portici,* Overture.

Aubert, Louis. *Habañera.*

Bach, Johann Christian. Sinfonia for Double Orchestra, op. 18, no. 1.

Bach, Johann Sebastian. Cantata no. 53, *Jauchzet Gott in allen Landen*; (arr. ?) Cantata no. 147, *Herz und Mund und Tat und Leben,* "Jesu, Joy of Man's Desiring"; Cantata no. 210, *O holder Tag, erwünschte Zeit,* nos. 1 and 9; (arr. Dubensky) Chorale Prelude, *Vater unser im Himmelreich*; (arr. Gui) Three Chorale Preludes; (arr. ?) Two Chorale Preludes; (arr. Stravinsky) Chorale Variations on *Vom Himmel hoch da komm' ich her,* BWV 769; Christmas Oratorio, BWV 248, "Pastorale"; Christmas Oratorio, BWV 248, Chorale "Brich an, O schönes Morgenlicht"; Brandenburg Concerto no. 1 in F Major, BWV 1046; Brandenburg Concerto no. 2 in F Major, BWV 1047; Brandenburg Concerto no. 3 in G Major, BWV 1048; Brandenburg Concerto no. 4 in G Major, BWV 1049; Brandenburg Concerto no. 5 in D Major, BWV 1050; Brandenburg Concerto no. 6 in B-flat Major, BWV 1051; Concerto for Piano no. 1 in D Minor, BWV 1052; Concerto for Piano no. 5 in F Minor, BWV 1056; Concerto for Violin no. 2 in E Major, BWV 1042; Concerto for Two Violins in D Minor, BWV 1043; (arr. Goedicke) Fantasy and Fugue in G Minor, BWV 542; (arr. Cailliet) Fugue in G Minor ("Little"), BWV 578; (arr. ?) *Komm, süsser Tod,* BWV 478;

Mass in B Minor, BWV 232, "Cum sanctu spiritu"; Mass in B Minor, BWV 232, "Sanctus"; Motet, *Fürchte dich nicht,* BWV 238; (arr. Webern) *Musikalisches Opfer,* BWV 1079, Ricercare a 6; (arr. Mangiagali) Partita no. 1 in E Major, BWV 1004, Prelude; (arr. Weiner) Partita no. 1 in E Major, BWV 1004, Prelude; (arr. Hubay) Partita no. 3 in D Minor, BWV 1006, Chaconne; (arr. Goedicke) Passacaglia in C Minor, BWV 582; (arr. Respighi) Passacaglia in C Minor, BWV 582; (arr. Respighi) Prelude and Fugue in D Major, BWV 532; (arr. Feldman) Prelude in E-flat Major; (arr. Stock) Prelude and Fugue in E-flat Major, "St. Anne," BWV 552; Suite no. 1 in C Major, BWV 1066; Suite no. 2 in B Minor, BWV 1067; Suite no. 3 in D Major, BWV 1068; (arr. Reger) Suite no. 3 in D, BWV 1068; Suite no. 4 in D Major, BWV 1069; (arr. Weiner) Toccata, Adagio, and Fugue in C Major, BWV 564; (arr. Cailliet) Toccata and Fugue in D Minor, BWV 565; (arr. Leonardi) Toccata and Fugue in D Minor, BWV 565.

Balakirev, Mily (arr. Casella). *Islamey.*

Ballantine, Edward. *From the Garden of Hellas,* Suite for Orchestra.

Bantock, Granville. *Omar Khayyam,* Part II.

Barber, Samuel. Adagio for Strings; *Medea's Meditation and Dance of Vengeance; Prayers of Kierkegaard; The School for Scandal,* Overture; *Souvenirs.*

Barstow. *Where the Lover Shall Rest.*

Barth, Hams. Concerto for Quarter-Tone Piano and Strings.

Bartók, Béla. Concerto for Orchestra; Concerto for Piano no. 1; Concerto for Piano no. 2; Concerto for Piano no. 3; Concerto for Two Pianos; Concerto for Viola; Concerto for Violin no. 2; Dance Suite; Divertimento for Strings; *Deux images,* op. 10; Hungarian Sketches; *The Miraculous Mandarin,* Suite; Music for Strings, Percussion, and Celesta; Portrait no. 1, op. 5, no. 1; Rhapsody for Piano; Suite no. 1, op. 3; Suite no. 2, op. 4; Two Hungarian Dances; (arr. Weiner) Two Rumanian Dances.

Bassani, Giovanni Battista (arr. Malipiero). Cantata for One Voice.

Bax, Arnold. Fantasy for Viola; *The Garden of Fand.*

Beethoven, Ludwig van. Concerto for Piano no. 1 in C Major, op. 15; Concerto for Piano no. 2 in B-flat Major, op. 19; Concerto for Piano no. 3 in C Minor, op. 37; Concerto for Piano no. 4 in G Major, op. 58; Concerto for Piano no. 5 in E-flat Major, op. 73; Concerto for Piano, Violin, and Violoncello in C Major, op. 56; Concerto for Violin in D Major, op. 61; *Coriolan,* Overture, op. 62; *Egmont,* op. 84, Overture; *Fidelio,* op. 72; *Die Geschöpfe des Prometheus,* op. 43, excerpts; *Grosse Fuge,* op. 133; *Leonore* Overture no. 2, op. 72; *Leonore* Overture no. 3, op. 72a; *Meeresstille und glückliche Fahrt* Overture, op. 112; *Missa solemnis,* op. 123, "Benedictus"; Romance no. 1 in G Major, op. 40; Romance no. 2 in F Major, op. 50; *Die Ruinen des Athens,* Turkish March; Symphony no. 1 in C Major, op. 21; Symphony no. 2 in D Major, op. 36; Symphony no. 3 in E-flat Major, op. 55; Symphony no. 4 in B-flat Major, op. 60; Symphony no. 5 in C Minor, op. 67; Symphony no. 6 in F Major, op. 68; Symphony no. 7 in A Major, op. 92; Symphony no. 8 in F Major, op. 93; Symphony no. 9 in D Minor, op. 125; *Die Weihe des Hauses* Overture, op. 124.

Bennett, Robert Russell. Eight Etudes; Symphony.

Berg, Alban. *Wozzeck,* Three Fragments.

Berlioz, Hector. *Béatrice et Bénédict,* Overture; *Benvenuto Cellini,* op. 23, Overture; *La captive; Le carnaval romain* Overture, op. 9; *Le corsaire* Overture, op. 21; *Le damnation de Faust,* op. 24, Marche hongroise, Ballet des sylphes, Menuet des follets; *Harold en Italie,* op. 16; *Les nuits d'été,* op. 7; *Roméo et Juliette,* op. 17; *Symphonie fantastique,* op. 14; *Les Troyens,* Marche.

Bizet, Georges. *L'Arlésienne,* Suite no. 1; *L'Arlésienne,* Suite no. 2; *Carmen; Les pecheurs de perles,* "Je crois entendre encore."

Blacher, Boris. Variations on a Theme of Paganini.

Bloch, Ernest. *America;* Concerto Grosso, no. 1; *Macbeth,* Two Symphonic Interludes; *Schelomo; Trois poèmes juifs,* "Cortège"; *The Twenty-second Psalm.*

Boccherini, Luigi (arr. Grutzmacher). Concerto for Violoncello in B-flat Major.

Borodin, Alexander. *Prince Igor,* Polovtsi March; *Prince Igor,* Polovtsi Dances; Symphony no. 2 in B Minor.

Borowski, Felix. *The Mirror.*

Bossi, Enrico. Theme and Variations, op. 131.

Brahms, Johannes. *Academische Festouvertüre,* op. 80; *Alto Rhapsody,* op. 53; (arr. Thomson) Eight Chorale Preludes, op. 122; Concerto for Piano no. 1 in D Minor, op. 15; Concerto for Piano no. 2 in B-flat Major, op. 83; Concerto for Violin in D Major, op. 77; Concerto for Violin and Violoncello in A Minor, op. 102; *Ein deutsches Requiem,* op. 45; *Gesang der Parzen,* op. 89; Hungarian Dances no. 1 in G Minor; no. 5 in G Minor; no. 6 in D Major; no. 7 in A Major; no. 12 in D Minor; no. 13 in D Major; no. 19 in B Minor; no. 21 in E Minor; *Schicksalslied,* op. 89; Serenade no. 2 in A Major, op. 16; *Spanisches Lied;* Symphony no. 1 in C Minor, op. 68; Symphony no. 2 in D Major, op. 73; Symphony no. 3 in F Major, op. 90; Symphony no. 4 in E Minor, op. 98; *Tragisches Ouvertüre,* op. 81; Four Trios for Ladies' Voices; Variations on a Theme by Haydn, op. 56a; *Vier ernste Gesänge,* op. 121; *Von ewiger Liebe; Willst du, dass ich geh'? Zigeunerlieder* (5), op. 103.

Brant, Henry. *Dedication.*

Britten, Benjamin. *Peter Grimes,* Passacaglia; *Peter Grimes,* Sea Interludes; Variations on a Theme of Frank Bridge.

Bruch, Max. *Achilles,* Lament of Andromache; Concerto for Violin no. 1 in G Minor, op. 26; *Scottish Fantasy* for Violin.

Bruckner, Anton. Symphony no. 3 in D Minor; Symphony no. 4 in E-flat Major; Symphony no. 7 in E Major; Symphony no. 8 in C Minor; Symphony no. 9 in D Minor; *Te Deum.*

Burleigh, Cecil. *Ghost Dance.*

Busoni, Ferruccio. Concerto for Piano, with Male Chorus.

Byrd, William (arr. Jacob) Suite.

Cadman, Charles W. *American Suite.*

Carpenter, John Alden. *Krazy Kat,* A Jazz Pantomime; *Skyscrapers,* excerpts; Symphony.

Casella, Alfredo. *La donna serpente,* Symphonic Fragments, Suite no. 1; *Italia* Rhapsody; *Paganiniana,* op. 65; *Pupazzetti;* Serenade for Little Orchestra.

Castelnuovo-Tedesco, Mario. Concerto for Guitar.

Chabrier, Emmanuel. *Bourrée fantastique; España; Gwendoline,* Overture.

Chadwick, George W. *Symphonic Sketches,* "Jubilee."

Charpentier, Gustave. *Louise,* "Depuis le jour."

Chausson, Ernest. *Poème de l'amour et de la mer; Poème* for Violin.

Chopin, François. *Andante spinato et Polonaise,* op. 22.

Chou Wen-Chung. *Landscapes*.

Clement, Károly. *Radda*.

Clementi, Muzio (arr. Casella). Symphony in C Major.

Copland, Aaron. *Appalachian Spring*, Suite; *Billy the Kid*, Suite; Concerto for Clarinet; *An Outdoor Overture*; *El salón México*; Scherzo for Orchestra; *The Tender Land*, Suite.

Corelli, Arcangelo. Concerto grosso in G Major, op. 6, no. 8, "Christmas." *La follia*, op. 5, no. 12.

Cornelius, Peter (arr. Mottl). *Der Barbier von Bagdad*, Overture; Ballad, *The Hero's Rest*.

Creston, Paul. *Threnody*.

Debussy, Claude (arr. Caplet). *Children's Corner*, excerpts; (arr. Ravel) *Danse*; *Danses sacre et profane*; *Images*, "Ibéria"; *Images*, "Rondes de printemps"; *La Mer*; *Nocturnes*; (arr. Busser) *Petite Suite*; *Prélude à l'après-midi d'un faune*.

Delage, Maurice. Two Hindu Poems.

Delibes, Léo. *Coppélia*, Suite; *Lakmé*, Aria; *Sylvia*, Suite.

Delius, Frederick. Concerto for Violoncello; *In a Summer Garden*; *Irmelin*, Prelude.

Dello Joio, Norman. Concert Music for Orchestra; Three Symphonic Dances.

Dohnányi, Ernö von. Concerto for Piano no. 2; Concerto for Violin; *Ruralia hungarica*, op. 32a; *Der Schleier der Pierrette*, op. 19; Suite for Orchestra in F-sharp Minor, op. 20; Variations on a Nursery Tune, op. 25.

Donato, Anthony. Sinfonietta no. 2.

Donizetti, Gaetano. *L'elisir d'amore*, "Una furtiva lagrima"; *La fille du régiment*; *Lucia di Lammermoor*.

Draeseke, Felix. Serenade in D Major, op. 49; *Symphonia tragica*, op. 40.

Dubensky, Arcady. Fugue for Violins.

Dukas, Paul. *L'apprenti sorcier*.

Duparc, Henri. *Chanson triste*; *Phidyle*.

Dvořák, Antonin. *Carnival* Overture, op. 92; Concerto for Piano in G Minor, op. 33; Concerto for Violin in A Minor, op. 53; Concerto for Violoncello in B Minor, op. 104; *Othello* Overture, op. 93; Slavonic Dances in C Major, op. 46, no. 1; in A-flat Major, op. 46, no. 3; in G Minor; in D Major, op. 46, no. 6; in G Minor, op. 46, no. 8; in B Major, op. 72, no. 1; in E Minor, op. 72, no. 2; Symphony no. 8 in G Major, op. 88; Symphony no. 9 in E Minor, op. 95.

Einem, Gottfried von. *Capriccio* for Orchestra.

Elgar, Edward. *Cockaigne* Overture, op. 40; *Enigma Variations*, op. 36; *Pomp and Circumstance*, March no. 1.

Enesco, Georges. Rumanian Rhapsody no. 1 in A Major, op. 11.

Eppert, Carl. *Speed*.

Erdmann, Eduard. Symphony in D Major, op. 10.

Etler, Alvin. Symphonietta no. 2; Symphony no. 1.

Fall, Leo. *Die Dollarprinzessen*.

Falla, Manuel de. *El amor brujo*; *Noches en los jardines de España*; *El sombrero de tres picos*, Three Dances; *La vida breve*, Interlude and Dance.

Flotow, Friedrich von. *Martha*.

Foote, Arthur. *Four Character Pieces*.

Foss, Lukas. Concerto for Piano no. 2; Symphony in G Major.

Franck, César. Symphonic Variations for Piano; Symphony in D Minor.

Franckenstein, Clemens von. *Rabab.*

Ganz, Rudolph. *Laughter . . . Yet Love* Overture.

Gershwin, George. *An American in Paris;* Concerto for Piano in F; *Rhapsody in Blue;* (arr. Bennett) *A Symphonic Picture of Porgy and Bess.*

Ginastera, Alberto. *Variaciones concertantes.*

Ginde. *Marche Lorainne.*

Glazounov, Alexander. Concerto for Violin in A Minor, op. 82; Symphony no. 3 in D Major, op. 33.

Glière, Reinhold. *The Red Poppy,* Russian Sailors' Dance; Symphony no. 3 in B Minor, *Ilya Mourametz,* op. 42, Scherzo.

Glinka, Mikhail. *Kamarinskaya; Ruslan and Ludmila,* Overture.

Gluck, Christoph. *Iphigénie en Aulide,* Overture; *O mio amato ben; Orfeo ed Euridice,* "Che farò senza Euridice?"; *Orfeo ed Euridice,* "Che puro ciel"; *Orphée et Euridice.*

Gohler, Georg. Symphony in F Major.

Goldmark, Karl. Concerto for Violin in A Minor, op. 28; *Im Frühling,* op. 36; *Die Königen von Saba,* op. 27; *Sakuntala,* op. 13.

Gould, Morton. *American Salute,* "When Johnny Comes Marching Home"; *Foster Gallery; Red Cavalry March; American Symphonette* no. 2; Symphony no. 1.

Gounod, Charles. *Faust; Le Médecin malgré lui; La Reine de Saba,* "Plus grande dans son obscurité."

Graener, Paul. *Schirin und Gertraude;* Sinfonietta for Strings and Harp, op. 27; *Theophano.*

Grainger, Percy (arr.) *Irish Tune; Molly on the Shore;* Shepherd's Tune.

Granados, Enrique. *Goyescas,* Intermezzo; (arr. Byrns) Spanish Dance no. 10 in G Major.

Grétry, André (arr. Mottl). *Céphale et Procris,* Ballet Suite.

Grieg, Edvard. Concerto for Piano in A Minor, op. 16; *Ich liebe dich; Peer Gynt,* Suite no. 1; *Ein Traum.*

Griffes, Charles T. *The Pleasure-Dome of Kubla Khan.*

Grimm, C. Hugo. *Erotic Poem.*

Gruenberg, Louis. Jazz Suite.

Hadley, Henry. Overture, *In Bohemia; Streets of Pekin,* Suite for Orchestra.

Hageman, Richard. *Me Company Along.*

Haieff, Alexei. Symphony no. 2.

Handel, George Frideric. *Acis and Galatea;* (arr. Casadesus) Concerto for Viola in B Minor; Concerto grosso in D Major, op. 6, no. 5; (arr. Seiffert) Concerto grosso, no. 16. *Israel in Egypt; Judas Maccabaeus; Messiah; Music for the Royal Fireworks,* excerpts; *Solomon,* Entrance of the Queen of Sheba; (arr. Harty) *Water Music,* Suite.

Hanson, Howard. *Elegy in Memory of Serge Koussevitzky;* Symphony no. 2.

Haydn, Franz Joseph. *Der Apotheke;* Concerto for Trumpet in E-flat Major; Concerto for Violoncello in D Major; *Die Jahreszeiten,* "Willkommen jetzt . . ."; *Sieben letzte Wörter,* "Elegie" for Wind Instruments; Sinfonia Concertante for Violin, Violoncello, Oboe, and Bassoon in B-flat Major, op. 84; Symphony no. 31 in D Major; Symphony no. 45 in F-sharp Minor; Symphony no. 82 in C Major; Symphony no. 88 in G Major; Symphony no. 94 in G Major; Symphony no. 95 in C Minor; Symphony no. 97 in C Major; Symphony no. 98 in B-flat Major; Symphony no. 100 in G Major; Symphony no. 101 in D Major; Symphony no. 102 in B-flat Major; Symphony no. 103 in E-flat Major; Symphony no. 104 in D Major.

Heiden, Bernard. *Euphorion*.

Hellmesberger, Georg. *Ball Scene*.

Herbert, Victor. Irish Rhapsody.

Herzfeld, Victor von. *Festmarsch in ungarische Weise*.

Hill, Edward Burlingame. *Stevensoniana* Suite no. 2, op. 29.

Hindemith, Paul. Concerto for Violin; Concerto for Violoncello; Kammermusik no. 1 for Small Orchestra, op. 24, no. 1; Kammermusik no. 2 (Klavierkonzert), op. 36, no. 1; Kammermusik no. 3 (Violoncellokonzert), op. 36, no. 2; *Das Marienleben*, "Nativity of Mary," "Joseph's Doubt," "Nativity of Christ"; *Mathis der Maler*, Symphony; *Neues von der Tage*, Overture; *Nobilissima Visione; Der Schwanendreher*, for Viola; Symphonic Metamorphosis on Themes by Carl Maria von Weber; Symphony, *Die Harmonie der Welt;* Theme and Four Variations, *Die vier Temperamente; When Lilacs Last in Dooryard Bloom'd*, Prelude.

Hofmann, Josef. *Chromaticon*.

Holst, Gustav. "Now Sleeps the Crimson Petal."

Honegger, Arthur. Concertino for Piano; *Pacific 231; Le roi David*.

Hovhaness, Alan. Symphony no. 2, "Mysterious Mountain."

Humperdinck, Engelbert. *Hänsel und Gretel*, Prelude; *Hänsel und Gretel*, "Dream Pantomime"; *Die Königskinder*, Overture.

Ibert, Jacques. *Escales*.

Indy, Vincent d'. *Istar*, Symphonic Variations.

Järnefelt, Armas. *Praeludium*.

Kabalevsky, Dmitri. *Colas Breugnon*, Overture; Symphony no. 2, op. 19.

Kálmán, Imre. *Die Herbstmanöver*.

Kann, Hugo. *Der Fremde;* Symphony no. 3 in E Major, op. 96.

Karg-Elert, Sigfrid. *Kammersinfonietta* in A Major.

Kelley, Edgar Stillman. *The Pit and the Pendulum*.

Khachaturian, Aram. Concerto for Piano.

Knipper, Lev. *Maku*, Suite on Iranian Themes.

Kodály, Zoltán. Galánta Dances; *Háry János*, Suite; *Marosszék Dances; Psalmus hungaricus;* Variations on a Hungarian Folksong, "Peacock Variations."

Koessler, Hans. Symphonic Variations.

Korngold, Erich. *Liebesbriefchen; Sommer*.

Kreisler, Fritz. *Aucassin et Nicolette*.

Lalo, Édouard. Concerto for Violoncello in D Minor; *Symphonie espagnole* for Violin, op. 21.

Langley, Lincoln. Waltz, *Children's Songs*.

Lazăr, Filip. *Tziganes*, Scherzo for Orchestra.

Lederer, Joseph. *Eine Nachtmusik*.

Lehár, Franz. *Das Fürstenkind; Der Graf von Luxemburg; Der Land des Lachelns*, "Dein ist mein ganzes Herz"; Waltz, *Gold and Silver*.

Liadov, Anatol. *Valse badinage;* Eight Russian Folksongs.

Liebermann, Rolf. Concerto for Jazzband and Symphony Orchestra.

Liszt, Franz. Concerto for Piano no. 1 in E-flat Major; Concerto for Piano no. 2 in A Major; *Die drei Zigeuner; Eine Faust-Symphonie;* Hungarian Fantasy; Hungarian Rhapsody no. 1 in F Minor; Hungarian Rhapsody no. 2 in A Major; Hungarian

Rhapsody no. 3 in D Major; *Die Lorelei; Mazzeppa; Mephisto* Waltz no. 1; *Les Préludes; Totentanz; Was man auf den Berge hört;* (arr. Weiner) *Weinen, Klagen, Sorge, Zagen; Die Zigeunerin.*

Locatelli, Pietro. Concerto grosso, no. 12 in F Major.

Lopotnikoff, Nikolai. Concertino for Orchestra, op. 30; Sinfonietta, op. 27.

Lualdi, Adriano. *Suite Adriatica.*

McBride, Robert. *Swing Stuff.*

MacDowell, Edward. Romance; Suite no. 2 in E Major, "Indian"; *The Song of Roland,* "The Lovely Alda," "The Saracens."

Mahler, Gustav. *Ich atmet' einen Linden Duft; Kindertotenlieder; Das Lied von der Erde; Lieder eines fahrendes Gesellen; Rheinlegendchen;* Symphony no. 2 in C Minor; Symphony no. 4 in G Major; Symphony no. 7 in E Minor; *Um Mitternacht; Wer hat des Liedlein erdacht?*

Malipiero, Gian Francesco. *Concerti; Impressioni dal vero.*

Marcello, Benedetto. *O Thou Beloved.*

Marschner, Heinrich. *Hans Heiling.*

Martinu, Bohuslav. Concerto grosso; Symphony no. 2.

Marx, Joseph. *Ach, gestern hat er mir Rosen gebracht; Hat dich die Liebe beruhrt? Marienlied; Selige Nacht; Venetianisches Wiegenlied; Waldseligkeit.*

Mason, Daniel Gregory. *Chanticleer* Overture; Suite after English Folksongs, op. 32; Symphony no. 2 in A Major.

Massenet, Jules. *Hérodiade,* "Il est doux"; *Manon,* La rêve.

Mendelssohn-Bartholdy, Felix. Concerto for Piano no. 1 in G Minor, op. 25; Concerto for Violin in E Minor, op. 64; *The Hebrides* ("Fingal's Cave") Overture, op. 26; *Meeresstille und glückliche Fahrt* Overture, op. 27; *A Midsummer Night's Dream,* op. 61, Incidental Music; Octet, "Scherzo"; *Ruy Blas* Overture; Symphony no. 3 in A Minor, op. 56; Symphony no. 4 in A Major, op. 90; Symphony no. 5 in D Major, op. 107.

Menotti, Gian Carlo. *Amelia al ballo.*

Meyerbeer, Giacomo. *L'Africaine; Les Huguenots.*

Miaskowsky, Nikolai. Symphony no. 5 in D Major.

Mihalovich, Ödön. Ballade, *Die Nixe.*

Milhaud, Darius. Concerto for Two Pianos; Concerto for Viola; *Le pauvre matelot; Suite française;* Symphony no. 7.

Mohaupt, Richard. Concerto for Violin; *The Landlady of Pinsk,* Overture; *Lysistrata,* Four Dances.

Moore, Douglas. *The Devil and Daniel Webster.*

Mozart, Wolfgang Amadeus. Concert Aria, *Ch'io mi scordi di te,* K. 505; Concerto for Bassoon in B-flat Major, K. 191; Concerto for Flute no. 1 in G Major, K. 313; Concerto for Flute and Harp in C Major, K. 299; Concerto for Piano no. 9 in E-flat Major, K. 271; Concerto for Piano no. 15 in B-flat Major, K. 450; Concerto for Piano no. 17 in G Major, K. 453; Concerto for Piano no. 20 in D Minor, K. 466; Concerto for Piano no. 21 in C Major, K. 467; Concerto for Piano no. 22 in E-flat Major, K. 482; Concerto for Piano no. 23 in A Major, K. 488; Concerto for Piano no. 24 in C Minor, K. 491; Concerto for Piano no. 25 in C Major, K. 503; Concerto for Piano no. 26 in D Major, K. 537; Concerto for Piano no. 27 in B-flat Major, K. 595;

Concerto for Two Pianos in E-flat Major, K. 365; Concerto for Violin no. 3 in G Major, K. 216; Concerto for Violin no. 4 in D Major, K. 218; Concerto for Violin no. 5 in A Major, K. 219; *Così fan tutte*, K. 588, Overture; Divertimento no. 11 in D Major, K. 251; Divertimento no. 15 in B-flat Major, K. 287; Divertimento no. 17 in D Major, K. 334; *Don Giovanni*, K. 527; *Die Entführung aus dem Serail*, K. 384, Overture; *Exultate, jubilate*, K. 165, "Alleluia"; *La finta giardiniera*, K. 196, Aria; German Dances, K. 605; *Idomeneo*, K. 366, Gavotte; Recitative and Aria, *Ma che vi fece, o stelle*, K. 368; Concert Aria, *Mentre ti lascia, o figlia*, K. 513; Concert Aria, *Mia speranza adorata*, K. 416; *Ein musikalischer Spass*, K. 522; *Le nozze di Figaro*, K. 492; *Les petits riens*, K. 299b, Overture; *Il rè pastore*, K. 208, "L'amerò, sarò costante"; *Der Schauspieldirektor*, K. 486, Overture; Serenade no. 9 in D Major, K. 320; Serenade no. 13 in G Major, K. 525; Sinfonia Concertante in E-flat Major for Oboe, Clarinet, Bassoon, and Horn, K. Anh. 9; Symphony no. 25 in G Minor, K. 183; Symphony no. 29 in A Major, K. 201; Symphony no. 31 in D Major, K. 297; Symphony no. 32 in B-flat Major, K. 319; Symphony no. 35 in D Major, K. 385; Symphony no. 36 in C Major, K. 425; Symphony no. 38 in D Major, K. 504; Symphony no. 39 in E-flat Major, K. 543; Symphony no. 40 in G Minor, K. 550; Symphony no. 41 in C Major, K. 551; *Die Zauberflöte*, K. 620.

Mraczek, Joseph. *Eva; Ikdar; Orientalische Skizzen für Kammerorchester.*

Mussorgsky, Modest (arr. Rimsky-Korsakov). *Boris Godunov;* (arr. Shostakovich) *Boris Godunov,* Monologue, Hallucination Scene, Farewell; *The Classicist; Khovanshchina,* Prelude; (arr. Rimsky-Korsakov) *A Night on Bare Mountain; Pain; On the Dnieper;* (arr. Ravel) *Pictures at an Exhibition.*

Nicodé, Jean-Louis. *Zwei fromme Gesänge,* op. 41; *Zwei dramatische Gesänge.*

Nicolai, Otto. *Die lustigen Weiber von Windsor,* Overture.

Offenbach, Jacques. *Les contes d'Hoffmann; Orphée aux enfers,* Overture.

Oldberg, Arne. Dramatic Overture, *Paolo and Francesca; St. Francis of Assisi.*

Orff, Carl. *Carmina burana.*

Otey, ?. Variations for Orchestra.

Paganini, Niccolò. Concerto for Violin no. 1 in E-flat Major, op. 6; (arr. Manen) Concerto no. 2 for Violin in B Minor, op. 7; (arr. Molinari) *Moto perpetuo.*

Pfitzner, Hans. *Blutenwunder; Das Christelflein; Klage; Die Rose vom Liebesgarten,* Trauermarsch.

Phillips, Burrill. *Selections from McGuffey's Reader.*

Pierné, Gabriel. Concert Piece for Harp.

Piston, Walter. Concerto for Violin; *The Incredible Flutist,* Suite; Symphony no. 2.

Pizzetti, Ildebrando. *La pisanelle,* Suite.

Planquette, Jean-Robert. *Les cloches de Courneville.*

Plüddemann, Martin. *Vollens Nachtgesang.*

Poldini, Ede. *Vagabund und Prinzessen.*

Ponce, Manuel. *Concierto du sur.*

Prokofiev, Sergei. *Ala et Lolly,* "Scythian" Suite, op. 20; *Alexander Nevsky,* op. 78; Concerto for Piano no. 2 in G Minor, op. 16; Concerto for Piano no. 3 in C Major, op. 26; Concerto for Violin no. 1 in D Major, op. 19; Concerto for Violin no. 2 in G Minor, op. 63; Concerto for Violoncello, op. 58; *Lieutenant Kijé,* Suite, op. 60;

The Love of Three Oranges, Suite, op. 33bis; *Peter and the Wolf,* op. 67; *Romeo and Juliet,* Suite no. 1; *Semyon Kotko,* Symphonic Suite; Symphony no. 1 in D Major, op. 25; Symphony no. 5 in B-flat Major, op. 100; Symphony no. 7 in C-sharp Minor, op. 131.

Puccini, Giacomo. *La bohème; Madama Butterfly,* "Un bel dì"; *Madama Butterfly,* Flower Duet; *Manon Lescaut,* Intermezzo; *Tosca.*

Purcell, Henry (arr. Grace). Evening Hymn; *Saint Cecilia,* "Soul of the World."

Rachmaninoff, Sergei. Concerto for Piano no. 1 in F-sharp Minor, op. 1; Concerto for Piano no. 2 in C Minor, op. 18; Concerto for Piano no. 3 in D Minor, op. 30; *Fate; The Isle of the Dead;* Motet, *To Thee O Lord;* Rhapsody on a Theme of Paganini, op. 43.

Rameau, Jean-Philippe. *Dardanus,* Ballet.

Ravel, Maurice. *Alborada del grazioso; Boléro;* Concerto for Piano in G Major; Concerto for Piano, Left-Hand; *Daphnis et Chloé,* Suite no. 2; Introduction and Allegro for Flute, Harp, and Strings; *Ma mère l'oye,* Suite; *Mélodies hébraïques; Menuet antique; Pavane pour une infante défunte; Rapsodie espagnole; Shéhérazade; Le tombeau de Couperin; Tzigane; La valse; Valses nobles et sentimentales.*

Read, Gardner. *Pennsylvaniana,* op. 67; Prelude and Toccata, op. 43.

Reger, Max. *Marias Wiegenlied; Symphonischer Prolog zu einer Tragödie,* op. 108; Variations on a Theme by Hiller, op. 100; Variations on a Theme of Mozart, op. 132; Vier Tondichtunge nach Böcklin, op. 128.

Respighi, Ottorino. *Antiche arie e danze per liuto; Ballata delle gnomidi; Fontane di Roma; I pini di Roma; Gli uccelli.*

Revueltas, Silvestre. *Janitzio.*

Rezniček, Emil von. *Donna Diana,* Overture.

Riegger, Wallingford. New Dance; *Dance Rhythms.*

Rieti, Vittorio. Concerto for Wind Instruments; Suite, *Noah's Ark.*

Riisager, Knudåge. *Fools Paradise.*

Rimsky-Korsakov, Nikolai. *Antar* Symphony, "Alla marcia"; *Capriccio espagnole,* op. 34; Concert Fantasy for Violin, op. 33; *May Night,* Overture; *May Night,* Aria?; *Russian Easter* Overture, op. 36; *Sadko,* "Flight of the Bumble-Bee"; *Scheherazade,* op. 35; *The Snow Maiden,* "Dance of the Tumblers."

Rodgers, Richard (arr. Walker). *Carousel,* Waltz.

Roger-Ducasse, Jean-Jules (arr. Ravel). Danse.

Rorem, Ned. *Design for Orchestra.*

Rosenstock, Josef. *Sinfonisches Konzert für Klavier und Orchester,* op. 4.

Rossini, Gioacchino. *Il barbiere di Siviglia; La Cenerentola,* Overture; *La Cenerentola,* "Non più mesta"; *La gazza ladra,* Overture; *Guillaume Tell,* Overture; *L'Italiana in Algeri,* Overture; *La scala di seta,* Overture; *Semiramide,* Overture; *Il Signor Bruschino,* Overture.

Roussel, Albert. *Bacchus et Ariadne,* Suite no. 2.

Rubinstein, Anton. Concerto for Piano no. 3 in G Major, op. 45; Concerto for Piano no. 4 in D Minor, op. 70.

Saint-Saëns, Camille. Concerto for Piano no. 2 in G Minor, op. 22; Concerto for Piano no. 4 in C Minor, op. 44; Concerto for Violin no. 3 in B Minor, op. 61; Concerto for Violoncello in A Minor, op. 33; *Danse macabre;* Introduction and Rondo capriccioso, for Violin; *Samson et Dalila,* "Amour, viens aider"; *Samson et Dalila,* Bacchanale; Symphony no. 3 in C Minor, op. 44.

Satie, Erik (arr. Debussy). *Gymnopédies* nos. 1, 3.

Scarlatti, Domenico (arr. Tommasini). *Le donne di buon umore,* Ballet Suite.

Schanze, Johannes. *Kindheit; Der Musikant; Symphonischen Prolog.*

Schoenberg, Arnold. *Pelleas und Melisande;* Theme and Variations for Orchestra, op. 43b; *Verklärte Nacht.*

Schreiber, Frederick. Concerto grosso for Four Solo Instruments.

Schreker, Franz. *Der ferne Klang.*

Schubert, Franz (arr. Cassado). Concerto for Violoncello in A Minor, D. 821; (arr. ?) *Dem Unendlichen,* D. 291; (arr. ?) *Erlkönig,* D. 328; (arr. Dohnányi) Fantasy in F Minor, D. 940; (arr. Liszt) *Marche militaire* in B Minor, D. 733; *Rosamunde,* Overture, D. 797; *Rosamunde,* Entr'acte and Ballet Music, D. 797; (arr. ?) *Ständchen,* D. 957, no. 4; Symphony no. 5 in B-flat Major, D. 485; Symphony no. 8 in B Minor, D. 759; Symphony no. 9 in C Major, D. 944; (arr. ?) *Ungeduld,* D. 795, no. 7.

Schuman, William. *American Festival* Overture; *Prayer in Time of War; Side Show for Orchestra.*

Schumann, Georg. *Im ringen um ein Ideal,* op. 40.

Schumann, Robert. Concerto for Piano in A Minor, op. 54; Concerto for Violoncello in A Minor, op. 129; *Genoveva,* Overture; Introduction and Allegro Appassionato in G Major, op. 92; *Konzertstück* for Four Horns in F Major, op. 86; *Manfred,* Overture; Overture, Scherzo, and Finale, op. 52; Symphony no. 1 in B-flat Major, op. 38; Symphony no. 2 in C Major, op. 61; Symphony no. 3 in E-flat Major, op. 97; Symphony no. 4 in D Minor, op. 120.

Sessions, Roger. *The Black Maskers,* Suite.

Shostakovich, Dmitri. *The Age of Gold,* Polka, Russian Dance; Concerto for Piano, Trumpet, and Strings no. 1 in C Minor, op. 35; Symphony no. 1 in F Minor, op. 10; Symphony no. 5 in D Minor, op. 47; Symphony no. 6 in B Minor, op. 54; Symphony no. 9 in E-flat Major, op. 70.

Sibelius, Jean. Concerto for Violin in D Minor, op. 47; *Finlandia; Karelia* Suite, "Alla marcia"; *The Swan of Tuonela;* Symphony no. 1 in E Minor, op. 39; Symphony no. 2 in D Major, op. 43; Symphony no. 4 in A Minor, op. 63; Symphony no. 5 in E-flat Major, op. 82; *Valse triste.*

Sinigaglia, Leone. *Le baruffe chiozzotte,* Overture, op. 32.

Smetana, Bedřich. *The Bartered Bride,* Overture; *The Bartered Bride,* "Ach warst du untreu mir"; *Dalibor; The Moldau.*

Smith, David Stanley. *Credo,* Poem for Orchestra, op. 83

Sowerby, Leo. *Money Music;* Passacaglia, Interlude, and Fugue; Suite, *From the Northland.*

Spohr, Louis. Concerto for Violin no. 9 in D Major, op. 55; *Notturno und Janitscharen Musik,* op. 34.

Still, William Grant. *Plain Chant for America.*

Strauss, Johann (The Elder). *Radetzky* March, op. 228.

Strauss, Johann (The Younger). Waltz, *Auf dem schönem blauen Donau,* op. 314; *Die Fledermaus;* Waltz, *Frühlingstimmen,* op. 410; Waltz, *Geschichte aus der Wienerwald,* op. 325; *Kaiser-Walzer,* op. 437; Waltz, *Kunstlerleben,* op. 316; Waltz, *Morgen-*

blätter, op. 279; *Perpetuum mobile,* op. 257; Waltz, *Rosen aus der Süden,* op. 388; *Schatzwalzer,* op. 418; Polka, *Unter Donner und Blitz,* op. 324; Waltz, *Wiener Blut,* op. 354.

Strauss, Joseph. Waltz, *Dorfschwalben aus Österreich,* op. 164; Waltz, *Mein Lebenslauf ist Lieb und Lust,* op. 263.

Strauss, Richard. *Allerseelen; Eine Alpensinfonie,* op. 64; *Also sprach Zarathustra,* op. 30; *Amor; Ariadne auf Naxos,* op. 60, "Grossmächtige Prinzessin"; *Ariadne auf Naxos,* op. 60, "Es gibt ein Reich"; *Le bourgeois gentilhomme,* op. 60, Suite; *Burleske* for Piano and Orchestra; *Capriccio,* op. 85, Closing Scene; *Caecilie;* Concerto for Oboe; *Don Juan,* op. 20; *Don Quixote,* op. 35; Duet-Concertino for Clarinet, Bassoon, Strings, and Harp; *Elektra,* op. 58; *Die Frau ohne Schatten; Heimliche Aufforderung; Ein Heldenleben,* op. 40; *Ich trage meine Minne; Morgen; Der Rosenkavalier,* op. 53; *Salome,* op. 54; *Säusle, liebe Myrthe; Die schweigsame Frau,* op. 80, "Potpourri"; *Ständchen; Sinfonia domestica,* op. 53; *Till Eulenspiegels lustige Streiche,* op. 28; *Tod und Verklärung,* op. 24; *Vier letzte Lieder; Wanderlied; Wiegenlied; Zueignung.*

Stravinsky, Igor. *Agon;* Concerto for Piano and Winds; Concerto for Strings in D Major; Divertimento (arr. from *The Fairy's Kiss*); *The Firebird,* Suite (1919); *The Firebird,* Suite (1947); *Fireworks,* op. 4; *Mavra; Petrushka,* Suite (1911); *Petrushka,* (1947); Three Poems on Japanese Lyrics; *Pulcinella,* Suite; *The Rake's Progress; A Soldier's Tale; The Song of the Nightingale;* Suite no. 1 for Small Orchestra; Suite no. 2 for Small Orchestra; Symphony of Psalms.

Suppé, Franz von. *Die schöne Galatea,* Overture.

Tartini, Giuseppe. Concerto for Violin in D Major.

Taylor, Deems. *Circus Days,* excerpts; *Through the Looking-Glass,* Suite.

Tchaikovsky, Peter. *Capriccio italien; Christmas Eve;* Concerto for Piano in B-flat Minor, op. 23; Concerto for Violin in D Major, op. 35; *1812 Overture,* op. 49; *Eugene Onegin; Francesca da Rimini,* op. 32; *Manfred* Symphony, op. 58; *Marche slave,* op. 31; *The Nutcracker,* op. 71, excerpts; Overture Fantasy, *Romeo and Juliet,* op. 47; Serenade for Strings in C Major, op. 48; *The Sleeping Beauty,* op. 66, Waltz; Suite no. 1 in D Major, op. 43, "Marche miniature"; Suite no. 3 in G Major, op. 55, Theme and Variations; *Swan Lake,* op. 20, Waltz; Symphony no. 4 in F Minor, op. 36; Symphony no. 5 in E Minor, op. 64; Symphony no. 6 in B Minor, op. 74; Variations on a Rococo Theme for Violoncello, op. 33.

Tcherepnin, Alexander. Divertimento; Five Russian Dances; Suite, op. 87.

Thomas, Ambroise. *Hamlet; Mignon; Raymond,* Overture.

Thompson, Randall. *Americana;* Symphony no. 2.

Thomson, Virgil. Concerto for Violoncello; Suite, *The Plow That Broke the Plains; The Seine at Night.*

Toch, Ernst. *The Fan,* A Little Overture; *Pinocchio,* A Merry Overture.

Turina, Joaquin. *Canto a Sevilla,* Four Songs.

Turner, Charles. *Encounter.*

Vaughan Williams, Ralph. Fantasy on a Theme of Thomas Tallis; Symphony no. 3, "Pastoral."

Verdi, Giuseppe. *Aida; Un ballo in maschera; Don Carlo,* "O don fatale"; *Falstaff; Messa da Requiem; Nabucco,* Overture; *Rigoletto; La traviata; Il trovatore; Les vêpres siciliennes,* Overture.

Vieuxtemps, Henri. Concerto for Violin no. 4 in D Minor, op. 31; Concerto for Violin no. 5 in A Minor, op. 37.

Villa-Lobos, Heitor. *Bachianas brasileiras* no. 2; *Bachianas brasilieras* no. 5.

Vivaldi, Antonio. Concerto grosso, op. 3 no. 11; Concerto for Piccolo; Concerto for Violin in A; *Le quattro stagioni*.

Volkmann, Robert. Concerto for Violoncello in A Minor, op. 33; Serenade in F Major, op. 63.

Wagner, Richard. *Eine Faust-Ouvertüre; Die Feen,* Overture; *Der fliegende Holländer; Götterdämmerung; Lohengrin; Die Meistersinger von Nürnberg; Parsifal; Das Rhein-gold; Rienzi; Siegfried; Siegfried Idyll;* Symphony in C Major; *Tannhäuser; Tristan und Isolde; Die Walküre; Wesendonck Lieder.*

Wagner, Siegfried. *Der Bärenhäuter; Sonnenflammen.*

Walton, William. *Façade* Suite.

Weber, Carl Maria von. *Abu Hassan,* Overture; (arr. Berlioz) *Aufforderung zum Tanz;* (arr. Weingartner) *Aufforderung zum Tanz; Euryanthe,* Overture; *Der Freischütz; Jubel* Overture; *Oberon,* Overture; (arr. Liszt) Polonaise brilliante for Piano and Orchestra.

Webern, Anton von. Six Pieces for Orchestra, op. 6.

Weill, Kurt. Concerto for Violin.

Weinberger, Jaromír. *Schwanda,* Polka and Fugue.

Weiner, Leo. *Carnival,* Humoresque for Small Orchestra, op. 5; Divertimento after Old Hungarian Dances, op. 20a; Pastorale, Fantasy, and Fugue, op. 23; Serenade for Small Orchestra; Suite, Old Hungarian Folk Dances, op. 18; *Toldi* Suite.

Weismann, Julius. Concerto for Violin in D Major, op. 36.

Wetzler, Hermann. *As You Like It,* Overture.

Wieniawski, Henri. Concerto for Violin no. 2 in D Minor, op. 22.

Wolf, Hugo. *Anakreons Grab; An Frühling; Elfenlied; Er ist's; Der Freund; In der Frühe; Italienische Serenade; Morgenhymnus; Der Rattenfänger; Schlafendes Jesuskind; Ver-borgenheit; Weylas Gesang.*

Wolf-Ferrari, Ermanno. *I gioielli della Madonna; Il segreto di Susanna,* Overture.

Aitay, Victor. Interview in *Podium,* Fall/Winter 1986.

Appia, Adolphe. *Music and the Art of Theater.* Translated by Robert W. Corrigan, Mary Douglas, and Walter R. Volbach, with a foreword by Lee Simonson. Coral Gables, Fla.: University of Miami Press, 1962.

Asbell, Bernard. "Claudia Cassidy: The Queen of Culture and Her Reign of Terror." *Chicago,* June 1956.

Assejew, Vladimir. Interview with author and copies of family documents and photos. Ljubljana, Yugoslavia. October 1984.

Bartenstein, Eva Reiner. Interview with author and copies of documents and photos. Zurich, Switzerland. October 1984.

Bartók, Béla. *Béla Bartók Letters.* Edited by János Demény. New York: St. Martin's Press, 1971.

Beacham, Richard C. *Adolphe Appia, Theater Artist.* Cambridge: Cambridge University Press, 1987.

Beckett, Lucy. *Richard Wagner, Parsifal.* Cambridge: Cambridge University Press, 1981.

Biancolli, Louis. *The Flagstad Manuscript.* New York: Putnam, 1952.

Bing, Rudolf. *5000 Nights at the Opera.* Garden City, N.Y.: Doubleday and Company, 1972.

——— . *A Knight at the Opera.* New York: J. P. Putnam's Sons, 1981.

Bloomfield, Arthur. *50 Years of the San Francisco Opera.* San Francisco: San Francisco Book Company, 1972.

Bónis, Ferenc. "Reiner Frigyes." In *Zenei lexicon,* edited by Denes Barthes. Budapest, 1965.

Boult, Sir Adrian. *Boult on Music.* London: Toccata Press, 1983.

——— . *My Own Trumpet.* London: Hamish Hamilton, 1973.

——— . *Thoughts on Conducting.* London: Phoenix House, 1963.

Breuer, János. *A Budapesti Filharmónica Társagáz zenekarának 125 Esztendeje, 1853–1978.* Budapest, 1978.

Brody, Clark. Interview with author. Evanston, Illinois. January 1987.

——— . Interview in *Podium,* Fall/Winter 1982, Spring/Summer 1983.

Brown, Howard Mayer. "Pedantry or Liberation? A Sketch of the Historical Performance Movement." In *Authenticity and Early Music,* edited by Nicholas Kenyon. Oxford: Oxford University Press, 1988.

Butera, Kathleen. "The History of the Pittsburgh Symphony." Unpublished typescript in the University of Pittsburgh, Hillman Library, Archives of Industrial Society.

Caratelli, Sebastian. *A Musician's Odyssey*. New York: Vantage Press, 1983.

Chicago Symphony Orchestra: The First 100 Years. (Booklet issued with recordings in CSO 90/12.) Chicago, 1990.

Chicago Symphony Orchestra. Bound volumes of concert programs, 1891–1963; press clippings, in scrapbooks and on microfilm, 1891–.

Cincinnati Historical Society, Cincinnati, Ohio. Press clippings, in scrapbooks, for Cincinnati Symphony Orchestra, 1922–1931.

Cincinnati Symphony Orchestra, Cincinnati, Ohio. Bound volumes of concert programs, 1922–1931.

Columbia Records. "Lab sheets" containing detailed entries made at the time of Reiner's recordings in Pittsburgh and New York, 1941–1950.

Columbia University, New York, New York. Fritz Reiner Center for Contemporary Music. Correspondence, photographs, and other documents. (Not available for study.)

Conductors' Guild. Reiner Retrospective, held at Columbia University, 9 January 1988. Remarks by Adele Addison, Lukas Foss, Philip Hart, Herbert Levy, and Regina Resnik. Transcript in *Podium*, Spring/Summer 1988.

Culshaw, John. *The Ring Resounding*. New York: Viking Press, 1967.

Curtis Institute of Music, Philadelphia, Pennsylvania. Program books, press clippings, photographs, correspondence, sound recordings, videotapes.

Daniel, Oliver. *Stokowski: A Counterpoint of View*. New York: Dodd, Mead, 1982.

Davis, Roland L. *Opera in Chicago*. New York: Appleton-Century, 1966.

Detroit Public Library, Detroit, Michigan. Concert programs, Ford Sunday Evening Hour, 1946.

Detroit Symphony Orchestra, Detroit, Michigan. Concert programs, Ford Sunday Evening Hour, 1936–1941.

Dettmer, Roger. Taped interviews of Herbert Tiemeyer and Herbert Silbersack.

———. "Kaviar fürs Volk." *Podium*, Spring 1981.

Dorian, Frederick, and Judith Meibach. "A Short History of the Pittsburgh Symphony Orchestra." *Carnegie Magazine*, January–February and March–April 1986.

Downes, Edward. Interview with Fritz Reiner, Weston, Connecticut, 13 March 1963; radio broadcast during Metropolitan Opera intermission, 23 March 1963.

Dresden Opera, Dresden, Germany. Sächsische Hof (later Staats) Oper. Posters, press clippings, Tagebücher, 1914–1921.

Druzinsky, Edward. Interview in *Podium*, Fall/Winter 1983.

Eaton, Quaintance. *Opera Caravan*. New York: Farrar, Straus and Cudahy, 1957.

Edwards, John. Interview with author. Chicago, Illinois. 1984.

———. Interview with Jim Unrath of WFMT, transcribed in *Podium*, Spring/Summer 1985.

Erskine, John. *The Philharmonic-Symphony Society of New York*. New York: Macmillan, 1943.

Fitzgerald, Gerald, éd. *Annals of the Metropolitan Opera*. Boston: G. K. Hall, 1989.

Francos, Alexis. "To Research a Symphony: Some Resources and Tools Available on the History of the Pittsburgh Symphony Orchestra." Unpublished typescript in the University of Pittsburgh, Hillman Library, Archives of Industrial Society.

Franz Liszt Academy of Music (Liszt F. Zenemüv Föiskola Evkönve), Budapest. Yearbooks, 1903–1910.

"Fritz Reiner Remembered." WQXR, New York, radio broadcast with Robert Sherman, Carlotta Reiner, and Chicago Symphony Orchestra musicians. Transcribed in *Podium* 1, no. 1 (1976); 1, no. 2 (1977).

Fritz Reiner Society. Newsletter. Nos. 1–16. [Chicago,] 1975–1982.

———. *Podium.* 22 issues. [Chicago,] 1976–1988.

Galkin, Elliott W. *The History of Orchestral Conducting.* New York: Pendragon Press, 1988.

Gelatt, Roland. *The Fabulous Phonograph.* Philadelphia. J. B. Lippincott Company, 1955.

Goldin, Milton. *The Music Merchants.* New York: W. W. Norton and Company, 1969.

Goldovsky, Boris. Interview with author. Santa Fe, New Mexico. August 1984.

———. *My Road to Opera.* Boston: Houghton Mifflin Company, 1979.

Gould, Morton. Interview with author. San Francisco. June 1984.

Grant, Margaret, and Herman S. Hechinger. *American Symphony Orchestras.* New York: W. W. Norton and Company, 1940.

Gray, Michael H. "Recording Reiner." *Absolute Sound* 49, Fall 1987.

Hamilton, David. Record review of *Tristan und Isolde. Opera Quarterly* 9, no. 3 (Spring 1993): 162.

———. "*Tristan* in the Thirties." *Musical Newsletter,* Fall 1976, Spring 1977.

———, ed. *The Metropolitan Opera Encyclopedia.* New York: Simon and Schuster, 1987.

Harrison, Jay S. "Return of Reiner." *Musical America,* October 1963.

Hart, Philip. "CSO/Reiner from the Archives." *ARSC Journal* 19, nos. 2–3 (February 1989).

———. *Orpheus in the New World: The Symphony Orchestra as an American Cultural Institution.* New York: W. W. Norton and Company, 1974.

———. "Towards a Reiner Discography." *ARSC Journal* 19, no. 1 (May 1988).

Helmbrecht, Arthur J., Jr. *Fritz Reiner: The Comprehensive Discography of His Recordings.* Privately printed, 1978.

Hendl, Walter. Interview in *Podium,* Spring/Summer, Fall/Winter 1984.

Herseth, Adolph. Interview with Kathy Frumkin of WFMT, transcribed in *Podium,* Fall/Winter 1981.

Heyworth, Peter. Review of *Die Meistersinger. Opera,* January 1956.

Hillis, Margaret. Interview in *Podium,* Spring/Summer, Fall/Winter 1983.

Hillyer, Stephen C. "FRS Centenary Tape Features Reiner's Earliest Recordings," *Podium,* Spring/Summer 1988.

Hitchcock, H. Wiley, and Stanley Sadie, eds. *The New Grove Dictionary of American Music.* 4 vols. London: Macmillan, 1986.

Holmes, John L. *Conductors on Record.* Westport, Conn.: Greenwood Press, 1982.

Horowitz, Joseph. *Understanding Toscanini.* New York: Alfred A. Knopf, 1987.

Hungarian National Library, Department of History of Theater, Budapest, Hungary. Népopera posters, 1912–1914.

Jablonski, Edward. *Gershwin.* Garden City, N.Y.: Doubleday and Company, 1987.

Judson, Arthur. Interviews with author. Harrison, New York. 1969 and 1970.

Kenyon, Nicholas, ed. *Authenticity and Early Music.* Oxford: Oxford University Press, 1988.

Klinger, Erzsebét Szebestyén. Interview with author. Vancouver, British Columbia. July 1984.

Kolodin, Irving. *The Metropolitan Opera.* New York: Alfred A. Knopf, 1966.

Kozma, Tibor. "Ave Atque Vale: Fritz Reiner." *Opera News,* 6 April 1953.

Krupicka, Frank Rainer. Correspondence and telephone conversations with author, Spring 1992. Interview with author, Santa Fe, New Mexico, July 1992.

Kupferberg, Herbert. *Those Fabulous Philadelphians*. New York: Charles Scribner's Sons, 1969.

Leiter, Robert D. *The Musicians and Petrillo*. New York: Bookman, 1953.

Library of Congress, Music Division, Washington, D.C. Fritz Reiner's and others' correspondence, sound recordings.

Los Angeles Philharmonic Orchestra. Copies of Reiner programs, 1959; Hollywood Bowl programs.

Lukacs, John. *Budapest, 1900*. New York: Weidenfeld and Nicholson, 1988.

Mayer, Martin. *The Met: One Hundred Years of Grand Opera*. New York: Simon and Schuster, 1983.

Metropolitan Opera Association Archives, New York, New York. Correspondence, contracts, press clippings on microfilm, photographs.

Newberry Library, Chicago. Chicago Symphony Orchestra press clippings, 1891–, in scrapbooks and on microfilm; photographs, programs, and other historical material related to music in Chicago.

New York Philharmonic Archives, New York, New York. New York Philharmonic–Symphony Orchestra and Stadium Concert programs, sound recordings.

New York Public Library, Library of the Performing Arts at Lincoln Center, New York, New York. Press clippings, programs, photographs, and sound recordings.

Northwestern University, Evanston, Illinois. Fritz Reiner Library in the Music Library. Correspondence and other personal papers, diaries, personal library of scores and books, photographs, programs and press clippings, sound and video recordings.

Oldberg, Richard. "The Oldberg Discography of the Chicago Symphony Orchestra." Unpublished typescript. Chicago, Illinois.

The Orchestral Association, Chicago, Illinois. Minutes of the meetings of the Board of Trustees, 1946–1963.

Otis, Philo Adams. *The Chicago Symphony Orchestra: Its Organization, Growth, and Development, 1891–1924*. Chicago: Clayton Summy, 1925.

Peck, Donald. Interview in *Podium* 3 (1979); Autumn 1980.

Peters, Gordon. Interview in *Podium*, Fall/Winter 1984.

Peyser, Joan. *Bernstein: A Biography*. New York: Birch Tree Books, William Morrow, 1987.

Philadelphia Orchestra. Programs, including those from the Robin Hood Dell concerts.

Phillips, Edna. Interview with author. Philadelphia, Pennsylvania. May 1987.

Pittsburgh Symphony Orchestra, Pittsburgh, Pennsylvania. Program books, press clippings, 1939–1949.

Potter, Rollin R. "Fritz Reiner: Conductor, Teacher, Musical Innovator." Ph.D. dissertation, Northwestern University, 1980.

Prokofiev, Serge. *Autobiography*. Moscow: Foreign Languages Publishing House, n.d.

Reid, Charles. *Thomas Beecham*. New York: E. P. Dutton, 1962.

Reiner, Carlotta. Interview with Al Schlachtmeyer, "Sunshine and Twilight in Weston: An Interview with Carlotta Reiner." *Podium* 2, no. 1 (1978).

———. "Last Will and Testament of Carlotta Reiner." Dated 14 May 1981. Office of the probate judge, Westport, Connecticut.

Reiner, Fritz. Interview with Gertrude Guthrie-Treadway. Cincinnati *Enquirer,* 25 September 1927.

———. "Last Will and Testament of Fritz Reiner." Dated 27 September 1962. Office of the probate judge, Westport, Connecticut.

————. "Outline for Course in Conducting." Unpublished manuscript in Northwestern University, Music Library.

————. "Reiner Discusses the Making of a Conductor." *Musical America*, 25 October 1941.

————. "The Technique of Conducting." *Étude*, October 1951.

————. *Wagner*. New York: Columbia Masterworks, n.d.

Reiner Symposium in Bloomington. Participants: Philip Farkas, George Gaber, Murray Grodner, Bernard Portnoy, Elvin Clearfield. Transcribed in *Podium* 2, no. 2 (1978); 3 (1979).

Répertoar Slovenskih Gledalisc, 1867–1967. Ljubljana, 1967.

Robbins Landon, H. C. *Mozart's Last Year*. New York: Schirmer Books, 1988.

Rochester Philharmonic Orchestra, Rochester, New York. Programs.

Rosenthal, Harold. *Two Centuries of Opera at Covent Garden*. London: Putnam, 1958.

Royal Opera House, Covent Garden, London, England. Programs.

Rudolf, Max. Interview with author. Philadelphia, Pennsylvania. January 1988.

————. *The Grammar of Conducting*. New York: G. Schirmer, 1950.

Russell, Charles E. *The American Orchestra and Theodore Thomas*. Garden City, N.Y.: Doubleday and Company, 1927.

Sachs, Harvey. *Music in Fascist Italy*. New York: W. W. Norton and Company, 1987.

————. *Reflections on Toscanini*. New York: Grove Weidenfeld, 1991.

————. *Toscanini*. Philadelphia: J. B. Lippincott Company, 1978.

Sadie, Stanley, ed. *The New Grove Dictionary of Music and Musicians*. 20 vols. London: Macmillan, 1980.

————, ed. *The New Grove Dictionary of Opera*. London: Macmillan, 1992.

Saerchinger, Cesar. "Fritz Reiner: Perpetual Prodigy." *Saturday Review*, 31 May 1952.

Schabas, Ezra. *Theodore Thomas*. Urbana: University of Illinois Press, 1989.

Schickel, Richard, and Michael Walsh. *Carnegie Hall: The First Hundred Years*. New York: Henry N. Abrams, 1987.

Schoenberg, Arnold. *Arnold Schoenberg Letters*. Edited by Erwin Stein. New York: St. Martin's Press, 1965.

Schonberg, Harold C. *The Great Conductors*. New York: Simon and Schuster, 1967.

Schwarzkopf, Elisabeth. Interview with Rudolf Sabor. *Records and Recording*, May 1980.

Seltsam, William H. *Metropolitan Opera Annals: First Supplement, 1947–1957*. New York: H. W. Wilson Company, 1957.

Shanet, Howard. *Philharmonic: A History of New York's Orchestra*. Garden City, N.Y.: Doubleday and Company, 1975.

Slonimsky, Nicolas. *Baker's Biographical Dictionary of Musicians*. 6th ed. New York: Schirmer Books, 1978.

————. *Music since 1900*. 4th ed. New York: Charles Scribner's Sons, 1971.

Smith, Marjorie Garrigue. Interview with author. Elizabethtown, New York. November 1986.

Smith, Sally Bedell. *In All His Glory: The Life of William Paley*. New York: Simon and Schuster, 1990.

Starker, János. Interview with author. Santa Fe, New Mexico, 1984.

————. Interview with Bruce Welleck, "János Starker Speaks about His Reiner Years." *Podium* 1, no. 2 (1977); 2, no. 1 (1978).

Staud, Géza. *A Budapest Opera Ház 100 Éve*. Budapest, 1984.

Stevens, Halsey. *The Life and Works of Béla Bartók*. New York: Oxford University Press, 1953.

Stoddard, Hope. *Symphony Conductors of the U.S.A.* New York: Thomas Y. Crowell Company, 1957.

Stravinsky, Igor. *Autobiography*. New York: Simon and Schuster, 1936.

——. *Selected Correspondence*. Edited by Robert Craft. Vol. 2. New York: Alfred A. Knopf, 1982.

Stravinsky, Igor, and Robert Craft. *Themes and Episodes*. New York: Alfred A. Knopf, 1966.

Stravinsky, Vera, and Robert Craft. *Stravinsky in Pictures and Documents*. New York: Simon and Schuster, 1978.

Swoboda, Henry, ed. *The American Symphony Orchestra*. New York: Basic Books, 1967.

Szigeti, Joseph. *With Strings Attached*. 2d ed. New York: Alfred A. Knopf, 1967.

Tait, Don. *Chicago Symphony Orchestra Discography*. Westport, Conn.: Greenwood Press, 1994.

Taruskin, Richard. "The Dark Side of Modern Music." *New Republic*, 5 September 1988.

——. "The Pastness of the Present and the Presence of the Past." In *Authenticity and Early Music*, edited by Nicholas Kenyon. Oxford: Oxford University Press, 1988.

Teatro Colón, Buenos Aires, Argentina. Programs, 1926.

Temple University, Philadelphia, Pennsylvania. Urban Archives Center. Press clippings.

Thomas, Louis Russell. "A History of the Cincinnati Symphony Orchestra to 1931." Ph.D. dissertation, University of Cincinnati, 1972.

Thomas, Rose Fay. *Memoirs of Theodore Thomas*. New York: Moffat, Yard and Company, 1911.

Thomas, Theodore. *A Musical Autobiography*. Edited by G. P. Upton. Chicago: McClurg, 1905.

Thomson, Virgil. *Selected Letters of Virgil Thomson*. Edited by T. Page and V. W. Page. New York: Summit Books, 1988.

——. *A Virgil Thomson Reader*. Boston: Houghton Mifflin Company, 1981.

Tintori, Giampiero. *Cronologia: opera, balletti, concerti, 1778–1977*. Milan: Teatro alla Scala, 1978.

Totels, Robert E. "Reiner at the Met." *Podium* 1, no. 1 (1976); 1, no. 2 (1977).

University of Cincinnati, Cincinnati, Ohio. Music Library. Publicity folders.

University of Pittsburgh, Pittsburgh, Pennsylvania. Hillman Library, Archives of Industrial Society. Pittsburgh Symphony Orchestra press clippings, unpublished manuscripts, and other archival material.

Valin, Jonathan. *The RCA Bible*. Cincinnati: The Music Lovers Press, 1993.

Viles, Eliza Ann. "Mary Louise Curtis Bok Zimbalist: Founder of the Curtis Institute of Music and Patron of American Arts." Ph.D. dissertation, Bryn Mawr College, 1983.

Welte-Mignon, licensee. *Catalog*. New York, 1927.

Whyte, Bert. "The Roots of High Fidelity Sound." *Audio*, June 1981.

Willis, Thomas. "Reiner Library Gift to N.U." Chicago *Tribune*, 28 December 1969.

The abbreviations in this index are mainly FR for Fritz Reiner, O for Orchestra, and SO for Symphony Orchestra. Music mentioned in the text is listed by composer; except where noted, Fritz Reiner was the conductor. Names of composers whose music Reiner conducted are in small capital letters.

Suite, 105; Symphony no. 1 in D Major, 117; Symphony no. 5 in B-flat Major, 105

Prude, Walter, 127, 233

PUCCINI, GIACOMO: *La bohème,* 7; —, FR Dresden anecdote, 22; *Tosca,* 7, 15

Pulido, Esperanza, 133

Pulley, Al, 184

Pullman Building (Chicago), 183

Rachlin, Ezra, 64, 108

RACHMANINOFF, SERGEI: Concerto for Piano no. 2 in C Minor, 128, 135, 174; Concerto for Piano no. 3 in D Minor, 139; Rhapsody on a Theme of Paganini, 136, 174

Radio City Music Hall, 79, 85

Rainer, Erika (daughter of FR and Charlotte Benedict), 19

Ralf, Torsten, 91

Rambleside, 97–99, 107, 115, 116, 121, 123, 133; Eva and Hans Bartenstein visit, 134; Monika Bartenstein visits, 238; *Carmen* cast party, 140; Carlotta Reiner ownership, 182, 239; sale, 242, 244

RAVEL, MAURICE, 203; *Boléro,* 33; Concerto for Piano in G Major (c. Leonard Bernstein), 108; *Daphnis et Chloé,* Suite no. 2, 33, 128; *Ma mère l'oye,* 33; *Rapsodie Espagnole,* 33; FR in, 204; FR visits, 54; *Le tombeau de Couperin,* 33; *La valse,* 33, 111

Raven, Seymour, 228, 231; and Claudia Cassidy, 223; Chicago SO manager, 222, 223, 225–26, 228, 228–29; labor relations, 228–29; on Orchestra Hall, 183; and Orchestral Association, 222; at *Tribune,* 161, 166, 167, 221

Ravinia Festival, 84; FR guest, 156, 164; union negotiations, 212

RCA-Victor, 86, 87, 108, 109, 111, 138–40, 171–75; and Claudia Cassidy, 223; and concert repertory, 173, 198; and Chicago SO touring, 184, 185; concerto recordings, 174; and Decca Records (U.K.), 219; *Die Fledermaus,* excerpts, 139, 141; Hendl/CSO recordings, 162;

and Orchestra Hall, 184; and FR, 137, 138, 141, 171, 231–32; repertory, 173; *Reader's Digest* recordings, 231; Robin Hood Dell SO, 136; royalties, 241; soloists, 198, 218

RCA-Victor SO, 140

READ, GARDNER, 107

Reader's Digest recordings, 231

Recordings, FR preparation, 197

Reddick, William J., 88

REGER, MAX: songs, 84

Reidel, Kurt, 93, 94

Reiner, Berta Gerster-Gardini, 41–42, 115, 123, 128; in Cincinnati, 28, 41; Cincinnati SO offer received, 23; divorces FR, 53; finances, 42; in New York, 53; marries FR, 21; and Tuśy Assejew, 51

Reiner, Berta (Tuśy). *See* Assejew, Tuśy

Reiner, Carlotta Irwin, 41, 51, 52, 53, 54, 57, 79; acting career, 52; and Berta Reiner compared, 52; and Claudia Cassidy, 156, 167, 176; Columbia University trust, 240; on conductor training, 238, 239; on Europe/Russia tour, 214; and Arthur Judson, 83, 123; last years, 237–39, 240, 241, 243; marries FR, 54; on medicine, 182; and Richard Mohr, 172; Northwestern University gift, 239; in Pittsburgh, 116; and press, 166, 177; at Rambleside, 98, 99, 121; and FR, 98, 124; FR's death, 233; on FR health, 224; FR's secretary, 179; and FR will, 239, 240; on Artur Rubinstein, 174; meets Richard Strauss, 54; and touring, 113, 114; and Tuśy Assejew, 122, 226–27; widow at Rambleside, 237; will, 182, 241; WQXR interview, 237

Reiner, Elca (Angela) Jelacin, 42, 50; marriage to FR, 7, 20

Reiner, Frederick Martin. *See* Reiner, Fritz

Reiner, Friderik. *See* Reiner, Fritz

Reiner Frigyes. *See* Reiner, Fritz

Reiner, Fritz, business: American Lyric Theater fee, 121; *Carnegie Hall* fee, 121; Chicago expenses, 180; Chicago SO contracts, 158, 187; Chicago television

Cassidy, 183, 184, 185; Carlotta Reiner to/from Ann Gaito, 181; Carlotta Reiner to Art Buchwald, 174; Carlotta Reiner to Lacy Hermann, 176; Carlotta Reiner to Mrs. Bok, 79; Carlotta Reiner to Edith Mason Ragland, 178; Carlotta Reiner to RCA-Victor, 166; Carlotta Reiner to Tuśy Assejew, 122, 221; FR/composer correspondence, 243; FR to/from Samuel Barber, 160; FR to/from Marshall Field, Jr., 209–10; FR to/from George Kuyper, 187; FR notes for Eric Oldberg meeting, 187; FR to/from Edward Specter, 115, 124; FR to Alexander Archipenko, 73; FR to Arthur Judson, 48; FR to Garson Kanin, 142; FR to J. P. Maxfield, 86; FR to New York *Times*, 213; FR to Seymour Raven at *Tribune*, 221; FR to Kurt Reidel, 94; FR to Igor Stravinsky, 117; FR notes for Thruston Wright meeting, 123; FR to Bruno Zirato (not sent), 113; Cesar Saerchinger to FR, 23; Robert Schnitzer to George Kuyper, 206, 208; Roger Sessions to FR, 34; Risë Stevens to FR, 145; Richard Strauss to FR, 70, 129; Igor Stravinsky to FR, 148

Reiner, Fritz, critical response to: "a master of his art" (Virgil Thomson), 108; "all not well at Orchestra Hall" (Claudia Cassidy), 223; Bartók Concerto for Piano no. 1 (J. Herman Thuman), 37; Bartók Concerto for Two Pianos (Olin Downes), 118; Beethoven Symphony no. 9 (Dresden), 18; Leonard Bernstein on FR (New York Philharmonic telecast), 234; Brahms Symphony no. 3 (Paul Henry Lang), 186, 192; Brahms Symphony no. 4 (J. Herman Thuman), 28; *Carmen* (Virgil Thomson), 145; *Carnegie Hall* (James Agee), 121; —, *Variety*, 121; Cincinnati May Festival, 1923 (New York *Times*), 30; Cincinnati SO debut, 28; —, farewell concert, 56; —, New York concerts, 35, (Olin Downes) 36; —, Philadel-

phia concert, 46; —, Deems Taylor, 29; Dresden press, 13, 18; *Elektra* (Olin Downes), 70, 145, (Irving Kolodin) 145, (Samuel Laciar) 74; Europe/Russia tour (Claudia Cassidy), 213, (Roger Dettmer) 212, (Robert Marsh) 212; *Falstaff* (Olin Downes), 130, (Virgil Thomson) 130; *Der fliegende Holländer* (Richard Capell), 92, (Met, mixed reception) 143; FR and Nikisch (Harold Schonberg), 17; *Die Meistersinger* (Henry de la Grange), 177, (Peter Heyworth) 176, (Vienna press) 176; New York Philharmonic-SO 1943 (Virgil Thomson), 118; obituary (Harold Schonberg), 189; *Parsifal* (Ernest Newman), 91, Philadelphia 0 (Ross Parmenter), 178; FR baroque style (Richard Taruskin), 199–200; Robin Hood Dell SO (Max de Schauensee), 136; *Salome* (Olin Downes), 130, (Irving Kolodin) 130, (Martin Mayer) 129, (Virgil Thomson) 130; *The Rake's Progress* (Olin Downes), 147, (Irving Kolodin) 147, (Virgil Thomson) 147; *Der Rosenkavalier* (Chicago), 117, (Olin Downes) 131, (Irving Kolodin) 131, 146; Toscanini influence on FR (Joseph Horowitz), 203; *Tristan und Isolde* (Dresden), 18, (Irving Kolodin) 143, (San Francisco) 94, (Virgil Thomson) 143; Vienna Philharmonic (John Culshaw), 175

Reiner, Fritz, family. *See* Assejew, Tuśy (daughter); Assejew, Vladimir (grandson); Bartenstein, Eva (daughter); Bartenstein, Fritz (grandson); Bartenstein, Hans (grandson); Bartenstein, Monika (granddaughter); Benedict, Charlotte; Krupicka, Frank Rainer (grandson); Reiner, Berta Gerster-Gardini (second wife); Reiner, Carlotta Irwin (third wife); Reiner, Elca Jelacin (first wife); Reiner, Ignácz (father); Reiner, Irma Polak (mother)

Reiner, Fritz, significant biographical events: arrival in America, 27; automo-

Reiner, Fritz (*continued*)
biles, 42, 88, 239; baptized, 3; born, 1;
Budapest to Dresden, 13; Chicago, 168,
179, 180, 188; childhood, 1; Cincinnati,
41, 54, 55; citizenship (United States),
28; daughters to Dresden, 20; Dresden,
18, 20; Dresden to Cincinnati, 31; Franz
Liszt Academy of Music, 3; funeral, 233;
health, 182–83, 224, 226, 231, 232; —, final
illness, 233; —, heart attack, 224, 225;
—, muscular pain, 133, 135; honorary
degrees, 81, 221; —, Loyola University, 221; —, Northwestern University,
221; —, University of Pennsylvania,
81, 221; —, University of Pittsburgh,
81, 221; Jewish ancestry, 1; law study,
3; lifestyle, 42; Manhattan apartments,
133; —, Park Avenue, 58; marries Berta
Gerster-Gardini, 21; —, divorced, 53;
marries Carlotta Irwin, 54; marries Elca
Jelacin, 7; —, divorced, 20; Mussolini
audience, 58; New York, first visit, 28;
Officer of the Order of the King of Italy,
58; photography, 42, 98; Pittsburgh, 101;
Rambleside, 97–99, 121, 221; seventieth
birthday, 186–87; wartime concern for
relatives, 122
Reiner, Fritz, and media: film, 85; —,
Carnegie Hall, 120; radio, 87–89, 119–
20; —, BBC, 92; —, Boston SO, 119; —,
Cincinnati SO, 47; —, Cleveland O, 119;
—, Curtis CBS broadcasts, 61; —, *Die
Walküre,* act II, 94; —, Firestone Hour,
48; —, Ford Sunday Evening Hour,
87–89, 116; —, Metropolitan Opera,
137; —, Metropolitan Opera *(Falstaff),*
130; —, Metropolitan Opera *(Salome),*
130; —, NBC SO, 116, 136; —, New
York Philharmonic-SO, 116, 118, 119;
—, *The Rake's Progress* (Metropolitan
Opera), 147; —, WBAI-FM (Chicago
SO), 170; recordings, Bell Laboratories,
Philadelphia O, 80, 86, 203; —, Chicago
SO, 170–75, 230–31; —, no Cincinnati
SO, 30, 48; —, Cleveland O (refused),
118; —, Columbia Records, 108–11,

137–38; —, Covent Garden, 91, 203; —,
Decca Records (British), 175; —, *Die
Fledermaus,* excerpts, 141; —, HMV *Tris-
tan und Isolde,* 91; —, New York *Post,*
86, 203; —, Pittsburgh SO, 108–11; —,
RCA-Victor, 138–39, 140, 170–75, 230–32;
—, *Reader's Digest,* 231; —, Robin Hood
Dell SO, 136; —, Royal Philharmonic
Orchestra, 231; —, underground recordings, 94; —, Welte-Mignon player-piano
rolls, 48; television, *Carmen* (Metropolitan Opera), 146; —, Chicago SO
(WGN-TV), 169–70, 220; —, copies at
Curtis and Northwestern, 243; —, *Der
Rosenkavalier* (Metropolitan Opera),
131
Reiner, Fritz, music: 189–205; chamber
music, 197; dynamics, 194; expression,
190, 191, 204, 205; Arthur Nikisch influence on FR, 16, 203; phrasing, 190;
preparation, 195–97; recitative continuo,
201; FR on conducting, 62, 63; FR and
players, 197–98; FR and soloists, 198–
99; rhythm and structure, 191, 192, 196;
Schumann Symphony no. 2 revised, 104;
"self-controlled control," 204; Richard
Strauss influence on FR, 16; structure,
192; style, 138, 199–203, (Austro-German
tradition) 199, (baroque) 138, 199,
200, (classical) 202, (contemporary)
199, (French) 199, 203, (Italian) 199,
(Romantic) 202, (Russian) 199, 202;
technique, 189–90, 191, 192, 193, 195, 196;
tone color, 194
Reiner, Fritz, opinions: America, 27;
American career in retrospect, 148; Beethoven Symphony no. 3 in E-flat Major,
75; Leonard Bernstein, 66; Maria Callas,
165; Alfredo Casella, 28; Claudia Cassidy,
167; Cincinnati SO, 29, 36, 37; conducting, 62–63, 189, 190, 191; conductor
training, 6, 230; contemporary music,
28; Paul Hindemith, 27; jazz, 27; Monteux criticized, 47; Arthur Nikisch
described, 16, 17; Papini aphorism, 75;
Goffredo Petrassi, 28; Philadelphia

Saxon Court (later State) Opera (Sächsiche Hofoper, Staatsoper, currently Dresden Opera), 9, 11, 12, 13; postwar changes, 21; FR and Kutzschbach letter, 21

Saxon Court/State Orchestra, 13

Sayão, Bidú, 131, 137

Schick, George, 155, 161

Schnabel, Artur, 154

Schnitzer, Robert F., 206, 207, 211, 214

Schoeffler, Paul, 132, 143, 160, 174

SCHOENBERG, ARNOLD, 27, 81; Erwartung (not FR), 43; letters to FR, 105, 241; Moses und Aron, "Golden Calf" (proposed), 160; Pelleas und Melisande, 105; Theme and Variations, 105; Verklärte Nacht, 105; —, (not recorded), 111

Schonberg, Harold, 17, 189

Schorr, Friedrich, 43

SCHREKER, FRANZ: Die ferne Klang, 15

SCHUBERT, FRANZ: Symphony no. 5 in B-flat Major, 219; Symphony no. 8 in B Minor, 33, 219; Symphony no. 9 in C Major, 33, 202

Schuch, Ernst von, 9, 12, 13, 21

Schulhof, Andrew, 123–24

Schuller, Gunther, 132

Schulthess, Walter, 177, 178, 205

SCHUMAN, WILLIAM, 107; American Festival Overture, 108; Prayer in Time of War, 1943, 108; FR eulogized, 233; Side Show for Orchestra, 108, 118

Schumann, Elisabeth, 60, 72

SCHUMANN, ROBERT, 17; Concerto for Piano in A Minor, 133; Symphony no. 1 in B-flat major, 33; Symphony no. 2 in C Major, 33, 104, 225; —, "retouched," 196; Symphony no. 3 in E-flat Major, 33; Symphony no. 4 in D Minor, 33

Schützendorf, Gustav, 43

Schwarzkopf, Elisabeth, 144, 147, 180, 194, 199

Schweitzer, Louis, 170

See, Arthur, 74

Seebach, Count Nikolaus von, 9, 14, 21

Seinemeyer, Meta, 43

Selby, John, 122

Selective Service (Draft), 103

Semper Theater (Dresden), 11, 12

Serkin, Rudolf, 59, 111, 217, 220, 227

SESSIONS, ROGER, 34, 81; The Black Maskers, Suite, 34

Severence Hall (Cleveland), 118

Sharrow, Leonard, 158

Shea, Nora, 123, 156

Sheridan, Frank, 81

Sherman, Robert, 237

SHOSTAKOVICH, DIMITRI, 194; Concerto for Piano no. 1, 106; Symphony no. 1, 106; Symphony no. 5, 106; Symphony no. 6, 106, 111, 118, 119, 216; Symphony no. 9, 106, 120

Shrine Auditorium (Los Angeles), 94

SIBELIUS, JEAN: Concerto for Violin in D Minor, 104; —, (not FR), 162; Symphony no. 1 in E Minor, 104; Symphony no. 2 in D Major, 104

Siems, Margarete, 14

Siepi, Cesare, 144

Simionato, Giulietta, 149

Slezak, Leo, 8

Smallens, Alexander, 71, 72

SMETANA, BEDŘICH: Dalibor, 6

SMITH, DAVID STANLEY, 107

Smith, Kenneth, 216

Smith, Moses, 109

Soria, Dario, 138

Soria, Dorle Jarmel, 233

Southern California Symphony Association, 222

South Pacific, 137

Sovern, Michael J., 241

Specter, Edward, 99–100, 105, 115; and FR, 102, 113, 115, 123, 124

Stader, Maria, 216

Starker, János, 158, 164; on FR music, 190, 196, 197, 204

State Department. See United States Department of State

Steber, Eleanor, 129, 131

Stern, Isaac, 127, 159, 160, 181, 198

Steschenko, Ivan, 70